# The News Gap

# The News Gap

## When the Information Preferences of the Media and the Public Diverge

Pablo Javier Boczkowski and Eugenia Mitchelstein

The MIT Press
Cambridge, Massachusetts
London, England

MIT Press books may be purchased at special quantity discounts for business or sales promotional use. For information, please email special_sales@mitpress.mit.edu or write to Special Sales Department, The MIT Press, 55 Hayward Street, Cambridge, MA 02142.

Set in Stone Sans and Stone Serif by Toppan Best-set Premedia Limited. Printed and bound in the United States of America.

Library of Congress Cataloging-in-Publication Data

Boczkowski, Pablo J.
The news gap : when the information preferences of the media and the public diverge / by Pablo Javier Boczkowski and Eugenia Mitchelstein.
pages cm
Includes bibliographical references and index.
ISBN 978-0-262-01983-5 (hardcover : alk. paper) 1. Online journalism. 2. Online journalism—Social aspects. 3. Online journalism—Political aspects. 4. News audiences.
I. Mitchelstein, Eugenia, 1979– II. Title.
PN4784.O62B63 2013
070.4—dc23
2013010262

10 9 8 7 6 5 4 3 2 1

para nuestras hijas, Sofía y Emma Boczkowski y Matilda Villán Mitchelstein, por el idioma de la infancia y el reino del revés

## Contents

# Acknowledgments

This book reports findings from a large-scale multi-year research endeavor. Because of its scale and complexity, this endeavor would not have been possible without substantive financial assistance. The majority of our support came from the Robert and Kaye Hiatt Fund for Research on Media, Technology, and Society at Northwestern University. In addition to providing funding, Bob and Kaye gave us helpful feedback on the evolution of our studies during our progress report meetings. Barbara O'Keefe, Dean of the School of Communication, created the scholarly environment that made the existence of this fund at Northwestern possible in the first place, and championed our research with her unique blend of unparalleled enthusiasm and sharp critique. We received additional support from the John S. and James L. Knight Foundation, through the Carnegie-Knight Initiative on the Future of Journalism Education, from the Innovation Fund (through Northwestern University's School of Communication), and from Northwestern's Media Management Center. We express our deepest gratitude to all these sources of financial support.

The idea to analyze the most clicked stories emerged in discussions that Pablo had with two research assistants, Romina Frazzetta and Victoria Mansur, for his previous book, *News at Work: Imitation in an Age of Information Abundance*. Romina and Victoria made important additions to the first iteration of the data-collection and coding protocols. The initial instantiation of a project directly comparing the most newsworthy and most clicked stories was pursued jointly with Limor Peer, who was of great help in refining these protocols and developing the conceptual framework. The subsequent projects were made possible by the outstanding technical, methodological, and logistical contributions of Martin Walter. He went above and beyond the call of duty even when his formal involvement with the research had ended. The studies reported in this book benefited from the research assistance of Pedro Arieira, Santiago De Simone, Denis Djapo, Borja del Olmo, Dan Ellman, Elena Fields, Lindsay Fullerton, Hilary Gifford, Louisa McClintock, Sacramento Rosello-Martinez, Michaela Soyer, Salvador Vazquez del Mercado, Celeste Wagner, Matt Weir, and Alberto Wolberg Casado.

We wholeheartedly thank the journalists and members of the public who agreed to share their experiences of and their thoughts about online news. In the early stages of the writing, Eszter Hargittai helped us to figure out the best way to tell a story with numbers during many conversations at monthly meetings of Eszter's and Pablo's "book writing club." Later, Ignacio Siles kindly read the first full draft of the manuscript and improved it with thoughtful and incisive suggestions. The book also benefited from discussions with John Alderman, Chris Anderson, Alice Antheaume, Lance Bennett, Josh Benton, Jeremy Birnholtz, Sofia Boczkowski, Jim Brady, Erik Bucy, Nosh Contractor, Eric Dagiral, Michael Delli Carpini, Mark Deuze, Jason DiSanto, Jamie Druckman, Jim Ettema, Patrice Flichy, Jean- François Fogel, Jeremy Freese, Janet Fulk, Megan Garber, Darren Gergle, Rich Gordon, Betsi Grabe, Doris Graber, Shane Greenstein, Larry Gross, Jay Hamilton, Keith Hampton, Bob Hariman, Pierre Haski, Shanto Iyengar, Josiane Jouët, Jim Katz, Laurent Mauriac, Ericka Menchen-Trevino, Peter Monge, Russ Neuman, Dan O'Keefe, Sylvain Parasie, Evan Parker-Stephen, Bruno Patino, John Pavlik, Trevor Pinch, Elena Raviola, Pascal Riche, Lauren Rivera, Dietram Scheufele, Phoebe Sengers, Jack Shafer, Pam Shoemaker, Susan Silbey, Verónica Silva, Aram Sinnreich, Adlai Stevenson III, Nancy Stevenson, David Thorburn, Joe Turow, William Uricchio, Thierry Vedel, Silvio Waisbord, Matt Weber, Jim Webster, and Owen Youngman.

We profited hugely from comments received during seminars at the Massachusetts Institute of Technology, Harvard University, Cornell University, Northwestern University, the University of Wisconsin at Madison, the University of Southern California, Rutgers University, Indiana University at Bloomington, the Institut d'Etudes Politics de Paris, the Université Marne-la-Vallée, La Cantine, Rue89, the Adlai Stevenson Center for Democracy, and the Universidad de San Andrés. We also benefited from feedback during talks at the annual meetings of the International Communication Association, the American Sociological Association, the National Communication Association, the Latin American Studies Association, and the Midwest Political Science Association.

As we noted above, Northwestern University provided a most auspicious context for the research presented in this book. In addition to Dean Barbara O'Keefe, we also want to mention our department chair, Bob Hariman, for supporting this research, Jane Rankin and Sheri Carsello for helping with funding issues, and Madeleine Agaton, JaTaune Bobsy, and Sharron Shepard for providing able administrative assistance.

We greatly enjoyed working with the MIT Press. We thank the one and only Margy Avery for her vision, her insight, and her enthusiasm for this project. Three anonymous reviewers greatly improved the manuscript with their helpful suggestions and exacting criticisms. During the early stages of the editorial process we also received helpful feedback from Joe Calamia at Yale University Press, Angela Chnapko and Andy Chadwick at Oxford University Press, and the anonymous reviewers commissioned by those two presses. During these early stages we also gained from the sage advice received in conversations with Tarleton Gillespie, Matt Hindman, Phil Howard, Dave Karpf, Dave Tewksbury, and Fred Turner. Last but not least, we whole-heartedly thank Kay Mansfield and Paul Bethge, who made a text written by two non-native English speakers clearer and more straightforward.

We are both fortunate to have great friends who provided help and encouragement during the research and writing process. They are too numerous to be named individually here, but our utmost gratitude goes to all of them. Our families provided their loving support throughout this project. Pablo thanks his mother, Aída Schvartz, his brother, Jorge Boczkowski, and, in particular, his daughters Sofía and Emma Boczkowski, who, among many other wonderful things they did over the past couple of years, patiently waited for the manuscript to be done before welcoming a puppy. Eugenia thanks her father, Enrique Mitchelstein, her sisters, Andrea, Paula, and Luisa, and particularly her husband, Rubén Octavio Villán, and their daughter, Matilda, who spent many Saturday and Sunday mornings in the park while she worked on the manuscript.

Portions of chapters 2–5 were published in earlier form in the following articles:

Pablo J. Boczkowski, "The divergent online news preferences of journalists and readers," *Communications of the ACM* 53 (2010), no. 11: 24–26

Pablo J. Boczkowski, Eugenia Mitchelstein, and Martin Walter, "Convergence across divergence: Understanding the gap in the online news choices of journalists and consumers in Western Europe and Latin America," *Communication Research* 38 (2011), no. 3: 376–396

Pablo J. Boczkowski and Limor Peer, "The choice gap: The divergent online news preferences of journalists and consumers," *Journal of Communication* 61 (2011), no. 5: 857–876

Pablo J. Boczkowski and Eugenia Mitchelstein, "Is there a gap between the news choices of journalists and consumers? A relational and dynamic approach," *International Journal of Press/Politics* 15 (2010), no. 4: 420–440

Pablo J. Boczkowski, Eugenia Mitchelstein, and Martin Walter, "When burglar alarms sound, do monitorial citizens pay attention to them? The online news choices of journalists and consumers during and after the 2008 U.S. election cycle," *Political Communication* 29 (2012), no. 4: 347–366

Pablo J. Boczkowski and Eugenia Mitchelstein, "How users take advantage of different forms of interactivity on online news sites: Clicking, e-mailing, and commenting," *Human Communication Research* 38 (2012), no. 1: 1–22

Material from these articles is presented here with permission from the respective publishers:

the Association for Computer Machinery

Sage Publications

the International Communication Association and Blackwell Publishing

Sage Publications

the International Communication Association and Blackwell Publishing

the International Communication Association and Blackwell Publishing

## A Note About the Figures

In figures that reproduce online content, dashed frames indicate stories on public-affairs topics; solid frames indicate stories on non-public-affairs topics. In other figures, PA always stands for public-affairs and NPA for non-public-affairs.

# 1 When Supply and Demand Don't Meet

A certain bakery has long been a fixture of daily life in a neighborhood. Legend has it that the founders decided, when they opened the bakery, that in addition to making money they wanted to contribute to the well-being of their customers. To that end, in addition to bread and pastries made with refined flour they also featured a wide selection of healthier goods made with whole-wheat flour. After a while, about 60 percent of their baked goods were made with refined flour and about 40 percent with whole-wheat flour. The items made with refined flour usually sold out before the end of each business day. The healthier items did well during certain periods, but were usually not as successful. On average, over the course of a year, 10–20 percent of all daily production went unsold, and that represented a major loss of ingredients and a misuse of labor and other expenses. Yet the founders persisted with their strategy because business was good and they believed in their social mission.

However, things have changed in the past few decades. The neighborhood has continued to grow at a normal pace, but the bakery now has much more competition from other bakeries. In addition, convenience stores offer mostly the top-selling breads and make it easier for customers to avoid the healthier options. This has decreased the revenues of the neighborhood bakery and threatened the viability of its business. The people currently in charge of the bakery would like to keep its social mission alive. Should they go on making about 40 percent of their goods with whole-wheat flour, with the expectation that the preferences of consumers may change? Or should they cut their losses and give customers more of what they want, even though that may not be conducive to their well-being?

This book is not about the bread and pastries sold by a neighborhood bakery; it is about the news produced by the leading media organizations on the World Wide Web. However, the example of the bakery parallels the predicament of the media organizations. They provide readers with much of the news that circulates in society, particularly the news that is essential for healthy functioning of the body politic. But online readers have shown a preference for something other than what news organizations give them. Although the news organizations disseminate news about politics, international, and economic matters, the stories that garner the most attention from the public tend to be about sports, crime, entertainment, and weather. As in the case of the bakery, this creates a gap between supply and demand—that is, between the news that is supplied and the news that is demanded. The idea of such a gap has been around for quite some time. More than 70 years ago, Robert Park, a leading figure of the Chicago School of Sociology and a former journalist, wrote: "The things which most of us would like to publish are not the things that most of us want to read. We may be eager to get into print what is, or seems to be, edifying, but we want to read what is interesting."[1] Although that is a truism among many academics and practitioners (a truism that studies have not unanimously supported), there has been only limited empirical research into whether this perceived gap actually exists in a particular medium and, if it does exist, how big it is and what factors appear to increase or decrease it.

The supply-demand gap in the case of news allows us to explore larger conceptual issues about media, technology, and society. One such issue, addressed years ago by Walter Lippmann[2] and John Dewey,[3] is whether is it feasible and desirable for the public to obtain the information required to participate adequately in matters of the polity. Writing during the consolidation of mass society, when the dominant communication technologies were newspapers and radio, Lippmann and Dewey presented differing visions of what news organizations and their publics wanted and needed and what the difference meant for liberal democracy. Lippmann argued that the majority of citizens were neither willing nor able to comprehend and address the complex issues that modern democracies faced, and asserted that broad dissemination of information by the media wasn't likely to solve the problem. Dewey suggested that, although citizens were capable of understanding public affairs and acting upon that knowledge, the media didn't serve them adequately. He maintained that the public needed full information, because "whatever obstructs and restricts publicity limits and distorts public opinion and checks and distorts thinking on social affairs."[4] The positions represented by Lippmann and Dewey have informed scholarship for decades. (Some of that scholarship is summarized in the next section.) In this book, we offer an empirical account of the gap between the supply of online news and the demand for it that provides new insights into this and other long-standing conceptual discussions. These insights help us to rethink fundamental elements of the matrix of communication and politics that has been essential to liberal democracy.

We live in an era of digital media and in a fragmented postindustrial society, in contrast with the newspapers and radio and industrial mass society of Lippmann's and Dewey's era. We point this out because many analysts and commentators have failed to recognize that the meaning of the news gap has changed. As our hypothetical example of the bakery suggests, to ignore consumers' preferences has different implications when there is only one vendor, or only a few, than it has when there are many competitors in a media environment in which consumers can easily avoid the kinds of news they don't want to read. Through most of the twentieth century, the strong market position of the leading print and broadcast news organizations enabled them to tell the public what they thought the public needed to know, despite their perception that the public preferred something else.[5] Merchants still had to advertise their products and services in newspapers, on radio, and on television to reach their customers. To learn about a sporting event, a reader had to buy an entire newspaper. To catch a weather report, a viewer of a newscast had to watch earlier segments, and she had few options for where to get her news. The public had only a limited ability to ignore other topics, even if it preferred to do so. For traditional media organizations, this contributed to the existence of a tolerable gap between the supply of and the demand for news. It helped those organizations to fulfill a public-service mission that was consistent with the prevalent journalistic ideology while enjoying big profits.

The recent evolution of news has changed the picture dramatically. Cable television and online news have brought huge increases in competition and in the ability of consumers to get the news they want and ignore the rest. These changes have reframed the dilemma of the gap for media organizations in the digital age and for society as a whole. In a highly competitive environment, how long can the leading suppliers of news about the polity sustain a gap between what they offer as the most newsworthy stories and what their audiences find appealing? What does this reframed dilemma mean for the body politic, which needs this information much as the human body needs the nutrients of bread baked with whole-wheat flour?

In this book we present the most comprehensive account to date of the gap between the kind of news that is supplied and the kind that is demanded. We concentrate on what could be called the "informational" dimension of the news by looking at the topics covered in a story and how they are presented to the public. Returning to the bakery analogy, we suggest that information in a news story is akin to ingredients in a meal. In the same way that the nutritional value of a meal doesn't get at all the ways in which food is intertwined with everyday culture, the information in a story doesn't get at all that the news means in social life. News and food are used to partake in social rituals, to signal social capital, to engage in conversation, and to mobilize political action. But the informational dimension of the news media is foundational to these other roles, which could not be enacted without the information used to ritualize, stratify, talk, mobilize, and so on.[6]

To examine what we call "the news gap," we developed a novel methodology that examines the news choices of journalists and consumers and deployed it in large-scale comparative studies of twenty leading news sites in seven countries in three regions in the world. The results of our research show that a sizable supply-demand gap is a common element of the news environment, cutting across sites that have divergent ideological orientations and are located in countries with diverse media systems and cultures. They also reveal that the gap decreases during periods of heightened political activity, such as national elections or government crises, owing to consumers' increased interest in news about the polity. Furthermore, they suggest that the gap isn't affected by novel storytelling formats such as user-generated content, in view of their low level of popularity among users of leading mainstream media sites.

We draw on these findings to rethink conceptual tools such as agenda setting,[7] monitorial citizenship,[8] and the role of storytelling formats in the news.[9] Contrary to the notion that the leading media have a strong and fairly uniform agenda-setting power, we contend that their power to set the agenda depends on context and is quite limited during periods of normal political activity. This is so because citizens adopt a monitorial stance, paying restricted attention to matters of the polity except during periods of heightened political activity. This monitorial stance, which challenges the idea that citizens either avoid public-affairs news or can't get enough of it,[10] is facilitated by the affordances of online news that allow consumers to focus on the stories that interest them and avoid the rest. But not all affordances matter equally. Contrary to the notion that "soft" news formats entice consumers to learn news about the polity and the notion that user-generated content venues yield a bottom-up, widespread sociopolitical agenda, we show that neither option captures the interest of the public substantively, and that consumers of the leading sites gravitate toward non-public-affairs content told in straight-news fashion.

In today's media environment, the supply-demand gap undermines the public-service orientation of leading media outlets and their contributions to the democratic process. The erosion of these outlets' agenda-setting power during periods of normal political activity and the limited impact of consumer-driven alternatives could accelerate the deterioration of shared discourse on matters of wide-ranging significance. This would weaken the search for common ground on such matters and exacerbate social division. Decision makers in the public, non-profit, and private sectors will remain interested in public-affairs news. But the leading media might lose their clout as agenda setters with them too, because the ability of the media to influence the elite public is premised on the size and the composition of their mass public. Thus, the news gap might jeopardize the role of the media as a liaison between elite decision makers and consumers.

The news gap also poses challenges to two other roles that news organizations play in the public sphere: providing information and providing spaces for public deliberation.[11] Lack of interest in public-affairs topics may lead to a citizenry that is neither prepared nor willing to discuss these topics, and fragmentation of the audience may undermine the position of the media in the circuit of public deliberation. The gap may also be a disincentive for the leading media to perform their traditional watchdog function, by which they help to hold government officials and other large collective actors accountable.[12] Since watchdog journalism is rarely cost effective for the organizations that undertake it,[13] the gap may increase pressure for these organizations to reduce the resources they devote to it. That would shift the balance of power further in favor of large collective actors, to the detriment of social accountability.

What is at stake, therefore, is not only the fate of the media, but also that of the matrix of communication and politics that subtended democratic practices in the twentieth century. The gap illuminates not only the current challenges to the public-service mission of journalism but also the current challenges to the feasibility of a particular information regime that once animated liberal democratic visions of society.

## What We Know about the News Gap

Producing and consuming news are important aspects of everyday life in modern societies. Their dynamics have attracted significant attention from social scientists and cultural analysts.[14] Within this broad area of inquiry, two widely researched topics are the role of journalists as sources of information for the citizenry and the significance of the information they provide for the democratic process.[15] Scholars have tried to ascertain whether journalists supply the news that citizens need and whether citizens want such information or prefer information on sports, crime, and entertainment—subjects that are interesting but don't contribute to the health of a democratic society. Over time, a debate emerged among researchers about whether there is a gap between the stories that journalists consider most newsworthy and those that capture the attention of consumers most strongly.[16]

Research has consistently shown that journalists at generalist, mainstream news organizations consider stories about politics, economics, and international matters (hereafter characterized as public-affairs news) to be more newsworthy than articles about subjects such as crime, entertainment, sports, and the weather (hereafter characterized as non-public-affairs news).[17] The preference of news producers for public-affairs topics results from professional and organizational norms that are at the core of the occupational identity of modern journalism.[18] According to Herbert Gans, journalists "expect, as an integral part of their professional identities, to provide [public-affairs stories]."[19] These norms are linked to the perceived significance of these topics[20] and to reporters' dependence on sources in business and in government.[21] John Zaller has written that journalists "want to be freed from the subservience to the mass audience, so that they can provide the public with the kind of news that they . . . feel the public needs."[22] W. Lance Bennett has noted that "the public relations machinery of government and business readily fills [the news media] organizational needs by producing events that are cheap, easy to report, numerous, and predictable."[23] Studies have shown that journalists are more influenced by other news workers, such as editors, peers, and competitors, than by the preferences of their audiences.[24] Robert Darnton, recalling his days at the *New York Times* and the *Newark Star-Ledger*, observed that journalists "really wrote for one another."[25] This disregard for what consumers might want from their news sources was made possible by the monopoly or oligopoly position of most mainstream media before the advent of cable television and, especially, the Internet.[26]

Studies of the behavior of news audiences have yielded conflicting findings. One stream of research has argued that news consumers are mostly interested in public-affairs content.[27] Klaus Bruhn Jensen has suggested that television viewers "place a particular emphasis on the traditional political relevance of news."[28] In his study of news consumption habits among young people, Edgar Huang found that "they tried to keep up to date with current events because they felt as though they owed it to themselves to be informed citizens."[29] However, a contending stream of research has argued that news audiences prefer non-public-affairs news stories.[30] Jane Singer reports that on British local media sites "user preferences leaned heavily toward coverage of quirkiness, sport, crime and death—plus a smattering of sex."[31] Some scholars have suggested that lack of attention to public-affairs matters may be a sign of rational ignorance in which consumers largely avoid learning about these matters because they perceive that the cost of acquiring and interpreting the relevant news outweighs the potential benefits.[32]

These conflicting findings about the behavior of audiences have led to inconclusive accounts as to whether there is a supply-demand gap in the case of online news. If consumers have a high level of demand for public-affairs reportage, there should be no major gap, because there seems to be a consensus that journalists supply a significant dose of such content. If the second camp is correct and consumers are mostly interested in non-public-affairs stories, there should be a major gap between the kind of news that is supplied and the kind that is demanded.

Some analysts have argued that the content of news stories isn't the main factor in whether the audience acquires information, and that the main factor is the format in which stories are disseminated.[33] In the frame of our hypothetical example, these analysts have suggested that the presentation of the news may be at least as meaningful as its ingredients. They have suggested that novel formats, such as talk shows and feature-style storytelling, may help to convey political public-affairs news to otherwise inattentive consumers.[34] According to Matthew Baum, "the rise of a new class of entertainment-oriented, quasi-news and information programs . . . has had the unintended effect of increasing the likelihood that . . . a given foreign policy crisis will become a water-cooler event. They have done so by attracting greater public attentiveness to foreign crises . . . particularly among segments of the population not typically interested in politics or foreign policy."[35]

Scholars and commentators have suggested that "softer" news formats have been on the rise in recent decades.[36] If Baum and the other proponents of the thesis of the increased importance of these formats for conveying public-affairs news are right, this should affect the supply-demand gap in the case of public-affairs news.

The gap acquires new dimensions in the online media environment. Thanks to the common technological affordances of websites, selecting articles to read is only one of several ways the public has to engage with the news.[37] Other options include forwarding an article via email, posting a comment about it on a website, and creating news content to be accessed by fellow news consumers. Thus, there may be a supply-demand gap in the case of articles consumers choose to read, but not in the case of articles they choose to share by email or in the case of articles about which they post comments.

However, research on whether news consumers take advantage of interactive features to share, comment on, or create public-affairs content has failed to produce conclusive findings. Some studies have found that media audiences focus on public-affairs news when creating online content.[38] Carlos Ruiz and his colleagues analyzed readers' comments on five online newspapers from the United States and Europe and found that "politics (in some cases with connection to economy) was the most discussed topic."[39] Other research on user-generated content has found that members of the public privilege non-public-affairs topics, such as personal life and entertainment, in their participatory practices.[40] Henrik Ornebring analyzed users' blogs in Swedish and British newspapers and found that they "mostly function as an online diary where the most popular topics are every-day life things such as love, work, children, etc."[41] Herbert Gans noted that citizen journalists "cover the informally organized parts of society, the 'private' worlds of family, friends, compatible neighbors, work colleagues."[42] Thus, whether there is a supply-demand gap in the case of online news remains an open question even when the stories consumers read, email, or comment on are examined.

Three main limitations have contributed to the inability to settle the scholarly debate about the existence and nature of the news gap.

First, most of the research relies on survey, circulation, and ratings data that measure consumers' choices in the aggregate. However, in an increasingly competitive market in which consumers have a growing array of unbundling techniques—from remote controls to Really Simple Syndication (RSS) feeds—at their disposal, surveys of preferences or ratings and circulation data at the outlet level or the program level are too aggregate to assess the effectiveness of the supply of news on consumption choices, which often are made at the story level. The use of survey research is particularly problematic in light of the inaccuracy of audience self-reports of media use.[43] Because of the perceived social desirability of knowledge of public-affairs content, some audiences may report accessing such content in higher proportions than they actually do. Conversely, they may underreport their consumption of non-public-affairs content.

Second, research has focused on the news preferences of journalists or that of consumers, not on the preferences of both within a single study. This tendency is partly a legacy of a division of labor between scholarship on production and scholarship on consumption. That division made some sense when journalists ignored consumers' preferences and selected what news to communicate almost entirely on the basis of occupational and institutional imperatives.[44] However, technological developments have given journalists, particularly those in online newsrooms, access to more volume and detail of information about news audiences' choices than they previously had access to.[45] Therefore, the present-day context challenges the desirability of studying the choices of news producers and news consumers separately rather than as inextricable parts of a single research project.[46]

Third, most studies have assumed that the news choices of journalists and consumers are relatively stable. However, these choices can change under a number of conditions.[47] For instance, research has found that the amount of political reportage tends to increase in relation to the progress of a presidential campaign, particularly as Election Day approaches.[48] Other studies have shown that news coverage can also vary in relation to "particularly dramatic events (e.g., the 2009 Iranian elections . . . [and] the devastating 2010 earthquake in Haiti)" during which "various information sources coalesce around a single topic."[49] Changes in the news environment can also affect consumption patterns. Research has shown that the public is more attentive during the final stages of electoral campaigns or national crises.[50] This is an example of "monitorial citizenship," in which members of the public who generally tune out public-affairs news turn more of their attention to such news at times of heightened political activity.[51] Thus, research should examine the possibility of temporal variations in online news choices, rather than assuming that they are static.

Beyond specific studies about the news preferences of journalists and their audiences and their interrelationships, there have been no general accounts that have directly examined the historical emergence and evolution of the supply-demand gap. From the available relevant scholarship, it can be inferred that the gap originated from developments in intersecting characteristics of the relationship between the media and their publics: the privileged market position enjoyed by most traditional media organizations, the jurisdictional strength of modern journalism as purveyor of news about the polity, the relatively low visibility of consumers' preferences in the daily routines of the newsroom, and the public's long-standing tendency to gravitate toward stories about leisurely aspects of daily life rather than news about the polity. The gap persisted because news organizations were thriving economically and journalists could enact their public-service mission even though audiences weren't paying much attention to the main public-affairs stories disseminated by the elite media.[52] However, the gap means something different in the current scenario. Recent social and technological developments have lowered the barriers to entry into the news business and increased the competitive pressures for leading players in the field. These developments have increased the ability of bloggers and amateurs to challenge the privileged status of journalists as information

**Table 1.1**
Conditions of emergence and evolution of the supply-demand gap in the case of online news.

| | Environment: Market power | Journalists: Occupational identity | Consumers: Avoidance of politics |
|---|---|---|---|
| Past | High market power (few or no competitors) | Strong jurisdictional space (limited competition from outside the occupation) Disregard for consumers' preferences easier to enact (limited knowledge of these preferences in the newsroom) | More difficult to enact (fewer choices and products more difficult to unbundle) |
| Present | Low market power (many competitors) | Weakening of jurisdictional space (greater competition from outside the occupation) Disregard for consumers' preferences more difficult to enact (extensive knowledge of these preferences in the newsroom) | Easier to enact (many more choices and products easier to unbundle) |

providers. They have also made consumers' preferences evident in the newsroom and thus much harder for journalists to ignore than in the past, and they have made it easier for consumers to avoid the kinds of stories that don't interest them. (See table 1.1.)

A few decades ago, the leading media organizations in print, radio, and television operated with very little competition.[53] For instance, in the United States only a few metropolitan areas had more than one newspaper. This meant that these media companies operated more like utilities than like firms in competitive sectors of the economy. The production of public-affairs news and the enactment of the public-service mission associated with it were supported by the market power that the leading organizations in traditional media enjoyed. Cable television and the Internet changed the situation radically. Competition has increased greatly within the media industry and in other industries too. That Yahoo News (an online-only enterprise with a small newsroom) would be the top news site for 2011, or that Google News (an online-only endeavor that runs on an algorithm and has no original reporting) would be the tenth most popular news site that year, was unthinkable at the dawn of the commercial Internet, less than two decades ago.[54] This dramatic growth in competition has increasingly made giving the public what they need, especially if that isn't what they want, a luxury for media organizations that see their profits in peril.

There have also been major changes in the conditions of journalistic work during the past ten years or so. Two of the changes are particularly relevant for the issues addressed in this book. First, bloggers, citizen journalists, and amateurs engaged in news production have challenged the jurisdictional space once enjoyed by the reporters and editors who worked for established news organizations.[55] Voices don't count equally, but there are many more voices clamoring for attention now than there once were. This has had a cumulative effect on the exclusivity of the journalistic domain. Second, in the past newsroom staffers had a distant and fairly abstract sense that consumers weren't very interested in public-affairs news. Today, detailed reminders of consumers' preferences surround reporters and editors working in online newsrooms.[56] The widespread adoption of tools such as Chartbeat and Google Analytics and the routine of circulating information about the popularity of stories among staffers have made the divergence in the news choices of journalists and consumers daily fodder in online newsrooms around the world. Together, these two trends make it much more difficult than it once was for journalists to ignore consumers' preferences and (to paraphrase Darnton) "really write for one another."

The relative linearity of information delivery in print media and (especially) broadcast media and the fact that the leading organizations in these media bundled different kinds of news into a product that wasn't easily disassembled made incidental exposure to public-affairs stories a routine aspect of news consumption.[57] However, things have changed dramatically in the online news environment because information presentation is nonlinear (a consumer doesn't have to flip through pages or skip television stories to find what she wants) and quite easy to unbundle (consumers have a vast array of technical and social tools with which they can assemble their own personal news menu, from RSS feeds to recommendations on Facebook pages). In addition, the proliferation of sites on the Web has made it possible for a consumer to find outlets that cater to what she wants to learn about and disregard the rest.[58] In this context, avoiding public-affairs information has become much easier than it once was.

In view of what the supply-demand gap means in the current media landscape, we have developed a series of studies that overcome the limitations of the available scholarship. We hope to settle the scholarly debate about whether the gap exists and, if it does exist, to establish its magnitude and ascertain what factors affect it.

## How We Conducted Our Research

We conducted a series of studies between spring 2007 and fall 2009 to examine the news choices of journalists and consumers on twenty websites in seven countries. Nine of these sites are based in the United States: abcnews.com (hereafter referred to as ABC), cbsnews.com (CBS), chicagotribune.com (Chicago), cnn.com (CNN), foxnews.com (Fox), news.yahoo.com (Yahoo), seattlepi.com (Seattle PI), usatoday.com (USA Today), and washingtonpost.com (Washington Post). Six are based in Western Europe: Welt.de (Welt) and tagesspiegel.de (Tagesspiegel) in Germany, Elmundo.es (Mundo) and Elpais.es (País) in Spain, and Guardian.co.uk (Guardian) and Times.co.uk (Times) in the United Kingdom. The remaining five are based in Latin America: Clarín.com (Clarín) and Nacion.com (Nación) in Argentina, Folha.com (Folha) in Brazil, and Eluniversal.com.mx (Universal) and Reforma.com (Reforma) in Mexico. We describe the rationale for choosing these sites in greater detail in the chapters in which we first present the results from each study. In general terms, we selected them because they converge and diverge on a number of critical dimensions.

These sites belong to mainstream and leading media organizations in the countries in which they are located. In the chapters in which we first introduce the findings from these studies, we report the sizes of their respective audiences when we collected data for each study. As a measure of the overall popularity of our entire sample, it is worth noting that in June 2012, when the initial version of this chapter was written, together these sites had 256 million visitors per month.[59] We wanted to examine the gap in some of the organizations that set the news agendas in their respective countries and, to a certain extent, for the rest of the world too. Once the possibility of duplication of audiences and the complications that arise from relying on audience data from different reporting agencies is acknowledged, this combined figure is an undeniable indicator of the power of the selected sites to provide information in and about the polity.

Another reason we selected these sites is that they differ in several respects. They are based in countries and regions of the world that have diverse political cultures and media systems. They also differ in their intended geographic scope. Some aim primarily at metropolitan markets; others have a national reach; still others, among them CNN and Yahoo, target both national and global audiences. The sites also have different ideological outlooks. Some are identified with conservative or right-wing perspectives and some with liberal, centrist, or left-leaning positions; others have no clear ideological affinity. In addition, there is some variation in the degree of concentration on certain types of news. Although they are all generalist sites in the sense that they report on all kinds of events, some (e.g., Washington Post) focus quite heavily on public-affairs topics and some (e.g., USA Today) do the opposite; others are between the two extremes. Some of the selected sites are tied to print newspapers and some to broadcast and cable news organizations; one (Yahoo) is part of an online-only enterprise. Selecting sites that differed in the aforementioned ways enabled us to probe the extent to which each variable had any implications for the existence, magnitude, and variability of the supply-demand gap.

In addition to the variation across sites, we selected different periods in which to gather information in order to see whether the news choices of journalists and consumers changed in relation to changes in the political context. In most cases, we looked at periods of relatively normal political activity. But we also examined the news choices of journalists and consumers during two periods of heightened political activity: a major scheduled event (the 2008 presidential election in the United States) and an unforeseen nationwide political crisis (large political protests against the national government of Argentina triggered by an increase in agricultural export taxes, also in 2008).

We followed a similar procedure across the various studies we conducted. (We describe the distinct characteristics of the studies in the respective chapters in which we first introduce findings from them.) For each of the sites and for each data-collection day, we identified the top stories selected by journalists and the top stories selected by consumers. The journalists' selections consist of the first ten stories on the homepage, counting from left to right and from the top down in a grid-like manner. These are the stories usually placed on the first screen of a homepage. Akin to above-the-fold stories on the front pages of newspapers, they represent a suitable approximation to journalists' choices of the most newsworthy stories of the day. The consumers' selections are the top four, five, or ten stories in the "most read" list made publicly available by each site. In addition, we collected the articles on the "most emailed" and "most commented" lists on three sites (CNN, USA Today, and Washington Post) to gauge the potential effect of variation in technological affordances on consumers' choices. In all, we collected 39,132 news articles: 18,138 from the journalists' lists, 15,461 from the "most clicked" lists, 2,763 from the "most emailed" lists, and 2,770 from the "most commented" lists.[60, 61]

Each of the fifteen people who analyzed various parts of this body of information was either a national of a country whose news sites were included in the study or someone who had lived in one of those countries. They had firsthand knowledge of the political, social, and cultural circumstances of the various countries and experience interpreting the news "as locals." Each story was assessed according to two variables. First, analysts looked at the content of the story and classified it as one that addressed either a public-affairs issue or a non-public-affairs issue. Second, they examined the format of each article and categorized it as belonging to one of four or five (depending on the study) typical news storytelling alternatives: straight news, feature style, opinion, blogs, and user-generated content. By examining the content of the articles and the main storytelling formats, we were able to ascertain the existence and the magnitude of the supply-demand gap in either or both of these important aspects of the news—content and format.

In light of the book's main empirical goals, we rely mostly on data about the actual news choices of journalists and consumers, as described above. We use quantitative and qualitative content-analysis techniques to examine these data.

In addition, we undertook a smaller ethnographic study to make connections between our major findings and how journalists and consumers interpret the production and consumption of online news, respectively. In conjunction with the content analysis of news choices before and during the nationwide political crisis in Argentina mentioned above, we conducted 37 in-depth interviews with editors of news sites and members of their public. The interviewees included 12 editors of the two news sites examined for the content-analysis study and of four competitor outlets and 25 consumers of all of these news sites. (The methodological details of this study are presented in chapter 3.) Combining the results from the content analysis and the ethnographic inquiry improved the validity of our interpretation.[62] Most important, it shed new light on the divergent and dynamic interpretive and experiential logics that affect the supply-demand gap during ordinary times and during periods of heightened political interest.

Our research methods permitted us to overcome the limitations of the existing scholarship mentioned in the previous section. First, we examined the supply-demand gap at the level of the story rather than in the aggregate. By using the story as the unit of analysis, we obtained a finer-grained picture of the news choices of producers and consumers. Moreover, by relying on the placement of stories on the homepage and on the "most clicked" lists, we avoided the inaccuracy of self-reported preferences. Second, we analyzed journalists' and consumers' choices concurrently and within a single study. Third, rather than assuming that the news choices of both groups were static, we looked at whether they changed between periods of routine political activity and periods of heightened political activity. This enabled us to ascertain to what degree the choices were dynamic.

In the chapters that follow, we present the main results of a series of large-scale comparative studies of the supply-demand gap. We used content analyses of nearly 40,000 stories deemed newsworthy by journalists, popular by consumers, or both. We complemented these studies with a smaller-scale ethnographic inquiry into some aspects of the interpretive and experiential aspects of the production and consumption of online news that subtend this gap. We conceived our research approach with an eye to overcoming the limitations of existent relevant scholarship. The outcome is the most comprehensive account yet offered of the supply-demand gap and of its implications for the future of the media industry and its role in liberal democracies.

## What We Found and Why It Matters

We begin our empirical journey in chapter 2, in which we look at the existence and size of the supply-demand gap. We show that the thematic content preferences of journalists and consumers on leading sites whose headquarters are located in the United States, in Western Europe, and in Latin America diverge markedly. Whereas journalists exhibit a strong preference for public-affairs news in the articles they consider most newsworthy, consumers lean toward non-public-affairs subjects in the stories they click most often. The magnitude of this gap is quite large, ranging from 9 to 30 percentage points and averaging 18 percentage points across sites. We find that the gap is quite immune to geographic and ideological variations. For instance, during periods of relatively routine political activity this gap existed on all the sites we studied. There was a gap despite the presence of substantive differences in the media systems among the countries in which sites are located and in the sites' ideological orientations. Moreover, the lack of major geographic variation persists at the regional level. When the findings from the Western European and Latin American sites are aggregated, there is a difference of one percentage point in the gaps of each region. A similar lack of variation is evident when the news choices of journalists and consumers of all the conservative and liberal sites are pooled in their respective ideological categories. Thus, chapter 2 establishes that the gap exists, that it is a sizable and regular feature of mainstream online news during periods of routine political activity, and that it is largely unaffected by geographic and ideological factors.

In chapter 3 we examine what happens to the thematic preferences of journalists and consumers during periods of heightened political activity. We look at two kinds of change in the political context: scheduled events (exemplified by the 2008 presidential election in the United States) and unforeseen nationwide political crises (exemplified by a crisis that occurred in Argentina in the same year). We show that in both situations the respective preferences of both groups deviated from the norm during periods of more routine political activity in the direction of a greater selection of public-affairs news. For instance, when we contrast the presence of public-affairs news in the top news choices of journalists and consumers of six leading sites during the fourteen days surrounding election day in 2008 and the same fourteen days in 2009, we find that the size of the gap is, on average, 11 percentage points smaller in the former period than in the latter period. This is due primarily to changes in the nature of demand, because the news choices of journalists changed less than those of consumers. Overall, in two countries with different political and media systems and in relation to contextual transformations of a different kind, the news choices of both journalists and consumers exhibit changes with relatively similar characteristics. This leads us to conclude that these choices can be dynamic.

Interviews with journalists and consumers provide insight into interpretive and experiential factors that shape their respective news choices during periods of routine political activity and into how those choices change when the sociopolitical context changes. There are intersecting tensions that characterize the predicament of each group. In the case of journalists, there is a tension between what might be labeled the "logic of the occupation" (marked by the prevalence of traditional editorial criteria) and "the logic of the market" (signaled by recognition that consumers tend to prefer non-public-affairs stories).[63] Our finding that the logic of the occupation prevail over that of the market within leading mainstream media organizations such as those we studied is consistent with the continued dominance of the modern journalistic identity. This phenomenon is amplified somewhat during periods of heightened political activity. A different but related tension marks the experience of consumers. Most of the people we interviewed felt a tension between consuming public-affairs news that generate anxiety and demand substantive interpretive effort and reading non-public-affairs stories that generate relaxation and make lesser cognitive demands. During normal times consumers gravitate toward non-public-affairs news, but during periods of heightened political activity they want to inform themselves about public affairs in order to maintain their self-image by observing socially desirable norms of civic duty and in order to navigate the political landscape more successfully.

In chapter 4 we switch from the ingredients of the news to its presentation, examining the storytelling preferences of journalists and consumers. The traditional straight-news format is the leading option for both groups across the 20 sites we studied during periods of routine and heightened political activity. This finding belies accounts that news has gone soft, at least for online news. On average, 72 percent of the ten most newsworthy articles and 61 percent of the ten most clicked articles are straight news across sites; the second most popular option—feature-style narratives—amount to 15 percent and 24 percent, respectively. These differences in format are smaller than the differences in content discussed in chapter 2. Novel, born-on-the-Web options aren't popular with journalists or with consumers. Across sites, blogs account for 4 percent of the journalists' choices and 3 percent of those of consumers, and user-generated content averages 1 percent and 0.26 percent respectively. Despite the hype about these storytelling options among some academics and practitioners, the levels of supply and demand suggest that they aren't a real competitor to traditional formats.[64] In addition, storytelling formats are somewhat independent of sociopolitical changes. Within this limited variance, there is more contextual dependency in the choices of consumers than in those of journalists. This suggests that journalists are less adaptable to changes in circumstances than consumers.

We also examine content and storytelling preferences together. We find that journalists oversupply straight news that deals with public-affairs topics and undersupply all the other permutations. But the gap between journalists' and consumers' choices when the analysis considers combinations of content and format is significantly smaller than the content gap identified in chapters 2 and 3. The storytelling preferences of journalists and consumers diverge less than those related to their thematic choices, even when both dimensions of the news are taken into account. This leads us to the conclusion that the supply-demand gap is attributable primarily to divergent content preferences and secondarily to the dynamics of storytelling.

In chapter 5, we explore whether differences in technology are related to variations in the thematic and storytelling preferences of consumers and what this might mean for the disparity between the stories considered most newsworthy by journalists and those preferred by consumers. We contrast the most clicked stories with their most emailed and most commented counterparts. We find that consumers usually click on what they deem interesting—most frequently, non-public-affairs stories in straight-news format. They often email articles that are bizarre or useful—non-public-affairs stories told in feature style. They comment on controversial stories—opinion or straight-news pieces about high-profile public-affairs topics. We also find that these three modes of consuming online news are more dependent on context than the stories supplied by journalists, but that commenting and clicking change more radically than emailing when there are changes in the sociopolitical environment. In a comparison of the difference between the most newsworthy and the most clicked stories, the gap between the content choices of journalists and consumers increases when one juxtaposes the journalists' top choices with the most emailed articles and decreases when journalists' top preferences are contrasted with the most commented on stories. Thus, these various uses of the different affordances made available by most sites indicate that technological factors are important for understanding the supply-demand gap in online news.

These findings are important for theorizing about the gap and its implications for long-standing debates at the intersection of communication, technology, and society. They also afford an opportunity for reflection on what they might mean with respect to the future of the media and their role in the democratic process.

We make two distinct theoretical contributions. First, we conceptualize some of the factors that affect the existence and magnitude of the gap. Contextual, technological, interpretive, and experiential dynamics affect the gap, but their geographic and ideological counterparts do not. In subsequent chapters, we shed light on the tendency of news consumers to activate different information practices in environments marked by ordinary and extraordinary sociopolitical circumstances and in relation to the various material properties of media artifacts. We also elaborate on the interpretive and experiential factors that subtend the prevalence of rational ignorance during ordinary circumstances and monitorial citizenship during extraordinary times. We argue that the lack of significance of geographic and ideological variations might be due to the power of two related trends: a trend toward the convergence of media systems and a trend toward the globalization of consumers' tastes.

Second, as was mentioned above, our exploration of the supply-demand gap has implications for at least three broader theoretical discussions at the intersection of communication and politics. They pertain to issues of agenda setting, monitorial citizenship, and the role of storytelling formats. First, we argue that the gap is linked to a potential limitation in the agenda-setting power of mainstream media with respect to public-affairs topics during periods of routine political activity. In view of the extremely limited public appeal of blogs and user-generated content, this limitation doesn't seem to be offset by a gain in consumer-driven efforts. Moreover, agenda setting should be understood as a function of the media that is highly dependent on context. Second, political communication scholars have recently been engaged in a normative debate about whether citizens want the media to provide comprehensive information about public affairs continually (the "full information" thesis) or only when critical dynamics of the polity are at stake (the "monitorial citizenship" thesis). Our account of variations in the size of the gap between periods of routine and heightened political activity contributes a unique perspective to this debate and supports the "monitorial citizenship" thesis. Third, contrary to the notions that "the news has gone soft" and that blogs and user-generated content are the way of the future, our analysis indicates that when we examine what people actually do, instead of what they say they do or what the pundits think they would want to do, journalists gravitate to straight-news accounts of public-affairs topics and consumers to straight-news accounts of non-public-affairs topics. Content is king in an age marked by an abundance of information available in a growing array of outlets, and members of each group lean toward the type of content that better resonates with their respective interpretive, experiential, and contextual circumstances.

In chapter 6 we summarize the descriptive, methodological, and theoretical contributions outlined above and explain how they are helpful in understanding the future of media and democracy. The supply-demand gap may have existed for a long time, although its magnitude in the past can't be ascertained. What is different now is that it threatens the public-service mission of mainstream news organizations in a time of increased market competition, rising challenges to traditional journalistic roles (including heightened awareness in newsrooms of consumers' preferences), and a greater ability of consumers to avoid the news they aren't interested in. We explore four possible ways to solve the problem that the gap presents for these organizations: to try to enact their public-service mission primarily through innovation in storytelling formats, to shift from generalist to niche strategies of news making, to give consumers more of the news they want and less of the information they need to function as informed members of the citizenry, and to make the production of news more flexible so as to be better able to deal with both periods of routine political activity and periods of heightened activity. We argue that the last option is the most promising one, because it matches the alternation between rational ignorance and monitorial citizenship that characterizes the behavior of demand. A flexible system of news production would allow mainstream media organizations to tailor their output to the behavior of consumers and to maintain their standing in the democratic process.

Regardless of how news organizations deal with a problem that may become more and more pressing, the potential consequences for the body politic are concerning. They include a loss in news organizations' agenda-setting power and a lack of effective participatory venues that would allow citizens to renew the agenda-setting process. Additional consequences are a reduction in the provision and the circulation of information that is critical to democratic deliberation and decision making and a growing disincentive for news organizations to play their watchdog role when it comes to matters of the polity. In the end, society's appetite for information may become satiated by news about weather, sports, crime, entertainment, or what Lippmann called "the curious trivial."[65] But the contributions of these symbolic nutrients aren't enough for the healthy functioning of the body politic. Much as we are what we eat, we are the news that we consume. And when the online news that is supplied fails to meet the demand, it isn't only leading media organizations that might suffer, but all of us.

# 2 The Divergence in the Content Choices of Journalists and Consumers

March 17, 2008 was a fairly typical news day in Germany, and it is precisely this typical quality that makes the findings in this chapter revealing. At least that might be the impression a reader would get from a cursory glance at the top screen of Tagesspiegel, the website of *Der Tagesspiegel*, one of country's leading dailies. (See figure 2.1.) Such a glance would show also that the thematic composition of the stories on this first screen of the homepage lean heavily toward public-affairs news. Seven of the first ten stories on the homepage are about public-affairs news; the remaining three are about non-public-affairs topics.

Placed in the top left corner of the screen, the top story of the day addresses a case with both international and political characteristics and is a typical example of the kind of public-affairs subjects that journalists tend to favor. Drawing on copy from news agencies, the article reports that NATO placed the Kosovo town of Mitrovica under *de facto* military law after riots by a Serb population hostile to independence attacked the UN police force and caused it to withdraw. It begins by providing factual information about the incident: "about 100 Serbs" attacked the UN personnel with stones and Molotov cocktails, injuring at least 30 police officers. The article closes by giving an account of the causes of violence: although the majority of the population is Albanian, 20 percent are ethnic Serbs opposing independence from Serbia, which had already been recognized by more than 20 countries, "including the United States and Germany."[1]

The most viewed stories on Tagesspiegel that day showed that consumers had markedly different thematic preferences than journalists. Unlike the journalists' top choices, the readers' top choices are marked by a strong predilection for non-public-affairs topics and "news you can use" (meaning stories with direct implications for everyday life). Six of the ten most

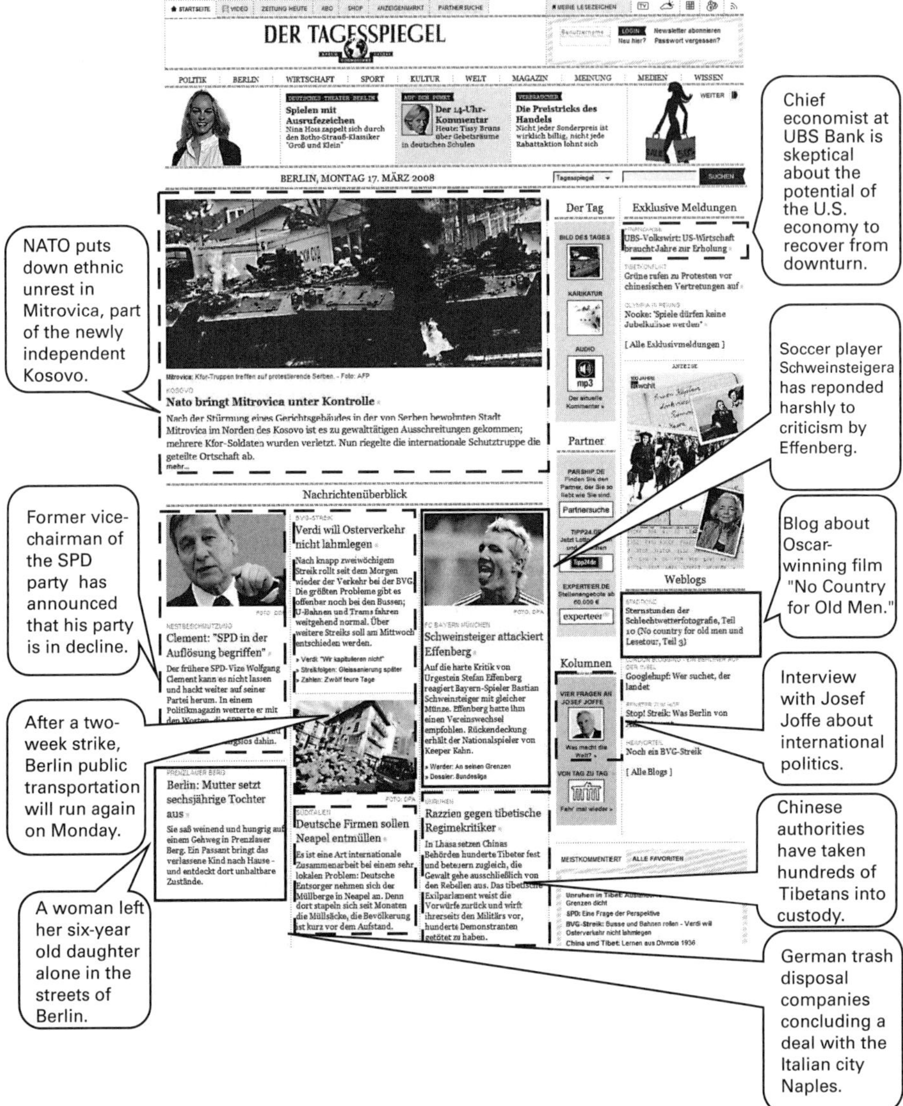


**Figure 2.1**
Homepage of Tagesspiegel on March 17, 2008. Dashed frames indicate stories on public-affairs topics; solid frames indicate stories on non-public-affairs topics.

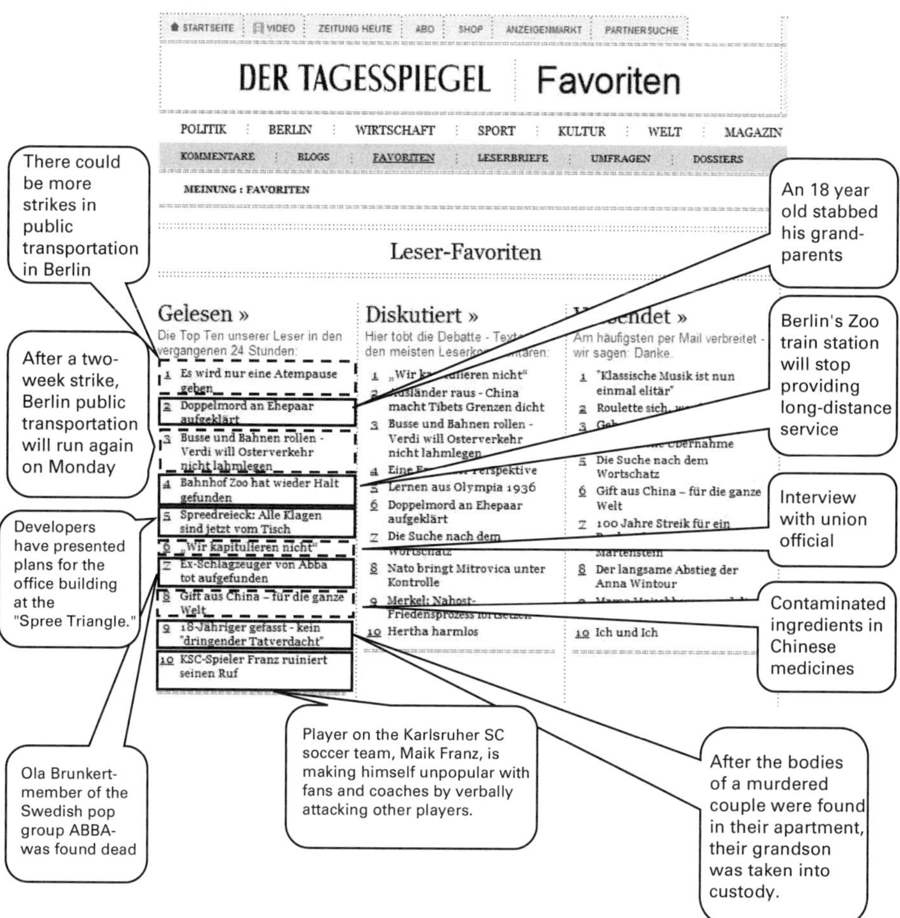


**Figure 2.2**
Top ten most viewed stories on Tagesspiegel on March 17, 2008.

viewed stories are not about public affairs. The remaining four stories address public affairs, including three stories on a Berlin transportation strike and a business piece on possible contamination of medicines imported from China. The latter are also examples of "news you can use."

The second most viewed story on Tagesspiegel that day is illustrative of consumers' preference for non-public-affairs news. It reports the murder of a 74-year-old woman and her 64-year-old husband in the Rudow neighborhood of Berlin. The elderly couple had been stabbed to death by their 18-year-old grandson. The story describes how "neighbors had heard cries for help" and called the police. It goes on to note that when investigators arrived at the crime scene "traces of blood" led them to the grandson, who confessed immediately.[2] The young man had previously been involved in another stabbing—he had helped his father attack his mother's new boyfriend.

The contrast between the media's provision of public-affairs news and the public's predilection for non-public-affairs stories also plays out across the Atlantic and south of the equator. The most prominently displayed stories on the homepage of Folha (the online counterpart of *Folha de S. Paulo,* one of Brazil's leading dailies) that day are evenly split between public-affairs stories and non-public-affairs stories. (See figure 2.3.) A look at the top five most viewed stories on Folha (located in the middle portion of the left side of the homepage) that same day reveals a dramatically different set of content preferences among the public. All of the most popular stories addressed non-public-affairs subjects. They included four entertainment stories and a report of a crime that had occurred in a McDonald's restaurant.

One of the most prominently placed public-affairs articles is a report on the looming international financial crisis. The story begins by quoting the director of the International Monetary Fund, Dominique Strauss-Kahn, who warned at an OECD conference that the "crisis would last a long time" and would have "serious consequences," which would also affect "emerging countries" such as Brazil. The article then describes how the United States Federal Reserve had lowered the discount rate a quarter of a percentage "to bolster liquidity and promote orderly functioning in financial markets."[3] Although the article describes a situation that would surely affect the economy of Brazil and the daily lives of Brazilians, it is noticeably absent among the five most viewed stories on that day. Faced with an

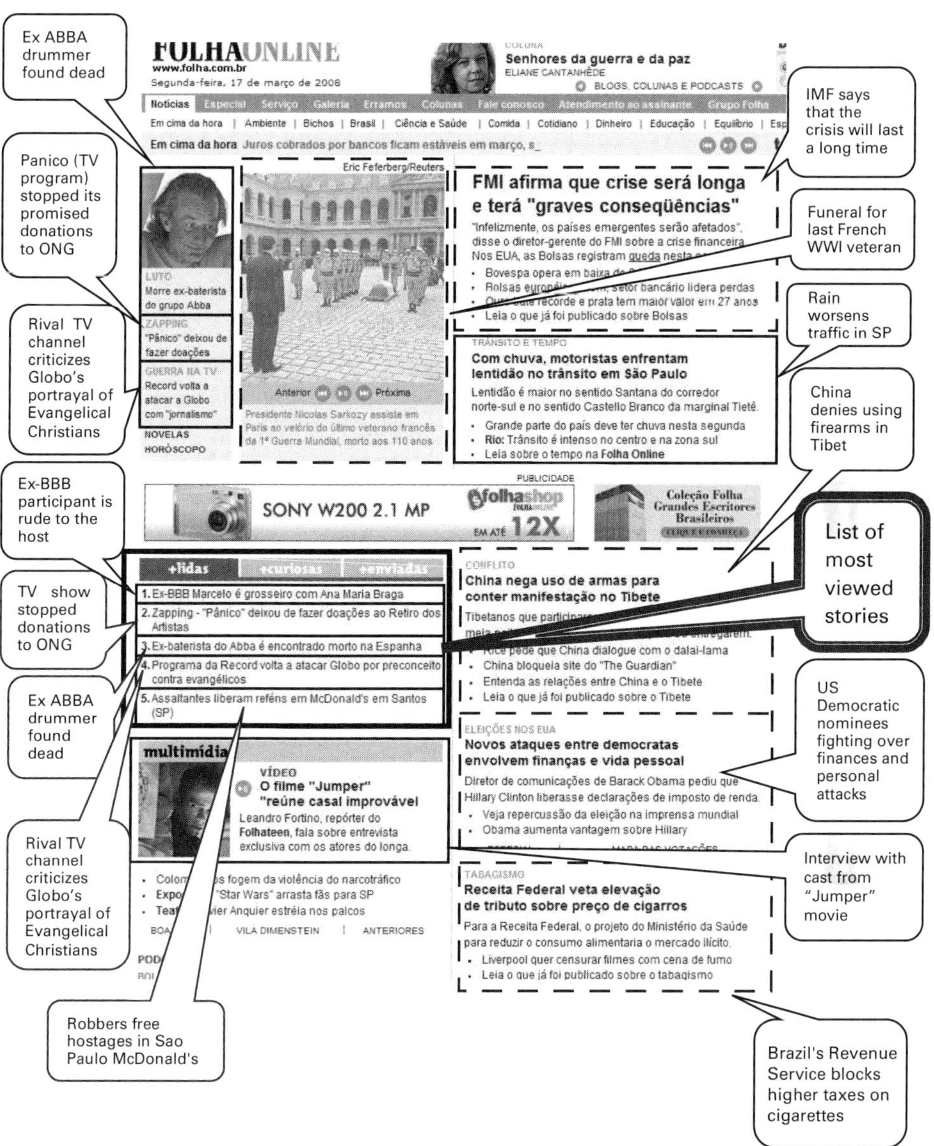


**Figure 2.3**

Homepage and top five most viewed stories on Folha on March 17, 2008.

approaching financial crisis, Folha consumers chose to devote their attention to the latest developments in show business. In fact, the most viewed story describes the rudeness of a former Big Brother Brazil contestant, a miner named Marcelo Arantes, to the show's host, Ana Maria Braga, when he refused to answer her question about the fights in which he was involved during his stay in "the house." The article includes speculations about Marcelo's sexual orientation and his intention to date a fellow contestant after she left the house.[4]

Tagesspiegel and Folha are located in countries with very different historical trajectories, cultural configurations, and structural compositions. They are also located on different continents and address different publics in different languages. Beneath these differences, however, journalists at Tagesspiegel and Folha share thematic preferences for news, which in turn diverge from the content choices of readers on both sites. Journalists at both sites feature a strong dose of public-affairs news in the main editorial offerings of the day: seven out of the ten stories that appear first on Tagesspiegel and five out of ten on Folha are about this kind of news. However, readers of both sites click most often on non-public-affairs stories; news of that kind constitutes the majority of the top ten most viewed stories on Tagesspiegel and all of the most popular stories on Folha. Whereas journalists give prominence to international conflicts and financial crises, consumers gravitate toward gory crimes and reality shows. A sizable supply-demand gap in content in the market for news results from these divergent thematic choices. As we stated in chapter 1, this gap is not a random occurrence; it is a regular feature among the mainstream news media. In the remainder of this chapter we document the existence of this gap, assess its magnitude, and show that it is largely unaffected by geographic and ideological factors.

These findings are relevant to two matters of ongoing discussions about media and society: whether there is convergence or divergence across media systems of different geographic locations and ideological orientations and whether the media continue to have a strong agenda-setting power in the digital age. We argue that the growing homogenization of journalism education and management, the rising dependence on news-agency copy, and the emergence of a high-choice media environment that allows consumers to focus on the stories they want and avoid the rest may contribute to the convergence. We suggest also that a gap as large, widespread, and consistent as the one we document indicates that leading media organizations may not be able to fulfill their traditional agenda-setting role, at least when it comes to online news. This, in turn, has significant implications for the matrix of political communication that connects collective actors, the media, and the public in contemporary societies.

## Measuring the Gap

The two illustrations that open this chapter represent larger trends that characterize the news choices of journalists and consumers that we found in a study of eleven online newspapers from six countries: Clarín[5] and Nación[6] from Argentina, Folha[7] from Brazil, Welt[8] and Tagesspiegel[9] from Germany, Universal[10] and Reforma[11] from Mexico, Mundo[12] and País[13] from Spain, and Guardian[14] and Times[15] from the United Kingdom. The countries in which these sites are published represent widely different media systems and political cultures.[16] Despite the differences among them, these sites are comparable in the sense that they are the online editions of leading generalist and mainstream newspapers that have national reach in their respective countries. Furthermore, in the five countries from which two news sites were sampled, the pairs had somewhat divergent ideological outlooks—either one member of the pair was conservative and the other liberal or one was conservative and the other centrist.

Data from these sites were collected between November 2007 and May 2008.[17] For each data-collection day, we identified and contrasted the top stories selected by journalists and consumers as introduced in chapter 1 and shown in figures 2.1–2.3. We focused on these stories because they are deemed the most newsworthy by journalists and they garner the most attention from consumers, respectively. For each story, we examined whether the main topic was or wasn't a public-affairs matter.[18, 19]

Our analysis shows some variance in the prevalence of public-affairs news in the top choices of both journalists and consumers. (See figure 2.4.) For example, on a site such as Universal in Mexico, journalists selected public-affairs stories as the most newsworthy stories of the day in more than 70 percent of all cases and consumers in more than 50 percent. The comparable numbers for Folha were above 40 percent and below 20 percent.[20] However, consistent with the pairs of illustrations that open this chapter, beneath this variation across sites there was a sizable and

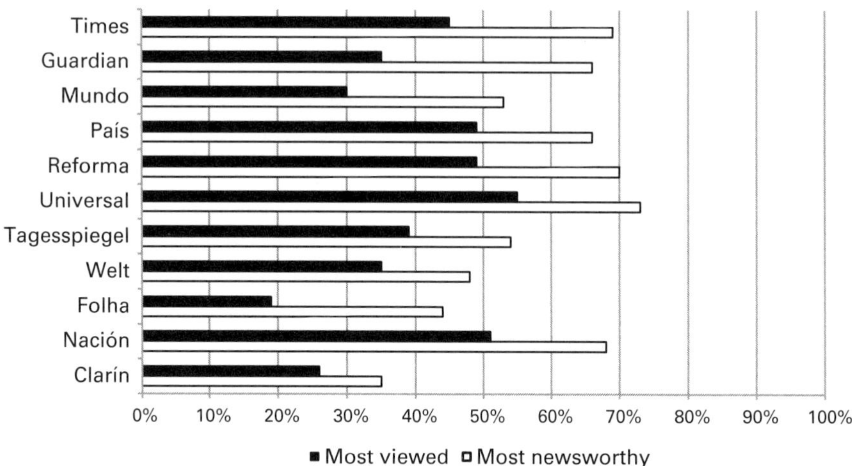


**Figure 2.4**
Percentage of public-affairs topics in the stories deemed most newsworthy by journalists and the articles most viewed by consumers on Times, Guardian, Mundo, País, Reforma, Universal, Tagesspiegel, Welt, Folha, Nación, and Clarín, all stories.

significant thematic gap between the news choices of journalists and those of consumers on all sites. News producers selected substantially more public-affairs stories than their audiences did. The difference between the choices of journalists and consumers ranged from 9 percentage points at Clarín to 31 percentage points at Guardian and reached an average of 19 percentage points across sites.[21, 22]

That news sites based in six different countries on two different continents converge to exhibit a thematic gap between the top news choices of journalists and their publics underscores the regularity of the thematic disparity. It also begins to give us an idea of that disparity's magnitude. These issues of regularity and magnitude are also present if we examine four leading online news sites based in the United States. As with the illustrations from Tagesspiegel and Folha, it is helpful to first look at concrete examples from a fairly typical news day in the United States. Table 2.1 displays the information about the ten articles that appear first on the homepages of four sites alongside the top ten most viewed stories on each of these sites on May 2, 2007. The sites are Chicago,[23] Seattle,[24] CNN,[25] and Yahoo.[26] They have different parent companies and different extents of geographic reach: two are affiliated with metropolitan print newspapers, one with a national cable channel of international reach, and one with a global search engine. Thus, it is not surprising that the news stories that these sites disseminate and those that capture the attention of their respective publics differ, as table 2.1 clearly illustrates. Beneath this difference, however, again there is a pattern of thematic divergence between the news preferences of journalists and consumers that cuts across all four sites; the journalists choose a higher proportion of public-affairs news than the consumers.

Even though the top stories of the day and the most viewed stories on CNN, Seattle, and Yahoo are about public affairs, their contents vary greatly. Journalists choose stories with strong policy overtones concerning congressional negotiations, immigration protests, and military conflicts. The public favors articles with an element of controversy, such as one on the decision not to allow the anti-war singer Joan Baez to perform at the Walter Reed Medical Center, which was the most viewed story on CNN. The difference between journalists' and consumers' preferences is brought to light by contrasting the most newsworthy story with the second most viewed story on CNN that day. The former, "Bush veto forces Dems to weigh difficult concessions," deals with foreign affairs and national politics; it reports on the negotiations between the Republican president and the Democratic congress regarding funding for the war in Iraq. In a matter-of-fact style, it depicts how President George W. Bush had vetoed an "Iraq war spending bill that set timelines for U.S. troop withdrawals," thus putting pressure on Congress to reach a compromise. Relying on a familiar "us-versus-them" trope, the article continues by quoting Speaker of the House Nancy Pelosi as having said that, although Democrats are willing to work with the White House, "the president wants a blank check [and] Congress is not going to give it to him."[27] The second most viewed story on CNN that day focused on Britney Spears' return to the stage after a hiatus of several years. In a marked contrast with the tone of the previous article, this story opens by colorfully describing how "Spears strutted her way back to center stage with a short, sexy set . . . wearing nothing more than knee-high go-go boots with a short white skirt and a sparkly pink bra top that showed off her belly button ring—and no evidence of the weight gain that landed her on celebrity tabloid covers last year." For background information, CNN offered details of the singer's latest stint in a rehabilitation center, mentioned "photographs splashed across the Internet" of her

**Table 2.1**

Top ten most newsworthy and most viewed stories on CNN, Chicago Tribune, Seattle PI, and Yahoo News, May 2, 2007. (Headlines with grey background refer to stories about public affairs, such as politics, economics, business, and international news. Headlines with white background refer to stories about non-public-affairs topics, such as sports, weather, entertainment, crime, science, and technology.)

| CNN | | Chicago Tribune | | Seattle PI | | Yahoo News | |
|---|---|---|---|---|---|---|---|
| Most newsworthy | Most viewed | Most newsworthy | Most viewed | Most newsworthy | Most viewed | Most newsworthy | Most viewed |
| Bush veto forces Dems to weigh difficult concessions | Baez: Why was I not in Walter Reed concert? | Drinking starts in the clubhouse: Hancock's death brings questions about alcohol use | Drinking starts in the clubhouse: Hancock's death brings questions about alcohol use | Immigration protests smaller, just as passionate | Appeals court rules against McDermott in phone call case | 4,000 U.S. soldiers arrive in Baghdad | IRS: Man ran secret bank from Wash. home |
| FDA: Contaminated feed could affect farms nationwide | Britney Spears takes baby step back on stage | House OKs smoking ban | Skulls found in man's apartment | Worth a million? Many are in King County | Des Moines home was a "bank" | Bush, Democrats to meet today on Iraq | Britney performs at California nightclub |
| Dobbs: A peculiar day for immigration rallies | Driver of exploded Bay Area truck had long criminal record | Associates call "ladies' man" an equal-opportunity cad | Associates call "ladies' man" an equal-opportunity cad | Appeals court reverses marijuana conviction on medical grounds | Mariners' Notebook: Hargrove tight-lipped on Weaver situation | International court issues first Darfur arrest warrants | "Reggie" the alligator reappears in L.A. |
| Israeli foreign minister joins calls for Olmert to resign | Father, relative charged in 10-year-old's scalding death | Cars in Printers Row hit with graffiti | House OKs smoking ban | Des Moines home was a "bank" | Mariners win, eclipse .500; Washburn good again | Ally of Israeli leader seeks resignation | 4,000 U.S. soldiers arrive in Baghdad |

| | | | | | | | |
|---|---|---|---|---|---|---|---|
| Panel cites gross violations of religious freedom in Iraq | Court file: Colleague suspected astronaut's affair | Skulls found in man's apartment | Study Suggests Racial Bias in NBA Calls | Supply keeps brakes on downtown housing | Worth a million? Many are in King County | Time Warner 1Q profit slips 18 percent | Kent State audio tape released |
| Court file: Colleague suspected astronaut's affair | Bush veto forces Dems to weigh difficult concessions | Police arrest slaying suspect holed up in building | Hancock reportedly offered cab ride home | Judge OKs class-action suit against Carrier over furnaces | Stanback sees many Cowboys hats | Spears gives brief concert at SoCal club | Study: Heart attack death rate declines |
| Driver of exploded Bay Area truck had long criminal record | Dobbs: A peculiar day for immigration rallies | Separate fires kill 1, injure 2 | Cars in Printers Row hit with graffiti | Edwards met with raucous applause at Seattle stop | Gig Harbor students protest surveillance of two girls kissing | What's US economy's future? Ask illegal immigrants. | Police to review clash at May Day rally |
| Ethics chief: Wolfowitz broke rules | "Dancing with the Stars" dismisses another | Warrants Issued for 2 Darfur Suspects | Police arrest slaying suspect holed up in building | Pike Place Market leaders list desired fixes | Go 2 Guy: Weaver will make a believer out of you, too | Musicians unlock mystery melody in Scottish chapel | Iran arrests former nuclear negotiator |
| Britney Spears takes baby step back on stage | FDA: Contaminated feed could affect farms nationwide | Study Suggests Racial Bias in NBA Calls | Sad goodbyes follow layoffs at hospital | Microsoft pushes next-gen ads | Good Samaritan canoeists get $85 tickets | On trip to Mars, NASA must rethink death | Couple touring home find woman's body |
| Thompson: Potential GOP opponents digging up dirt | Kent State tape: "Get set! Point! Fire!" | "We're proud of our lives" | Tom Poston; comic actor on "Newhart" | Eggs Benedict show Mom she's worth your time and effort | Cocaine, opiates killed UW's Brasier | Arctic ice cap melting 30 years ahead of forecast | Historian claims to ID Jack the Ripper |

"wearing nothing underneath her short skirts," and the divorce settlement she had just reached with the father of her two young children.[28]

A quantitative analysis[29] of the data collected from these sites between April and June 2007 shows that on each of the sites journalists chose significantly more public-affairs stories than consumers. (See figure 2.5.) As with the sites from Western Europe and Latin America, there were variations in the prevalence of public-affairs news among the top stories for both journalists and consumers. However, consistent with the illustration presented in table 2.1, these differences in the thematic choices of journalists and consumers resulted in disparities of ten or more percentage points across all sites.

A second examination of these data looks at the stories chosen exclusively by journalists or consumers on each site but not by both. It provides a distilled picture of the choices of each group by focusing on the subset of stories that journalists displayed prominently but that had low levels of demand among consumers, or on the subset of stories that had high levels of demand among consumers although journalists didn't display them prominently. For example, table 2.2 shows how the CNN homepage and the list of the most clicked stories looked on May 2, 2007 after the stories

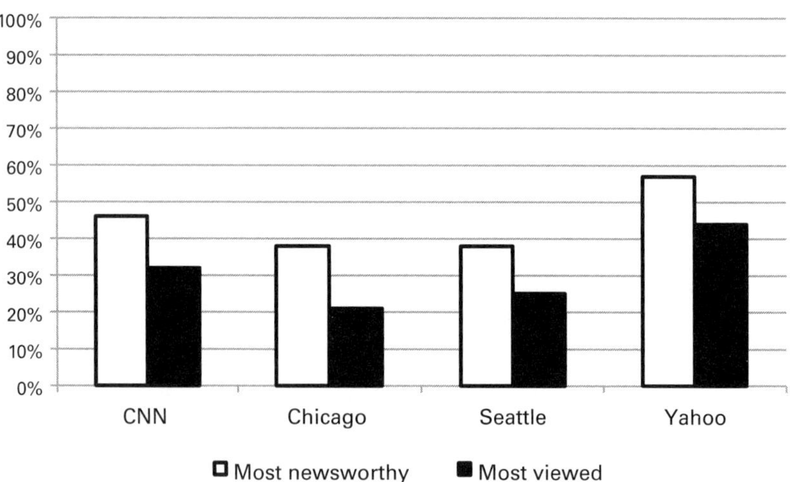


**Figure 2.5**
Percentage of public-affairs topics in the stories deemed most newsworthy by journalists and the articles most viewed by consumers on CNN, Seattle, Chicago, and Yahoo, all stories.

**Table 2.2**

Top ten most newsworthy and most viewed stories on CNN, May 2, 2007, before and after excluding articles with overlap in the most newsworthy and "most viewed" lists. (Headlines with grey background refer to stories about public affairs, such as politics, economics, business, and international news. Headlines with white background refer to stories about non-public-affairs topics, such as sports, weather, entertainment, crime, science, and technology. Headlines in bold refer to stories that are part of both the "most newsworthy" list and the "most viewed" list in the same period of data collection.)

| Before | | After | |
|---|---|---|---|
| Most newsworthy | Most viewed | Most newsworthy | Most viewed |
| **Bush veto forces Dems to weigh difficult concessions** | Baez: Why was I not in Walter Reed concert? | | Baez: Why was I not in Walter Reed concert? |
| **FDA: Contaminated feed could affect farms nationwide** | **Britney Spears takes baby step back on stage** | | |
| **Dobbs: A peculiar day for immigration rallies** | **Driver of exploded Bay Area truck had long criminal record** | | |
| Israeli foreign minister joins calls for Olmert to resign | Father, relative charged in 10-year-old's scalding death | Israeli foreign minister joins calls for Olmert to resign | Father, relative charged in 10-year-old's scalding death |
| Panel cites gross violations of religious freedom in Iraq | **Court file: Colleague suspected astronauts' affair** | Panel cites gross violations of religious freedom in Iraq | |
| **Court file: Colleague suspected astronaut's affair** | **Bush veto forces Dems to weigh difficult concessions** | | |
| **Driver of exploded Bay Area truck had long criminal record** | **Dobbs: A peculiar day for immigration rallies** | | |
| Ethics chief: Wolfowitz broke rules | "Dancing with the Stars" dismisses another | Ethics chief: Wolfowitz broke rules | "Dancing with the Stars" dismisses another |
| **Britney Spears takes baby step back on stage** | **FDA: Contaminated feed could affect farms nationwide** | | |
| Thompson: Potential GOP opponents digging up dirt | Kent State tape: "Get set! Point! Fire!" | Thompson: Potential GOP opponents digging up dirt | Kent State tape: "Get set! Point! Fire!" |

with overlap between journalists and consumers had been removed. Only four stories remained on each list. The journalists' choices were four stories about public affairs: one on a political crisis in Israel, one on religious freedom in Iraq, one on an ethics scandal at the World Bank, and one on a Republican presidential hopeful, Senator Fred Thompson. In contrast, only two of the four remaining stories on the consumer side were about public affairs: one on Joan Baez' not being allowed to perform in a concert for veterans and one on new revelations about the Kent State University shootings of 1970. The two other stories were about the murder of a child and the weekly outcome of the television program "Dancing with the Stars."

For the second analysis, we examined only 26 percent of the stories on CNN, 46 percent on Chicago, 60 percent on Seattle, and 67 percent on Yahoo—the stories on each site without overlap between the two lists. Consistent with the examples presented in table 2.2, the results from the second analysis show that the thematic gap between journalists' and consumers' choices increased on all sites when compared with the findings from the full data set summarized in figure 2.5. The gap increased from 14 to 51 percentage points on CNN, from 17 to 38 percentage points on Chicago, from 13 to 23 percentage points on Seattle, and from 13 to 19 percentage points on Yahoo.[30] (See figure 2.6.) Thus, patterns that existed when all stories were included in the analysis become magnified after stories with overlap were removed. This suggests that if the potential influence of each group on the other were to diminish, the choices of journalists and consumers would be even more divergent than they currently are. Furthermore, on three of the four sites journalists' choices moved in the direction of public-affairs stories, and on all sites consumers' choices moved toward non-public-affairs stories. On CNN, Chicago, and Seattle, this widening arose from increases in both journalists' share of public-affairs stories and consumers' share of non-public-affairs news. On Yahoo, the proportion of public-affairs stories decreased for both journalists and consumers, with a more pronounced decrease for consumers. In addition, as the number of stories chosen exclusively by journalists and by consumers decreased, the disparity between them increased. For example, journalists chose only 165 stories that weren't also selected by consumers on CNN, versus 424 on Yahoo, and their respective gaps with consumer choices increased by 37 and 6 percentage points. This indicates that when the

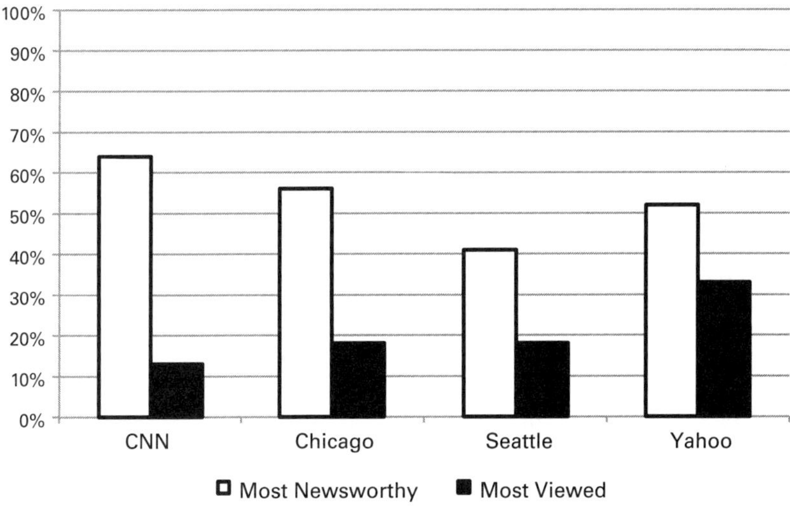


**Figure 2.6**
Percentage of public-affairs topics in the stories deemed most newsworthy by journalists and the articles most viewed by consumers on CNN, Seattle, Chicago, and Yahoo, excluding stories with overlap.

overlap between journalists' and consumers' preferences is larger, the most newsworthy stories that are not among the most viewed articles lean strongly toward public-affairs news, whereas the most popular stories that are not featured prominently on the homepage tend to be about non-public-affairs topics.

This two-step analysis of the data from four leading online news sites based in the United States is highly consistent with the trends from the sites in Western Europe and Latin America. The thematic gap between the top news choices of journalists and their publics is a regular phenomenon in the media environment, and its magnitude reached double digits in all but one of the fifteen sites examined. Looking at the gap *across* the sites, rather than *within* them, provides further confirmation of these findings. To this end, we examined the stories that appeared on either the journalists' or the consumers' lists of more than one site in a country.[31] This gives us a measure of the convergent news interests across the journalistic field and/or the public at large. In the six countries in which two or more one sites were analyzed, there is a significant gap between the convergent choices made by journalists and consumers, ranging from 8 percentage points in Argentina to 26 percentage points in Spain. Public-affairs topics occupied the majority of journalists' convergent news choices in all the cases analyzed, ranging from 56 percent of the stories in the United States to 76 percent in the United Kingdom. Public affairs also occupied the majority of audiences' shared choices in four of the countries, although to a lesser extent than in the journalists' lists, ranging from 51 percent of the convergent news choices in Argentina to 64 percent in the United Kingdom. In contrast, non-public-affairs stories occupied most of consumers' convergent preferences in Spain and the United States.

In sum, this analysis of the convergent news choices of journalists and consumers demonstrates that the supply-demand gap characterizes the editorial space not only in its persistence from one site to the next but also in the inter-site convergence of news preferences among the two groups.

## Do Ideology and Geography Affect the Supply-Demand Gap?

We returned to the data from the comparative study of Western European and Latin American media to examine whether ideological differences might affect the presence and/or magnitude of the gap. We found that the thematic disparity between the online news choices of journalists and consumers remained quite immune to the ideological orientation of the sites—that is, differences between journalists' and consumers' choices also existed, and their sizes were comparable, when news sites of opposed ideological stances were contrasted. (See figure 2.7.) On conservative sites (Mundo, Nación, Reforma, Times, Welt), the difference between journalists' and consumers' choices was 21 percentage points. On centrist and liberal sites (Clarín, Guardian, País, Tagesspiegel, Universal) this difference was 19 percentage points. Ideology's lack of relevance to journalists' and consumers' thematic preferences is also underscored by the finding that the prevalence of public-affairs news is almost identical for journalists of conservative and liberal sites as well as for consumers of each of these sites.

Contrasting Spain's two leading online newspaper sites, Mundo and País, illustrates this pattern of similarity across the ideological divide. On March 24, 2008, Mundo, Spain's major conservative site, featured six public-affairs news stories among the ten most prominently displayed stories. These included the two main stories of the day, displayed on the top left side of the screen, about the new speakers of the ruling Spanish

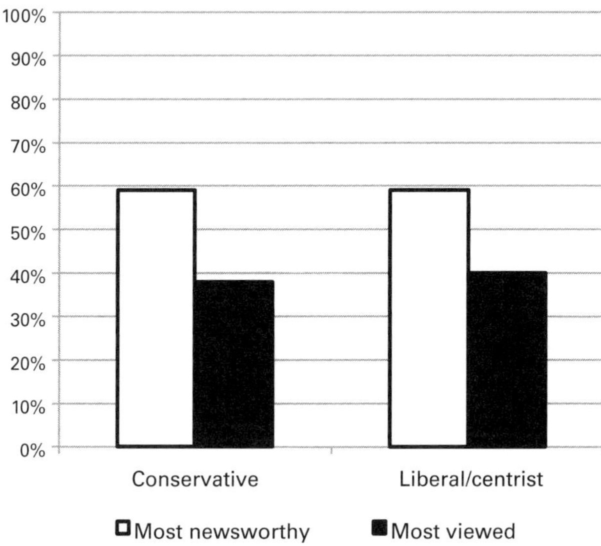


**Figure 2.7**
Percentage of public-affairs topics in the stories deemed most newsworthy by journalists and the articles most viewed by consumers in conservative and liberal/centrist online news sites.

Socialist Party (PSOE) in Congress and in the Senate—José Alonso and Carmen Silva, respectively. Both stories are replete with factual information on their previous appointments, the names of the officials they replaced, and the naming of their deputies. For instance, the article on Alonso noted that he had represented the province of León in the Congreso de los Diputados (Congress of Deputies) and had served as Minister of Defense, and that "deputy Ramón Jáuregui will occupy the position of secretary general of the Parliamentary caucus, thus becoming 'number two' in the caucus' leadership." Likewise, the article on Silva's appointment reveals that she had been "councilwoman in charge of Urbanism and Housing in the town of Vigo," and that she planned to appoint "an experienced team to lead the Socialist caucus in the Senate."[32]

Things weren't much different across the ideological aisle on the homepage of País, Spain's top left-leaning news organization, which was updated only 6 minutes later than the homepage of Mundo. As on Mundo, six of the ten most prominently displayed stories on País were about public affairs. Furthermore, the top two stories of the day coincided with those of Mundo, were placed in the same order on the screen, and had nearly identical headlines. The articles about Alonso and Silva were very similar in structure, describing their careers, who they were replacing, and who would be joining them on their leadership teams.

A simple comparison between these two homepages shows a remarkable degree of convergence in the top editorial choices of journalists on two sites with markedly divergent ideological positions. First, both sites exhibit a 60–40 mix of public-affairs and non-public-affairs news. Second, the sites coincide in the selection of four of the ten most prominently displayed stories. This coincidence is particularly strong regarding public-affairs news. It holds for three out of six stories, including the top two stories of the day, which are constructed with similar language and presented in similar order. Third, placement on the screen also follows a similar logic on both sites. Public-affairs stories dominate the column on the left side, and the top non-public-affairs stories—a piece about Britney Spears on Mundo and one on fiscal fraud by the soccer club Betis on País—are located to their right to "soften" the initial visual impression of what would otherwise be a top homepage screen marked by "harder" public-affairs topics.

An examination of the most popular stories on these two sites reveals other similarities of a different kind. On Mundo, seven of the ten most viewed stories are about non-public-affairs topics. The top two are about sports and have provocative headlines. The top story (about recent poor race performances by the Formula One driver Fernando Alonso) is titled "Fernando Alonso: 'I feel impotence.'" The second most viewed story, headlined "'If my swim suit tears, I'll swim without it,'" and reports on a "wardrobe malfunction" that happened to the swimmer Rafael Muñoz. The article describes Muñoz's performance in the 2008 European Aquatics Championships, in which he won a bronze medal in the 50-meter butterfly race. The story reports that Muñoz had to compete in a borrowed suit—he "was hoping to race in the new suit, but when [he] got there, it was torn. [He] returned to change to his spare suit, but when [he] tried it on it tore, too, and [he] said 'well, let's swim without a swim suit.'"[33]

Non-public-affairs news also constitutes the majority of the ten most viewed stories on País. Six of these stories are about these same topics, including four of the top five. The top story addresses a timeless topic with the headline "Confirmed: 'Love is blind.'" It is a report on research at an academic center in Barcelona on the increases in dopamine and serotonin experienced by people who are in love. According to the most popular article on the site that day, researchers found that "people who are really in love lose the ability to criticize their partners, that is, they are incapable of noticing their partner's defects, which confirms the popular saying, 'love is blind.'"[34] Thus, although journalists at Mundo and País emphasized the trials and tribulations of the ruling political party in their editorial offerings for that day, consumers of both sites showed a preference for sports, scandal, and romance.

Moreover, there are interesting similarities between the preferences of consumers of Mundo and País. Unlike journalists, consumers gravitate toward non-public-affairs topics—seven out of ten and six out of ten of the most viewed stories on Mundo and País, respectively, are about such topics. In addition, headlines with sexual implications (e.g., "I feel impotence," "Love is blind," "If my swim suit breaks, I'll swim without it") seem to garner substantive attention. And the popular stories that touch on topics commonly considered "unsexy," such as political and financial matters, tend to be about matters that are closer to people's everyday lives (for example, the practical implications of the real estate crisis) rather than about the loftier matters often favored by journalists (such as the appointment of new socialist speakers in the Spanish Congress). In view of the similarity between the choices of journalists of both sites and between the consumers of both sites, it is not surprising that the quantitative evidence indicates that ideology doesn't affect the supply-demand gap in the case of online news.

As was mentioned in chapter 1, the geographical locations of news sites, considered as a proxy for cultural and structural features of the media, could also influence the existence and size of the supply-demand gap. We find that there are some superficial differences in the prevalence of public-affairs news across sites and across countries in Western Europe, Latin America, and the United States. The data show that journalists and consumers in Western Europe and Latin America choose a higher proportion of public-affairs news than their counterparts in the United States. (See figure 2.8.) The prevalence of this type of news among the most newsworthy stories reaches nearly 60 percentage points in the first two regions; it averages only 45 percentage points across the four American sites. Consumers of the Western European and Latin American include 40 percent

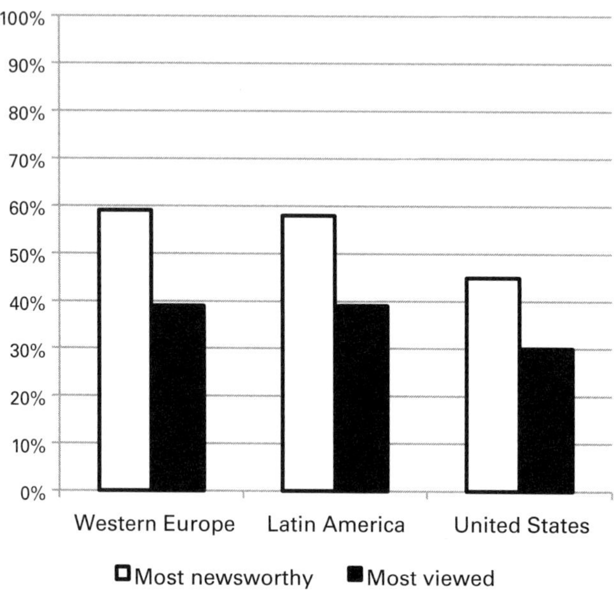


**Figure 2.8**
Percentage of public-affairs topics in the stories deemed most newsworthy by journalists and the articles most viewed by consumers in Western Europe, Latin America, and United States.

of public-affairs stories in their "most viewed" lists; the comparable figure for American consumers is 30.5 percent. Yet a very strong and consistent pattern cuts across the three parts of the Western hemisphere beneath this disparity in journalists' and consumers' lists. There is a disparity of more than 10 percent in the prevalence of public-affairs subjects among the top online news choices of both groups. When the fifteen sites are grouped by region, it becomes obvious that journalists choose public-affairs news 20 percentage points more often than consumers in Western Europe, 19 percentage points more often in Latin America, and 14 percentage points more often in the United States.

The homepages and "most viewed" lists of Times and Nación on March 17, 2008 illustrate the lack of major variance across regions in the existence and relative magnitude of this gap. Although both Times and Nación share a conservative ideological orientation, the United Kingdom and Argentina have markedly different national media systems and occupational cultures. However, on that day the thematic composition of the pairs of homepages and "most viewed" lists was quite convergent, even though the actual stories differed by site. Six of the ten most newsworthy stories on the Times homepage were about public-affairs topics, including two articles on foreign news, two on the financial crisis, and two on business news. The most prominently displayed public-affairs story reports the incidents in Kosovo. It is a typical article about foreign affairs, providing first the most important facts ("the UN ordered its police to pull out of a Serb-dominated town in northern Kosovo—today after troops and officers were injured in a riot by hundreds of nationalists opposed to the country's independence") and noting that "twenty-two Polish UN police and eight French NATO troops" had been injured, "while reports suggest that at least one UN van and one NATO lorry had been seized, set on fire, and the detainees freed.[35]

Across the Atlantic and south of the equator, the most prominently displayed stories on the homepage of Nación exhibited an almost identical thematic mix on that day; seven out of ten articles were about public-affairs news, including four pieces on national news, one on international news, another about economic news, and a public policy story about the mayor of Buenos Aires. The most prominently placed article about public affairs reports the repeal by a Circuit Court of the statute of limitations for crimes committed by the Alianza Anticomunista Argentina between 1973 and 1976. The court had decided that those acts of torture and murder constituted "crimes against humanity" and thus could not be subject to the statute of limitation, as regular crimes are. Finally, the piece describes how Juan Domingo Perón's third wife, and president from 1974 until 1976, Isabelita Martínez, risked being detained for these crimes if she ever returned to Argentina.[36]

The homepages of Times and Nación reveal quite comparable forms of editorial construction in two organizations located in countries with different media systems, traditions, and histories. In both cases, public-affairs news dominates the top editorial offerings. Furthermore, those stories tend to concern important topics and dense policy issues that range from the financial crisis to international conflicts. In addition, a handful of non-public-affairs news stories soften the top editorial offerings. They include—in both cases—a major story about a figure with a significant presence in the public imagination of his respective country—the former Beatle Paul McCartney on Times and the former soccer superstar Diego Maradona on Nación.

Consumers' news preferences differ dramatically. The most popular story of the day among online readers of Times was a feature on the difficulties of erasing one's existence from Facebook. First, the article describes how some social networking sites, such as Facebook and MySpace, had suffered losses in membership during the previous year. It then wonders "whether many people have grown weary of being contacted by complete strangers, invited to join wacky-sounding groups or asked to play silly vampire-bite games where you receive points for the number of strangers you can 'infect.'" According to the writer, the main rationale for trying to leave social networks was the need to remove embarrassing posts from public view. The story finishes by describing the difficulties some Facebook users had when they tried to delete their Facebook profiles, and provides tips on how to achieve that end.[37] A public-affairs piece on the global financial crisis and two other non-public-affairs articles completed the top four "most read" stories list: an article about ten things that will get passengers kicked off an airplane and a review of a new Renault sedan.

Although there are important cultural differences between the United Kingdom and Argentina, the thematic preferences of the online readers of Nación and of Times didn't differ much on March 17, 2008. Eight of the most viewed stories were about non-public-affairs news. The most viewed article was about people who had taken up new activities after retiring. For instance, the story describes how Norma, "a retired math teacher," opened an organic food business at the age of 65, and how Alberto, a 74-year-old architect, had moved to a seaside town and completed two postgraduate degrees after his children had left the family home. The article finishes by quoting Alberto, who says that "taking up the books again, spending the night finishing an assignment . . . makes you forget you are 70 years old. If you feel good, you are never old."[38]

These examples illustrate a strong pattern in the data: the thematic preferences of readers of sites based in two very different countries, on different continents, and publishing in two different languages converge to a remarkable degree. In both cases, the most viewed stories are dominated by non-public-affairs topics: three out of four on Times, and eight out of ten on Nación. Furthermore, these stories tend to focus on "light," humorous, and practical topics, such as how to remove one's profile from Facebook, how a new car performs, how to avoid being kicked off a plane, how to install a home network, and how to find a new life after retirement.

The contrast between the similarities across homepages of sites of two different countries and the similarities between the "most viewed" lists of these sites reveals a thematic gap between supply and demand that seems quite independent of geographic factors.

## Concluding Remarks

In chapter 1 we noted the existence of a debate in scholarly circles about whether there is a gap between the thematic news preferences of journalists and those of consumers. The evidence presented in this chapter clearly establishes that this gap exists, that it is sizable, and that it appears to be fairly immune to variations in regional provenance and ideological leaning of the media in question. This was true for the fifteen leading media outlets that we examined in seven countries in three quite diverse parts of the Western hemisphere.

On all of the news sites included in this chapter, journalists selected as the most newsworthy articles substantially more public-affairs stories than did their public. The gap was fairly large, ranging from 9 to 30 percentage points, with an average of 18 percentage points across all sites. Furthermore, the gap increased when we removed stories that overlapped the "most newsworthy" and "most read" lists. This suggests that if they were more sheltered from knowing what the other group wants, journalists and consumers would diverge even more in their thematic choices for news. The gap was also present when we looked at the convergent news choices of journalists and consumers across sites in the same country, not just within a particular site. In sum, three different perspectives on the evidence—when all stories within sites are analyzed, when only stories without overlap within a given site are considered, and when only the stories that converge across two or more sites per country are examined—yield essentially the same result: the presence of a sizable thematic gap in the online news choices of journalists and consumers. Thus, in terms of the debate mentioned above and discussed in chapter 1, this analysis provides strong support for the thesis that news audiences, in contrast with journalists, are mostly interested in non-public-affairs stories.

Our test for the existence of a thematic gap between the content preferences of journalists and consumers is a cautious one. First, whereas journalists choose which stories to cover from the universe of possible newsworthy events, consumers make their selection within each site among the choices offered by journalists. On the basis of findings from this study, it is reasonable to expect that if audiences were presented with more non-public-affairs stories they might choose an even lower proportion of public-affairs news. Second, leading online news sites account for only a portion of consumers' media diet. Recent scholarship has shown that audiences tend to privilege entertainment over news.[39] In light of this research, the thematic gap might be larger than what this study shows if the entire universe of media choices for audiences were compared against journalists' choices.

The gap doesn't vary when sites are grouped according to the region in which they are based. This finding is relevant to another topic of ongoing debate in the literature: whether there is convergence or divergence of national and regional media systems. Some scholars have argued that journalistic practices and media content are becoming increasingly similar across nations because of the expansion of the market society and the secularization of politics after World War II. Worldwide communication has gone through a process of modernization or professionalization,[40] and journalists from all over the world have embraced the Anglo-American ideal of objectivity and facticity.[41] A second notion suggests that transnational media conglomerates, which appeared in the last three or four decades of the twentieth century, exploit content by repurposing it for distribution across multiple platforms in different countries[42] and promote the adoption of a stronger commercial orientation and the values of free-market capitalism.[43] Other analysts have proposed that different countries have distinct media cultures[44] that are in turn influenced by political and legal institutions that vary across nations. This constitutes a barrier against the homogenization of journalistic work and news content.[45]

A cursory look at the results shows that there is some variance in the proportion of public-affairs news in the top choices of journalists and consumers on different sites.[46] However, beneath this expression of divergence lies a more fundamental pattern of convergence, represented by the presence of the gap in news choices on all the sites, regardless of geographical region. The evidence of the existence of a thematic gap between journalists' and consumers' choices on fifteen news sites across seven countries is highly robust and provides support for the convergence thesis, at least regarding the issue of the thematic gap in online news.

That the divergence between journalists' and consumers' choices doesn't vary when sites are grouped according to their ideological stances reinforces the convergence thesis. The size of the gap between the stories considered most newsworthy by journalists and the articles most viewed by consumers on conservative and liberal sites differed by only two percentage points. This is consistent with the research that indicates that mainstream online media tend to cover the same topics, although their opinions on those issues may vary.[47] Although some scholars have found that consumers select news sources that match their political beliefs,[48] there are no ideological differences between audiences that prefer coverage of public-affairs issues and those that lean toward entertainment topics.[49] Two factors contribute to explain this convergence. First, journalists from different parts of the world have increasingly embraced the same values and professional practices,[50] shaped by patterns such as the growing homogenization of journalism education and management[51] and the increasing dependence on the same pool of correspondents and news-agency copy.[52] These values include privileging public-affairs news content and relying on politicians and government officials as the main sources of news. Second, in a high-choice media environment,[53] consumers all over the world are more capable of following their interests, which, according to this study, don't coincide with those of journalists.

As was discussed in chapter 1, the existence of a thematic gap between journalists' and consumers' choices has multiple implications for our understanding of the internal dynamics and the broader societal role of the news media. One implication concerns the agenda-setting function of the press in the digital era. Agenda-setting theory proposes that news media influence which issues or events are the most important at the moment and thus deserve public attention.[54] Although some authors have proposed that the use of online sources of information[55] doesn't diminish the influence of the media on the public's agenda, others have hypothesized that the online environment may erode editorial influence over the public's agenda as a result of the multiplication of news outlets and the resulting fragmentation of the audience.[56] Our findings suggest that the leading mainstream news media may not fulfill their agenda-setting role—at least when it comes to online news—because consumers' news preferences diverge from those of journalists. In other words, the media may very well attempt to set an agenda that is focused on public-affairs topics, but a sizable portion of their audiences seems to be spending most of their attention on sports, weather, crime, and entertainment news. What can be said about the power of the media to set the agenda when there is an 18-percentage-point gulf, on average, between what those media say and what their publics appear to be listening to? In this sense, the media seem to be talking to themselves and to the political and economic elites, rather than to their broad base of consumers. Moreover, the ability of the media to influence the elites is somewhat dependent on the size and composition of their audience. Because news outlets with large and resourceful audiences are more likely to influence decision makers than those that don't have such audiences,[57] their power to set the agenda for both the elite and the mass public on the Web may be compromised by the supply-demand gap in online news. The erosion of the agenda-setting influence of mainstream media organizations could lead to the disappearance of broadly shared national concerns, thus diminishing the ability of the public to come together on common issues and maximizing social polarization.[58]

The conceptual and political import of a diminution in the power of the media to set the agenda is particularly critical during periods when the citizenry could benefit most from information about public affairs—periods marked by major political or economic events, such as elections or crises, a matter we address in the next chapter.

# 3 The Difference Politics Makes

November 4, 2008 was an extraordinary day in recent American history. More than 130 million Americans went to the polls to elect the first African-American president in the country's history in what was the highest turnout for a presidential election since 1968.[1] It was also the first election in 56 years in which neither an incumbent president nor a vice-president ran for office. If these aspects of the electoral process weren't enough to generate major interest in public-affairs reportage, in the same year fifteen banks failed, the federal government rescued many others, and the Dow Jones Industrial Average fell 18 percent between October 6 and October 10 in its worst weekly decline ever.[2] The combination of a high-profile political campaign and the worst recession since the Great Depression of the 1930s[3] created the conditions for a quasi-experiment on how high-profile political and economic developments might affect the news choices of journalists and consumers.[4] The occurrence of these two events made it possible to study in a "natural" setting the evolution of the supply-demand gap in preferences for online news during a period of heightened activity in public-affairs matters.

Journalists' choices at two of the top U.S. news sites, Washington Post and CNN, on November 4, 2008 illustrate the importance of public-affairs matters that fall. The *Washington Post* is known for its strong focus on political coverage. That day, all the stories in its online edition were about public affairs, in general, and the election, in particular. (See figure 3.1.) From the top of the page down and from left to right, the most prominently displayed article focused on heavy voter turnout and isolated malfunctions in the voting process in Virginia, Maryland, and the District of Columbia. The article begins by describing how "voters driven by the historic presidential election waited up to several hours

» Hello valt | Change Preferences | Sign out
» Make Us Your Home Page
» U.S./World Home Page | Change to Washington Home Page

washingtonpost.com

The Washington Post
Today's Paper | Subscribe | PostPoints

NEWS | POLITICS | OPINIONS | LOCAL | SPORTS | ARTS & LIVING | GOING OUT GUIDE | JOBS | CARS | REAL ESTATE | RENTALS | SHOPPING

SEARCH: go washingtonpost.com Web: Results by Google

Tuesday, November 4, 2008 | 3:56 p.m. ET

ELECTION 2008

Landmark Election Draws Eager Voters

Voters wait to cast ballots in Md. (Susan Biddle/Post)

Lines Long for Washington Area Voters

Voters go out of their way to make sure ballots are cast; minor problems reported in Fairfax and Prince George's.
» Debbi Wilgoren | 12:06 p.m. ET
• E-Mail Hoax at GMU | Before You Venture Out | Kelly
• The Fix | Va. Politics | Md. Moment | D.C. Wire | Raw Fisher

Your Guide to Election Night

Sign up to follow coverage throughout the day via Twitter and alerts by e-mail and text. Also, send us your video comments and polling place reports at Vote Monitor.
• An Armchair Pundit's Plan | Where the Candidates Stand

Isolated Problems Amid Heavy Voter Turnout

Lines form early at many voting sites and experts caution that the day could be marked by long delays.
» Mary Pat Flaherty | 1:42 p.m. ET
• The Trail: Live Updates
• Polls Show Obama With Advantage

At the End of an Extraordinary Ride

THE TRAIL | Election Day is always a moment of great anticipation. This Election Day may be among most anticipated as any in memory.
» Dan Balz | 10:25 a.m. ET
• Death Casts Pall on Obama Camp
• Media Notes | At the Polls

A Breakdown of Races You'll Want to Watch

THE FIX | An hour-by-hour look at the contests and places that will redraw the nation's political landscape.
» Chris Cillizza | 1:15 p.m. ET
• McCain Undertakes 7-State Swing
• Authorities Eye Voter Perks
• Sketch: Where's Whatshisname?

INTERACTIVE
Political Landscape 2008

GALLERY
Voters Crowd Polling Stations

VIDEO
Area Voters Flood Polls Early

POLITICS » Complete election coverage | D.C. Area Elections » Va. Senate race, Md. slots and more

OPINIONS
A Confirmational Election
Cohen: Beyond Karl Rove's gaze, America has been changing.
Robinson: A New Pride | Q&A
PostPartisan: Limerick Contest

Stocks Stage Election Day Rally

Dow up 3 percent, despite growing evidence that the country may be slipping into a recession.
» Renae Merle | 3:18 p.m. ET
• China Faces Faltering Economy | Economy Watch

TALK BACK
Defend your vote, post your election reports, chat with other users. More »

LIVE WEBCAST
Our video coverage and analysis of the election starts at 6 p.m. ET.

Advertisement

VIDEO SERIES
Voices on Leadership
Looking to build your business or take your management skills to a higher level? CEOs from recognizable companies and leadership experts weigh in on what skills are needed to succeed.
Voices on
• Blog: The Intelligent Leader• Voices on Green
• Voices on Small Business• Voices on Personal Tech

E-MAIL NEWSLETTERS
Sign Up for Your Newsletters Today
Specialized e-mail newsletters produced exclusively for washingtonpost.com readers.
• News: Breaking News Alert | TechNews Daily Report
• News: Sights & Sounds
• Politics & Opinion: Politics News & Analysis
• Politics & Opinion: Federal Insider• Today's Opinions
• Arts & Living: Washington City Guide
• Arts & Living: Movies | Travel | Home
• Arts & Living: DC Scout - Hip Local Finds
• Sports: Redskins• News for Life: Health - Lean Plate Club
• News for Life: Personal Finance | Jobs

**Figure 3.1**
Homepage of Washington Post on November 4, 2008.

in line at polling stations starting before sunrise" on that day. It then introduces several voters and the reasons for their respective choices. For instance, we read about 79-year-old Mildred Benning, an African-American woman who had "lived through the civil rights struggle in North Carolina, an experience that [had] shattered her faith in the goodness of American people—for a while." Benning, who had turned out to vote for Obama, is reported to have exclaimed "Who among us ever thought we would live to see this day? I've never been so proud of my country."[5]

On that day, the thematic preferences of Washington Post's consumers coincided with those of journalists. (See figure 3.2.) The most read article of the day is an analysis of the latest survey results, which "underscored the steep hill" the Republican presidential candidate, John McCain, had to "climb in the final hours to reach the 270 electoral votes needed to win the White House."[6] The article focuses on the horse-race aspect of the electoral contest, rather than on substantive differences between the two candidates or potential policy outcomes of the election. It cites the Washington Post/ABC News tracking poll, which showed Obama leading by 9 percentage points, and remarks that all the latest national polls showed a lead of between 5 and 11 percentage points for Obama. But it then states that "until the polls close and the final votes are tallied, nothing is certain in Campaign 2008," and concludes on a rather gloomy note that "the remaining mysteries are how voters ultimately will respond to the prospect of the nation's first African American president and whether any racial resistance to his candidacy can be offset by the Obama campaign's effort to expand the electorate." All the remaining stories in the "most viewed" list were about the election and addressed topics such as the possibility of heavy voter turnout and the wariness of authorities concerning gifts offered to voters by certain companies, such as Starbucks and Ben & Jerry's.

Although CNN is considered more a generalist than a politics-oriented news site,[7] on November 4, 2008 all the stories that journalists selected to appear in the top portion of the site's homepage were also about public affairs. (See figure 3.3.) The top article of the day referred to the "excitement" of voters as they arrived at various polling stations across the United States. It coincides with Washington Post's appraisal of the election as "historic": "When the ballots are counted, the United States will have elected either its first African-American president, or its oldest first-term president and first female vice president."[8] It also features the testimonials of enthusiastic voters. For instance, "Jude Elliot, an 8th-grade social studies teacher in Orangeburg, South Carolina" is reported to have said that it felt "great to be an American today," and that the time he spent voting had been "the best hour and a half of my life." Juan Bedoya Castano, a Colombian immigrant who had just become a citizen of the United States a month before the election, said that he had "never voted for something" and "this actually mean[t] something."

washingtonpost.com Hello valt
Change Preferences | Sign Out
The Washington Post
Print Edition | Subscribe | PostPoints

NEWS | POLITICS | OPINIONS | LOCAL | SPORTS | ARTS & LIVING | GOING OUT GUIDE | JOB

SEARCH: go washingtonpost.com Web: Results by Google | Search A

washingtonpost.com

**Most Viewed Articles**
Updated 3:00 p.m. ET

**1) Polls Show Obama With Clear Advantage**
By Dan Balz
Washington Post Staff Writer
November 3, 2008 1:49 PM

Democrat Barack Obama, seeking a history-making victory in a presidential campaign that has captivated the country as few others ever have, maintained a clear advantage over Republican John McCain yesterday as the two made final appeals in battleground states and readied massive get-out-the-vote ...

**2) Americans Cast Ballots Across the Country**
By Mary Pat Flaherty
Washington Post Staff Writer
November 4, 2008 6:25 AM

Polls opened across the country today amid signs of heavy turnout for the election between Republican John McCain and Democrat Barack Obama, with lines forming early at many voting sites and experts cautioning that the day could be marked by long delays in casting votes and getting them counted

**3) Authorities Eye Voter Perks**
By Frank Ahrens
Washington Post Staff Writer
November 4, 2008 12:26 PM

Businesses that hope to reward voters today for exercising their patriotic right might be committing a felony.

**4) The Election That LBJ Won**
By Richard Cohen

November 3, 2008 7:06 PM

Somewhere beyond the gaze of Karl Rove, America's been changing.

**5) Five Election Myths**
By Anne Applebaum

November 3, 2008 7:06 PM

Beware the hopeful, reassuring cliches that will be passed around today and tomorrow.

**6) Voters Experience Long Lines With Minor Problems in Fairfax, Pr. George's**
By Debbi Wilgoren
Washington Post Staff Writer
November 4, 2008 6:58 AM

Virginia, Maryland and District voters lined up at polling stations hours before the doors opened this morning, braced for unprecedented turnout and eager to cast their ballots in a historic presidential election.

**7) Chatological Humor**
Gene Weingarten
Washington Post Staff Writer
October 28, 2008 6:59 PM

Post columnist Gene Weingarten answers your questions about his column, "Below the Beltway," and more. Funny? You should ask.

**8) A New Kind of Pride**
By Eugene Robinson

November 3, 2008 7:29 PM

I know what Obama meant when he said his faith had been 'vindicated.'

**9) The Final Push**
By Shailagh Murray and Robert Barnes
Washington Post Staff Writers
November 3, 2008 10:22 PM

It took nearly two years, many ups and downs, countless smart moves, missed chances and lucky breaks. But finally Barack Obama could say the words: "One more day."

**10) Election 2008: Early Voting and Exit Polling**
Michael McDonald
George Mason University
October 31, 2008 6:29 PM

George Mason University Associate Professor Michael McDonald, who runs the school's United States Elections Project, discusses the results of early voting in the 2008 campaign and what they mean for races around the country, as well as how exit-polling will work Tuesday night.

**Figure 3.2**
Ten most viewed stories on Washington Post on November 4, 2008.

**Figure 3.3**
Homepage of CNN on November 4, 2008.

Consumers of CNN were also interested mostly in public-affairs topics that day, although less so than journalists: eight of the ten most viewed stories were also about the election, whereas all of the journalists' choices were. (See figure 3.4.) These eight stories included the piece based on the testimonies of excited voters that was featured on the homepage, one on possible tie scenarios in the Electoral College, one on Barack Obama casting his vote, one on technical glitches in the voting process, one on the final campaign appearance by John McCain, one on the feelings of camaraderie among voters, and one on the Democratic Party's chances of attaining a large majority in the Senate. The second most viewed story on Election Day 2008 examined the "social issues[,] including abortion rights, affirmative action and same-sex marriage" being decided through ballot measures in 33 states. These referenda included moves to outlaw abortion in Colorado and South Dakota, California's Proposition 8 on same-sex marriage, and a "variety of proposals related to animal rights, gambling, marijuana and renewable energy."[9] The piece cited a remark by an "elections analyst" named Jenny Bowser that "the potential to effect change should encourage people to vote." The two stories in the "most read" list that weren't about public affairs were an interview with the inventor of the multi-touch screen that CNN used in its coverage of the elections and an article about the murder of a teenager in Brooklyn.

Washington Post and CNN are similar in certain ways and different in others. Both are leading and mainstream media outlets with national reach in the United States. (CNN also has a major global presence.) However, Washington Post has a stronger focus on political coverage because it is located in the nation's capital and is read by many politicians and policy makers,[10] and it has liberal leanings.[11] In contrast, CNN is a generalist outlet whose audience includes mostly Democrats and Independents.[12] The respective news choices of journalists and consumers on November 4, 2008 reflected this combination of similarities and differences. Journalists on both sites selected public-affairs topics for all of the ten most newsworthy stories, and public-affairs news accounted for the majority of the consumers' ten most popular stories (80 percent on CNN, 100 percent on Washington Post). Although there was a 20-percentage-point disparity between consumers' and journalists' news choices on CNN, there was no gap on Washington Post. This constitutes a major difference from the uniform situation presented in the previous chapter. Developing the

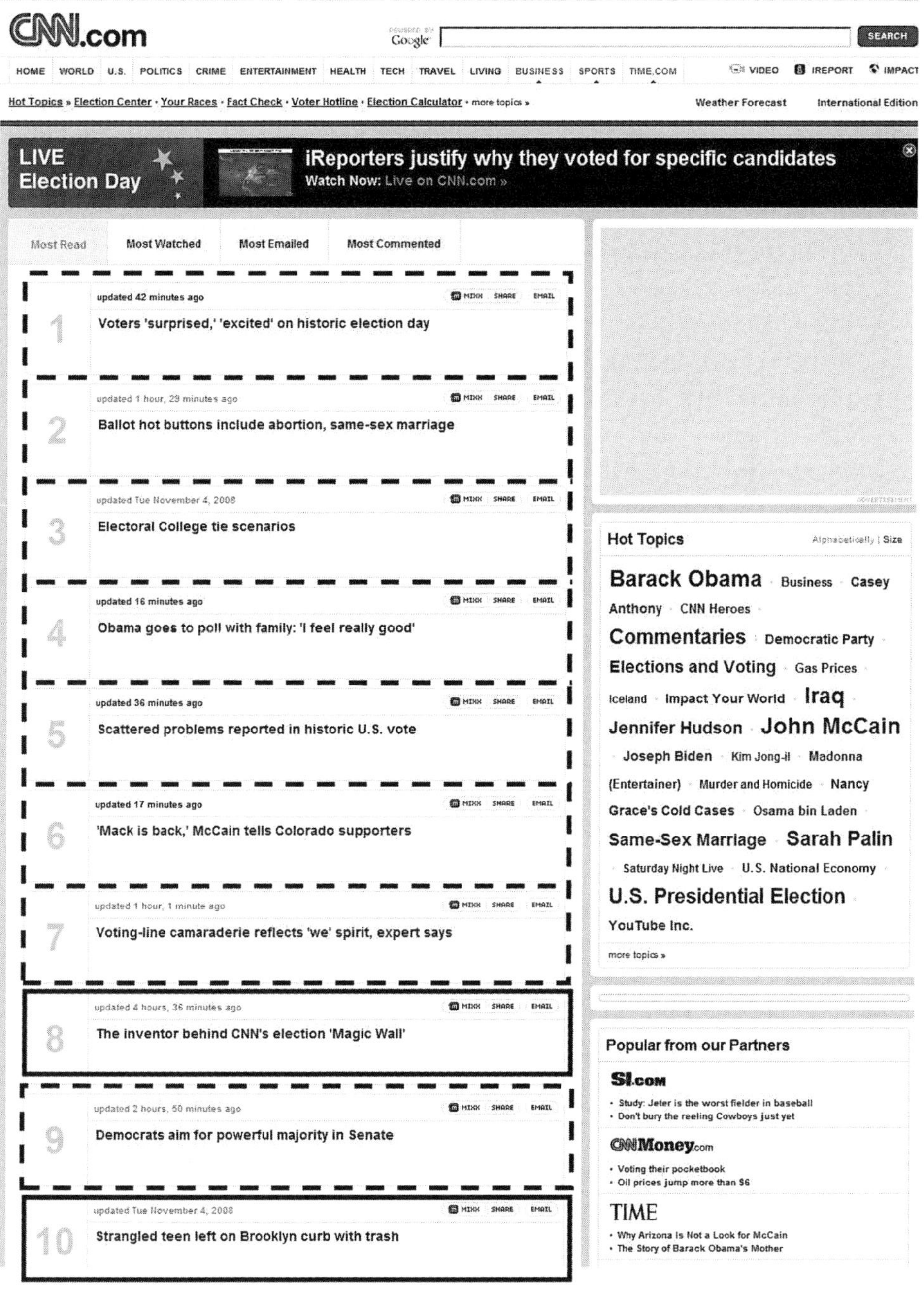


**Figure 3.4**
Ten most viewed stories on CNN on November 4, 2008.

themes suggested in these illustrations, the current chapter aims to elucidate the difference that major political events, either planned (such as a presidential election) or unforeseen (such as a sudden nationwide political crisis), might make in the existence and size of the thematic gap between journalists' and consumers' news choices. We find that both during the 2008 election in the United States and during a political crisis in Argentina in the same year the respective preferences of both groups changed from the norm during periods of more routine political activity in the direction of a greater prevalence of public-affairs news. That this was due primarily to alterations in the nature of demand is evident from the finding that that the news choices of journalists didn't change as much as those of consumers. That, in turn, resulted in an overall reduction of the size of the gap. Therefore, the chapter addresses two more fundamental issues: whether this gap is dynamic or static (that is, whether it changes in relation to contextual transformations) and what role the political process plays in whatever dynamism there is.

We argue that the diminished agenda-setting power of the media during normal times—discussed in the previous chapter—gets a boost during periods of heightened political activity, at least in the case of online news. Thus, in the digital age the agenda-setting function of the news media should be seen as highly context-dependent. Furthermore, this dependence on context, as noted above, is primarily premised on fluctuations in the public's interest. Thus, our account also suggests that—contrary to idealized notions of "fully informed" consumers who want more political information than the media provide and "rationally ignorant" audiences who disregard political matters that they cannot influence—people behave as monitorial citizens by increasing their attention to public affairs during periods of heightened political activity and decreasing it during more ordinary times.

## The 2008 U.S. Presidential Election

The illustrations presented above are from a project that examined the news choices of journalists and consumers in six American English-language sites affiliated with cable, television, and print news outlets: ABC,[13] CBS,[14] CNN,[15] Fox,[16] USA Today,[17] and Washington Post.[18] These sites all have national reach and made the relevant information about consumers' news choices publicly available for the duration of the project. Yet they differ in catering to different types of audiences, in degree of concentration on public-affairs news, and in their ideological leanings. Analyzing diverse news outlets allowed us to ascertain whether the differences between journalists' and consumers' choices share fundamental characteristics across the sites selected, in spite of the existence of these variations. We looked at the news choices of journalists and consumers from August 1, 2008 to December 1, 2008 and sampled between four and five times per week, with one exception: we sampled fourteen consecutive days surrounding Election Day (from October 27, 2008 to November 9, 2008).[19] We then collected data on these same sites almost exactly a year later (from October 26, 2009 to November 8, 2009) to examine whether there were differences between periods of heightened and more routine political activity.[20] We conducted two waves of analysis. First, we compared the two sets of fourteen days in 2008 and 2009 to ascertain any patterns of inter-annual variation. Then, we examined the complete four months of data from 2008 to look at changes within the campaign cycle. We present the main findings from these two waves of analysis in the remainder of this section.

The analysis of the fourteen days surrounding Election Day indicates that at the six sites journalists published a higher percentage of public-affairs stories than of non-public-affairs stories, ranging from 64 percent at ABC to 79 percent at Washington Post. (See figure 3.5.) At five out of the six sites, consumers selected a greater percentage of public-affairs stories, ranging from 59 percent at CNN to 91 percent at Washington Post. At Fox, consumers selected only 25 percent of public-affairs stories. Even in the two final weeks of the campaign, Fox consumers, who tend to hold a conservative ideology,[21] exhibited a low level of interest in public-affairs news. This could have been a result of the frustration of these consumers with the Republican Party's chances in the presidential election. In spite of journalists' and audiences' shared preferences for public-affairs topics during the fourteen days surrounding Election Day, at four of the sites there was a gap between the thematic choices of news producers and consumers. Journalists selected more public-affairs topics than consumers, and the difference ranged from 11 percentage points on CBS to 50 on Fox. In contrast, at ABC there was no statistically significant difference between journalists' and consumers' preferences. At Washington

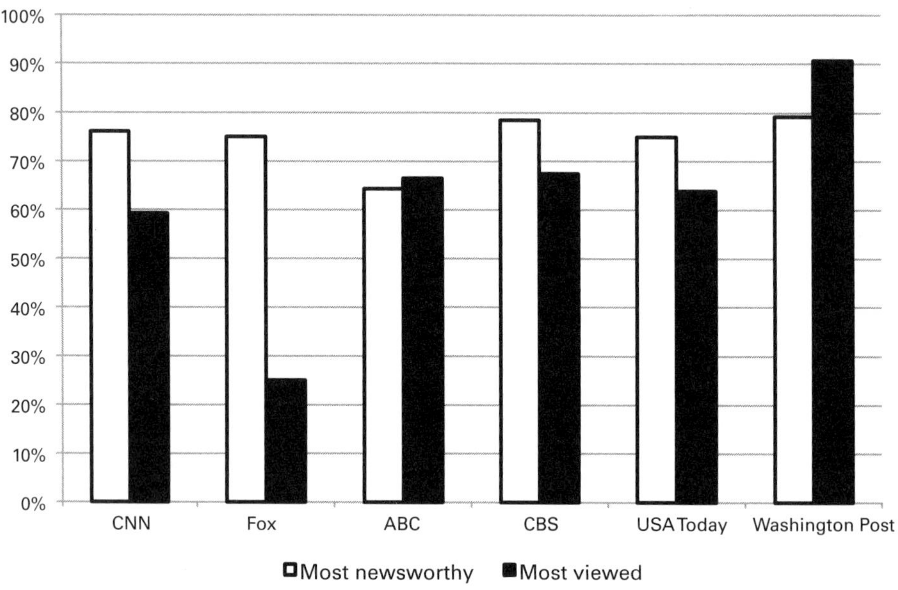


**Figure 3.5**
Percentage of public-affairs topics in the stories deemed most newsworthy by journalists and the articles most viewed by consumers on CNN, Fox, ABC, CBS, USA Today, and Washington Post, October 27–November 9, 2008.

Post the trend reversed, and consumers selected 12 percentage points more of public-affairs topics than journalists.

The situation at the peak of the election cycle has differences and similarities with the scenarios in the United States, Western Europe, and Latin America that we presented in chapter 2. Three patterns of difference are most noteworthy. The first is heightened interest in public-affairs news among both journalists and consumers (with the exception of Fox for the latter). The second is the disappearance of the gap on one site. The third is the fact that on Washington Post, the site most devoted to politics among the six sites sampled, consumers selected more public-affairs topics than journalists. The main pattern of similarity is the existence of double-digit gaps on the majority of the sites, even in an extraordinarily fertile context of interest in public-affairs reportage.

But how stable are these patterns of similarity and difference? A look at the choices of journalists and consumers during the two weeks in 2009 that match the fourteen-day period surrounding Election Day in 2008 provides useful information. An examination of the homepages and the most viewed stories at Washington Post and CNN on November 4, 2009 illustrates the difference in the news choices of journalists and consumers between periods of extraordinary political activity and periods of more routine political activity.

At Washington Post, journalists selected ten public-affairs news stories as the most newsworthy stories of the day, as they had done exactly a year before. (See figure 3.6.) The leading article, placed on the top left corner of the site, covered the reaction of the chairman of the Republican National Committee, Michael Steele, to the victories of Republicans in gubernatorial elections in Virginia and New Jersey. The piece reports that Steele, interviewed on a television show the morning after Election Day, "crowed,

The Washington Post

TODAY'S NEWSPAPER
Subscribe | PostPoints

NEWS | POLITICS | OPINIONS | BUSINESS | LOCAL | SPORTS | ARTS & LIVING | GOING OUT GUIDE | JOBS | CARS | REAL ESTATE | RENTALS | CLASSIFIEDS

SEARCH: go washingtonpost.com Web: Results by Google

Wednesday, November 4, 2009

Markets: DJIA +25.92 NASDAQ -2.11 S&P 500 +0.68

(Photo: Getty)

RNC's Steele takes a victory lap
44 | Crowing over GOP victories in Va. and N.J., chairman declares wins a rebuke to "incredibly arrogant government in Washington."

After celebration: GOP faces ideological fissures
Reenergized Republicans are savoring a "renaissance," but soon they will face questions over how best to lead the party back to power.
» Philip Rucker and Perry Bacon Jr. | 2:30 p.m. ET

- Christie bests Corzine in race for N.J. governor
- N.Y.'s Bloomberg narrowly reelected to third term
- The Fix: Former CEO Fiorina announces Senate bid

West Wing: Too much hype
Aides state they're unconcerned about what losses might portend for their boss and his policies.
» Michael D. Shear | 2:15 p.m. ET

- Media Notes: The non-referendum | Full Coverage

Cracks in Obama coalition
ANALYSIS | Republicans have the more energized constituency heading into midterm elections.
» Dan Balz

OPINIONS
The electoral aftermath
Marcus: Ignore the hype
Capehart: Fed-up nation
Dionne: Conservatives lost
Broder: Trouble ahead for Dems

- Milbank: Michael Steele's gotta crow
- Will: Obama looks for unicorns in Afghanistan
- Pundit Contestant 5: Grade your citizenship
- Pundit Contestant 6: America's Afghan 'victory'

PLUS » Telnaes Animation: GOP attention deficit

Editorials, Opinions, Columns, and Blogs

- Ombudsman: Blog | Latest Column | Feedback

Conviction in CIA rendition case
22 agents guilty of kidnapping cleric in Milan, sending him to Egypt without judicial oversight.
» Craig Whitlock | 2:52 p.m. ET

Fed holds rates near zero
Federal Reserve still views recovery as fragile and pledges to keep interest rates low for some time.
» Neil Irwin | 2:54 p.m. ET

- New York files antitrust suit against Intel
- Chrysler unveils business plan | Stocks jump

MOST VIEWED ARTICLES
- One daughter's secret revealed, ultimately too late
- Contests serve as warning to Democrats: It's not 2008 anymore
- Great whites near shore more often than believed
- Italian court convicts 23 Americans in CIA rendition case

Most Popular: What's hot on washingtonpost.com

Advertisement

SPECIAL FEATURES
Innovations in News
Experience the next generation in online news and see behind-the-scenes of the latest projects.

**Figure 3.6**
Homepage of Washington Post on November 4, 2009.

'Yeah, baby. That's my moment.'"[22] The article then deals with Steele's statements in a news conference at which he "declared the wins a rebuke to the 'incredibly arrogant government in Washington.'" He blamed a "botched process" for the Republican loss in a congressional district in New York where conservatives unhappy with the moderate candidate had supported a candidate favored by the Tea Party movement.

In contrast, the most read story that day among Washington Post consumers was a feature piece about a couple coming to terms with their daughter's drug addiction. (See figure 3.7.) The article chronicles the transformation of Alicia Lannes from an "outgoing young woman who loved to pull pranks and spend time with her family" to "a hysterical junkie overwhelmed by despair."[23] It also focuses on the role her boyfriend, Skylar Schnippel, played by first introducing her to the drug and then "distributing to her." It conveys the main facts in the case through an interview with Alicia's parents and through an account of the criminal case against Schnippel. After describing a series of heroin overdoses leading up to the final, fatal one, the piece concludes by describing how, every night, Alicia's father pauses outside his daughter's bedroom and softly bids her good night. More generally, of the ten stories in the "most viewed" list, six were about public affairs, including one analyzing the results of various gubernatorial elections, one on the reaction to these results at the White House, and one on the Republican victory in Virginia. The remaining four articles were about non-public-affairs topics, including the feature piece about the girl who died of an overdose, a story about sharks approaching the coastline more often than previously thought, a story about a heroin ring connected to four deaths by overdose, and a question-and-answer session with two Washington Post celebrity-news columnists.

At CNN, seven of the ten stories deemed most newsworthy by journalists were about public-affairs matters. (See figure 3.8.) The most visible story on the homepage concerned the former Hewlett-Packard CEO Carly Fiorina's intention to run as a Republican senatorial candidate in California. It described how Fiorina made the announcement at "an event in conservative Orange County, pledging that her focus [would] be on economic recovery and fiscal accountability."[24] The article then explained that Fiorina would have to compete "against conservative California Assemblyman Chuck DeVore for the GOP nomination," then "face three-term Sen. Barbara Boxer in November."

washingtonpost.com

**Most Viewed Articles**
Updated 3:00 p.m. ET

**1) One daughter's secret revealed, ultimately too late**
By Caitlin Gibson

November 3, 2009 9:00 PM

Greg and Donna Lannes sat on either side of their daughter in the Bethesda office of psychiatrist Steven Pankopf. Between them, Alicia was composed, her head up and her voice steady.

**2) Contests serve as warning to Democrats: It's not 2008 anymore**
By Dan Balz
Washington Post Staff Writer
November 3, 2009 11:07 PM

Off-year elections can be notoriously unreliable as predictors of the future, but as a window on how the political landscape may have changed in the year since President Obama won the White House, Tuesday's Republican victories in Virginia and New Jersey delivered clear warnings for the Democrats.

**3) Great whites near shore more often than believed**
By Juliet Eilperin
Washington Post Staff Writer
November 3, 2009 6:37 PM

For years, humans have thought of great white sharks wandering the sea at random, only occasionally venturing close to shore.

**4) Italian court convicts 23 Americans in CIA rendition case; extradition undecided**
By Craig Whitlock
Washington Post Foreign Service
November 4, 2009 5:30 AM

MILAN — An Italian court on Wednesday convicted 22 CIA operatives and a U.S. Air Force colonel of orchestrating the kidnapping of a Muslim cleric here in 2003 and flying him to Egypt, where he said he was tortured.

**5) Obama's brother speaks out for first time**
By Keith B. Richburg
Washington Post Staff Writer
November 4, 2009 8:18 AM

GUANGZHOU, China — The mixed-race son of a brilliant but troubled Kenyan academic and a white American woman writes an emotionally moving book about his search for identity and self.

**6) White House tries to shrug off Democratic election losses**
By Michael D. Shear
Washington Post Staff Writer
November 4, 2009 1:12 PM

President Obama's top advisers closed ranks around their boss Wednesday, declaring themselves unconcerned by Tuesday night's Democratic losses as they attempted to insulate the president from any political damage to his reputation and his legislative agenda.

**7) Teen Heroin Ring in Centreville: Parents Talk**
Caitlin Gibson and Greg and Donna Lannes
Writer and parents of Alicia Lannes
November 2, 2009 4:30 PM

Greg and Donna Lannes, the parents of Alicia Lannes, who was one of four fatal overdose victims connected to a heroin ring that operated among a group of more than 50 teens and young adults in Centreville, Va., will be online with writer Caitlin Gibson to discuss the story.

**8) GOP reclaims Virginia**
By Rosalind S. Helderman and Anita Kumar
Washington Post Staff Writers
November 3, 2009 6:01 AM

Virginians elected Republican Robert F. McDonnell the commonwealth's 71st governor Tuesday, sweeping the GOP to power and emphatically halting a decade of Democratic advances in the critical swing state.

**9) As Virginia goes, so goes not much**
By Ruth Marcus

November 3, 2009 5:11 PM

Tuesday's election results won't forecast much for anyone.

**10) The Reliable Source: Scientology church, Sasha and Malia, Agassi, January Jones, Mel Gibson, more**
Amy Argetsinger and Roxanne Roberts
Washington Post Staff Writers
November 3, 2009 10:40 AM

**Figure 3.7**
Ten most viewed stories on Washington Post on November 4, 2009.

**Figure 3.8**

Homepage of CNN on November 4, 2009.

The list of the most read articles at CNN on November 4, 2009 (figure 3.9) shows a dramatically different set of thematic preferences among consumers than among journalists. The most read story was a short piece that described a Twitter exchange between Jessica Simpson and Dolly Parton on the subject of their breasts. The article begins by reporting that Parton tweeted "Aahhh chiropractor... Hurts so good:-) you lug these around and see if your back don't hurt!" and Simpson replied "Amen sister:)."[25] It then reports on previous situations that centered on the singers' "double-D breasts"—for instance, that Simpson "offended some of her new [country] fan base by showing off too much cleavage." Six off the remaining most popular stories were also non-public-affairs stories.

The distance that separates the potential electoral contest between Carly Fiorina and Barbara Boxer from the breast-size communion of Dolly Parton and Jessica Simpson on November 4, 2009 is a powerful illustration of the widening of the gap in preferences from a period of extraordinary political activity to a more ordinary period. A cursory comparison of figure 3.5 (a bar graph of data from the period October 27–November 9, 2008) and figure 3.10 (October 26–November 8, 2009) reveals a general decline of interest in public-affairs news (with some notable exceptions). The decline is far less pronounced for journalists than for consumers. At four of the six sites—CNN, Fox, CBS, and Washington Post—journalists prioritized public-affairs news when selecting articles for the top portions of their respective homepages, ranging from 57 percent at CNN to 82 percent at Washington Post. At ABC and USA Today, half of the items deemed most newsworthy by editors concerned public affairs. In contrast, at five of the six sites (CNN, Fox, ABC, CBS, and USA Today) the top news choices of consumers exhibited a much lower level of prevalence of public-affairs stories than non-public-affairs stories, ranging from 26 percent at Fox to 46 percent at CBS. The exception to this trend was Washington Post, where more than two-thirds of consumers' top choices consisted of public-affairs news.

Between 2008 and 2009 at four of the six sites—CNN, ABC, CBS, and USA Today—journalists' prioritization of public-affairs news decreased an average of at least 10 percentage points less than consumers' appetite for this type of content. The two exceptions were Washington Post (at which the provision of public-affairs news among the most newsworthy stories remained similarly high) and Fox (at which consumers' interest in public-affairs news stayed equally low). Thus, in the fall of 2009 there was a large

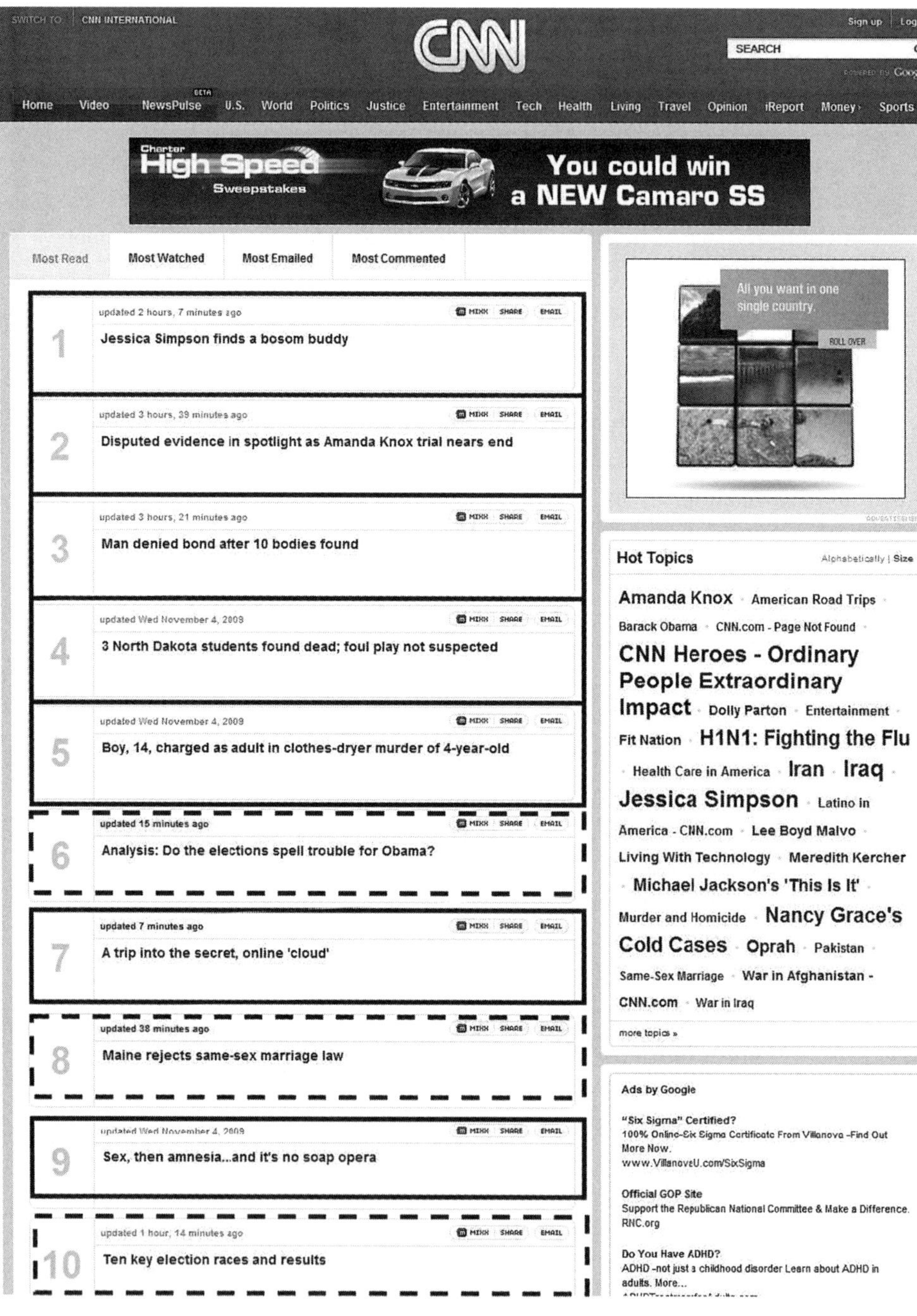


**Figure 3.9**

Ten most viewed stories on CNN on November 4, 2009.

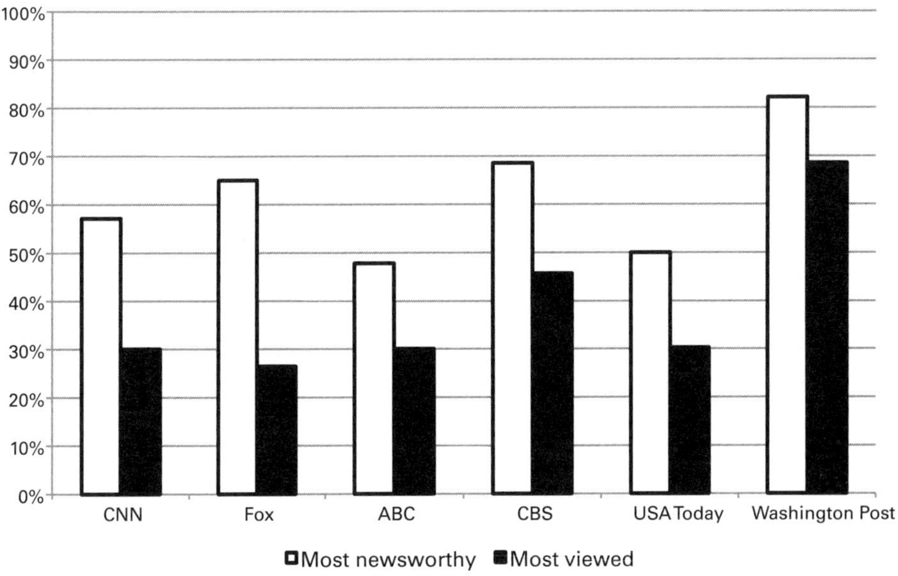


**Figure 3.10**

Percentage of public-affairs topics in the stories deemed most newsworthy by journalists and the articles most viewed by consumers on CNN, Fox, ABC, CBS, USA Today, and Washington Post, October 26–November 8, 2009.

thematic gap between journalists' and consumers' preferences for public-affairs news at all six sites and in the usual direction (journalists > consumers). This gap erased the various effects that the peak of the 2008 election cycle had had on these choices on the same sites. The most extreme change occurred in the case of Washington Post, where the gap swung 25 percentage points and changed signs. These findings suggest that the news choices of journalists and consumers are quite dynamic. They also indicate that this dynamism appears to be more marked for consumers than for journalists. Moreover, major political events seem to trigger changes in the news choices of both groups. The dynamism of the gap at sites with very different ideological orientations, such as Fox and CNN, confirms the notion put forward in chapter 2 that ideology doesn't seem to have a major effect on the existence or the size of the gap.

Looking at how the news choices of journalists and consumers unfold during the presidential campaign is a different way to ascertain the potential effect of political activity on their news choices. To this end, we examined the period that began on August 1 (roughly three weeks before the first national convention) and ended on December 1 (approximately three weeks after the election). We focused on whether the choices of journalists and consumers changed as Election Day approached and, if they did change, to what extent and in what direction.

A look at the stories on Washington Post's and CNN's homepages and their respective "most read" lists at the start of the national campaign season reveals that they resemble the illustrations from fall 2009 more than those from Election Day 2008. On August 1, 2008 the top story of the day at Washington Post, placed at top left on the homepage, was a profile of the athlete Usain Bolt featuring his native village in Jamaica and his meteoric rise to fame. The piece also examined Jamaica's success in producing "a disproportionate number of the world's elite sprinters . . . while largely avoiding the stain from the drug scandals that have plagued the sport."[26] The second most prominently displayed article was on the suicide of an Army scientist who had been suspected of anthrax terrorism. Written in a factual tone, the article reports that before his death the scientist "was about to be indicted in connection with the 2001 anthrax attacks that killed five people and terrorized the country" and notes that what motivated his alleged involvement in the anthrax mailings remained unclear.[27] Of the remaining eight stories among the ten that received prominent placement on the homepage, seven were on public-affairs topics.

Among the ten most viewed stories at Washington Post, seven were on public-affairs topics, and three of those were on the suicide of the anthrax suspect. The three other articles were on non-public-affairs topics. One was a highly personal article (titled "It's Hannah again. Should we take this?") in which a journalist commented on a wake-up service featuring the voice of the television character Hannah Montana.[28] The journalist began by making fun of the cheerful prerecorded message telling the recipient "I know it's early, but you have an awesome day ahead of you! Right. When's the last time you were a sixth-grader with braces in public school?" She concludes: "Just when it seemed Hannah Montana (Miley Cyrus's alter ego) had reached the saturation point in your child's life, a revelation: The teen singer's voice can be the throaty alarm clock that rouses your offspring, via telephone, in the morning."

Editors at CNN selected as the most prominently placed story of the day a science article about a patient reading aloud during brain surgery. It chronicles a young college student's discovery that he had a brain tumor and the surgical procedure he underwent. According to the article, "because the tumor was located in a very delicate area of the brain, his surgeon recommended a procedure called 'awake craniotomy with mapping.'" During such a procedure, "doctors perform surgery on patients who are awake in order to see what functions the surgeon may be affecting while eradicating the tumor."[29] Three of the remaining nine stories at the top of the homepage were also about non-public-affairs topics. The other six stories dealt with public-affairs matters, among them plunging car sales, the quarterly losses at General Motors, and the suicide of the anthrax suspect.

An analysis of the "most read" list on CNN reveals a sizable gap between the thematic choices of journalists and those of consumers. Seven of the ten stories that CNN consumers clicked most often were on non-public-affairs topics, including the most viewed article, which reported on the appearance in court of a man suspected of decapitation. The article describes how the 40-year-old suspect, who had stayed silent during the first stage of the trial, had "repeatedly stab[bed] and then decapitate[d] the man sitting next to him on a Greyhound Canada bus."[30] The remaining non-public-affairs stories included one on the arrest of a person suspected of killing swimmers. The three stories about public-affairs issues concerned an assault with racial overtones on a black man in Toronto; the claim by the former Bosnian Serb leader Radovan Karadzic that he had made a deal with the United States to disappear from public life, and the suicide of the anthrax suspect.

Far from the hegemony of election-related stories that dominated the news agenda on election day, the thematic mix of top stories for both journalists and consumers before the beginning of the campaign cycle illustrates a trajectory in which the news choices of journalists and consumers became progressively more focused on public-affairs stories at the time of the election than three months earlier. Moreover, although both groups adapted their news preferences to the proximity of the election, consumers did so more markedly than journalists. Therefore, because audiences increased their interest in public-affairs topics, the gap between the thematic choices of journalists and consumers tended to diminish as the election approached.

This evolution can be visualized by comparing the patterns shown in figures 3.11 and 3.12, which track the temporal trajectory of journalists' (figure 3.11) and consumers' (figure 3.12) choices from week 1 (three weeks before the first national convention) to week 18 (about three weeks after Election Day). The journalists' level of preference for public-affairs news exhibited a somewhat consistent pattern across sites, but the consumers' level of preference showed much greater variation across the same sites. Whereas the journalists' minimum and maximum values for the selection of public-affairs news were 35 and 88 percentage points (depending on the week), the consumers' minimum and maximum values were 2 and 95 percentage points. The odds of a story in the journalists' list being about public-affairs news increased significantly during all but one week from week 5 until week 15. The weekly percentage increase in the odds of a story

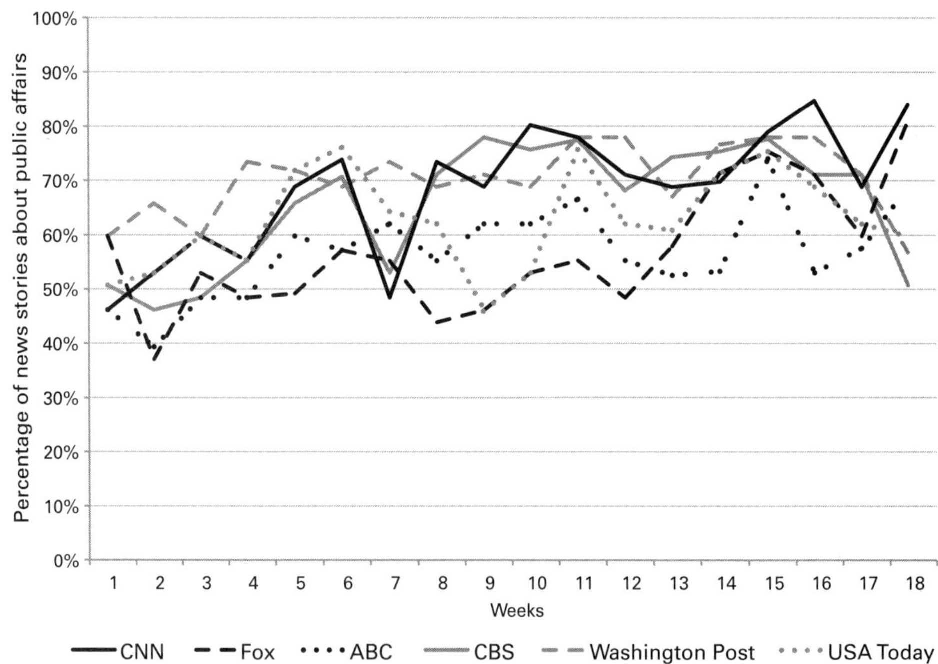


**Figure 3.11**
Percentage of public-affairs stories on the journalists' lists, August 1–December 1, 2008, by site and by week.

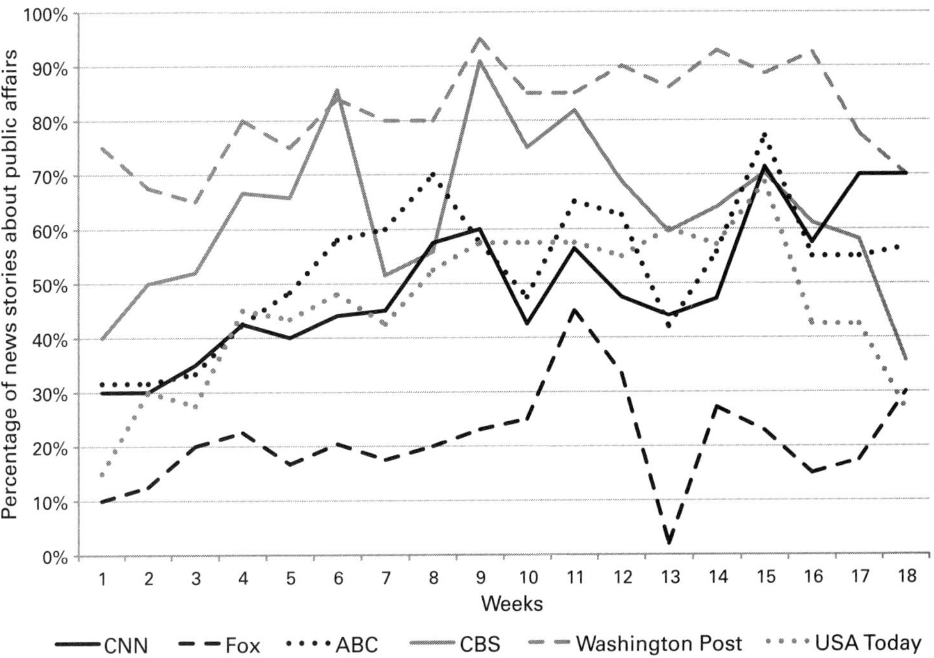


**Figure 3.12**
Percentage of public-affairs stories on the consumers' lists, August 1–December 1, 2008, by site and by week.

being about public affairs, relative to stories posted during week 1, ranged from 57 percent in week 9 to 249 percent in week 15.[31] Variation in the audiences' choices followed a similar pattern, although the values tend to be larger: the odds of a story on the consumers' list being about public affairs increased significantly during all weeks from week 4 to week 15, with percentage increases ranging from 98 percent in week 5 to 392 percent in week 15.[32]

Like the comparison between the peak of the political process and a more routine period exactly a year later, the analysis of journalists' and consumers' choices during the last three months of the 2008 presidential campaign reveals that there is significant dynamism in these choices and that this pattern is more pronounced for the latter than the former. However, these findings cannot account for the extent to which and the direction in which these choices vary when an unforeseen political crisis emerges and the signals that focus the attention of both groups on public-affairs topics are more sudden and easier to miss. In the next section we will address this matter by looking at how these choices changed during a major political crisis that erupted in Argentina in the spring of 2008. We will also explain why journalists and consumers said that they modified their news-production and news-consumption behaviors, respectively.

## The 2008 Political Crisis in Argentina

On March 12, 2008 a cursory glance at the top screen of Clarín revealed that one major event from the previous day was featured prominently on the homepage. In the upper left portion of the screen we read about the death of a popular local talk-show host, Jorge Guinzburg. The article eulogized Guinzburg as an "intelligent and informed" professional, noting that he had worked as a journalist, a radio and television host, a screen-writer, and an advertiser and thus was difficult to characterize.[33] It then chronicled his professional successes and awards and mentioned that his wife and children were with him until his final moments. A much smaller portion of the homepage was devoted to another event that had taken place the day before: the announcement by the Minister of Economy that export taxes for agricultural produce, mainly soybeans, were to be raised. The remainder of the ten most prominently displayed stories featured a mix of public-affairs and non-public-affairs topics. Four of them covered a wide array of public-affairs matters, including the resignation of the governor of New York, Eliot Spitzer, after allegations that he had hired a prostitute. The piece on Spitzer's fall from grace, headlined "Client 9 and Room 871: a sex and politics scandal in New York,"[34] was the only one apart from Jorge Guinzburg's obituary that featured a photograph on the homepage. The article described the content of the calls between the governor and the prostitution service, providing details such as the prostitute's name ("Kirsten") and her height, weight, and hair color. Four other stories addressed non-public-affairs matters: one consisted of reminiscences by friends and colleagues of a recently deceased celebrity, two concerned crimes, and one was about a sporting event.

The list of the ten most clicked stories that same day on Clarín, located in a box in the middle of the right column, presented a starkly different thematic mix, one which was similar to consumers' preferences described in the previous chapter. The most viewed story was Jorge Guinzburg's obituary. Among the remaining nine stories, seven were about non-public-affairs matters, including the second most viewed article, a very short piece describing how a premature newborn was found in a motel's parking-lot rest room by an unsuspecting customer. The two remaining stories in the list addressed public-affairs matters: the victory of Barack Obama in the Mississippi primary and the demand for salary increases by professors at Argentina's national public universities.

What began as a major yet ordinary policy change regarding taxes triggered a momentous national political crisis that spread rapidly. Argentina is one of the world's major agricultural exporters. Agriculture represents 9.5 percent of the country's gross domestic product and only 1 percent of its labor force[35] but about 22 percent of its total exports.[36] One of the traditional sources of political conflict in the country has been whether primary products should be exported and how the income from export taxes should be invested. When the government decided to increase export taxes, agricultural producers announced they would cease production and commercialization on the following day. During our data-collection period, this developing story captured the public agenda from the week after the lockout was announced until the Minister of Economy resigned, five weeks later. The political crisis continued for few months more, until the president decided to submit a bill raising export taxes to Congress. After being approved in the Chamber of Deputies, the bill reached a tie in the Senate, which was resolved, as Argentina's constitution mandates, by the vice-president. The vice-president voted against the administration, and the increase in export taxes was repealed. Public discontent with the administration lasted until the following year, when the party in power lost the midterm elections.

It isn't surprising that only two weeks later, on March 26, 2008, when the battle over agricultural export taxes had already become a major political crisis, the thematic choices of news consumers on the country's leading sites were drastically different. On Clarín, the gap between the thematic preferences of journalists and audiences had virtually disappeared. Eight out of the ten stories considered most newsworthy by editors addressed public-affairs topics. These eight stories all dealt with different aspects of the political crisis. The most prominently displayed article reported on the refusal by the administration to consider changes to the policy. It began by quoting Minister of Economy Martín Lousteau as having said that there was "absolutely no chance" of a change in course and having asked agricultural producers to return to "sanity."[37] The piece then reported that the Minister of Justice had said that there would be no violent repression of protesters but had suggested that picketing streets and roads was dangerous behavior. The remaining stories included one on an increase in consumer prices and one on an attack on demonstrators who favored the agricultural producers by a group of picketers aligned with the administration. There were two non-public-affairs stories, one a feature on the melting of the Antarctic ice sheet and the other a blog post analyzing a television advertisement.

Seven of the ten most read stories that day were about public-affairs topics. They addressed various aspects of the crisis, including the government's refusal to modify the policy, criticisms by leaders of the opposition of a speech by the president, and statements by a leader of the picketers' group supporting the government. The three remaining stories were about non-public-affairs topics; one covered the melting of the Antarctic ice sheet, one reported a car crash, and one gave the scores of National Basketball Association games.

These two sets of most newsworthy and most popular stories on Clarín capture the main differences in the thematic distribution of news choices by journalists and consumers between periods of routine and heightened political activity. A more systematic analysis of these choices on Clarín and its main competitor, Nación, over a 24-week period from November 2007 through May 2008 reveals two main trends. First, journalists selected more public-affairs news stories than consumers.[38] The difference between journalists' and consumers' lists is 9 percentage points on Clarín and 17 percentage points on Nación. This gap is robust enough to be present on two sites with markedly different ideological, editorial, and audience profiles, which resonates with patterns from comparable national settings presented in the previous chapter. Second, this gap changed dramatically at a time of heightened political activity during the fourth quarter of this 24-week period, following the rise in export taxes announced by the Argentine government on March 11, 2008. This developing story captured the public agenda from the week after the lockout was announced (week 18) until the Minister of Economy resigned on April 24 (week 23) because of the conflict. As was noted above, during these six weeks the crisis created an irreparable schism between the president and the vice-president, toppled the Minister of the Economy, energized what had been a relatively dormant and quite dispersed opposition in Congress, galvanized a groundswell movement of agricultural producers that took center stage and shook the national administration to its core, and led to huge and repeated demonstrations in cities across the country. This period is framed in figure 3.13. A comparison of the news choices during weeks 18–23 with those from the weeks before and after this period suggests two important patterns.

First, as is evident in figure 3.13, consumers' choices are more variable than those of journalists. A more precise indicator of this pattern is the weekly differences between the minimum and maximum percentages of public-affairs stories for the journalists and consumers of both sites. At Clarín, journalists' choices have a proportion of between 20 and 44 percentage points of public-affairs stories (depending on the week), but the proportion of consumers' selection of this type of content varies between

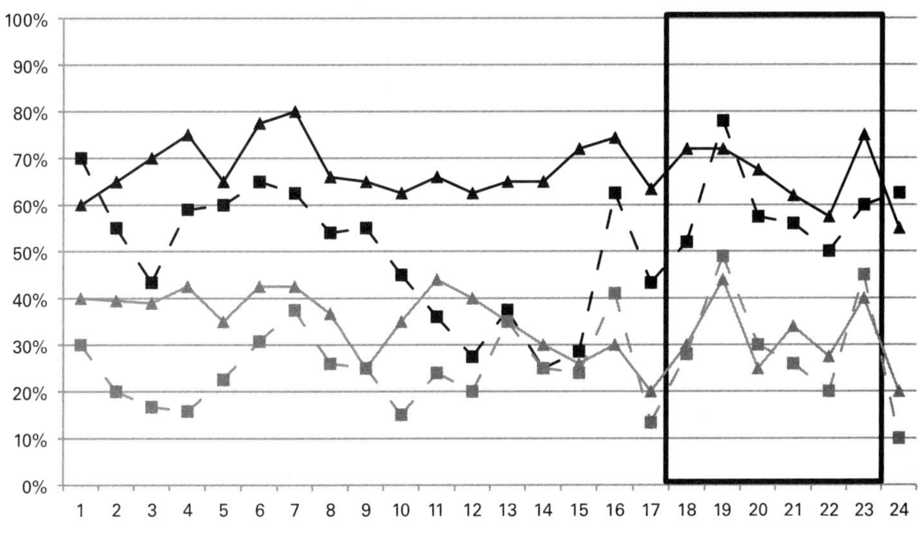


**Figure 3.13**

Percentage of public-affairs stories in journalists' and consumers' choices at Clarín and Nación, by week.

10 and 49 percentage points in a given week. At Nación, journalists' minimum and maximum values are between 50 and 80 percentage points, whereas those of consumers are between 25 and 78 percentage points. Thus, whereas journalists' choices vary 24 and 30 percentage points at Clarín and Nación, respectively, consumers' choices have oscillations of 39 and 52 percentage points at these sites, respectively.

Second, a comparison of the average news choices of both groups during periods of normal and heightened political activity shows that journalists' level of selection of public-affairs news doesn't vary by period. However, consumers' selection level changed significantly during a period of heightened political activity: it rose 8 percentage points at Clarín and 11 percentage points at Nación. (See figure 3.14.) As a result of these changes, the disparity between journalists' and consumers' lists diminished during the period of heightened political activity. During the weeks of normal levels of political activity, the difference between journalists' and consumers' lists was 12 percentage points on Clarín and 20 percentage points on Nación. During periods of high interest in politics, the difference between journalists' and consumers' lists narrowed to less than 1 percentage point on Clarín and 8 percentage points on Nación.

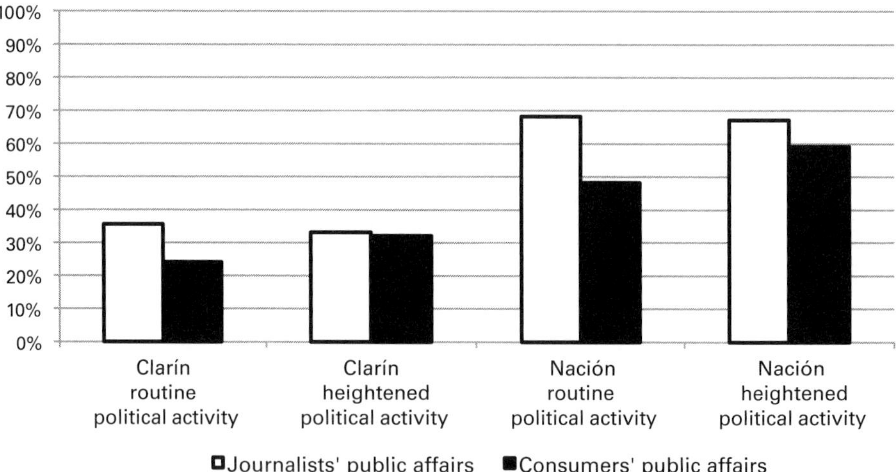


**Figure 3.14**
Percentage of public-affairs stories in the news choices of the journalists and consumers during periods of routine and heightened political activity, by site.

This analysis is analogous to the trends that emerged from the comparison of the thematic gap between journalists' and consumers' news choices during the 2008 presidential campaign in the United States and exactly one year later that were presented at the beginning of this chapter. It reveals that the gap between the news choices of journalists and consumers that characterizes relatively ordinary political periods either disappears or decreases markedly during an unexpected crisis of national proportions. The changes during the period of heightened political activity resulted mostly from transformations in the choices of consumers, whereas those of journalists remained largely unchanged.

Interviews with the editors of Clarín and Nación and four competitor sites and with consumers of all of these sites provide insight into the interpretive and experiential factors associated with their respective news choices.[39] Both groups are confronted by two cross-cutting tensions. For the journalists, there is tension between the logics of the occupation and the market. For consumers, there is tension between an approach to information acquisition marked by a sense of civic responsibility and self-preservation and a somewhat hedonistic alternative. In both cases, these tensions were often referred to as the conflict between what is important and what is interesting. In the remainder of this section we will unravel these tensions and reflect on what they mean for each group and how their intersection affects the thematic supply-demand gap in the case of online news.

Consistent with the analysis presented above, journalists say that they tend to privilege public-affairs news. Laura Eiranova, an editor at Crítica, says that "60% to 70% of their homepage addresses politics or economics, 20% to 30% metro and crime topics, and 10% sports and entertainment."[40] Darío Gallo, an editor at Perfil, comments "We prefer to leave the top of the home for the most important topics . . . in general, they have to do with political or international issues."[41] An editor at another online newspaper agrees: "It is rare that we 'open' [the homepage] with a topic that is not about politics or economics."[42]

Most journalists routinely look at the list of the most clicked stories on their respective sites. An editor at Nación says that he monitors the "most clicked" list "all the time."[43] Daniel Vittar, an editor at Clarín, notes that the Internet "allows us to check immediately, like the minute-by-minute television [ratings], which [stories] have an effect and which don't. You publish a story and see that within two hours it is among the most read . . . and you say to yourself 'Well, something is happening with this news.' So we pay attention to it."[44] Editors look at the lists of most read stories on their sites for two main reasons. The first is to validate their work. For instance, Natalia Zuazo, an editor at Perfil, remarks "I am attentive . . . mostly to confirm my [editorial] choices . . . [since] the most clicked list provides me with an indicator/parameter of whether consumers are reading more or less of what I publish."[45] The second reason is to strengthen the coverage of stories that prove to be popular among consumers. Darío D'Atri, managing editor at Clarín, says "If an article is doing well in the ranking, we feed into it [by] changing the focus, adding information and photographs, and so on, to keep drawing attention to it because we know people are interested in it."[46]

During ordinary news periods, paying attention to the popularity of stories on their news sites makes it visible to journalists that consumers' preferences gravitate toward non-public-affairs topics and therefore diverge markedly from the focus of the journalists' main editorial choices. "Most of the time," Gastón Roitberg of Nación comments, "entertainment and sports [stories are] first in the ranking of the most clicked stories."[47] An editor at an online newspaper concurs: "Entertainment topics always work; sport topics work . . . , and gory topics work. If someone relatively famous died, you know that the article will be clicked a lot."[48] Federico Kotlar of Clarín says "There is quite a lot of fascination with gory stuff. The other day we were laughing because four out of the ten most read stories included 'death' or 'died' in the headline."[49]

The divergence between journalists' selections marked by public-affairs stories and consumers' preferences dominated by non-public-affairs topics shows the journalists that a thematic gap exists in the news choices between the two groups. "More often than not," Gastón Roitberg of Nación explains, "entertainment and sports stories occupy the top places in the most read ranking. That does not mean that an article about politics is not as important as those stories about sports and entertainment. It's simply that online (news) consumption is marked by entertainment content, which entails solving leisure needs in an easy way."[50] When asked what he thinks about this gap, Kotlar answers "Well, it's the reality. . . . It's like discussing what I think about the fact that the Great Wall of China has the shape it has."[51]

Journalists also admit that this gap appears to narrow during periods of heightened political activity. Referring to the conflict between the government and the agricultural producers, Darío Gallo says "Our readers were interested in that issue."[52] An editor at another news organization states that during the conflict "politics stories . . . were the most read ones—not only the breaking news stories, but also the opinion pieces."[53] An editor at Nación agrees: "You looked at the ranking and, out of the 100 most clicked stories, 90 were about politics."[54] Consistent with the findings presented above, Daniel Vittar of Clarín comments that during the conflict between the national government and the agricultural producers "People were very interested [in that developing story]. . . . But [once the conflict was over] they became interested [again] in other things, such as a gory police story or in entertainment news."[55]

When asked why they believe that consumers' news preferences diverge from theirs during ordinary times, journalists often note that people seem to enjoy stories that entertain them, help them further their leisure interests, and connect with others at home and at work. They add that public-affairs news appears to be less suitable for these purposes than non-public-affairs stories. According to Daniel Vittar of Clarín, "People . . . want . . . things that have to do with their milieu, their taste, [and] their interest in music or entertainment."[56] His colleague Federico Kotlar mentions that one of the most read stories of that day was an article on kidney health. "That reveals people's needs," he comments. "You cannot ignore 'news you can use.' People have been looking at articles about politics and a lot of them say 'In reality, I'd like to know how to take care of my kidneys.'"[57] On the effectiveness of non-public-affairs content in fostering social interactions, an editor at Nación notes that "in general, people are more relaxed talking about soccer or about what happened in [the television series] *Lost* [than talking about national news]."[58]

Journalists experience a certain negative affect from the tension created by the divergence between the stories they consider most newsworthy and those that consumers click most often. "The truth," an editor at an online newspaper admits, "is that, sometimes, seeing that the most read article is about Brad Pitt's and Angelina Jolie's twins makes me feel a bit depressed."[59] Journalists emphasize that this tension is present in all media but is intensified online. Juan Schjaer, the top editor of Página 12, notes that "it is exactly the same tension"[60] that he experienced during his days in the print newsroom. But Clarín's editorial director, Darío D'Atri, says that because it is possible to update a site constantly, and because editors have more information about consumers' preferences than they once did, "this tension that you experience in the print newspaper at the most once a day; on the Web you can experience it several times a day."[61]

Journalists insist that, although this tension makes the public's preferences very visible, they normally choose stories according to traditional editorial criteria that often diverge from these preferences. When explaining their choices, editors often emphasize the importance of traditional journalistic norms. Nerina Sturgeon, an editor at Crítica, says "There are 1,600,000 readers. If I have to think about what they are going to like and what they are not going to like, I'd go crazy. Thus, I use the criteria that I have built during the fifteen years of my journalistic career."[62] "We cannot ignore what people are interested in," says Darío D'Atri of Clarín, "but we cannot make the news as a function of those interests either. . . . I believe that journalism has a role that is different from following those [consumer demand] trends. We should not make what I call 'Homer Simpson's car,' which has beer can holders and a place to store hamburgers but weighs 5 tons and doesn't work."[63, 64]

"I don't have any doubt that if you let a user be editor to put together the homepage for a day, he would probably [select] other topics," Gaston Roitberg of Nación comments. "But the reality is that the editors are here [in the newsroom], not outside of it. . . . [Also,] we respond to the print newspaper's editorial criterion, and, in fact, it is difficult for us to open the homepage with a subject not related to politics or the economy. It is an online version of the print newspaper, and we do not intend to change that."[65] Natalia Zuazo, at Perfil, goes a step further than Roitberg: "If it was for what readers say, I would have to edit a site full of scandal [news] and I can't do that."[66] Editors also claim that remaining consistent with their organization's identity is a reason to privilege their criteria over audiences' preferences. "We are guided by parameters that have to do with taking care of the brand," Federico Kotlar explains. "Clarín cannot publish just anything that is out there."[67]

This tension between what might be labeled the "logic of the occupation" (centered on the dominance of traditional editorial criteria) and "the logic of the market" (signaled by recognition of consumers' preferences oriented toward non-public-affairs topics) characterizes the predicament of journalists.[68] Our analysis shows that, consistent with what we argued in chapter 1, the logic of the occupation trumps that of the market. This has the effect of maintaining the centrality of the public-service mission to journalistic identity. From an interpretive standpoint, this happens even in the presence of many ubiquitous and constant indicators that the prevalence of public-affairs reportage conflicts with the interests of consumers. Experientially, this knowledge is accompanied by negative affect. That the public-service orientation prevails in spite of a plethora of reminders that it clashes with consumers' preferences, in a context of increasing market competition and of negative affect towards the changing circumstances of editorial labor, is a testimony of the power and durability of this orientation in the occupational identity of journalism.

A different but related tension marks the experience of consumers. In interviews, consumers often speak of a tension between what they call "important" stories (that is, public-affairs stories) and what they call "interesting" stories (that is, non-public-affairs) stories. Sebastián, a 25-year-old lawyer who visits news sites every morning, declares "First, I read all the most important headlines, which always are about national politics. Then, I look at those that interest me the most."[69] (In his case, the latter tend to be sports stories.) Andrés, a 22-year-old managerial worker says "What I look at more is sports. It's what I look at most often . . . but (the subject) to which I attach the least importance."[70]

Perceptions about what is interesting appear to be organized differently for men and women. Whereas men tend to focus primarily on sports, women seem to be drawn to other non-public-affairs topics. For instance, Simona, a 42-year-old economist, states that she reads only "the basics about politics" but that she "is very interested in science topics"; thus, she reads articles about "science and education."[71] Analía, a 39-year-old administrative assistant, remarks "There are few articles that I read in their entirety . . . but what I am most interested in are issues related to culture."[72] Alejandra, a 26-year-old college student, says "People don't use the newspaper to get to know about the economy, or politics, or 'big topics'. It is also a kind of distraction. I . . . read news stories about entertainment, a movie review, a particularly attention-catching headline."[73]

In spite of the differences in their respective preferred topics, the views of Sebastián, Andrés, Analía, Simona, and Alejandra represent those of most of the consumers who were interviewed for this project. Yet a small group of interviewees, also aware of the tension between public-affairs and non-public-affairs news, devote their attention first to public-affairs topics and then delve into non-public affairs stories. Carolina, a 22-year-old college student, normally focuses on public-affairs news and looks at arts and entertainment stories "only when I have time [on] Saturday and Sunday."[74] Lucila, a 25-year-old MBA student, remarks that she reads about "politics, more than anything." "But if I have more time," she continues, "I look for [articles] about entertainment or sports."[75] For some interviewees, importance and interest coincide. Diego, a 30-year-old human-resources consultant, says "Usually, the articles that interest me are those placed at the beginning of the homepage, because they are considered most important. They are (the stories about) national politics, international politics, eventually a crime story."[76]

Both groups of interviewees agree that most of the popular news on the sites they normally visit are non-public-affairs stories. Paola, a 30-year-old graduate student, says "Every time you look at the 'most read stories,' they are [composed of] some silly [stories] about health, sports, [and] entertainment."[77] Agustín, a 45-year-old economist, says "Always, or not always, but many times, the most read article features a pretty girl . . . or an article about 'how so-and-so was dressed,' and that is the most read [story]. It is surprising, but that's the way it is."[78]

Like journalists, consumers note that the disparity between public-affairs and non-public-affairs stories seems to narrow in periods of heightened political activity. Analía, the administrative assistant who most frequently reads stories about culture, arts, and entertainment, remarks "We have the agricultural producers' strike, [so] I follow the headlines [from this story], and, if there is something I can read [about it], I read it."[79] Nicolás, a 33-year-old engineer who is mostly interested in articles about technology, says "Lately, with the agricultural [conflict] I have even added [to his daily news budget] a blog related to agricultural issues."[80] Leandro, a 22-year-old college student, says "I read quite a lot of news about the agricultural producers. . . . It is, obviously, *the* topic to follow."[81] Interviewees are aware of how their content preferences and those of other consumers vary during periods of heightened political activity. Simona notes that during normal times "Most people are not interested in [public-affairs news]. . . . They read the newspaper to learn about soccer games. . . .

[But] when serious stuff happens, [these] people become more interested in it . . . and then everybody reads more or less the same [news]."[82]

Interviewees give divergent reasons for their consumption of public-affairs news and non-public-affairs news. A 22-year-old college student says that she consumes public-affairs news "as an obligation . . . to be informed, rather than as a distraction."[83] Nicolás also mentions that he reads online news "to be informed,"[84] and Sebastián declares that he doesn't like "to go out onto the street and have no idea of what is going on."[85] Andrés, a 22-year-old managerial worker, echoes this difference between a sense of civic duty and a feeling of personal enjoyment: "I don't like politics very much, but I have to pay a bit of attention to it . . . [whereas] I read 'bizarre' news to take a break from current events."[86]

These various reasons are tied to the divergent cognitive demands associated with the consumption of these two types of news. A 30-year-old clerical employee who regularly looks at Lanacion.com says "Other people might like that politics stories are [at the top of the homepage] because they understand [them]. But since I don't understand them well, I scroll down [looking for non-public-affairs news]. When I reach a story I like [at the bottom part of the homepage, mostly populated with sports and entertainment stories], I stop and read."[87] María, a 22-year-old college student, says "It's difficult for me to do a deep analysis of anything having to do with the economy and form an opinion because I don't understand much about economics. . . . [But entertainment stories] are understandable by everybody. They're very basic, and it's not necessary to do any analysis."[88] For Sebastián, "Reading a news story about international politics you have to pay more attention . . . and even go to another site to get information and only then you understand the article. . . . With sports [stories] it is much more simple; I follow them every day and I don't need an introduction to the subject."[89]

The tension between public-affairs stories and non-public-affairs stories is also related to the different affective states during the consumption of news and in its aftermath. Lilia, a 54-year-old lawyer, says that "reading about politics" causes her "anxiety." In contrast, looking at news about arts and culture, her favorite subjects, "gives me a lot of pleasure . . . you never get tired of that."[90] To Patricio, a 29-year-old employee in a financial services company, reading "political news makes me feel angry. You think, 'How come this is going on?' . . . You feel that the government is lying to you."[91] Javier, a 26-year-old clerical worker, concurs: "When you read sports there are no news stories that affect you too much, but [reading about] politics . . . depending on the article you read, you swear, you get angry."[92] In contrast, Diego, a 30-year-old human-resources consultant, routinely clicks on a small set of sports headlines usually placed at the bottom of the Lanacion.com homepage because "I laugh a lot with the pictures . . . it is a form of relaxation [while] reading [the news]."[93] Mauro, a 23-year-old intern at an investment bank, compares the "disappointment, sadness and powerlessness" that reading about politics makes him feel with the enjoyment provided by a "silly article" about the oldest joke in the world, which "gave [him] five minutes of satisfaction."[94]

In sum, most of the interviewees experienced tension between consuming public-affairs news (which demanded substantive interpretive effort and generated anxiety) and reading non-public-affairs stories (which made lower cognitive demands and helped them relax). Thus, consistent with what was expressed in chapter 1, a stance of "rational ignorance" dominates during normal times, and non-public-affairs news makes up a larger portion of people's news diet than public-affairs stories. Things change during periods of extraordinary sociopolitical activity. In line with the dynamics of monitorial citizenship, a combination of civic duty, a desire to participate in public conversations increasingly centered on the crisis, and a self-preservation mechanism triggering the acquisition of information with which to successfully navigate the changed landscape takes precedence over more hedonistic predispositions, and consumers change their information-acquisition patterns in the direction of greater consumption of public-affairs news.

## Concluding Remarks

In chapter 1 we argued that most studies of the thematic news preferences of journalists and audiences have assumed, explicitly or by omission, that the choices of both groups are stable. The findings presented in this chapter show that this may not be true, because the preferences of both groups changed (albeit in somewhat different ways) in connection with contextual transformations. During two kinds of alterations in the political landscape—a major, scheduled event such as a national election and an unforeseen nationwide political crisis—the thematic preferences of journalists and consumers changed significantly relative to the norm during periods of more routine political activity.

This dynamic character of the news choices during periods of heightened political activity results in reduction or disappearance of the thematic gap between what is supplied and what is demanded on the majority of the sites studied. A comparison of this gap on six mainstream generalist news sites in the United States between the peak of the 2008 electoral season and exactly a year later reveals that the gap was, on average, 12 percentage points smaller on four sites during the 2008 period, and that it swung 25 percentage points and changed signs on the Washington Post site. An analysis of trends within the 2008 campaign cycle shows that the prevalence of public-affairs news in the choices of both groups increased as Election Day approached. However, this pattern is less variable and more predictable across sites for journalists than for consumers. An examination of journalists' and audiences' preferences on two Argentine news sites before and during the outbreak of the agricultural taxation dispute reveals that the gap diminished by at least 11 percentage points on Argentina's two leading online news sites. In both the 2008 presidential election in the United States and the 2008 political crisis in Argentina, the changes in the gap were driven primarily by an increase in consumers' preferences for public-affairs news. The choices of journalists also changed, but much less so than those of their audiences. In sum, the findings that in two countries with different political and media systems, and in relation to contextual transformations of a different kind, the news choices of both journalists and consumers exhibit changes with relatively similar characteristics lead us to conclude that these choices should not be treated as static but as highly dynamic. Thus, contextual variations appear to influence the existence and the magnitude of the gap.

The interviews with news workers and members of the audience indicate that both the gap in news choices and its modification during a period of heightened political activity arise, in part, from divergent interpretive and experiential factors. Journalists prioritize public-affairs news at all times because of normative preferences associated with the centrality of a public-service mission within their occupational identity.[95] This trait endures even in a context marked by rising competition, greater knowledge about the divergence in consumers' preferences, and a certain negative affect, which is why journalists' news choices appear to be more stable than those of consumers. In contrast, during normal times, consumers adopt a stance of rational ignorance[96] toward public affairs, and privilege non-public-affairs stories that require lower cognitive demands than public-affairs topics and are connected to positive affect.[97] But during periods of heightened political activity, their preferences change because a combination of normative, conformity, and learning pressures acquire greater importance than during ordinary periods.[98]

We closed chapter 2 by suggesting the existence of a diminished effectiveness in the agenda-setting function of the news media in the online environment because the news preferences of audiences markedly diverge from those of journalists. The findings presented in this chapter add nuance to that assertion by positing that this agenda-setting power appears to depend, at least partly, on broader contextual dynamics. In a high-choice media environment, such as the Internet,[99] the media may be less effective in setting the agenda for the larger public during periods of relatively normal political activity than during times of heightened political activity. We have provided two types of evidence to support this claim. First, the results from the quantitative content analysis presented in this chapter show that as major political or economic events emerge and evolve, consumers of generalist, mainstream media shift their usual pattern of news choices to a much greater proportion of public-affairs stories. This leads to a closing of the typical gap in the supply of news by these media (and even the inversion of the gap when an outlet is heavily focused on political news, as Washington Post is) at the same time that the journalists working for these companies increase their provision of public-affairs reportage. Second, the outcome of our ethnographic inquiry suggests that consumers shift to a greater uptake of public-affairs news during the period dominated by these events as a result of a mix of normative, conformity, and self-preservation tendencies.

The role of contextual factors in the agenda-setting function of the online news media also illuminates the hitherto mostly normative debate between the "burglar alarm" model and the "full information" model for news. The "burglar alarm" model proposes that the news media should call citizens' attention to urgent matters rather than suppose that citizens follow all public-affairs news closely.[100] Supporters of the "full information" model, on the other hand, argue that citizens want a full-fledged provision of public-affairs reportage. They maintain that the underprovision of this content and the continual sounding of alarms might have the effect of diverting citizens' attention away from mainstream news media.[101] Despite the sometimes passionate nature of this debate among academics, there has been little research on the extent to which citizens modify their news-consumption practices when the media call attention to urgent public-affairs matters. The examination of consumers' behaviors, interpretations, and experience presented in this chapter provides, to the best of our knowledge, the first empirical exploration of this debate. Our results show that, at least for online news, audiences behave as "monitorial citizens," increasing the percentage of public-affairs topics in their news diets during periods of heightened political activity.[102] That is, our findings indicate that there is no enactment of the full-information standard or the rational-ignorance position at all times. Instead, consumers alternate between the two stances, paying more attention to public affairs during extraordinary periods, when they may feel there is more at stake, than during more ordinary times.[103]

The practice of monitorial citizenship is tied to the distribution of political knowledge in a society. Some scholars have recently warned about a trend toward widening inequalities in political knowledge and participation associated with greater levels of content choices in a media environment marked by the rising importance of cable and the Internet as sources of political news.[104] The enactment of monitorial citizenship during a period of high political activity might moderate this negative trend. The research presented in this chapter suggests the possibility that the relative entertainment preferences of news consumers[105] and their engagement with public-affairs issues might vary not only from person to person but also across temporal and contextual circumstances. This finding should be factored into accounts of the role of media consumption in the distribution of political knowledge among the citizenry.

Finally, in a polity in which presidential candidates court voters by playing saxophone with Arsenio Hall or chatting with Oprah Winfrey, analysts have argued that it is not necessarily, or even primarily, the content of news stories but rather the format in which news is disseminated that has now become crucial for conveying political information to a largely inattentive public.[106]

# 4 How Storytelling Matters

In chapters 2 and 3 we established that there is a gap between which news subjects garner the attention of journalists and which subjects garner the attention of consumers. However, news stories vary greatly, not only in the topics they address, but also in how they cover those topics. For instance, a single event, such as an earthquake, can be reported in several ways. A straight news story may present a summary of the main facts in a dispassionate voice; a feature article may adopt a narrative approach and concentrate on the human side of the event. A commentary article may discuss at some length a particular aspect of the event, for example the public-policy choices that undergird the region's preparedness for an emergency response. In the past three decades, the potential existence of major changes in various storytelling alternatives in the mainstream media has been under much discussion in scholarly circles.[1] Some analysts have argued that the news seems to have "gone soft" and, therefore, "soft" news formats appear to be useful to convey public-affairs topics to an otherwise inattentive audience.[2, 3] Others have suggested that the possibility to post comments on blog entries and (especially) to contribute material through various instantiations of user-generated content create opportunities for participation that may revitalize the public sphere.[4]

In this chapter, we examine, within this double context of the historic importance of storytelling in journalism and the ongoing scholarly debates about recent changes in storytelling patterns, whether there is a supply-demand gap in storytelling formats—in addition to and together with the gap in subject matter. We first look at the prevalence of various kinds of storytelling formats in the most newsworthy and most clicked stories on the sites discussed in chapters 2 and 3. Then we take a combined look at storytelling format and subject matter by analyzing the prevalence of public-affairs and non-public-affairs thematic choices within each of the main storytelling formats.

We uncover four main patterns of choice among journalists and consumers:

- The narratively sparse and fact-loaded straight-news format (defined more extensively in the next section) is by far the dominant storytelling option for both journalists and consumers across the twenty sites in seven different countries that we studied. By contrast, the newer storytelling options, such as blogs and user-generated content, exhibit extremely low levels of popularity among both journalists and consumers.
- When content and storytelling preferences are examined jointly, the straight-news format is utilized proportionally more often in reports on public-affairs topics than other formats. There is a similar association between feature-style pieces and non-public-affairs subjects.
- A comparison of the combined thematic and storytelling preferences of journalists and consumers reveals that journalists oversupply straight news that deal with public-affairs topics and undersupply all the other combinations. However, this content-plus-format gap is considerably smaller than the purely thematic gaps identified in chapters 2 and 3.
- Storytelling formats appear to be largely independent of variations in the sociopolitical context. This demonstrates that storytelling preferences are more stable than thematic preferences for both journalists and consumers.

These findings are relevant to an ongoing discussion about whether "soft" and participatory news formats may increase interest in public-affairs topics. Our findings show that, despite recurring suggestions from industry observers and scholars to journalists and media managers to innovate in aspects of the narrative and design of news articles and include user-generated content as a critical component of the information supply, consumers prefer non-public-affairs topics, regardless of the format. Content appears to be king in the digital age. This has implications for the agenda-setting function of the media. If, as we noted in chapter 2, the media have difficulty carrying on that function during normal political times, the unpopularity of blogs and user-generated content suggests that this loss might not be offset by an audience-driven agenda. Thus, the construction of an agenda centered on public-affairs news that would have wide reach appears to be difficult in the new media environment.

## Variations in Storytelling Formats in Online Journalism

We categorized the news articles according to the main storytelling technique the author or authors of each article employed. We considered between four and five main storytelling options, depending on the study: straight news, feature style, commentary, and one or two types of novel formats—blogs and user-generated content.

Straight news stories often begin with information about who, what, where, when, and why—the five W's of journalism.[5] An article on Guardian about protesters disrupting the Olympic flame ceremony on March 24, 2008 is an example of this storytelling technique.[6] It is worth noticing the popularity of this event among journalists on that day. Stories about the episode were among the ten most newsworthy articles on the eleven online newspapers included in our study of Western Europe and Latin America sites. In contrast, articles about it appeared in the "most clicked" lists of only two of those eleven sites, País and Tagesspiegel. Written in a dispassionate tone and a third-person voice, the Guardian piece offers in its first 58 words a concise summary of who, what, when, and where: "Pro-Tibetan protesters today disturbed a high security ceremony to light the Olympic flame in Greece. International dignitaries were gathered at Olympia, the site of the ancient Olympics, when three members of the Paris-based 'Reporters Without Borders' ran onto the field to disrupt a speech by Liu Qi, president of the Beijing organizing committee and Beijing Communist party secretary."

"Feature-style storytelling" alludes to pieces (often seen as indicative of the softening of news) that adopt narrative or other literary devices. The authors might also deploy a more personal tone than is common in straight news. Such pieces usually have a beginning-middle-end narrative structure and often lack a lead paragraph introducing the main facts of the story.[7] It is often assumed that feature-style stories tend to hold readers' attention better than straight news articles.[8] Contrast the Tibet story with the illustration we selected for the feature-style storytelling option: an article, published on ABC on September 28, 2008, on the popularity of virginity pledges. The sixth most clicked article on that site that day,[9] it begins by conveying the experience of one of the participants in a pledge ceremony, a Colorado father of five daughters: "For Keith Dorscht, escorting his daughters to the annual purity ball is about chivalry, not chastity. For his five girls—ages 10 years to 9 months—it's a fairy tale night filled with ball gowns, swirling ballerinas and dancing past midnight." The first part of the story is infused with human-interest touches and an array of narrative evocations, including Dorscht's reflection that for his daughters the event is not about sex; it is "just a father-daughter ball, and they are thinking Cinderella." The fairy tale theme is underscored by the description of the proceedings, which include the participants' attire ("he [will be] dressed like a prince, and she, in a flowing white dress, [will be] his princess") and their actions ("Dorscht walks through an arch of swords, as she lays a rose—the symbol of purity—on a Christian cross and he signs a covenant pledging to serve as her protector"). It is only after telling the story of another person, a married woman who had taken the pledge as a child and said she had "no regrets," that the article begins to provide some facts about teenage sexuality in the United States, including that "studies suggest those chastity programs aren't deterring young people from having sex."

A third format option, commentary, refers to stories with a pronounced point of view about a topic or a product. Emphasizing opinions and value judgments rather than factual information, such stories are traditionally differentiated from factual news articles by presentation and by placement.[10] This option includes editorials, columns, opinion articles, and reviews, among others. To illustrate the commentary format, we chose a column by Gerard Baker that was published in the Times of London on February 22, 2008. In that piece, which was ranked third among the five most read stories on that site that day, Baker criticizes the presidential candidate Barack Obama and his wife for not being patriotic enough. But instead of resorting to an array of facts or a narrative structure filled with attention-catching vignettes, Baker makes his case by offering a series of observations that express a strong and coherent point of view. Some of these observations are supported by facts, but others are not. In the opening salvo he states "For most ordinary Americans, those not encumbered with an expensive education or infected by prolonged exposure to cosmopolitan heterodoxy, patriotism is a consequence of birth." After outlining some reasons for that patriotism, Baker calls Michelle Obama's statement that the success of her husband's campaign "had marked the first time in her adult life that she had felt pride in her country" "the most revealing statement made by any political figure so far in this campaign season." He says it is instructive because first, it "reinforced the growing sense of unease that even some Obama supporters have felt about the increasingly messianic nature of the candidate's campaign." Second, it exposes "what the Obama family really thinks about the kind of nation that America is—a pretty wretched sort of place."[11] This kind of blunt evaluation is typical of the commentary option and showcases the primacy of the personal point of view.

In addition to the formats mentioned above, novel options include blogs and user-generated content.[12] We define blogs as frequently updated sections of news sites containing dated entries arranged in reverse chronological order and often employing a tone more informal than that of straight news, features, or commentary.[13] One of the most popular incarnations of the blog format across the various studies conducted for the book was USA Today's Lifeline blog, which was devoted to arts and entertainment. Entries for Lifeline were among the ten most clicked stories on USA Today during eleven of the fourteen days on which we collected data in 2009. For this illustration, we use a post about the sexual and marital meditations of the Australian actress Nicole Kidman. Fourth among the ten most read stories on this site on November 4, 2009, the article opens with a provocative headline: "Nicole Kidman: 'I've explored strange sexual fetish stuff.'" The body of the text is fairly short and consists of a series of quotations lifted from an interview with a magazine. Reading more like a teaser than an argument, they are stitched together by a few informal words from the journalist. For instance, we learn that Kidman burned her diaries when she remarried because "you're only going to find out bad things" and that, to her, marriage is "incredibly raw, incredibly dangerous, and you're very much out at sea."[14] Like the quotation used in the headline, statements of this kind represent an age-old media strategy of vicarious exposure to the fantastic world of famous people. The informality of the blog format makes this strategy especially suitable for quick news consumption on the Web.

The term "user-generated content" alludes to stories or material submitted by members of the public, which may include eyewitness footage or photos, accounts of experiences, and articles or commentary produced by members of the audience.[15] In the cases in which users' contributions were summarized and presented by a journalist, a story was coded as user-generated content only when the material authored by the user made up the majority of the text. To illustrate this alternative, we used CNN's much-touted iReport, an "umbrella space" on the site that incorporates stories contributed by users. We chose an article published on August 16, 2008 under the headline "iReporters: Turning 50 isn't what it used to be." Taking advantage of the fiftieth birthday of the pop singer Madonna, the article features a collection of users' vignettes about health and personal matters. The overall upbeat perspective of the article probably contributed to its popularity—it was number seven among the ten most read stories on CNN on the day it was published. For Becky Oliphant, a marketing professor at a university in Florida, turning 50 was "a very liberating feeling." This perspective is tied to matters of wellness, often couched in an inspirational, life-transforming tone. For example, we read that John Tackett Jr. from California shed 140 pounds a few years before turning 50 and celebrated his birthday by running a marathon. These accomplishments made him realize that he could "do now more than I ever thought I could do." This is perhaps why another contributor, Elondra Abrams from Oregon, calls Madonna "just one example of 'the 50, fit and foxy club.'"[16]

## The Popularity of Different Storytelling Alternatives

The straight-news format was the leading storytelling alternative for both journalists and consumers. It was the top choice for journalists on each of the twenty sites examined for this book. The popularity of this format ranged from 42 percent on Welt to 94 percent on Fox and averaged 72 percent of the ten most newsworthy stories across the sites sampled. (See table 4.1.) It was the dominant storytelling format on all but one of the "most clicked" lists. The exception to this pattern was Washington Post during the 2008 campaign, when commentary articles were more popular than straight news. For consumers, straight news stories ranged from 38 percent of the most clicked stories on Washington Post to 91 percent of the most clicked stories on Reforma, averaging 61 percent across the twenty sites.

The feature style was a distant second to the straight-news style among both journalists and consumers. That is, the feature style was the second

**Table 4.1**
Average, maximum, and minimum frequencies of different storytelling formats at all news sites studied.

| | Journalists | | | Consumers | | |
|---|---|---|---|---|---|---|
| | Average | Minimum | Maximum | Average | Minimum | Maximum |
| Straight news | 72% | 42% | 94% | 61% | 38% | 91% |
| Features | 14% | 4% | 31% | 24% | 8% | 41% |
| Commentary | 7% | 0% | 26% | 10% | 0% | 40% |
| Blogs | 4% | 0% | 19% | 3% | 0% | 26% |
| User-generated content | 1% | 0% | 5% | 0.26% | 0% | 1% |

most chosen storytelling style of the most newsworthy articles on most of the sites, averaging 14 percent across the sites sampled and ranging from 4 percent on Reforma to 31 percent on ABC. It was also the second most popular storytelling style for consumers on most of the sites, with an average of 24 percent, a low of 8 percent (on Reforma and Fox), and a high of 41 percent (on ABC).

The third most selected format, also for both journalists and consumers, was commentary. In the case of the most newsworthy stories, commentary was behind straight news and features on most of the sites. On average, this format was used in 7 percent of the most newsworthy stories, but there was wide variance in its popularity. For instance, whereas on Fox there were no commentary stories among the ten most newsworthy articles on all the days in 2009 on which we collected data, on Welt it accounted for 26 percent of the journalists' top choices. For consumers, commentary articles were the top choice on Washington Post in 2008, the second most selected choice on Folha, and below that on the remaining eighteen sites. Commentary reached an average of 10 percent of the most clicked stories across sites, also exhibiting significant variance: whereas it was absent among the ten most clicked stories on Universal, Reforma, and ABC in 2009, it reached 40 percent on Washington Post in 2008.

The newest storytelling formats—blogs and user-generated content—were, in general, not very popular among either journalists or consumers.

The blog as a storytelling format was included in the analysis of stories in the study of Western Europe and Latin America and in the 2008 and 2009 iterations of studies of media based in the United States. Many sites, including Welt, Folha, and Clarín, had no blog-format stories among the ten most newsworthy articles. But there were a few exceptions in our data set. (One exception was USA Today in 2009—that year, 19 percent of its ten most newsworthy articles were in blog format.) On average, 4 percent of the ten most newsworthy stories across sites were in blog format. Results were similar for the most read pieces. In 2008 Tagesspiegel, Welt, Times, Folha, Universal, Reforma, and CNN had no blogs among their top ten most popular stories. However, on USA Today in 2009, 26 percent of the most read stories were blogs. Overall, an average of 3 percent of the ten most read stories featured this format across all the sites studied.

User-generated content, which was included as a category in the 2008 and 2009 studies of media based in the United States, occurred in only 1 percent of the ten most newsworthy stories across sites. Furthermore, this format wasn't present at all among the ten most newsworthy stories on the CBS website in 2008. It appeared on only one of the sites in the 2009 iteration of the study: Washington Post, where 5 percent of the top journalistic choices were user-generated stories. User-generated content wasn't found among the most read stories on Fox, ABC, and CBS in 2008, or on any of the sites in the 2009 sample. Its highest popularity level, on CNN in 2008, was a meager 1 percent. On average, it accounted for only 0.26 percent of the most clicked stories across sites.

A site-by-site examination of the prevalence of these various storytelling formats affords a different way to visualize these remarkably constant patterns in the preferences of journalists and the public. Figures 4.1 and 4.2 reveal the overwhelming dominance of the straight-news format as the format of choice among journalists. There is some comparatively minor variance. For example, at Fox, in both 2008 and 2009, more than 90 percent of the articles selected by journalists as most newsworthy were in the straight-news format, whereas at Washington Post the comparable percentage was never greater than 48. There were also some cross-regional differences. The Western European sites tended to feature fewer stories in the straight-news format than their Latin American

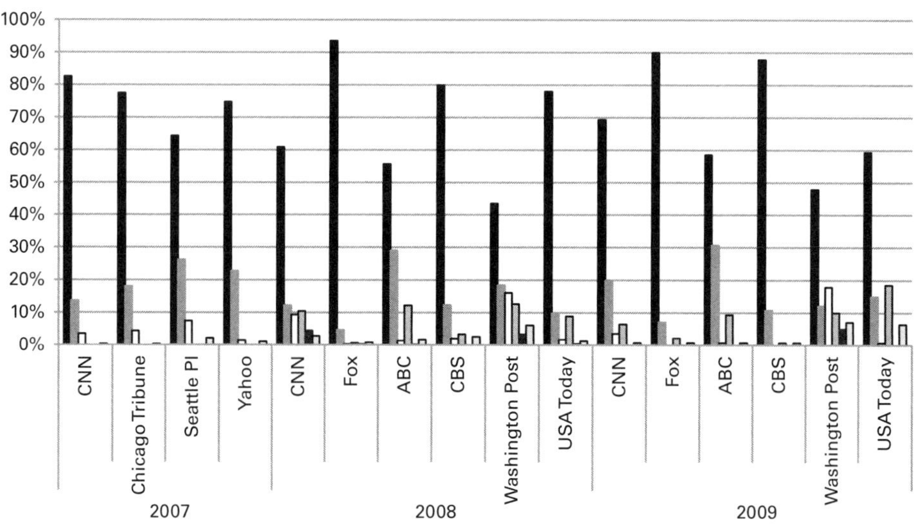


**Figure 4.1**
Percentage of straight-news, feature-style, commentary, and alternative formats in the stories deemed most newsworthy by journalists on CNN, Seattle, Chicago, and Yahoo, 2007, CNN, Fox, ABC, CBS, Washington Post, and USA Today, 2008 and 2009.

counterparts—42 percent at Welt and 80 percent at Guardian versus 77 percent at the Mexican site Universal and 92 percent at the Argentine site Clarín. Beneath these comparatively less important variations within and across countries and regions lies a highly consistent pattern of strong dominance by the straight-news style, followed in a distant second place by the feature style.

This pattern is also evident in the choices of consumers, but with some reduction in the size of the difference between the popularity of straight-news style and the feature style. (See figures 4.3 and 4.4.) There was also variation across news sites. For example, nearly 90 percent of the most clicked stories at Fox in 2008 and 80 percent of the most clicked articles in the 2007 sample at CNN were in the straight-news format. In 2008 the comparable percentage was 38 at Washington Post, the only site on which straight news wasn't the most popular for consumers that year. (They preferred commentary-style articles by two percentage points.) There

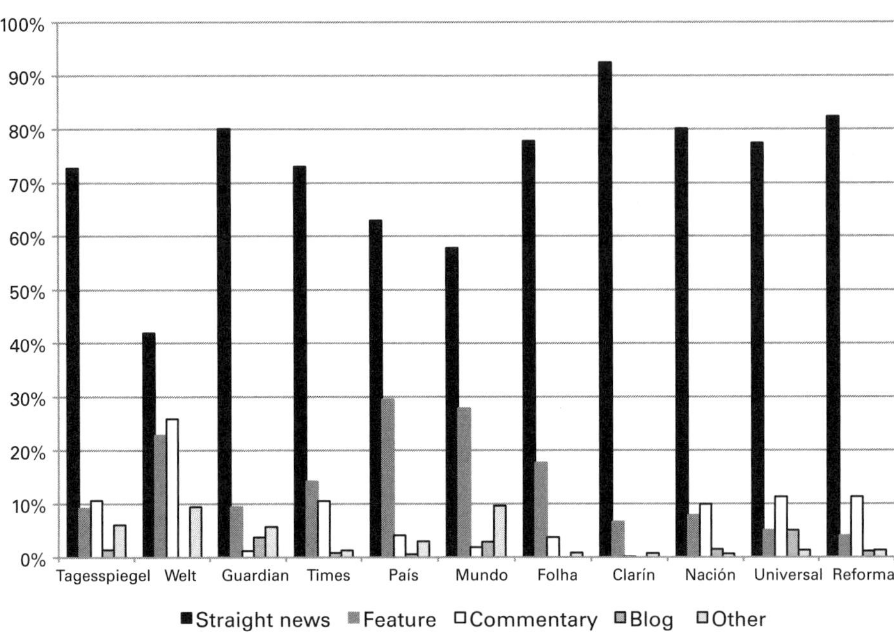


**Figure 4.2**
Percentage of straight-news, feature-style, commentary, and alternative formats in the stories deemed most newsworthy by journalists on Tagesspiegel, Welt, Guardian, Times, País Mundo, Folha, Clarín, Nación, Universal, and Reforma.

was also some variation in Latin America and in Western Europe, although not across neatly divided geographic lines. Of the ten most clicked stories on the German site Welt, 41 percent were straight-news articles; on the Argentine site Nación the comparable figure was 42 percent. On the Argentine site Clarín and on the Mexican sites Universal and Reforma, nearly 90 percent of the ten most clicked stories were straight news. But in figures 4.3 and 4.4, as was true of the journalists' top choices, the black bars representing straight news dominate the selections of consumers across all the sites, followed by feature-style articles.

The analysis presented in this section raises questions about two much-circulated assumptions: that the news has "gone soft" and that novel formats such as blogs and user-generated content are highly appealing to audiences. But what happens when we examine the popularity of these and other storytelling formats with respect to particular kinds of content?

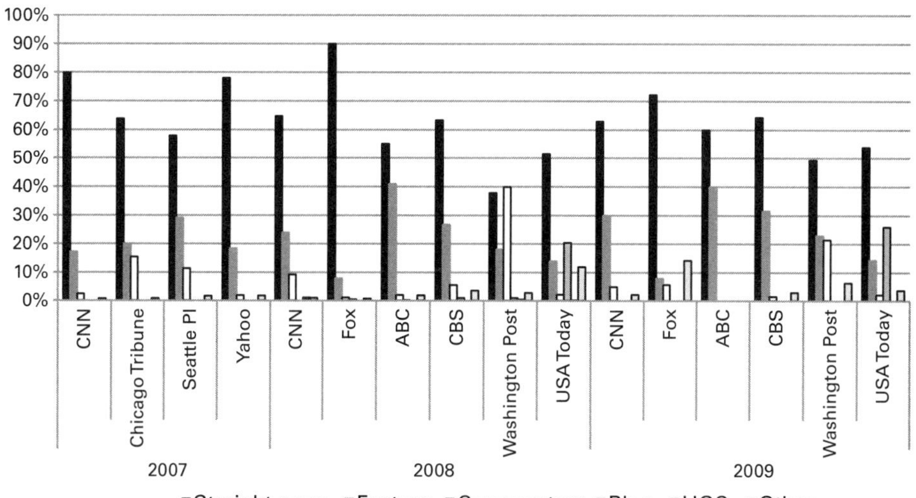


**Figure 4.3**
Percentage of straight-news, feature-style, commentary, and alternative formats in the stories most viewed by consumers on CNN, Seattle, Chicago, and Yahoo, 2007, and CNN, Fox, ABC, CBS, Washington Post, and USA Today, 2008 and 2009.

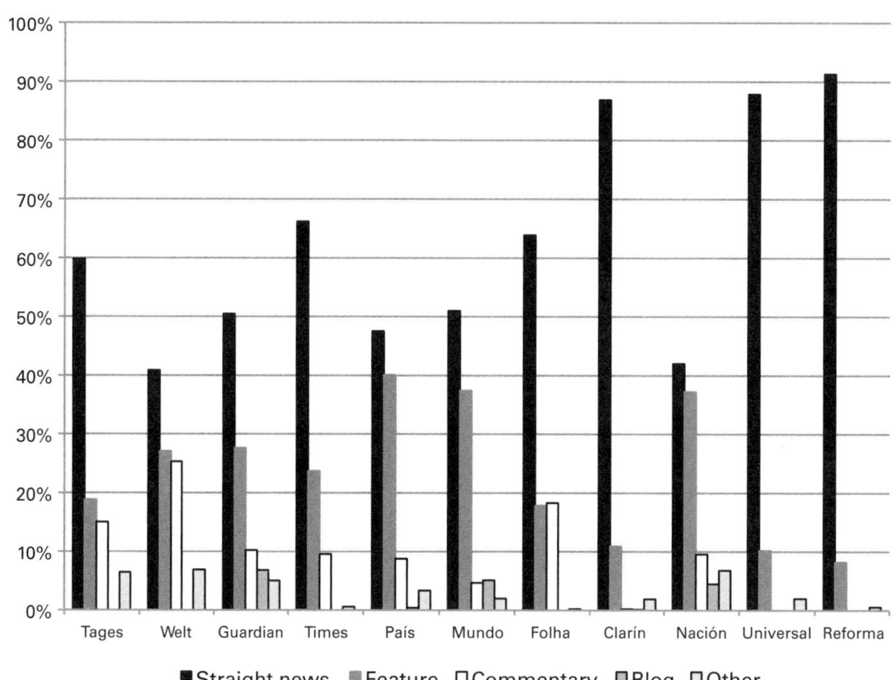


**Figure 4.4**
Percentage of straight-news, feature-style, commentary, and alternative formats in the stories most viewed by consumers on Tagesspiegel, Welt, Guardian, Times, País, Mundo, Folha, Clarín, Nación, Universal, and Reforma.

## Patterns of Interaction between Content and Storytelling

In the 2008 U.S. sample, there was only one article with public-affairs content that appeared on the "most clicked" lists on the six sites analyzed. Not even news of the election of Barack Obama as president made it onto the top ten lists of all six sites. The story also appeared on the "ten most newsworthy" lists of all six sites. The event in question was the confession by John Edwards, who had been the Democrats' vice-presidential candidate in 2004 and who had sought the presidential nomination that year and again in 2008, that he had had an extramarital affair. An article on this event, which appeared on the CBS website on August 8, 2008, addressed the intersection of private life and political dynamics of a major politician. It could have been a straight-news rendition of the main facts, a narrative that highlighted the colorful aspects of the situation, or a commentary piece to showcase the writer's strong point of view. The CBS article is a good illustration of the dominant choice among both journalists and consumers in general, particularly for public-affairs topics: an account that reports the main facts in a dispassionate tone and hides the author's perspective. It begins by identifying Edwards and describing the latest events in the scandal: "Former U.S. presidential candidate John Edwards, who won nationwide praise and sympathy as he campaigned side-by-side with his cancer-stricken wife, Elizabeth, admitted in shame Friday he had had an extramarital affair with a woman who produced videos for his campaign."[17] Despite the obvious presence of scandalous details and a topic that easily elicits emotional reaction, the article manages to tell the story within the conventions of straight news.

A different story has a non-public-affairs topic and involves another high-profile public figure: J. K. Rowling, author of the hugely popular Harry Potter novels. The article, which appeared on the London Times website on January 29, 2008, reports the novelist's decision to end the Harry Potter series. Under the headline "Split more painful than divorce," the piece opens with the following quotation from Rowling: "It has been the worst break-up of my life—far worse than splitting up with any man." It goes on to quote Rowling as having said "It has also been wonderful to stop and draw a breath and think, 'My God, look what has happened with an idea I had 17 years ago on a train.'" Although it could easily have focused on factual information, such as sales figures, revenues, expansion into movies, video games, and toys, the article was written in a light, tongue-in-cheek manner typical of feature-style storytelling.[18]

A comparison of these two articles encapsulates the main findings of a detailed analysis of the divergent prevalences of the main storytelling options in public-affairs and non-public-affairs news. Our research shows that, all else being equal, a public-affairs topic is more likely to be communicated in straight-news style than a non-public-affairs topic. Conversely, feature-style articles are more prevalent for non-public-affairs stories than for public-affairs matters. Although both patterns are present in the data, the association is stronger and more consistent for non-public-affairs news and the feature style than for public-affairs topics and the straight-news style. There is nothing intrinsic in most topics to predispose them to one particular storytelling technique. On the contrary, these associations between content and format result from choices that journalists make.

In the case of the top news choices of journalists, both patterns of association can be visualized in figure 4.5. (Since the trends regarding the associations between format and content are fairly comparable across sites, for clarity's sake in the remainder of this chapter we present aggregate information for each region and year of data collection.) First, public-affairs topics are more likely than non-public-affairs topics to be presented in a straight-news format in three of the main samples (2007 U.S., Latin America, Western Europe), equally likely in the 2009 U.S. sample, and less likely in the 2008 U.S. sample. Second, non-public-affairs topics are more likely to be presented in feature style consistently across the five samples. Third, there are no clear tendencies of association between commentary, blogs, and user-generated content and either public-affairs or non-public-affairs news. Commentary was more likely to be present in articles on public-affairs topics in the 2007 U.S. sample and the Latin American samples of this type of format. But the tendency was the opposite for the 2008 and 2009 U.S. samples and the Western European samples. There were comparable splits in the cases of blogs and user-generated content. In addition to the lack of a clear, directional effect, it is worth noticing that these three storytelling techniques—commentary, blogs, and user-generated content—amount to only 12 percent of all the articles analyzed. Thus, the lack of a clear trend in the association between these formats and either public-affairs content and

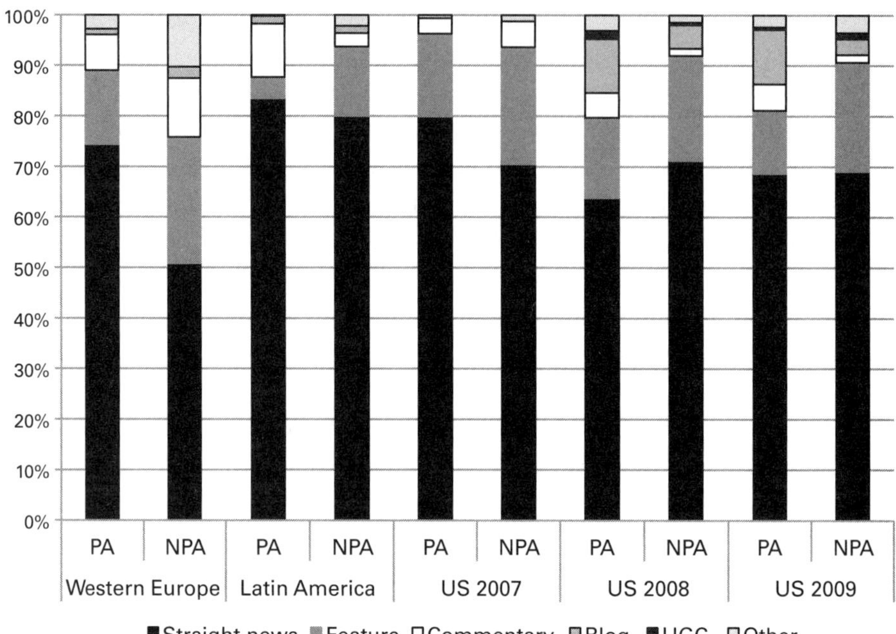


**Figure 4.5**
Associations between content and format, most newsworthy stories, Western Europe, Latin America, and United States. PA: public-affairs. NPA: non-public-affairs.

non-public-affairs content applies to a relatively small portion of the top online editorial offerings.

These same patterns also characterize the most popular news choices of consumers. (See figure 4.6.) Stories with a straight-news format are more prevalent when conveying information about public-affairs topics than about non-public-affairs topics in the same three samples—United States 2007, Latin America, and Western Europe. This news format is less prevalent in the U.S. 2008 data and equally likely in the U.S. 2009 sample. Moreover, feature-style articles are more likely to address non-public-affairs topics than public-affairs topics in all the cases, but with a small margin in the 2008 and 2009 data from the U.S. Finally, there is no clear direction in the associations between subject matter and commentary, blogs, and user-generated content formats. Like the most newsworthy stories, when combined, these three formats amount to a relatively small, thirteen percentage points of all the ten most clicked stories across all samples. The

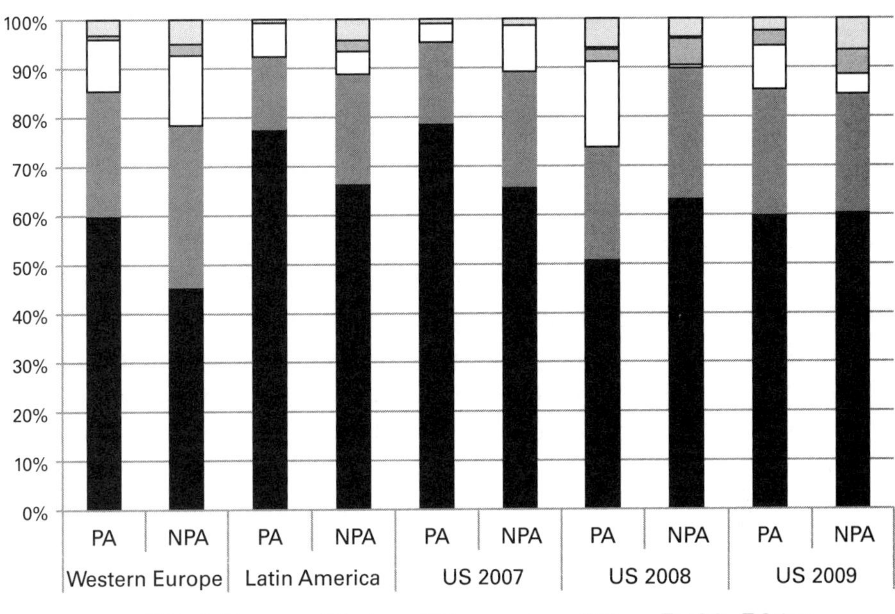


**Figure 4.6**
Associations between content and format, most viewed stories, Western Europe, Latin America, and United States.

lack of a clear effect regarding the commentary, blogs and user-generated content formats doesn't undermine the significance of the association between straight news and public-affairs reportage and that between feature-style storytelling and non-public-affairs topics.

We have established the existence of important interactions between storytelling techniques and subject matter, but are these interactions different for journalists and for consumers? In other words, is there a supply-demand gap not only in subject matter (as was established in chapters 2 and 3) but also in storytelling preferences, or in any combination of format and subject, or both?

## Disparities in the Storytelling Choices of Journalists and Consumers

We use a two-step analysis to address the question of a disparity in the storytelling preferences of journalists and consumers. First we examine whether there is a disparity in the storytelling formats of the top online news choices of journalists and consumers; then we focus on what happens when we combine storytelling formats with thematic preferences in the articles analyzed.

When we look only at storytelling formats, the first analysis indicates that journalists choose substantially more straight news among the most newsworthy stories than consumers do for the most clicked stories. There is a gap that is consistent across the five main sources of data we collected, ranging from 5 percentage points in the 2007 sample from the United States to 14 percentage points among the media from Western Europe, and reaching an average of 9 percentage points across sites. The flip side of this trend is the existence of a parallel and converse gap regarding feature-style stories. That is, the percentage of feature-style stories among consumers' ten most clicked articles exceeds the percentage of feature-style stories among the stories rated most newsworthy by journalists. This gap applies to four of the five data sources: the 2008 and 2009 U.S. samples and the samples from the Western European and Latin American media. There is a virtual tie in the case of the 2007 U.S. sample. The values are quite consistent across these four data sources, ranging from 7 percentage points in the 2008 sample from the United States to 11 percentage points among the Western European and Latin American media, with an average of 9 percentage points across these sources—or 8 percentage points including the 2007 U.S. sample. Finally, there is not such a clear-cut pattern regarding the commentary articles. The variance between the choices of journalists and consumers is fairly small—less than 4 percentage points—in four of the five data sources. The exception is the 2008 U.S. sample, in which consumers chose commentary stories 7 percentage points more often than journalists. This might be due to an increase in interest about explanatory content among the citizenry during a period of heightened political activity.[19]

An account of the interactions between storytelling and content preferences adds nuance and precision to this emerging picture of the differences between the choices of journalists and consumers. In particular, it suggests that the main gap is between journalists' selecting as the most newsworthy stories of the day stories on public-affairs topics presented in a straight-news format and the popularity of those stories among consumers. This gap is evident in the data from all five sources, ranging from 12 percentage points in the 2007 sample from the United States to 21 points among the Western European media and averaging 17 percentage points across sites. (See figure 4.7.) It is mostly offset by two other patterns. First, consumers choose more non-public-affairs stories told in a straight-news format than journalists, also across all the data sources. This pattern is fairly consistent across sites, ranging from 6 percentage points in the 2008 sample from the United States to 11 percentage points in that country's sample from a year later, with an average of 8 percentage points across sites. Second, consumers select more non-public affairs stories told in feature-style. This trend also affects all five data sources, ranging from 3 percentage points in the 2007 sample from the United States to 10 percentage points among the Western European media, and reaches an average of 6 percentage points across sites. Taken together, these two gaps in the direction of consumers choosing more stories of a certain kind than journalists offset 14 of the 17 percentage points of the gap in which journalists select more public-affairs articles told in a straight-news fashion than consumers. The remaining 3 percentage points are made up of much smaller gaps that affect the other combinations of subject matter and storytelling technique.

The articles presented earlier about pro-Tibet protests and John Edwards' confession showcase the dominant pattern in journalistic choice: the use of straight-news reportage to cover public-affairs events. In contrast, the

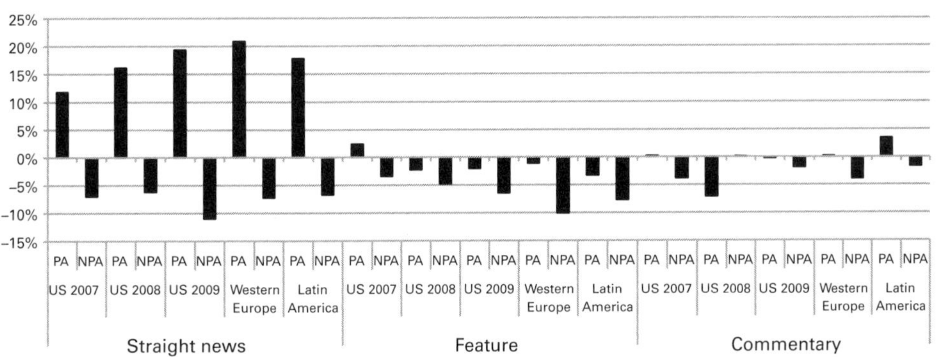


**Figure 4.7**
Gap in format and content choices between journalists and consumers, United States, Western Europe, and Latin America.

previously introduced pieces about virginity pledges and J. K. Rowling's reflections on ending the Harry Potter saga, which present stories that deal with non-public-affairs subjects told in a feature style, are examples of a type of story that is more popular among consumers than among journalists. But a more typical kind of story that consumers favor more than journalists is illustrated by a story about Hurricane Gustav that was published on USA Today. This article deals with a non-public-affairs topic in a straight-news format. The fact-loaded opening sentence conveys both the extent of the evacuation effort and the storm's main features: "Tens of thousands of residents of coastal parishes and cities streamed out of harm's way Saturday as Hurricane Gustav, with winds reaching 150 mph, swelled to an 'extremely dangerous' Category 4 and took dead aim at the Gulf Coast." The author then reports on experts' assessment of the storm, on evacuation procedures in Alabama and Mississippi and on the damage the storm had caused in Jamaica and in the Cayman islands.[20]

USA Today's story on Hurricane Gustav covered what was the most popular event across all the events that became news during the August-to-December period of our 2008 study. It was even more popular than the presidential election and the financial crisis. There were only eleven events reported in 66 stories that made it to the ten most read stories on all six sites included in the study of more than 4,500 top ten consumer-chosen stories that were analyzed. The largest topical category was natural disasters, the subject of stories that reported on five of these eleven events. Two of these events had to do with different moments in the evolution of Hurricane Gustav, and three with those of Hurricane Ike. Furthermore, the first wave of news about Hurricane Gustav received the highest average placement in the ranking of the most read stories that converged among all sites. It occupied the first place on ABC, CNN, and Fox, second place on CBS and USA Today, and third place on Washington Post. The remaining six events were the death of the actor Bernie Mac, the killing of a relative of an American athlete during the Beijing Olympics, the disappearance of a nephew of the actress Jennifer Hudson, a purported sighting of the legendary monster Bigfoot, terrorist attacks in Mumbai, and John Edwards' admission of his affair. As Barack Obama was about to be elected president and the markets were pulverizing the assets and dreams of thousands of businesspeople and millions of households, consumers of the country's leading online media were far more interested in straight-news accounts of rain, death, monsters, and sex than in the actions of Barack Obama or Ben Bernanke.

## Are Storytelling Preferences Static, or Dynamic?

In chapter 3 we showed that the content preferences of journalists and consumers vary in relation to contextual changes in the level of political activity. Are format preferences also influenced by changes in the political context? To answer this question, we compared the distribution of storytelling preferences among the top news choices of journalists and consumers in the two weeks surrounding the United States presidential election in 2008 and the corresponding fourteen-day period a year later. An initial analysis reveals two main trends.

The storytelling preferences of journalists don't appear to have changed from a period of heightened political activity in 2008 to one marked by a relatively routine level of political activity a year later. From 2008 to 2009, on the "most newsworthy" list, straight-news articles increased by a meager 3 percentage points, feature-style stories decreased by 1 percentage point, and commentary pieces showed almost no variation. (See figure 4.8.) In chapter 3 we showed that journalists changed their content preferences on four of the six sites by least 10 percentage points between 2008 and 2009.

Consumers' preferences in styles of storytelling appear to be more subject to change than those of journalists. From 2008 to 2009, on the respective "most clicked" lists there was a 5-point increase in the percentage of straight-news stories and a 5-point decrease in the percentage of commentary articles. As noted above, the greater presence of commentary pieces among the most popular stories in 2008 over 2009 could be due to the interest among audiences for articles that made sense of the various aspects of the political process. These results suggest that consumers modify their format preferences in relation to contextual variation, although to a much lesser extent than their content choices, which exhibited an average decrease of 22 percentage points in the popularity of public-affairs topics from 2008 to 2009. That the news choices of consumers are more subject to change than those of journalists is also consistent with the findings presented in chapter 3.

The intersection of content preferences and format preferences reveals that that journalists' preferences in storytelling techniques remained quite

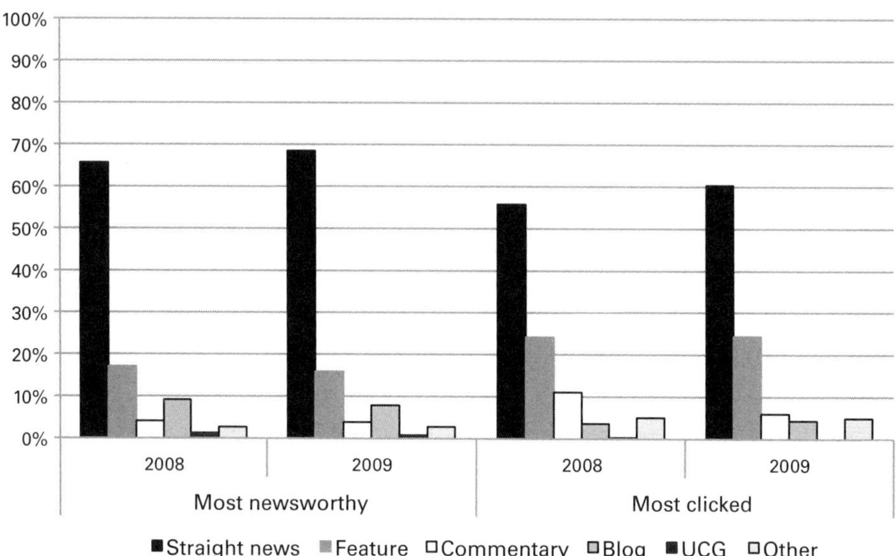


**Figure 4.8**
Percentage of straight-news, feature-style, commentary, blogs, user-generated content, and alternative formats in stories deemed most newsworthy by journalists and articles most viewed by consumers in U.S. samples, 2008 and 2009.

stable from 2008 to 2009. The changes averaged 2 percentage points and ranged from decreases of half a percentage point in public-affairs articles told in commentary format to increases of 8 percentage points in non-public-affairs topics told in straight-news format. (See figure 4.9.) In contrast, consumers' preferences regarding the combination of content and format choices varied more markedly than those of journalists between 2008 and 2009. In this case, the inter-annual modifications averaged 4 percentage points and ranged from an increase of 2 percentage points in the case of non-public-affairs commentary articles to an increase of 13 percentage point in the case of non-public-affairs topics told in a straight-news manner.

An examination of the evolution of the format choices of journalists and consumers during the final months of the 2008 presidential campaign provides another perspective on whether their respective choices vary in relation to changes in the sociopolitical context. The analysis shows that the preferences of both groups regarding storytelling formats remained

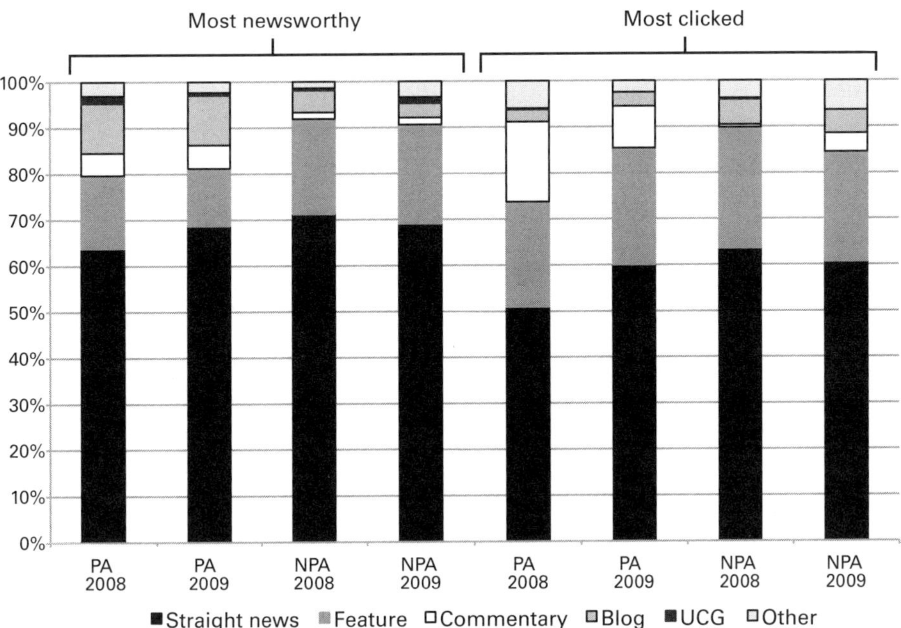


**Figure 4.9**
Associations between content and format in the stories deemed most newsworthy by journalists and the articles most viewed by consumers in U.S. samples, 2008 and 2009.

quite stable in the three months before Election Day as well as in the first few weeks that followed it. The stability regarding storytelling format choices differs from the relatively dynamic nature of their thematic preferences, which was documented in chapter 3. As the campaign progressed, there was no consistent increase or decrease in the likelihood that a story would be presented in straight-news style, in feature style, or in commentary style, either in the journalists' top editorial offerings or in the "most clicked" lists.[21]

This combination of inter-annual and intra-annual perspectives sheds light on whether the online news choices of journalists and consumers are static or dynamic when it comes to storytelling formats. The analysis suggests that, unlike the dynamism of content preferences, these formats appear to be largely static and fairly independent of variations in the sociopolitical context.

## Concluding Remarks

We have shown in this chapter that in online news the traditional storytelling styles are still preferred. The straight-news style was preferred by both journalists and consumers on all the sites sampled, and the feature style was a much less popular second choice for both groups. Several authors proposed that the development of online news would foster innovation in narrative and presentation techniques and formats.[22] As it turns out, however, straight-news articles, feature-style stories, and, to a much lesser extent, commentary pieces are still the dominant choices among journalists and consumers. The newest storytelling formats, such as blogs and user-generated content, are less popular among news producers and their audiences.

In chapter 1, we discussed how scholarly debate has been leaning in the past three decades towards a greater prevalence of feature-style storytelling.[23] Scholars have argued that the increase in competition has caused this trend by allowing a commercial logic to have more of an effect on editorial pursuits. This trend has also captured the imagination of students of media audiences.[24] Some analysts maintain that consumers want "softer" news, even in a higher proportion than they are offered by journalists.[25] Other scholars contend that interest in "harder" content is still paramount among consumers.[26] The results from the analysis of news formats in this chapter belie accounts of news' having "gone soft," at least in the case of online news. The straight-news format dominates the storytelling choices of journalists and consumers of news on twenty sites originating in seven different countries.

Do blogs and user-generated content constitute a scalable alternative to traditional storytelling techniques? Many scholars and media analysts have touted the transformative potential of blogs[27] and user-authored news as means by which members of the public can contribute information, either indirectly (via comments on blogs) or directly (as in the case of user-generated content).[28] However, some research has indicated that news organizations aren't enthusiastic about allowing audience members to become co-authors of content.[29] Other scholars maintain that members of the audience have shown only limited interest in contributing content to online news sites.[30] In this chapter, we have shown that blogs make up only 4 percent of the stories considered most newsworthy by journalists and 3 percent of the most read articles, and that user-generated content constitutes only 1 percent and 0.26 percent respectively. These findings suggest that, although it is certainly technically possible for blogs and user-authored content to become more prevalent storytelling alternatives for online news in the future, the present levels of supply and demand suggest that these formats are not real competitors to the straight-news, feature, and commentary formats.

We show that the supply-demand gap in the case of online news is much less pronounced for storytelling formats than the disparity in preferences for thematic content. Journalists tend to select straight-news storytelling techniques more than consumers choose to read them. However, those differences are less marked than the ones established by the findings in chapter 2 about the gap between the respective preferences of journalists and consumers for public-affairs and non-public-affairs news. Furthermore, the combination of storytelling format and thematic content preferences gives us a more precise view of the nature and size of the gaps. Across the twenty sites we looked at for this chapter, journalists tend to choose public-affairs topics told in straight-news style, whereas consumers consistently select more non-public-affairs stories told in both straight-news and feature styles. The oversupply of public-affairs stories told in straight-news style is attributable partly to their cheap availability (via wire services) to news sites[31] and partly to journalism's professional and organizational norms.[32]

As we showed in chapter 3, journalists' and consumers' content preferences are dynamic, responding to social and political changes. The account offered in this chapter indicates that format preferences appear to be less influenced by sociopolitical changes than by thematic preferences, and that once again the behavior of consumers is more subject to change than that of journalists. The format preferences of journalists changed only slightly in a comparison of the final fourteen days of the 2008 presidential campaign with the relatively uneventful two-week period a year later or when analyzing variations in the format of the most newsworthy stories in the fifteen weeks leading up to Election Day in 2008. On the other hand, audiences increased their consumption of straight-news stories and decreased their consumption of commentary articles from 2008 to 2009. But those changes were much smaller than the changes in their thematic preferences. Overall, the relatively limited variability of storytelling formats for both journalists and consumers indicates that their storytelling preferences are much more stable than their comparable preferences regarding the content of the news. Moreover, contrasting the behavior of journalists and consumers indicates that consumers have more variable storytelling preferences than journalists. This evidence underscores that journalists appear to be less able to adapt to changes in circumstances than consumers, which doesn't bode well for the future of traditional news production in a fast-paced and changing environment. We will address this issue again in the final chapter.

As we noted at the end of chapter 3, some scholars have argued that "soft" and participatory news formats may increase interest in and acquisition of information about public-affairs topics among otherwise inattentive members of the audience.[33] Over the past several decades, scholars and industry analysts have proposed that media outlets should change the nature of the news that is supplied because of changes in demand. The first calls for such a transformation came in the 1970s, when some suggested that newspapers make changes in graphic design and in narrative style as a strategy to compete with television news.[34] Another wave started in the 1990s with the emergence of notions of civic journalism. Calls for change have intensified since the early 2000s, when the emergence of participatory online platforms created the prospect that the traditional media system dominated by large bureaucratic firms might be transformed.[35]

The findings presented in this chapter indicate that consumers don't necessarily want public-affairs news told in "softer" or participatory formats, but that they prefer non-public-affairs topics regardless of the format. In fact, audiences prefer stories on non-public-affairs topics told in straight-news fashion. This, in turn, challenges the idea that "softer" or participatory formats could increase interest in public-affairs topics among news audiences, at least when it comes to online news consumption. Even though consumers have a slightly higher preference than journalists for feature-style stories, when they choose to read articles told in feature style they select non-public-affairs topics more often than public-affairs topics. Our findings indicate that, at least in the case of online news, content affects the consumption of news more than format does.

At the end of chapter 2 we suggested that the effectiveness of the agenda-setting function of the leading mainstream media was diminishing, as evidenced by findings that consumers' news preferences diverge strongly from those of journalists. The fact that blogs and user-generated content haven't become highly popular indicates that an audience-driven agenda isn't replacing the agenda-setting function of the news media. Instead, the idea of a broad and influential public agenda centered on matters of the polity, whether set by decision makers and journalists or by the consumers themselves, is disappearing in the new media environment, at least during periods of routine political activity.

# 5 Clicking on What's Interesting, Emailing What's Bizarre or Useful, and Commenting on What's Controversial

The accounts presented in the previous three chapters compared the stories that journalists deemed most newsworthy with the most clicked articles as a proxy for what consumers read. However, as we noted briefly in chapter 1, clicking isn't the only way for users to interact with articles on news sites. During the period of our study for this book, most leading sites offered at least two other forms of interaction with their news content. Consumers could email one or more articles to their friends and family members, or they could comment on the content of these articles, and the entire world could then see and respond to their comments.[1] These three widespread forms of interaction with online news content—clicking, emailing, and commenting—are expressions of general types of interactivity in news media.[2] Clicking on an article is a manifestation of "content interactivity," which is understood as the ability of users to select the information they want to consume.[3] Emailing a story to members of one's social network and commenting on an article for broad public visibility are examples of "human interactivity." This is defined as using media technologies to communicate between two or more users.[4] Although emailing and commenting on a news article share this human-to-human communication interactive aspect, from the perspective of the sender they differ in an important way: in the identity of the recipient of what is being communicated. Whereas emails are addressed to a smaller group of known individuals, comments are meant for consumption by a much larger audience composed mostly of unknown people.

In this chapter we analyze the differences in thematic and storytelling preferences that are linked to clicking, emailing, and online commenting. We use the findings from this analysis to probe what these differences mean for the supply-demand gap in the case of news on the Web. To accomplish these goals, we examine the thematic and format composition of the "most clicked," "most emailed," and "most commented" lists in 2008 and 2009 on three sites based in the United States: CNN, Washington Post, and USA Today.[5] This comparison of the most clicked, most emailed, and most commented on articles on the three sites reveals that users take advantage of these interactive features in different ways. They tend to click on what they deem interesting—most often non-public-affairs stories in the straight-news format. They prefer to email what they find either bizarre or useful—typically non-public-affairs stories told in feature style. They post comments on what they consider to be controversial—often commentary-style or straight-news-style articles about high-profile public-affairs topics. When compared with the difference between the most newsworthy and the most clicked stories, this pattern of consumers' preferences means that the thematic gap increases when one contrasts editorial choices with the most emailed articles, and decreases when journalists' preferences are contrasted with the most commented on stories.

An illustration of these patterns emerged when we contrasted the "most clicked," "most emailed," and "most commented" lists, and also when we contrasted the top stories in those lists, on CNN, USA Today, and Washington Post on August 1, 2008.

The ten most clicked stories on CNN on August 1, 2008 included eight pieces about non-public-affairs matters and nine articles told in straight-news fashion. (See table 5.1.) These thematic and storytelling preferences are consistent with the main findings presented in the previous three chapters. A closer examination of the most popular story on that day shows what interested the public when the United States was entering the final phase of the 2008 presidential election campaign and the financial markets were showing growing signs of distress. Using straight-news style, the story in question reports that "a 40-year-old man was charged with second-degree murder in connection with the stabbing and beheading death of his seatmate on a Greyhound Canada bus."[6] In rather graphic language, the article details how the 22-year-old victim "was repeatedly stabbed and then decapitated" and how fellow passengers exited the bus and used wrenches and crowbars to keep the suspect inside the vehicle "with the victim's body" until the arrival of the police. (See figure 5.1.)

The ten most emailed stories on USA Today on the same day are different from the ten most clicked articles on CNN. None of the most emailed

**Table 5.1**
"Most clicked" list on CNN, "most emailed" list on USA Today, and "most commented" list on Washington Post, August 1, 2008.

| Position | "Most clicked," CNN | "Most emailed," USA Today | "Most commented," Washington Post |
|---|---|---|---|
| 1 | Decapitation suspect appears in court | Foreclosed home caused 44-pound cat's abandonment | President Obama continues hectic victory tour |
| 2 | Judge taken off remaining 'Jena 6' cases | Richt, Georgia, ready to face expectations of being top dog | McCain charge against Obama lacks evidence |
| 3 | People magazine gets Pitt-Jolie baby pictures | A used Prius is a hot commodity these days | So much for St. John |
| 4 | Mayor: Attack on Toronto man has racial overtones | Overthinking may offer protection from dementia | McCain's true voice |
| 5 | Your parents named you what? The pros, cons of unusual names | "Twilight" author Stephanie Meyer unfazed as fame dawns | The curious mind of John McCain |
| 6 | Mom on YouTube begs ex to return girl | Witness: Man decapitated on Canadian Greyhound bus | As aides map aggressive race, McCain often steers off course |
| 7 | Karadzic details 'deal with US to vanish' | "Anne of Green Gables" still rules Prince Edward Island | Police raid Berwyn Heights Mayor's home, kill his 2 dogs |
| 8 | Suspect arrested in swimmer killings | Severe sleep apnea increases risk of death | Pelosi: Save the planet, let someone else drill |
| 9 | Anthrax suspect, scientist, kills self as FBI closes in | Built to swim, Phelps found a focus and refuge in water | Sen. Stevens indicted on 7 corruption counts |
| 10 | Man accused of decapitating British girlfriend | Three-way deal beats deadline, sends Ramirez to Dodgers | Workers' religious freedom vs. patients' rights |

**Figure 5.1**
The most clicked article on CNN, August 1, 2008.

stories were about public-affairs topics, and half were written in feature style. (See table 5.1.) The list combines bizarre stories; articles about celebrities, sports, and crime; and "news you can use" about health, the environment, and tourism. The most emailed article on that day (figure 5.2) took an original approach to an increasingly common topic in the news in the summer of 2008: the foreclosure of homes across America. It told the story of a 44-pound cat whose owner had abandoned when her home was foreclosed.[7] The "porky white cat," the article reported, was taken to a shelter and soon "became a local media sensation." Hundreds of people volunteered to adopt it. For reasons that the writer failed to explain, the cat, a male once known as Powder, was renamed "Princess Chunk." Quasi-celebrity status led to an appearance on the TV show "Live with Regis and Kelly" during which a veterinarian "examined him and determined he was indeed a male." Having put the issue of gender confusion to rest, the article closed with the equally puzzling matter of species confusion: the cat's temporary foster parent, a shelter worker, said that she intended to "walk her" on a leash, noting that "she could pass for a dog."

The ten stories on the "most commented" list on Washington Post on August 1, 2008 showed marked differences with the most clicked and most emailed stories on CNN and USA Today on that day, respectively. All ten stories concerned public-affairs subjects, and four appeared in commentary format. The list of these ten stories combines some of the latest news about the presidential campaign and some opinion pieces about various aspects of the unfolding electoral contest. (See table 5.1.) In the most commented on article on that list, Dana Milbank criticizes the campaign agenda and

■ Home ■ News ■ Travel ■ Money ■ Sports ■ Life ■ Tech ■ V

News » Offbeat

# Foreclosed home caused 44-pound cat's abandonment

Updated 1d 5h ago | Comment | Recommend

E-mail | Save | Print | RSS

Enlarge By Al Schell, Courier-Post/AP

BLACKWOOD, N.J. (AP) — A 44-pound cat found lumbering around New Jersey was abandoned by a woman who said her home was foreclosed, an animal shelter official said Thursday.

The porky white cat found Saturday became a local media sensation and was dubbed "Princess Chunk". But the animal is really a male whose name is Powder.

Jennifer Anderch, director of the Camden County Animal Shelter, said Thursday that the cat's owner came forward to describe the animal's background.

Anderch said she's received hundreds of calls from people seeking to adopt Powder.

Mixx it

Other ways to share:

Digg

Newsvine

Reddit

Facebook

What's this?

**Figure 5.2**

The most emailed article on USA Today, August 1, 2008.

style of the presidential candidate Barack Obama. (See figure 5.3.) The opening sentence reads "Barack Obama has long been his party's presumptive nominee. Now he's becoming its presumptuous nominee."[8] Milbank chides Obama for undertaking a "presidential-style world tour," meeting with Pakistan's president, and going to "Capitol Hill to be adored by House Democrats in a presidential-style pep rally." He closes as follows: "Some say the supremely confident Obama . . . has become president-in-waiting. But in truth, he doesn't need to wait: He has already amassed the trappings of the office, without those pesky decisions."

A comparison of the decapitation of a passenger on a bus, the discovery of an abandoned cat, and the criticism of a presidential candidate for behaving like a president-elect illustrates the main differences between the stories that consumers most often click, email, and comment. These findings suggest that divergent appropriation of technological affordances of online news sites affect the disparity between journalists' and consumers'

washingtonpost.com

The Washington Post
Print Edition | Subscribe | PostPoints

NEWS | POLITICS | OPINIONS | LOCAL | SPORTS | ARTS & LIVING | CITY GUIDE | CARS

SEARCH: go ◉ washingtonpost.com ◯ Web: Results by Google™ | Search Arch

washingtonpost.com > Columns

FEATU

**Washington Sketch**
Dana Milbank, Columnist

Sketch Archive | XML RSS | Live Politics Q & A | Politics Headlines | Politics E-Mail

CORRECTION TO THIS ARTICLE
This column incorrectly said that Sen. Barack Obama shared his views on how to avoid micromanagement with British Prime Minister Gordon Brown last Saturday. Obama shared those views with British opposition leader David Cameron.

**President Obama Continues Hectic Victory Tour**

*By Dana Milbank*
Wednesday, July 30, 2008; Page A03

Congress offers adulation to the self-elected president. (By Linda Davidson -- The Washington Post)
Buy Photo

Barack Obama has long been his party's presumptive nominee. Now he's becoming its presumptuous nominee.

Fresh from his presidential-style world tour, during which foreign leaders and American generals lined up to show him affection, Obama settled down to some presidential-style business in Washington yesterday. He ordered up a teleconference with the (current president's) Treasury secretary, granted an audience to the Pakistani prime minister and had his staff arrange for the chairman of the Federal Reserve to give him a briefing. Then, he went up to Capitol Hill to be adored by House Democrats in a presidential-style pep rally.

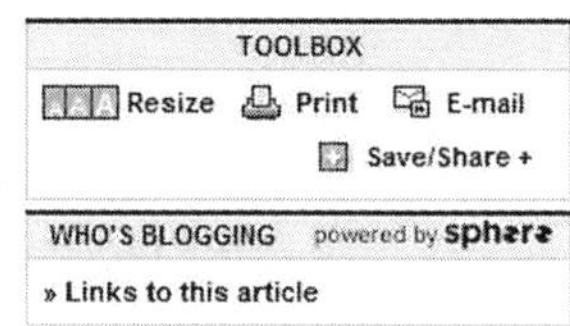

TOOLBOX
Resize | Print | E-mail
Save/Share +

WHO'S BLOGGING powered by sphere
» Links to this article

**Figure 5.3**
The most commented on article on Washington Post, August 1, 2008.

choices. But a notion of the gap remains across these multiple practices of media consumption.

## Content and Storytelling Patterns of the Most Clicked, Emailed, and Commented On Stories

Using a three-stage approach, this section examines the distribution of content and storytelling preferences among the stories on the "most clicked," "most emailed," and "most commented" lists on CNN, USA Today, and Washington Post. First, we examine patterns in the thematic content of the stories that appear on each of these lists. We then shift our gaze to storytelling preferences. Third, we focus on the interactions between thematic and content preferences. For each of these stages we also consider the disparities between these lists and the most newsworthy stories. Having discussed the most newsworthy and most clicked stories in chapters 2–4, in this chapter we are concerned primarily with the articles most emailed and most commented on.

Two patterns in the thematic content preferences appear consistently across all sites. In a rank ordering of the prevalence of public-affairs news among the three forms of interactive consumption, most commented on stories are first, the most clicked articles second, and the most emailed news third. (See figure 5.4.) The difference between the most commented on and most emailed stories runs from 18 percentage points on Washington Post to 44 percentage points on CNN. Second, across all sites the most commented on articles have a higher proportion of public-affairs news than those deemed most newsworthy by journalists. This disparity ranges from 10 percentage points on USA Today to 26 percentage points on Washington Post. The nature of this disparity, with consumers selecting to comment on a higher proportion of public-affairs topics than the proportion present in the most newsworthy articles, is different from the disparity between the most clicked and most newsworthy stories. In addition to these two patterns that exist across all sites, a third pattern is found only for CNN and USA Today. This third pattern shows a larger disparity between the most newsworthy and the most emailed articles than between the most newsworthy and the most clicked stories. That readers of Washington Post are highly interested in public-affairs news, especially during

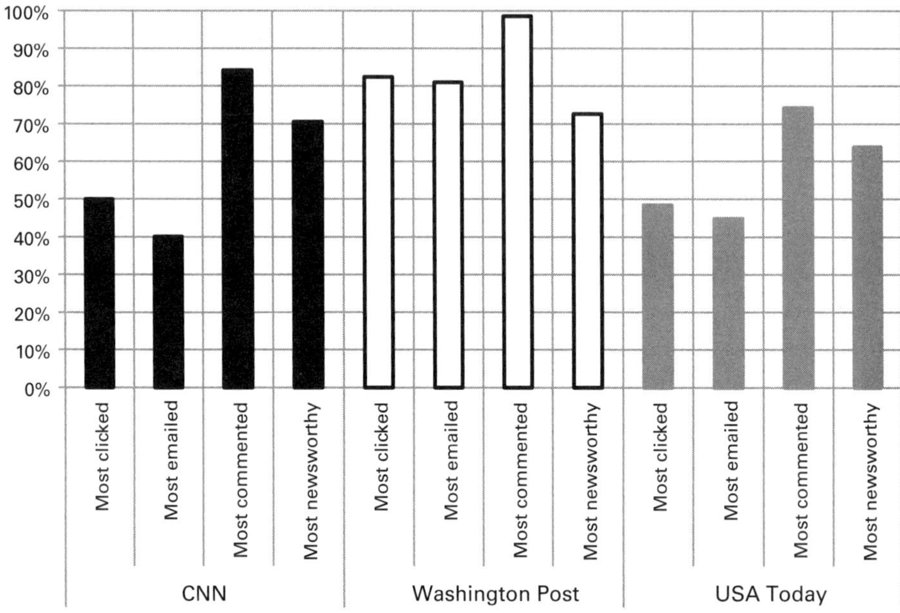


**Figure 5.4**
Percentage of public-affairs and non-public-affairs stories in the most clicked, most emailed, and most commented on stories on CNN, USA Today, and Washington Post, 2008.

a presidential-election year, might account for the parity between the most clicked and the most emailed stories on that site.

Two patterns that relate to storytelling are also present on all three sites. A rank ordering of the prevalence of feature-style storytelling shows that it is highest among the most emailed stories, followed by the most clicked stories, and last among the most commented on articles. (See figure 5.5.) The difference in the presence of this storytelling technique between the most emailed and most commented on stories ranges from 13 percentage points on Washington Post to 29 percentage points on USA Today. The second pattern follows from the first: the most emailed stories have a much higher proportion of feature-style news than the most newsworthy pieces. This disparity ranges from 5 percentage points on Washington Post to 31 percentage points on USA Today. An additional pattern concerning the prevalence of commentary pieces applied only to the two sites that carried a substantive proportion of such pieces during our study: CNN and

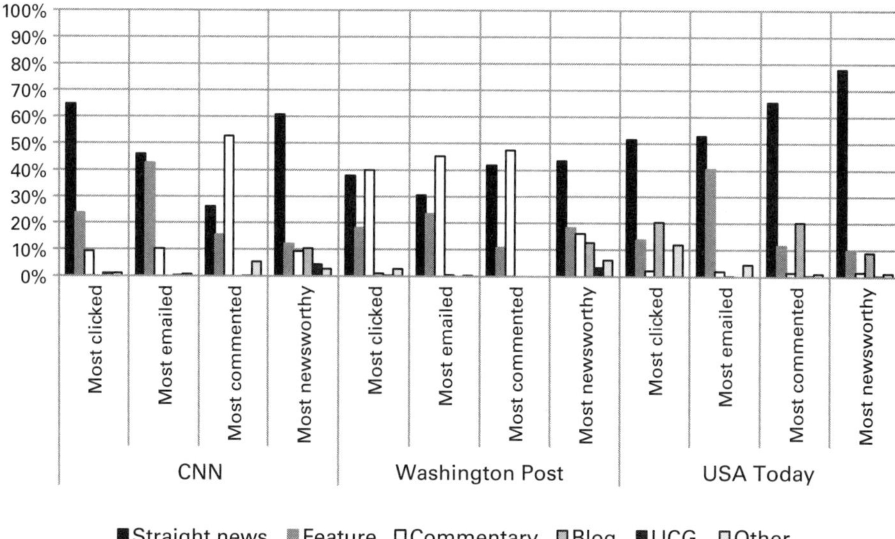


**Figure 5.5**
Percentage of straight-news, feature-style, commentary, and alternative formats in the most clicked, most emailed, and most commented on stories on CNN, USA, and Washington Post, 2008.

Washington Post. This storytelling format is more often present among the most commented on stories than the most newsworthy articles, which amounts to a difference of 31 percentage points on Washington Post and 43 percentage points on CNN.

An examination of the connections between content and format allows us to better characterize the differences among the articles that consumers most often click on, forward by email, and comment on. (In the remainder of this chapter, because the trends regarding these connections are relatively comparable across sites, we present aggregate information for the most clicked, emailed, commented, and newsworthy stories.) A cursory look at figure 5.6 reveals a distinct pattern of connection between content and format in the "most emailed" list and another one in the "most commented" list. More than half of the stories about non-public-affairs topics in the emailed articles use the feature style. This is the highest prevalence of the feature style across all four lists and both public-affairs and non-public-affairs content. There is a strong link between public-affairs content and commentary format in the most commented on stories. (There is also

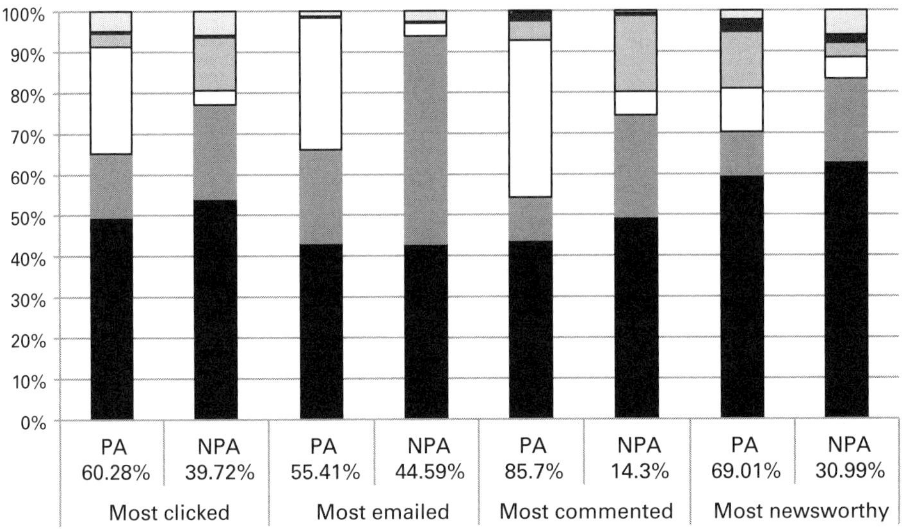


**Figure 5.6**
Associations between content and format, most clicked, most emailed, and most commented on stories, all three sites, 2008.

a strong association between public-affairs news and straight news, but this isn't unique to the most commented on stories.) Like the previous content-format pair, this is the highest level of prevalence of commentary format across lists and content options.

These two dominant patterns of consumer choice affect the size of the respective gaps between the most emailed and most commented on stories, on the one side, and the most newsworthy articles, on the other side. Regarding the comparison with the most emailed articles, our analysis indicates that journalists oversupply public-affairs stories told as straight news by 17 percentage points. We found that the "most emailed" list has 17 percentage points more non-public-affairs topics told in feature-style than the "most newsworthy" list. These are the largest gaps, but there are also other, smaller ones. When comparing with the most commented on stories, journalists oversupply non-public-affairs subjects told as straight news by 12 percentage points, but consumers include among their most commented on stories 26 percentage points more public-affairs topics presented in commentary style. There are also other, smaller gaps between the most newsworthy and most commented on articles. In addition, journalists tend to include as the most newsworthy stories more blog posts about public affairs than those included in the "most emailed" list and the "most commented" list, by 9 and 6 percentage points respectively.[9]

The combination of these two patterns of associations (non-public-affairs stories with feature-style stories for the most emailed news and public-affairs stories with commentary for the most commented on stories) and the qualitative evidence that emerged from reading the news we collected led to our conclusions. The most distinct attribute of the stories that are shared with friends and family is their bizarre or useful character; the most distinct attribute of the articles that are most discussed with the larger public is their high-profile, controversial nature. These trends apply even to sites that are sought after for other kinds of content. For instance, although consumers visit the Washington Post site primarily for its treatment of public affairs in straight-news and commentary formats, its non-public-affairs stories rendered in feature style are also prevalent among the most emailed articles. A feature-style article about beer made with yeast found preserved in million-decades-old amber was the most emailed article on that site on September 1, 2008. The article began as follows:

> Raul Cano is the real-life "Jurassic Park" scientist. Yes, there is one. A day before that movie opened in 1993, Cano announced that he had extracted DNA from an ancient Lebanese weevil entombed in amber, just as the fictional employees of InGen do with a mosquito to create their dino-amusement park. . . . But Cano was less interested in extinct reptiles than in Homo sapiens now roaming the earth.[10]

After recounting various unsuccessful endeavors that Cano (a professor at California Polytechnic State University in San Luis Obispo) pursued to exploit his discovery, the article revealed that "last month, a breakthrough" occurred. "The product? Beer. 'I was going through my collection, going, 'Gee whiz—this is pretty nifty. Maybe we could use it to make beer,'" Cano was quoted as saying. Partnering with another scientist and a lawyer, Cano developed "Fossil Fuels Brewing Co., which ferments a yeast strain . . . dating from about 25 million to 45 million years ago." "The real-life scientists," the story concludes, "are crafting a new legacy, in what may be the first *Jurassic Park* sequel you'll actually be able to swallow." Thus, although Washington Post consumers show a great deal interest in all matters political, the news that they share with their friends and family members suggests that they would also enjoy the "smooth and spicy" taste of a beer made with an ingredient originated long before the landscape was divided into blue and red territories.

In contrast, users often visit CNN for its up-to-date and comprehensive coverage that features mostly stories on public-affairs subjects told in a straight-news style. However, a relatively high proportion of the most commented on stories are commentaries on controversial, high-profile public-affairs topics. An example is Campbell Brown's column "Sexist treatment of Palin must end," which appeared on September 24, 2008 and was the most commented on article on the site for the next six days.[11] The piece began with a strong assertion that clearly conveyed the author's point of view: "Frankly I have had it, and I know a lot of other women out there who are with me on this. I have had enough of the sexist treatment of Sarah Palin. It has to end." Brown continues by detailing her frustration with the lack of direct contact between the Republican vice-presidential candidate and the media. She notes that at a campaign event in New York the campaign staffers "ban reporters from asking Gov. Palin any questions. I call upon the McCain campaign to stop treating Sarah Palin like she is a delicate flower who will wilt at any moment." After elaborating on why Palin should have increased, direct, and unfettered air time, Brown again emphasized her main point toward the end of the column: "Free Sarah Palin. Free her from the chauvinistic chains you are binding her with."

The analysis of the most clicked, most emailed, and most commented on stories shows that online news consumers enact different practices in relation to the various interactive options afforded by online news sites. In chapters 3 and 4 we established that consumers' thematic choices—and to a much lesser extent, their storytelling preferences—change as the socio-political context changes. Does this also apply to the stories they email and comment? We answer this question in the next section.

## The Dynamic Nature of Interacting with the News Online

Here, as in the previous two chapters, we take a two-pronged approach to this question. First, we examine whether there are any differences in the online news choices of the consumers between the fourteen days surrounding Election Day 2008 and the same fourteen days a year later. Then we look at whether there is any variation within the final four months of the presidential campaign.

An analysis of the thematic composition of the most clicked, most emailed, most commented on, and most newsworthy articles during the week before and the week after Election Day 2008 and the equivalent two weeks a year later reveals two main patterns of change in consumers' choices. (See figure 5.7.) First, all expressions of interactivity have dynamic qualities, but some change more than others. The prevalence of public-affairs news among the most emailed stories across the three sites decreased by an average 16 percentage points from 2008 to 2009. That proportion went down by 28 and 31 percentage points among the most clicked and most commented on stories, respectively. Thus, patterns of interactional connectivity via email appear to be more stable than patterns of one-to-many communication via commenting on the news. This is also true for person-to-document interactivity enacted by reading articles on a site.

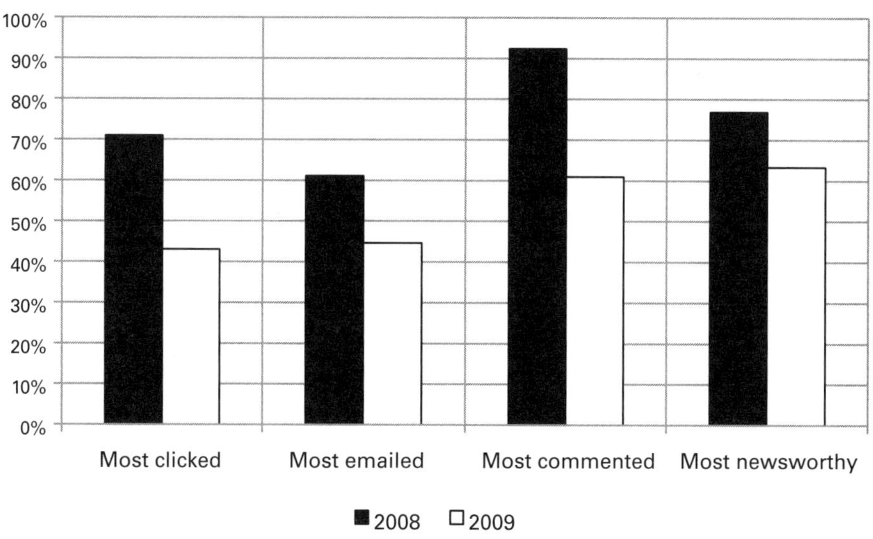


**Figure 5.7**

Percentage of public-affairs and non-public-affairs in the most clicked, most emailed, and most commented on stories on CNN, USA Today, and Washington Post during the fourteen days surrounding Election Day, 2008 and 2009.

Consistent with the trends established in chapters 3 and 4, the second pattern is that the three types of consumer choices are more dynamic than those of journalists. The inter-annual variance is higher for consumers than for journalists by a small margin when it comes to emailing the news (a difference of 3 percentage points) and by a large margin for clicking and commenting choices (differences of 15 and 18 percentage points, respectively).

An examination of the storytelling composition of the four lists reveals three main patterns. (See figure 5.8.) The first is a decrease in the prevalence of the commentary format from 2008 to 2009 across the three types of consumer interaction with the news. This suggests that the interest in articles that provide interpretation and analysis that signaled the peak of the electoral contest was no longer so marked during a period of more routine political activity in 2009. This decrease ranged from 4 percentage points in the "most emailed" list to 10 percentage points among the most clicked stories to 25 percentage points for the most commented on stories. The type of storytelling format that compensated for this loss on each list is indicative of the respective natures of the lists. Straight-news storytelling made up most of the difference among the most clicked and most commented on news, but feature-style storytelling filled the losses of

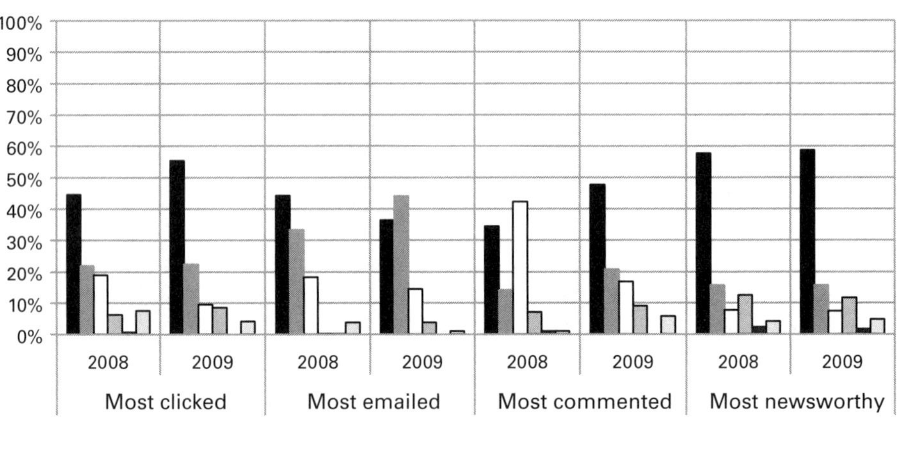


**Figure 5.8**
Percentage of straight-news, feature-style, commentary, and alternative formats in the most clicked, most emailed, and most commented on stories on CNN, USA and Washington Post, 2008 and 2009.

commentary and straight news among the most emailed stories between the final two weeks of the presidential campaign and the same two weeks a year later. Although all three forms of interactive choice exhibit dynamic qualities, the second pattern is a wider gap among the most clicked and most commented on stories than among the most emailed ones. Furthermore, these variations are less pronounced than the respective variations in the thematic choices of the three lists described in the previous paragraph. In contrast, the third pattern is that the "most newsworthy" list remained fairly stable with respect to storytelling format, with nearly the same percentage of straight-news, feature-style, and commentary articles in 2008 and 2009.

A cursory glance at the connections between thematic content and storytelling format permits a more nuanced account of the dynamism in the interactive practices of online news consumers during the peak of the fourteen-day period surrounding election day and exactly a year later. (See figure 5.9.) The largest inter-annual difference in the most clicked articles is the decrease in consumers' interest in public-affairs articles presented in commentary format—from 27 percent to 13 percent of the most viewed stories that dealt with public-affairs topics. This difference is made up

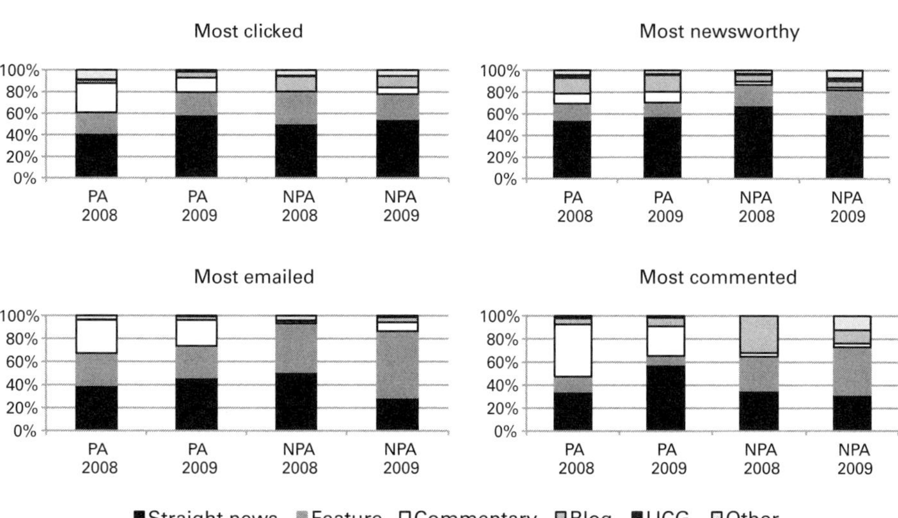


**Figure 5.9**
Association between content and format, 2008 and 2009.

largely by an increase in the proportion of straight news among the public-affairs stories. That same combination of theme and format also decreased from 46 percent to 26 percent of stories about public-affairs topics on the "most commented" lists from 2008 and 2009. This difference is also mostly offset by an increase in the prevalence of straight news within the public-affairs stories. The combination that experienced the most dramatic change among the most emailed articles was non-public-affairs pieces told in feature style. That combination occurred in 42 percent of the non-public-affairs stories on that list in 2008 and was the majority of the most emailed stories in 2009 with 58 percentage points. A loss in the presence of public-affairs topics told as straight news paralleled those gains. A decrease of interest in commentary pieces about public-affairs topics in the most read and most commented on news and a rise in the popularity of feature-style stories about non-public-affairs subjects in the news that consumers share with friends and family members characterize the passage from a period of heightened political activity in 2008 to a more normal period in 2009.

These dominant associations between thematic content and storytelling formats yield inter-annual variations in the gaps between the most newsworthy stories and the most emailed and most commented on articles. (See figure 5.10.) Concerning the gap between the most newsworthy and most emailed stories, the main difference between the fourteen-day period surrounding election day and the same fourteen days exactly a year later is an increase of 12 percentage points in the disparity for stories on non-public-affairs subjects rendered in feature style. In the case of the most newsworthy and most commented on stories, the main difference is a decrease of 26 percentage points in the number of commentary articles that deal with public-affairs topics. The most emailed choices are considerably more stable than the most commented on choices, which is consistent with divergent trends mentioned above.

The contrast between the ten most emailed stories on USA Today on Election Day 2008 and exactly a year later provides a powerful illustration of the dynamic patterns that characterize this type of interactive behavior among consumers. On November 4, 2008, eight of the ten most emailed stories weren't about public affairs, and three of the ten were written in feature style. (See table 5.2.) That day, the majority of the articles were

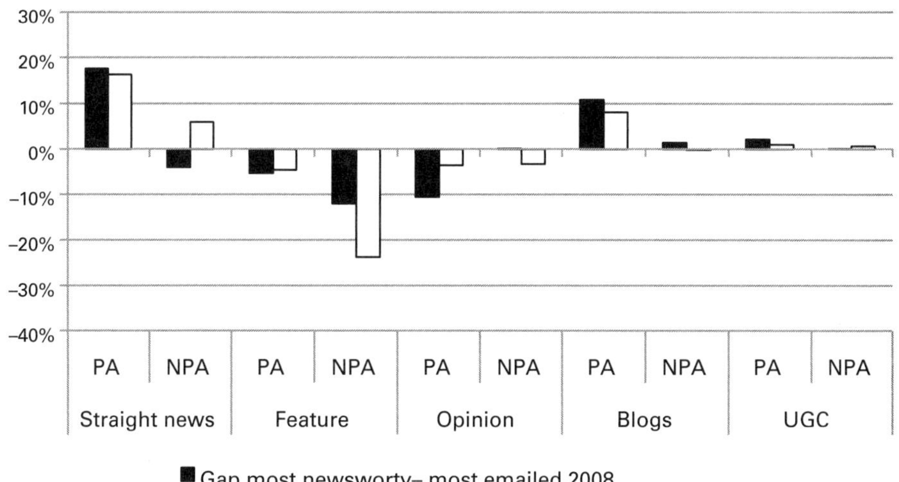


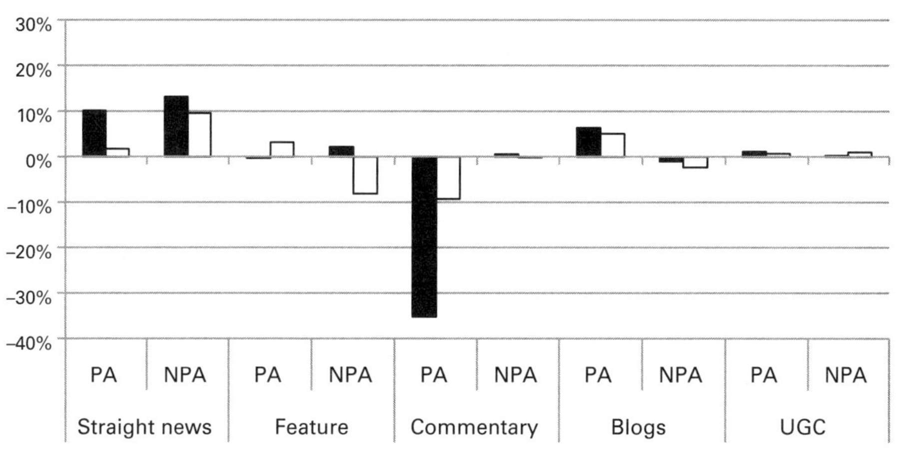


**Figure 5.10**
Gap between the most newsworthy and most emailed and most commented on stories, 2008 and 2009.

**Table 5.2**
"Most emailed" lists on November 4, 2008 and November 9, 2008, USA Today.

| Position | November 4, 2008 | November 4, 2009 |
|---|---|---|
| 1 | New ways to mitigate migraines | Beer with extra buzz on tap up to 16% |
| 2 | Study: counties with more rainfall have higher autism | Bill Clinton, George W. Bush debate in NYC |
| 3 | Voters can pick up free stuff on Election Day | More walk away from homes, mortgages |
| 4 | Neighbors at odd over noise from wind turbines | Older patients most likely to die from H1N1 influenza |
| 5 | Eating fish twice a week may help diabetes patients | At MIT, running back Brown discovers a formula for success |
| 6 | Brisk walking brings better health, less body fat | Dark matter "wrecking ball" may have hit Milky Way |
| 7 | "Grey's Anatomy" has change of heart about Dr. Hahn | Father of UCLA player uses Facebook to rip Neuheisel, coaching staff |
| 8 | Artificial pancreas would dial up diabetes control | High-definition equals high sales for wearable video camera |
| 9 | Dealerships empty as all major automakers see sales plunge | Analysis: Maine voters reject gay marriage law |
| 10 | Women caught dirt-handed with more types of bacteria, study finds | Royal Caribbean's Oasis of the Seas towers over English town during brief visit |

about health (including stories about migraines, autism, diabetes, and the benefits of walking), as if, after a long and draining electoral campaign that overlapped with a severe financial crisis, Americans were more concerned about their personal health than about the health of the body politic. The only story on the presidential election in that list was a prime example of "news you can use": an article about free items, such as Starbucks coffee and Ben & Jerry's ice cream, that were offered to voters. Exactly a year later, the thematic and format proportions in the "most emailed" list on USA Today were a bit different: seven out of the ten most emailed articles weren't about public affairs, and five were in feature style. That day the "most emailed" list was more varied than it had been on Election Day, but it still consisted largely of non-public-affairs news and feature-style stories: a story about allowing higher alcohol content in beer, two about college football, one about H1N1 influenza, and one about a canceled debate between former presidents George W. Bush and Bill Clinton.

On Election Day 2008, the most emailed article on USA Today was a feature-style story on new treatments for migraines. After stating that "headaches distract" and "migraines can debilitate,"[12] the article outlined several treatments—from the innovative, to the obvious, to the bizarre—and invited readers to comment. In a telling illustration of the differences between the most emailed and most commented on stories, only 51 users posted comments on that article. The most commented on article on that day—a straight news story about the presidential election—drew more than 4,000 posts. Although few consumers of USA Today felt compelled to comment on the migraine article, many shared it by email with their acquaintances, hoping to help friends and family members cope with their headaches (which the political campaign and the financial crisis had perhaps aggravated).

The most emailed item exactly a year later was a straight news story about states, including Alabama, West Virginia, and Vermont, that allowed higher alcohol content in beer than other states.[13] Did the changes in the subject matter from migraines to beer signal a shift in the mood of the population? The markets were rebounding, and things seemed more tranquil on the political front. In typical straight-news fashion, the relatively short article included quotations in favor of the motion by brewers' associations and quotations against it by advocates and substance-abuse experts. It also listed the states that had raised the maximum legal alcohol content for beer. Online news consumers may have emailed this article to their friends with humorous comments about getting an extra buzz from their beers, or gentle warnings about watching what they drink when visiting certain states.

A comparison of the "most commented" lists on Washington Post on November 4, 2008 and November 4, 2009 illustrates the types of stories that consumers chose to comment on. On Election Day 2008, all the stories on the "most commented" list were about public affairs, and three were written in commentary style. (See table 5.3.) The list included stories on the state of the election races and the latest polling results, stories on President Bush's visit to Republican headquarters in Washington, and a column characterizing Sarah Palin as "the last of the culture warriors." A year later, all the stories on the "most commented" list were, again, about public affairs, and four were commentaries. There were stories on the gubernatorial elections in Virginia and New Jersey and

**Table 5.3**
"Most commented lists" on November 4, 2008 and November 9, 2008, Washington Post.

| Position | November 4, 2008 | November 4, 2009 |
|---|---|---|
| 1 | The state of the races | Contests serve as warning to Democrats: It's not 2008 anymore |
| 2 | "My heart and my values didn't change" | Could America go broke? |
| 3 | Last of the culture warriors | GOP reclaims Virginia |
| 4 | A positively negative home stretch | A world of change in 287 days |
| 5 | Polls show Obama with clear advantage | Democrats' concerns over abortion may imperil health bill |
| 6 | Disclosure about Obama's aunt may have violated privacy policy | As Virginia goes, so goes not much |
| 7 | True believers in McCain flock to PA | Palin as politically charged lightning rod |
| 8 | The amazing race | Bullets are speeding faster out of gun shops in U.S. |
| 9 | A new kind of pride | Climate bill faces hurdles in Senate |
| 10 | Poll shows Obama deflected recent attacks | Maine set to vote on gay marriage |

on the gay-marriage referendum in Maine, and a review of two books about Sarah Palin.

The most commented on article on Election Day 2008 was an analysis of the presidential, congressional, and gubernatorial contests that had been published in the print edition of the *Washington Post* two days earlier.[14] The longevity of this article in terms of its popularity for commentary purposes is probably due to a number of concurrent factors, in addition to the salience of its topic for *Post* readers in particular and the public in general. These include the prestige of its authors (some of the best-known political journalists in the country, among them David Broder and Dan Balz), its placement on the front page of the print edition, and some of the controversial elements of analysis it contained. Among the controversial elements was the assertion that the uncertainty of "how voters [would] ultimately respond to the prospect of the first African American president in U.S. history . . . could make the contest closer than it appears." Assertions of this kind when discussing the highest political office can surely entice consumers to voice their opinions, regardless of whether these opinions are directly about racial matters or indirectly motivated by them.

The most commented on article exactly a year later was also an analysis of electoral politics, this one concerning the gubernatorial and congressional elections that had taken place the previous day.[15] Furthermore, like the 2008 article, it had been written by the noted *Post* staffer Dan Balz. Once again, the topic involved a series of high-profile political events (though obviously not as high-profile as those of 2008) analyzed in a dispassionate tone. Nonetheless, it contained a number of statements likely to generate controversy among people willing to voice their opinions on the site. Balz opened the article as follows: "Off-year elections can be notoriously unreliable as predictors of the future, but . . . Tuesday's Republican victories in Virginia and New Jersey delivered clear warnings for the Democrats." He went on to raise the stakes of what these signs might mean:

> Neither gubernatorial election amounted to a referendum on the president, but the changing shape of the electorate in both states and the shifts among key constituencies revealed cracks in the Obama 2008 faction and demonstrated that, at this point, Republicans have the more energized constituency heading into next year's midterm elections.

In chapter 3 we showed that the thematic composition of the top online news choices of journalists and consumers changed during the campaign cycle, and that the choices of journalists changed less than the choices of consumers. As Election Day approached, both groups gradually increased the proportion of public-affairs topics in the "most newsworthy" and "most clicked" lists, respectively. Our analysis shows that two additional forms of interactive behavior explored in this chapter—sharing stories by email and commenting on them on the site—also exhibited dynamic qualities in relation to the progress of the campaign. Figure 5.11 tracks the temporal trajectory of the thematic composition of the most newsworthy, most clicked, most emailed, and most commented on stories from week 1 (three weeks before the first national convention) to week 18 (approximately three weeks after Election Day). On all four lists, the prevalence of public-affairs topics increased as Election Day got closer.

The odds that a story on the "most clicked" list would be about public-affairs news increased in each week from week 6 to week 15. The weekly

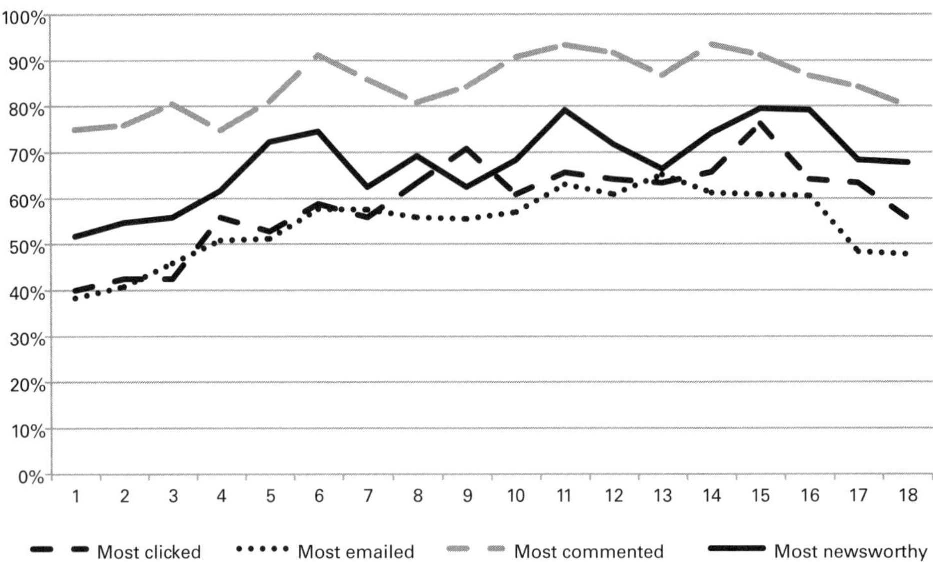


**Figure 5.11**
Percentage of public-affairs topics on "most clicked," "most emailed," "most commented," and "most newsworthy" lists, August 1 to December 1, 2008, United States, all sites, by week. (Election Day was during week 15.)

percentage increase in the odds of a story being about public affairs, relative to stories posted during week 1, ranged from 110 percent in week 7 to 487 percent in week 15.[16] Variation in the most emailed stories follows a similar pattern, although the values tend to be smaller. The odds that a story on the "most emailed" list would be about public affairs increased significantly during all weeks from week 6 to week 15, the increases ranging from 119 percent in week 9 to 264 percent in week 13.[17] Finally, the thematic composition of the "most commented" list showed consistent, significant increases in the odds of a story being about public affairs from week 10 to week 15, the increases ranging from 139 percent in week 13 to 452 percent in week 14.[18] In contrast, the increases in the odds a story on the "most newsworthy" list would be about public affairs were smaller, ranging from 86 percent in week 13 to 265 percent during week 15.[19] Thus, the three forms of interactivity in consumer choice are dynamic when it comes to the subject matter of the stories in question. But there are differences among these forms of interactivity; the most emailed stories are more stable than their most clicked and most commented on counterparts.

Consistent with what we showed in chapter 4 with respect to the most clicked stories, the storytelling preferences of consumers on the "most emailed" and "most commented" lists are more stable than their respective preferences regarding thematic content. Our analysis shows that the preferred storytelling formats of the articles that consumers most often read, email, and comment on remained quite constant in the three months before Election Day and in the first few weeks that followed it. The only list that showed some consistent change was the "most commented" list. At the very end of the campaign, the percentage of commentary articles went from 23 percent to 42 percent and the likelihood that a story in the "most commented" list was in commentary style was 241 percent in week 14 and 220 percent in week 15. This stability is also evident in the journalists' preferences. As the campaign progressed, there was no consistent increase or decrease in the odds of stories being presented as straight news, as features, or as commentary among either the stories in the "most newsworthy" list, those in the "most clicked" list, or those in the "most emailed" list.[20]

In sum, emailing behavior and commenting behavior exhibit dynamic qualities similar to those of clicking behavior in the sense that they react to changes in the sociopolitical context. This reactivity is more marked in the thematic content of the news than in their storytelling formats. Furthermore, the changes in the content and format of the most commented on and the most clicked articles are more pronounced than those in the most emailed articles.

## Concluding Remarks

In this chapter we have explored the similarities and differences between clicking, emailing, and commenting on stories and what they mean for the supply-demand gap in online news. We have shown that consumers tend to click on interesting public-affairs stories told in straight-news fashion, that they tend to email useful or bizarre non-public-affairs stories written in feature style, and that they tend to comment on high-profile, controversial public-affairs subjects presented as opinion or as straight news. This leads to a thematic disparity between the most newsworthy pieces and the most emailed articles, with a higher prevalence of public-affairs stories in the former. It also leads to a different thematic disparity between the most newsworthy and most commented on articles: the consumers choose a higher proportion of public-affairs topics than journalists. Thus, the findings presented in this chapter indicate that variations in the uptake of technological affordances are associated with variations in consumers' news choices.

The existence of differences in the subject matter and the storytelling formats of the articles that news consumers select to read, email, and comment on points toward the specificity of various interactive practices. It also underscores the explanatory value of combining research on the existence of various interactive features on leading news sites with research on the social practices associated with those features (that is, how people take advantage of them). Had this study focused on one type of interactivity, as most previous research has done,[21] it would not have elicited the differences in the thematic and format composition of the stories that were the focus of the three kinds of interactive behavior. Moreover, the divergence in the most emailed and most commented on stories, both considered by scholarship as instances of "user-to-user interactivity,"[22] suggests that in conceptualizing interactive practices it would be worthwhile to distinguish interaction with known and unknown users. When forwarding stories by email, online news consumers tended to focus on non-public-affairs articles told in feature style, usually about bizarre or useful topics. This evokes avoidance of potentially controversial topics in social interaction about the news, by which news audiences steer clear from discussing public-affairs subjects with people they know.[23] When commenting on news articles, consumers appear to take advantage of the relative anonymity afforded by online newspapers and do not shy away from controversial topics.[24, 25]

An examination of the variability of content and format choices across the most clicked, most emailed, and most commented on stories confirms the findings presented in chapter 3, namely that audiences modify their interactions with news sites according to the social and political context. This has three main theoretical implications. First, it provides further evidence for the notion that news audiences behave as monitorial citizens,[26] scanning their environment, consuming public-affairs content, and expressing their opinion about that type of content more frequently during times of heightened political activity. Second, the smaller variation in stories about public-affairs topics on the "most emailed" list indicates that, regardless of the context, the default behavior of online audiences is to avoid potentially controversial public-affairs topics in their social interactions. This finding challenges the widespread applicability of the notion that individuals who expose themselves to high levels of political information act as "influentials"[27] regarding political issues by relaying urgent political matters to their social contacts.[28] Third, the narrowing of the thematic disparity between the most newsworthy and the most clicked stories and the disappearance of the thematic disparity between the most newsworthy and the most commented on stories during the 2008 presidential campaign provide further support for the notion that in a high-choice media environment, such as the Internet,[29] media increase their ability to set the agenda for the larger public during times signaled by heightened political activity.

Our analysis of storytelling formats across the three types of interactive behavior sheds additional light on matters having to do with whether "the news has gone soft," a topic that we addressed in chapter 4. Consumers may prefer to email somewhat "softer" news to friends and family members, but they still select items in "hard" news formats, such as straight news and opinion articles, to read and to comment on. Although blogs and user-generated content occupy 11 percent and 3 percent of the "most newsworthy" list, respectively, these born-on-the-Web storytelling formats are still oversupplied in relation to all expressions of interactivity. This further confirms the notion, elaborated in chapter 4, that these newer formats have extremely limited appeal to consumers of online news. Blogs take up 7 percent of both the "most clicked" list and the "most commented" list and less than 1 percent of the "most emailed" list. Similarly, user-generated content takes up 2 percent of the most commented on stories and less than 1 percent of the most clicked and most emailed articles.

The information presented in this chapter adds another layer of complexity to our account of the supply-demand gap. In the previous chapters, we established that the stories that journalists selected to publish as the most newsworthy and the articles that consumers selected to read differed in thematic composition and, to a lesser extent, in storytelling style. In this chapter, we have shown that the disparity between journalists' and audiences' choices extends to other common activities that consumers undertake with online news, including emailing them to friends and family members and posting comments about them for a wider audience to read. Thus, even when we look at three different forms of interaction with digital media, the premise of this book holds: there is a supply-demand gap in the case of online news. The uptake of various technological affordances influences the choices of journalists and consumers, but the notion of the gap remains across these forms of media consumption.

# 6 The Meaning of the News Gap for Media and Democracy

We opened this book with the hypothetical example of a traditional neighborhood bakery. It seems fitting to close it by returning to that example to highlight four lessons that we learned in chapters 2–5.

First, the plight of that particular bakery isn't unique. Neighborhood bakeries in cities across countries and continents with different industry structures, culinary traditions, and taste cultures must deal with the gap between the supply of and the demand for bread and pastries made with whole-wheat flour and those made with refined flour.

Second, the gap is quite dynamic, mostly because of fluctuations in the nature of demand. Although the supply of baked goods changes with the typical patterns of daily life and also in response to unforeseen circumstances, such as a shortage of some ingredients, those changes are much smaller than changes in what customers purchase—changes, for instance, caused by a health scare that captures the attention of the public and triggers a temporary modification in eating practices. This isn't a positive sign when it comes to the prospects of adapting the rather stable production process of a traditional bakery to a changing and uncertain environment.

Third, we learned that it all comes down to the ingredients. For decades, owners of neighborhood bakeries and a plethora of critics and consultants have argued that changing the presentation of goods baked with whole-wheat flour would increase the demand for them. They offered creative designs of pastries for adults and animal-shaped confections for children, but those remained on the shelves while white-flour goods presented in traditional ways sold at much higher rates. More recently, customers have been invited to participate in the baking process in the hope that their recipes and their labor would be eagerly accepted by fellow customers.

However, most consumers have been reluctant to take up this invitation, and demand for baked goods prepared with input from customers has been minimal. After all these innovations, customers of bakeries have shown a marked and resilient preference for white-flour bread and pastries prepared by trained bakers and presented in tried and true ways.

Fourth, because of its size, regularity, and ubiquity, and in light of a competitive environment that allows patrons to avoid the healthy options more easily than previously, the gap may have major consequences for the sustainability of the traditional bakery's social mission and a balanced diet for society at large. Yesterday's gap and today's gap might be the same from an accounting standpoint, but the meanings of the two gaps differ. A dramatically altered context makes it more costly for traditional bakeries to continue performing their social mission as they did in the past. They might cater to a relatively small group of health-conscious customers but risk losing a portion of their wider clientele. This, in turn, might mean a significant decrease in the provision of healthy options and concomitant negative public-health consequences. The plight of the neighborhood bakery is not only the plight of many such bakeries, but also of society as a whole.

Neighborhood bakeries are not elite media organizations, whole-wheat flour is not public-affairs information, and bread and pastries are not news. But these four lessons encapsulate some of the main findings and implications learned from our empirical examination of the supply-demand gap in the case of online news. The gap is a regular feature of the leading news sites, its magnitude is quite large, and its existence cuts across geographic and ideological differences. The gap is also dependent on context, and consumers' choices are much more variable than those of journalists. How media organizations are going to be innovative when they can't keep up with their consumers in the first place is an alarming question. Furthermore, at least in the case of online news, content is king: consumers of leading mainstream sites gravitate toward non-public-affairs topics regardless of how they are presented. They show a marked preference for straight news over features and a strong disregard for participatory options such as user-generated content. Finally, the news gap threatens the sustainability of the public-service mission of the elite media, at least to the extent that was common during the twentieth century. By implication, this puts a question mark on taken-for-granted contributions of the media to the democratic process, such as the formation of a widespread and effective agenda on matters of the polity, the provision of a robust body of information about these matters to the public sphere, and the vibrant performance of a watchdog role. The possibility of decreased interest in public affairs, political deliberation and participation, and social accountability looms large, because the gap might become a normal feature of our high-competition, high-choice media landscape.

In the remainder of this chapter we address these and other lessons learned in our account of the news gap by first reviewing our findings systematically and then reflecting on what they mean for the matrix that connects media, technology, and society in the digital age.

## What We Now Know about the News Gap

During periods of normal political activity, the news gap is evident in regions that have different media systems, cultures, and histories. The magnitude of the thematic gap reaches nearly 20 percentage points across the sites we studied during ordinary times. Moreover, the account presented in chapter 2 which examined only journalists' and consumers' choices that did not overlap suggests that the divergence between journalists' and consumers' news choices would be even starker if each group were not potentially influenced by the preferences of the other. In contrast, the supply-demand gap in storytelling formats is smaller. Furthermore, the analysis of the combined content and storytelling preferences reveals that journalists oversupply public-affairs topics told in a straight-news format, whereas consumers routinely choose more non-public-affairs stories without regard to the format. This leads us to conclude that the gap is attributable mostly to thematic preferences, not to preferences for different styles of storytelling.

In this book we have made three methodological contributions to the study of the news gap in particular and to the production and consumption of news in general. First, relying on the story as the unit of analysis has enabled us to offer a fine-grained analysis of journalists' and consumers' news choices. We would not have been able to achieve this if we had relied on the more usual aggregate metrics, such as ratings and circulation figures, or on indirect ones, such as responses to surveys. Second, analyzing journalists' and consumers' news choices in relation to each other has allowed us to obtain a precise characterization of the gap. This would not have been possible if we had examined the preferences of either one of those two groups and inferred the size and composition of the gap on the basis of what is known about the other. Third, looking at the news selections of both groups during a period of relatively normal political activity and during a period of heightened political activity has enabled us to gauge variations in the gap from one period to the other and within the temporal evolution during the second period. It has also enabled us to show that the choices of journalists are less variable than those of consumers. Had we treated journalists' and consumers' news choices as static, and had the research been conducted only during a period of relatively normal political activity, or only during a period of heightened political activity, it would not have been possible to ascertain the dynamic nature of both groups' choices or the different degrees of variation in the two groups.

We have also made two theoretical contributions in this book. First, we have shed light on whether and how certain explanatory factors—geographic, ideological, contextual, technological, interpretive, and experiential—affect the news gap. Second, we have reflected on the news gap's implications for broader conceptual discussions of the dynamics of agenda setting, monitorial citizenship, and storytelling preferences.

Our analysis suggests that geographic and ideological factors do not seem to influence the size and variability (or lack thereof) of the gap. Overall, the divergence in the news choices of journalists and consumers was fairly immune to variations across countries and regions with different media cultures, histories, and structures and to whether the site or sites in question had conservative or liberal leanings. As we elaborated in chapter 2, this lack of variance seems to be attributable to two trends, one toward the convergence of media systems and one toward the globalization of consumers' tastes.

In contrast, we found that contextual, technological, interpretive, and experiential factors influence the existence and magnitude of the gap. The shift from a period of ordinary political activity to a period of heightened political activity and the evolution of events within the latter period affected the thematic composition of the news choices of journalists and consumers. As we noted above, the changes were much more pronounced for consumers than for journalists. Contextual transformations also shaped, albeit to a much lesser extent, the storytelling choices of consumers; the preferences of journalists didn't change significantly. Format preferences are more stable than content preferences because they are tied to long-standing cognitive schemas through which consumers apprehend many different kinds of stories.[1] Although these effects varied among the sites, the overall trends were still quite noticeable. In chapters 3–5 we argued that this contextual variability indicates the presence of a monitorial citizenship stance that motivates consumers to turn their attention to matters of the polity much more intensely during periods of heightened political activity.

Variations in technological affordances were associated with diversity of news choice on the part of consumers. As we showed in chapter 5, consumers tend to click on non-public-affairs stories told in straight-news fashion, to email articles that address non-public-affairs topics via feature-style storytelling, and to comment on high-profile public-affairs matters conveyed in either the straight-news format or the commentary format. These diverse realizations of the different interactive capabilities of news sites are anchored in pre-existent communication practices. We have already discussed how clicking on news stories is related to reading print newspapers and watching television newscasts. Scholars have argued that emailing patterns reproduce long-standing practices of interpersonal sociability that tend to be dominated by noncontroversial, helpful, and humorous topics.[2] Research has shown that commenting on public online spaces is shaped by the anonymity afforded by these digital settings and the desire of a vocal minority to take advantage of that anonymity to voice their opinions.[3]

Interviews with journalists and consumers revealed that interpretive and experiential factors also affect the gap. The prevalence of the public-service ethos at the core of the occupation's identity influences journalists' news choices. This ethos is enacted even in the presence of constant reminders that it conflicts with the preferences of consumers and the persistence of negative affect. Consumers' choices are tied to the sense that reading public-affairs news stories places greater demands and generates more anxiety than reading non-public-affairs stories. As was noted above, things change during periods marked by extraordinary social and political circumstances because a combination of civic duty, a desire to conform to a social mood centered on public-affairs topics, and the need to acquire information in order to successfully navigate the transformed environment take precedence over the hedonistic orientation that predominates during more normal periods.

In addition to theorizing about the factors that influence the gap, our account also contributes to broader scholarly work on media, technology, and society. One such development concerns the process of agenda setting. In chapter 3, we showed that the power of the media to set the public agenda is strongly moderated by contextual dynamics. During ordinary political times, the presence of a relatively uniform and sizable gap between journalists' and consumers' choices indicates that this power is low, or at least lower than the dominant views on media and society would have it. Moreover, even during extraordinary political periods during which the media's power to set the agenda is higher, there was a supply-demand gap in news content at a significant fraction of the sites we studied.

Alternative pathways that might lead to the formation of an agenda centered on public-affairs news are not without complications. There is the possibility that consumers might obtain this kind of content by glancing at the headlines on the homepage and then clicking mostly on non-public-affairs stories. Over time, this would lead to a hollowing or "twitterization" of the process of agenda setting: consumers would know that the issues exist, but would know little beyond that. However, there is no evidence that consumers are indeed paying attention to public-affairs headlines. Moreover, recent trends showing that Google searches and Facebook links are gaining in importance as ways for consumers to find stories contradicts this hypothetical scenario.[4] Another alternative pathway is that consumers obtain public-affairs content by talking to people in their social networks who have read stories rather than by clicking on stories. However, our findings on emailing behavior reported in chapter 5 cast doubt on the efficacy of this second-order effect.[5]

Interpretive and experiential mechanisms explain, in part, the relatively limited power of the media to set the agenda via online news during ordinary periods and its rise during extraordinary times. Our findings show that there is active avoidance of public-affairs stories rather than passive lack of interest in them, and that in a "high-choice" media environment[6] such avoidance is easier than it was in the past. This avoidance is an outcome of the perception among consumers that public-affairs stories make greater cognitive demands than stories on non-public-affairs topics.

Reading public-affairs stories is also associated with negative affect. Furthermore, the ability to "switch on" attention to public-affairs stories during extraordinary times leads to our contribution regarding an additional debate at the intersection of communication and politics: the dynamics of monitorial citizenship in a digital age.

As we noted in chapter 3, there has been an ongoing debate among some scholars of political communication about the "burglar alarm"[7] and "full information"[8] models for news. To date, this debate has been largely normative. In this book we provide an empirical test of which of the two standards holds, at least for online news. We also shed light on the interpretive and experiential mechanisms that subtend our empirical finding.

We find that neither the "full information" model nor the rational-ignorance model holds *at all times*. Instead, consumers move in and out of rational ignorance in a pattern that falls under the notion of monitorial citizenship; they pay more attention to matters of the polity during extraordinary periods than during more ordinary times. Furthermore, the enactment of monitorial citizenship is more pronounced for clicking and commenting than for email. The relative steadiness of emailing behavior is associated with the permanence of the conversational topics that characterize exchanges within well-established social networks.[9]

The ability of consumers to significantly alter the composition of their news diet is an additional indication of their active position within the larger ecology of news. In the specific case of monitorial citizenship, a combination of efforts to maintain and protect the self influences this high level of agency. As our interviews show, consumers maintain their self-image during extraordinary political times by abiding by socially desirable norms of civic duty and conforming to the changed social climate in which more attention is paid to public affairs than during ordinary times. The interviews also indicate that consumers change their behavior in extraordinary political times by focusing on a greater proportion of public-affairs stories in order to acquire information that can help them navigate an altered sociopolitical landscape.

The account of the relative stability of storytelling-format preferences links to a conceptual debate at the intersection of media and politics. When it comes to how journalistic stories are told, there has been considerable ferment in both scholarly and practitioner circles over the past few decades about the perception of transformation in the nature of demand as a justification for the need to change the nature of supply. As we argued in chapter 4, there has been a push for the softening of news ever since the 1970s, and since the early 2000s there have been calls to increase the presence of blogs and user-generated content on news sites. Despite the differences between the arguments related to both waves, there is a common, but implicit, denominator across them. When it comes to accessing the news about matters of the polity, there is significant demand for storytelling formats, such as feature-style narratives, blogs, and different embodiments of user-generated content. However, as we stated in the introduction to this chapter, our research shows that audiences don't prefer these alternative formats and mostly ignore user-generated content, at least in the case of online news. First, there is no major presence of feature style, blogs, and user-generated content in the supply of online news. On average, straight news accounts for four out of five of the most newsworthy stories on the sites we studied. More important, straight news dominates the demand for online news. Even though consumers choose more feature-style stories than journalists do, the appeal of these stories is still smaller than that of straight news. The extremely low interest in blogs and user-generated content among consumers of these news sites suggests that these options are, at best, still a nascent technology-driven possibility and, at worst, an ill-fated marketing ploy. There may be demand from some consumers to participate in news production, but very few fellow audience members seem willing to read the resulting stories.

Our account begins to shed light on why straight news still rules the day after decades of discussion to the contrary. Content is king, at least in the case of online news. Content drives consumption much more than format does because clicking behavior is based on the information contained in the headlines, and headlines are more suited to convey information about the thematic content than the storytelling format of the story. Content also affects consumption because the context of online news consumption, which occurs mostly at work, predisposes people to focus on short snippets of content instead of reading a longer piece, such as a feature.[10] Finally, blogs and user-generated content often have headlines that are low in information content.

## The Importance of the News Gap for the Future of the Media and for the Role of the Media in Democratic Life

As we argued in chapter 1, the news gap probably has existed for a long time. It was well tolerated by the elite media in light of their high market power, the strength of the occupational jurisdiction of their journalists and their low knowledge of their public's preferences, and the limited ability of consumers to enact a stance of rational ignorance. However, the latter-day media environment has altered that status quo through the combination of an increase in competition in the market for news among companies across the information industries, rising challenges to the occupational jurisdiction of journalists and increased visibility of the public's news choices within the newsroom, and the greater ease with which consumers can read the stories that interest them and ignore the rest. This "trifecta" of competitive, occupational, and consumer trends threatens the viability of the public-service mission of the leading elite media. How can they deal with this situation? We think the four most plausible alternatives are the following:

- Try to channel this mission through innovation in storytelling formats.
- Switch from generalist to niche strategies of content development.
- Go downstream and compete in the tabloid sector of the news market by giving the consumers more of what they want and less of what they need.
- Develop a mode of flexible news production that can easily alternate between periods of routine and heightened political activity.

As we noted in chapter 4, scholars and commentators have argued that a possible way forward for the leading mainstream news media would be to garner more attention from the mass audience via format innovations (primarily the use of feature style, blogs, and user-generated content) and/or to "smuggle" public-affairs content via these format choices. However, as we noted in the previous section, the findings presented in chapters 4 and 5 indicate that these strategies to soften the news supply, modernize it, and/or delegate part of its production to the mass public share a simple problem: consumers are not highly interested in any of them. These findings suggest that trying to solve the dilemma of the gap in the contemporary media environment by devoting renewed resources to format innovation would be inconsequential at best (and not increase consumers' interest) and detrimental at worst (and cause consumers to look elsewhere for news).

A second solution to the dilemma posed by the gap would be to switch from a generalist-oriented production strategy to a niche-oriented one. Our analysis in chapter 3 of the appeal of the Washington Post's website during the electoral cycle and the rise in importance of relatively novel sites focused on public-affairs news (such as Politico and Pro-Publica) suggests that the development of deep coverage of this kind of news has promise. Because resources are finite, devoting more of them to one particular subject means devoting fewer to the rest. Over time, this would entail a reorientation of the media organizations in question from generalists covering a wide array of topics to niche players concerned primarily with one topic. Research has demonstrated the limitation of this potential strategy by showing that the Web is a winner-take-all market (more than the markets in other media platforms), so that any content niche can ideally sustain a handful of players.[11] Even though a niche strategy might be suitable for a small number of news organizations, especially those that already have strong brand recognition in that content space, it is hardly ideal for the average player and the industry as a whole. Furthermore, it is conceivable that the high demand for public-affairs news on Washington Post during election time is related to a decrease in attention to these topics on smaller, generalist sites that cannot afford the depth and breadth of coverage of the more niche-oriented players. Thus, a hypothetical scenario in which some leading sites moved to niche strategies in the public-affairs arena might result in a broad, negative effect for the majority of the news industry, because they would "vacuum" attention to these topics away from the smaller sites.

A third way out of the dilemma posed by the gap would be to "go downstream," so to speak. This would entail giving consumers more of what they want (mostly stories about sports, entertainment, weather, and crime) and less of what the leading media believe they need to know to be well informed members of the polity (deep coverage of politics, economics, business, and international events). In a sense, this has been occurring for some time already, as a cursory comparison of the *New York Times* and the *Wall Street Journal* from the 1960s to the present shows. But deepening this strategy doesn't seem a fruitful way to move forward for two reasons.

First, there are plenty of news organizations that do this in a successful manner. The "tabloid" sector of the news industry is a thriving, well-populated market. Furthermore, the rise of "content farms" on the Web, such as Demand Media, adds another layer of difficulty to the strategy of moving downstream. From a competitive standpoint, entering the downstream market seems an uphill battle for sites such as those we studied for this book. Second, our interviews show that consumers who visit these sites do so because of the appeal of the brand identity of these organizations. This identity is intimately linked to the public-service mission embodied in much of their news coverage. Going downstream might risk diluting the identity of the brand and alienating typical consumers. Therefore, we don't believe that catering more directly to consumers' preferences would be a suitable way out of the dilemma posed by the gap for leading news organizations.

In our view, the fourth solution is the best one. It entails adding considerable flexibility to the currently dominant organization of news production, with its somewhat rigid beats and specializations. Our account shows that rational ignorance govern consumers' preferences during ordinary times, but that monitorial citizenship prevails during periods of extraordinary political activity. A flexible news-production system would be nimble enough to alter the supply of information to match the perceived changes in the nature of demand. To a certain extent, news organizations have always done this. For instance, during a crisis staffers from other beats are often reallocated to increase coverage of the crisis. However, our analysis of the differences between periods of routine political activity and periods of heightened political activity shows that at present there isn't much flexibility in the production processes of news organizations. Much more could be done to make the production process flexible in a way that will better meet consumers' demand.

The need to generate concomitant modifications in a number of aspects of the currently dominant news-production process potentially complicates the implementation of such a flexible production system. These modifications include alterations in organizational infrastructure (e.g., revisiting the location and focus of foreign bureaus), networks of sources (e.g., how to cultivate a diverse portfolio of sources for the different periods of political activity and how to keep the contacts "fresh" during idle reporting times), and technical knowledge (e.g., how to design training and on-the-job socialization programs that would facilitate achieving adequate levels of proficiency across disparate topics). These can be vexing issues, in particular for organizations that have long functioned in a different way, but they are not insurmountable. However, our research suggests that the pre-existing rigidity in editorial news choice is the thorniest obstacle to the successful implementation of a flexible production system. In all studies, during ordinary and extraordinary political times, and concerning content and storytelling preferences, consumers exhibited a much higher degree of variance than journalists. We suspect that this rigidity is associated with the values and beliefs of the occupation and organizations of journalism. The persistence of these values and beliefs would be the most difficult barrier to a flexible mode of production.

There seems to be no easy way out of the dilemma that the gap poses to the leading news organizations in the current media environment. Pursuing the alternatives discussed above would most likely involve major transformations of multiple kinds. Because a continuation of the current situation threatens the viability of the public-service mission in the short term or the medium term, the gap presents major challenges to three critical contributions that this public-service mission has historically made to the democratic process. The first contribution is the establishment of a somewhat cohesive news agenda centered on matters of the polity and of wide reach within the citizenry. The second is the provision of a fairly large volume of robust and diverse information about these matters to the public sphere that then aids political deliberation and civic participation. The third contribution of the public-service mission is the enactment of a vibrant watchdog function with respect to powerful actors in government, business, and the nonprofit sector. We now turn our attention to these vital aspects of the contribution of the media's public-service mission to the democratic process.

In the previous chapters we showed that the power of the media to set the agenda decreases during ordinary periods (and increases somewhat during extraordinary times), and this loss isn't offset by consumer-driven efforts via user-generated content. To assess what this might mean for society at large, it is important to view the media's function in the agenda-setting process from two concurrent but different roles they perform in the democratic process: as player and as intermediary.

The leading mainstream media organizations aim to influence two kinds of publics: the elite public (composed of decision makers in government, in business, and in the nonprofit sector) and the mass public. These two publics are interrelated. On the one hand, the ability to influence the elite public is premised on the size and composition of the mass public. A media outlet with a large and resourceful mass public is more likely to influence decision makers than otherwise. On the other hand, the mass public assigns value and credibility to the news carried by these media, partly on the basis of their ability to reach the elite public. Furthermore, the leading media remain influential with the elite public through their coverage of matters of the polity. But if the mass public isn't paying attention to public-affairs news, and these media and the journalists who work for them no longer have the kind of market power and jurisdictional strength that they once had to tolerate this discrepancy, then the public-service orientation at the heart of their organizational and occupational identities is at risk. Pablo Boczkowski has argued that this might affect the power of the media to set the news agenda.

> This interdependence between the elite and mass publics puts news organizations into a double bind when they are confronted with increased awareness of the mass public's preference for non–public affairs subjects. . . . On the one hand, to disregard the mass public's interests could lead to the erosion of its size, loyalty, and overall affect. This could, in turn, weaken news organizations' ability to influence the news agenda and the elite public. On the other hand, to cater to the mass public's preference for non–public affairs stories could also diminish news organizations' ability to influence the agenda. (2010, p. 178)

The leading media are the conduit that other large, powerful collective actors use to reach the public. As the existence and magnitude of the gap seem to suggest, if a significant portion of the news disseminated in this way goes unread or unheard, this leads to a suboptimal process of capturing the attention of the public. Thus, from the vantage point of these collective actors, who are trying to set an agenda favorable to their interests, the leading media might become progressively less desirable intermediaries. This might lead these large, collective actors to increase their attempts to bypass the leading media and reach the public directly.

The implications of the gap for the leading media (both as powerful political players and as intermediaries between other political players and the public in the agenda-setting process) suggest that one potential societal outcome is a deterioration of a cohesive agenda marked by matters of the polity and shared by major segments of the public. Another potential outcome is a rising disconnect between the public and the interests of these large, collective actors, with the concomitant decrease in shared centers of concern and action for society as a whole. Thus, a loss in the media's agenda-setting power might mean a crisis in the whole system of political communication that has long been central to the dynamics of a liberal democracy and the ability of complex societies to achieve common ground.

The leading mainstream media organizations also add to the welfare of the democratic process in at least two other ways: by contributing to the establishment and maintenance of a vibrant public sphere and by helping to control other powerful actors through their watchdog role.

The media are sources of information for the public sphere and focal points for deliberation about affairs of the polity. In terms of information provision, the news is an essential input for debate about public affairs,[12] because the information disseminated by mainstream media is crucial for citizens to engage in discussion about social and political issues.[13] This function is mostly performed by leading news organizations; smaller and tabloid outlets usually lack the resources needed to conduct public-affairs reportage. Moreover, mainstream media serve as privileged spaces for public deliberation in which citizens of modern democracies can come together to debate among themselves and with political leaders and other decision makers.[14] Discussion of public affairs, in turn, leads to higher levels of political knowledge and increased civic participation.[15] The loss of leading news media as sources of information for debate would lead to the overall impoverishment of public deliberation and the fragmentation of our shared public space, as national mainstream media are replaced by smaller niche outlets as scenarios for deliberation. According to Jürgen Habermas, "the rise of millions of fragmented chat rooms across the world tend . . . to lead to the fragmentation of large but politically focused mass audiences into a huge number of isolated issue publics. Within established national public spheres, the online debates of web users only promote political communication, when news groups crystallize around the focal points of the quality press, for example, national newspapers and political magazines."[16]

The challenge posed by the gap to the role of the media in the public sphere is twofold. First, lack of interest in public-affairs content might lead over time to a population that is less equipped to participate in discussions about crucial aspects of its shared social life. Second, a substantially reduced consumer base for public-affairs information and a related fragmentation of the audience endanger the leading mainstream media's function of providing a focal point for deliberation about these crucial aspects of social life. Together, these two challenges suggest a potential trajectory in a direction of decreased knowledge and a loss of common ground among the citizenry.

Another major contribution of the media to the democratic process is their watchdog role in holding state officials and other powerful actors accountable for their actions by promoting public scrutiny of those in authority.[17] The notion that the news media could limit excessive power by acting as an independent defender of the public interest was one of the earliest justifications for freedom of the press.[18] Mainstream news outlets help the citizenry to control influential people and organizations both directly (by exposing corruption in public administration and the corporate sector) and indirectly (by increasing the perceived social costs of being caught committing wrongful acts). Thus, the existence of a free press has been linked to increased rule of law, greater government efficiency in the policy process, and less corruption.[19] Watchdog journalism is costly because it demands that staff be devoted to investigating leads that may not be fruitful during long periods of time, and it constitutes a small part of public-affairs content disseminated by mainstream media.[20] If the media cut back on the production of public-affairs news, it is likely to result in a further decrease in the intensity of watchdog efforts. Smaller outlets would find it even more difficult to undertake watchdog journalism, a time-intense and resource-intense endeavor. Silvio Waisbord proposes that "the reluctance of news organizations to assign adequate resources puts pressures on reporters to produce fast and low-cost news, instead of time-consuming news-gathering," and that "consequently, a combination of shoddy reporting and editorial constraints produces superficial, inchoate, and incomplete coverage."[21]

The gap between journalists and consumers may increase the time and resources devoted to non-public-affairs topics and subsequently diminish public-affairs coverage in general and investigative reportage in particular. If the leading elite media were to abandon their watchdog function, the balance of power in democratic societies would shift further in favor of other large collective actors, who would then be able to proceed with fewer external controls.

In chapter 1 we noted that the existence of the news gap has long been a truism among both academics and practitioners—a "curious fact of human nature," as Robert Park wrote in the preface of Helen Hughes' book *News and the Human Interest Story*.[22] Like all truisms, it has been taken for granted, and its dynamics have gone unexplored. After all, business was good for the leading media, their public-service mission was good for the journalists who worked for them and for society at large, and the contributions of this mission to the democratic process were aligned with the belief system of most academics who study the imbrication of communication and politics. But in the past few decades, social and technological transformations have changed the media landscape drastically. As a result, the media system is in transition. Some elements of the old system will still remain, but many will not; it is not clear which ones will remain and what will replace those that will change. New logics will emerge, but they are impossible to foresee from the vantage point of the present.

It is noteworthy that some of these transformations have helped us to produce this first comprehensive account of the supply-demand gap in news. Without the tools that have made it possible to collect information about consumers' choices at the story level, and without the decisions by many leading news organizations to make this information available, our studies could not have been done, at least not in the way we undertook them. This is noteworthy because, although we find evidence of the gap, its meaning in the larger ecology of news, media, publics, and politics has been forever altered. More than a century ago, Ferdinand de Saussure argued that the meaning of a word is dependent on the sentence in which it is uttered.[23] Similarly, the meaning of a social phenomenon such as the news gap depends on the historical period in which it is considered. Yesterday's gap is not today's gap, even though the divergence in the choices of journalists and consumers might be similar. Yesterday, the gap signified the power of the leading media to set the agenda despite the public's wishes and the centrality of this phenomenon within the large matrix of mass-mediated political communication that undergirds liberal democracies. Today, the gap signifies the growing weakness of these media to set the agenda and the problems associated with maintaining their public-service mission in an increasingly unfavorable competitive landscape. By implication, the gap also allows us to examine the progressive disassembling of that matrix of political communication and the uncertainty about the circulation of information that connects large collective actors, the media, and their publics.

Thus, this book might be the first comprehensive examination of the news gap and perhaps also the last. A social science book about an important aspect of the current state of the media might well become a piece of media history in a few decades. As Marx and Engels wrote, "All that is solid melts in the air."[24]

# Coda

A central argument of this book was that the online news choices of journalists and consumers vary in relation to changes in the sociopolitical context. We established this pattern by comparing the evolution of these respective choices within a presidential-election year (2008) and between that year and a non-election year (2009). In this coda, we further elaborate our account of the dynamic character of the supply-demand gap in online news by extending our analysis to encompass a five-year sequence that starts and ends with presidential elections (2008 and 2012), has a congressional election in the middle (2010), and includes two non-election years (2009 and 2011). This enables us to assess similarities and differences in temporal patterns within two different presidential-election cycles. It also allows us to track the tendencies in online news choices that cut across the ups and downs in political activity during this modal five-year sequence in American politics. In addition, because of the recency of the 2012 election, this coda constitutes one of the first scholarly analyses of the media and public behavior during the political contest that ended with the reelection of Barack Obama as president of the United States.

To this end, we collected additional data to compare with our studies of ABC, CBS, CNN, Fox, USA Today, and Washington Post conducted in 2008 and 2009. We gathered information on the "most newsworthy" and "most clicked" lists during the two weeks surrounding the midterm congressional elections of 2010, the corresponding 14 days in 2011, and 89 days from August 1 to December 2, 2012—a period that included the Republican and Democratic conventions, the presidential and vice-presidential debates, and 14 consecutive days surrounding Election Day—thus replicating in 2012 the data-collection procedure we employed in 2008. This additional data-collection effort resulted in another 6,123 "most newsworthy" stories and 5,154 "most clicked" stories.[1] (Beginning in 2012, Fox no longer made its most viewed items public. For consistency in the presentation of findings, in what follows we will not include Fox in our account; however, additional analyses including Fox from 2008 to 2011 do not exhibit significant differences with the analyses without it for that four-year period.)

We show that the gap between the content choices of journalists and those of consumers was a consistent and defining trait of these sites during the five years analyzed, journalists selecting as most newsworthy more public-affairs stories than consumers selected. We also find that this gap varied in size quite predictably, and that it exhibited an inverse relationship with the ups and downs of the sociopolitical context: a heightened degree of political activity is tied to a narrowing of the gap, and a reduction in that activity is linked to an increase in the size of the gap. Furthermore, these rhythms in the supply and the demand of online news were shaped primarily by variations in the behavior of audiences, since the content choices of journalists were more stable. Thus, the gap was smaller during presidential-election years, was of intermediate size during the congressional-election year, and was larger during non-election years. Finally, the gap in content preferences was quite independent of storytelling issues because the relationships with variations in the sociopolitical context persisted despite some changes in the prevalence of some storytelling options. These four patterns of content choice both confirm and expand upon the findings we presented in chapters 2–4.

Straight news remained at the top of the preferences of both journalists and consumers across the five years. There were some changes in the presence of feature-style stories and blogs. The former showed an uptick in 2012, but it remains to be seen whether it is the beginning of a trend or an outlier. On the five sites examined, blogs morphed from a distinct and innovative format into an alternative strategy for conveying straight news. However, these changes in format didn't affect the content-and-format gap: whereas journalists disseminated as most newsworthy items on public affairs presented in straight-news format, consumers gravitated toward non-public-affairs topics, regardless of the format. Thus, with the exception of the transformation of blogs and the uptick of feature-style articles in 2012, the dominant storytelling patterns discussed in chapter 4 were confirmed for the entire 2008–2012 cycle.

## Content Choices of Journalists and Consumers over a Five-Year Period

Our analysis shows that interest in public-affairs news among both journalists and consumers is markedly cyclical, rising and falling in a highly predictable way in relation to the ups and downs of political activity. In addition, its variance is more pronounced for consumers than for journalists. On four of the five sites—CNN, CBS, Washington Post, and USA Today—public-affairs news articles constituted at least half of the ten most newsworthy articles during each of the five years, ranging from 50 percent on USA Today in 2009 to 83 percent on Washington Post in 2012. (See figure C.1.) On ABC, more than 60 percent of the journalists' most newsworthy stories in the two presidential-election years were public-affairs news, but the percentage fell to 47 in both 2009 and 2011 and to 39 in 2010. In contrast, on three of the five sites—CNN, ABC, and CBS—public-affairs content made up more than half of consumers' top news choices

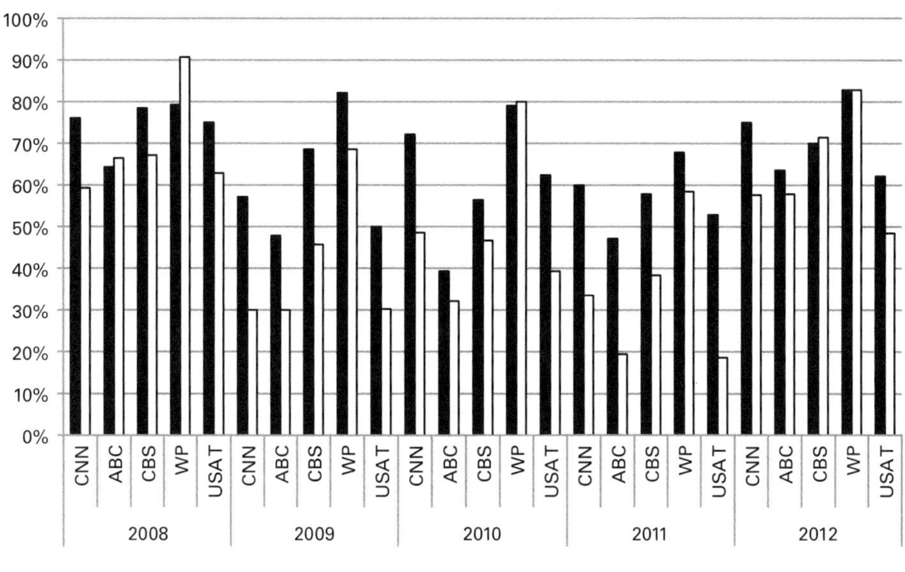


**Figure C.1**
Percentage of public-affairs topics in the stories deemed most newsworthy by journalists and the articles most viewed by consumers on CNN, ABC, CBS, USA, and Washington Post, 2008, 2009, 2010, 2011, and 2012.

only during presidential-election years. It fell well below the 50 percent threshold in 2009, 2010, and 2011, ranging from 19 percent on ABC in 2011 to 49 percent on CNN in 2010. On USA Today, it was below 50 percent in every year except 2008. Not surprisingly in light of the evidence presented in chapter 3, an exception to this pattern of lower interest in public-affairs topics among consumers was Washington Post, where public-affairs topics made up more than half of the most viewed stories during the five years examined, ranging from 58 percent in 2011 to 91 percent in 2008.

The news choices of both journalists and consumers exhibit a cyclical pattern, which is more pronounced for consumers than for journalists. (There is greater variance in the choices of the consumers than of the journalists.) These trends are evident in figure C.2, which shows the percentage of public-affairs content on all the sites combined during the five years that we studied. Among the stories deemed most newsworthy by journalists, the percentage of public-affairs stories was at least 70 in the two presidential-election years and was 62 in the midterm-election year. Public-affairs stories made up 61 percent of the stories in the top portion of the homepage in 2009 and 57 percent in 2011. Thus, the largest inter-

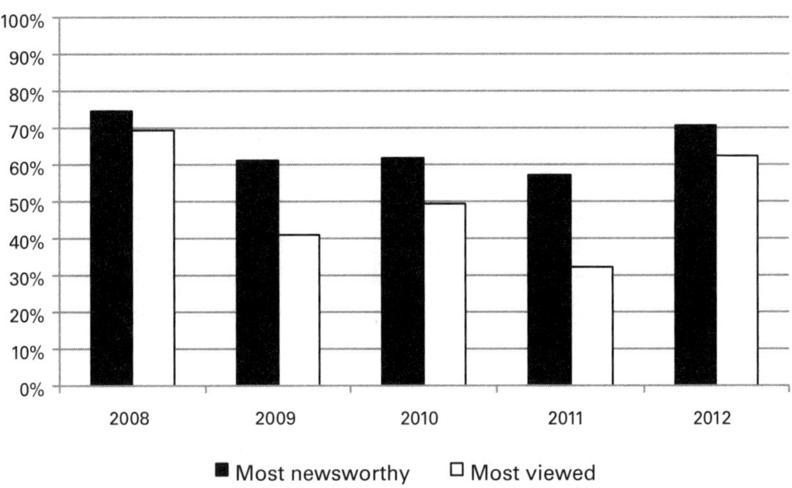


**Figure C.2**
Percentage of public-affairs topics in the stories deemed most newsworthy by journalists and the articles most viewed by consumers on CNN, ABC, CBS, USA, and Washington Post, 2008, 2009, 2010, 2011, and 2012.

annual variation for journalists—that between 2008 and 2011—was 18 percentage points. In contrast, public-affairs news accounted for more than 60 percent of consumers' most viewed stories only in the two presidential-election years; their preference for public-affairs content decreased to 49 percent in the midterm-election year and reached a low of 32 percent in 2011. The difference between the minimum and maximum percentages of public affairs in consumers' choices in 2008 and 2011 is 37 percentage points, more than twice the variance in journalists' choices between those two years.

A graphical representation of the gap between journalists' and consumers' news choices over the five-year period exhibits an M-shaped pattern that goes from a low point during presidential-election years (when political activity was at its peak) to a high point during non-election years (when political activity was at its lowest), reaching a middle point during the congressional-election year (when there was an intermediate level of political activity). This pattern was evident both within each site and across sites, as figure C.3 shows. For the five sites examined, the average gap between the supply and the demand for online news was only 5 percentage points in 2008 and 7 in 2012, increased to 13 percentage points in 2010, was 20 percentage points in 2009, and reached a high of 23 percentage points in 2011.

Interest in public-affairs news was higher for both journalists and consumers in 2008 than in 2012. This was probably influenced, at least in part, by the differences in the contests those two years: 2008 saw the first presidential election in 56 years in which neither an incumbent president nor a vice-president ran, and the turnout of voters was the highest since 1968. By contrast, in 2012 there was an incumbent running for reelection, most of the polls and statistical models predicted his victory, and the turnout was 5 percentage points lower than four years earlier.[2] Despite the lower level of interest in public-affairs news in 2012 than in 2008, intra-annual variations in news choices followed similar trajectories. (See figure C.4.) In 2008, the odds of a story in the journalists' list being about public-affairs news increased significantly during all but one week from week 5 until week 15, and the weekly percentage increase in the odds of a story being about public affairs, relative to stories posted during week 1, ranged from 54 in week 7 to 277 in week 15. Regarding audiences' choices, the odds of a story on the consumers' list being

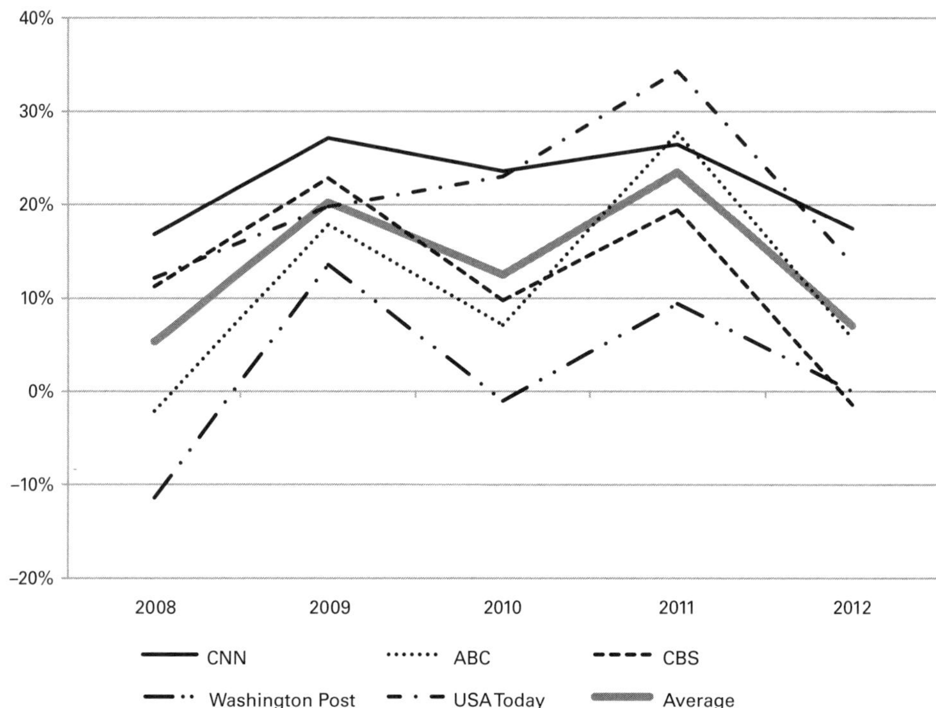


**Figure C.3**
Gap in public-affairs topics between the stories deemed most newsworthy by journalists and the articles most viewed by consumers on CNN, ABC, CBS, USA, and Washington Post, 2008, 2009, 2010, 2011, and 2012.

about public affairs increased significantly during all weeks from week 4 to week 15, the percentage increases ranging from 99 in week 5 to 456 in week 15.[3] Four years later, the odds of a story in the "most newsworthy" list being about public-affairs news increased significantly during all but three weeks from week 5 until week 15. The weekly percentage increase in the odds of a story being about public affairs, relative to stories posted during week 1, ranged from 55 in week 8 to 276 in week 15. The odds of a story on the consumers' "most viewed" list being about public affairs increased significantly during all weeks except one from week 4 to week 15, the percentage increases ranging from 61 in week 11 to 425 in week 15.[4]

In summary, a comparison of the prevalence of public-affairs content in the supply and the demand for online news from 2008 to 2012 reveals

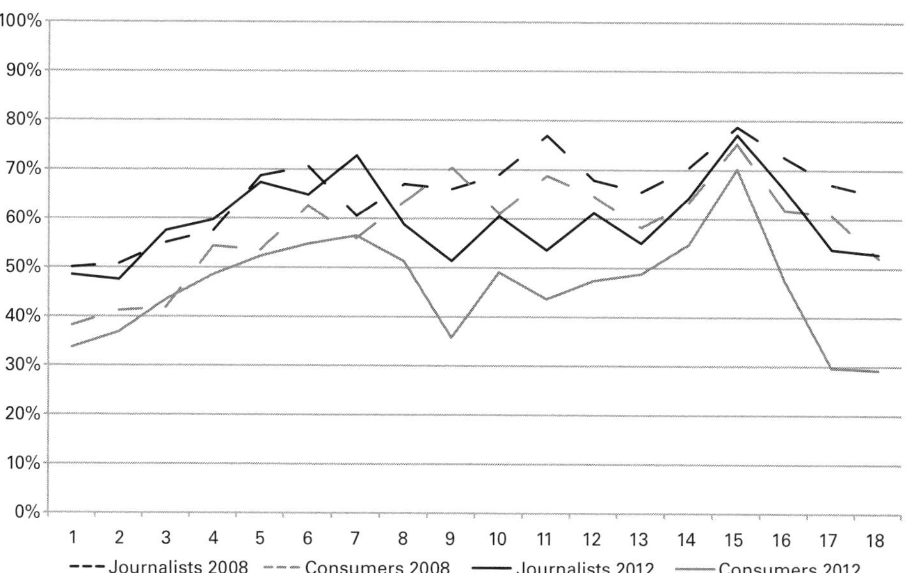


**Figure C.4**
Percentage of public-affairs stories on journalists' and consumers' lists in 2008, and 2012, by week.

that the preferences were cyclical and that there was more variance for consumers than for journalists. In each of the years analyzed there was a significant gap, but the size of the gap varied according to the political context in which journalists and consumers made their respective online news choices. The gap was also quite independent of changes in storytelling format.

## Storytelling Choices of Journalists and Consumers over a Five-Year Period

Our analyses indicate that when it comes to storytelling issues, the online news choices of journalists and consumers are quite stable and appear not to be greatly affected by variations in the sociopolitical context. Within this larger pattern, we find that straight news remained the leading storytelling format for both journalists and consumers across the five-year period analyzed, that blogs (a novel and distinct format in the early years of our sample) progressively became an alternative vessel for conveying straight news in the later years, and that feature-style storytelling experienced growth during the 2012 election season.

Straight news was the top storytelling option among the most newsworthy stories on all the sites in every year except on CNN in 2012, when features were the top choice. The prevalence of straight news ranged from 25 percent on CNN in 2012 to 88 percent on CBS in 2009 and averaged 58 percent of the ten most newsworthy stories across the sites sampled. (See figure C.5.) Straight news was also the dominant storytelling format on all but two of the "most viewed" lists during the five-year period we studied. The exceptions to this pattern were Washington Post during the 2008 presidential campaign, when commentary articles were more popular, and CNN during 2012, when feature-style articles were more popular. Among consumers, straight news stories ranged from 29 percent of the most clicked stories on Washington Post in 2008 to 71 percent on CNN in 2010, averaging 52 percent across the five sites. (See figure C.6.)

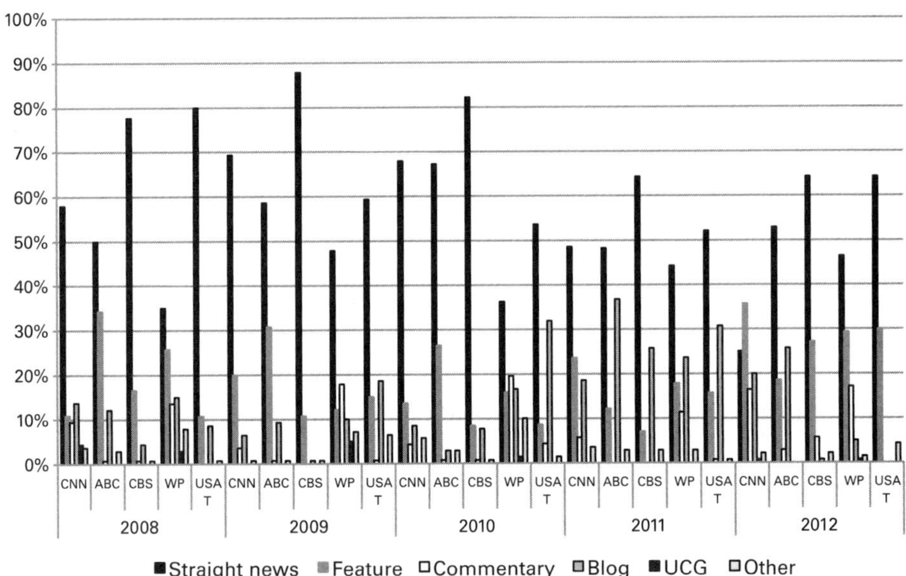


**Figure C.5**

Percentage of straight news, feature-style, commentary, blogs, and user-generated content in the stories deemed most newsworthy by journalists on CNN, ABC, CBS, Washington Post, and USA Today, 2008, 2009, 2010, 2011, and 2012.

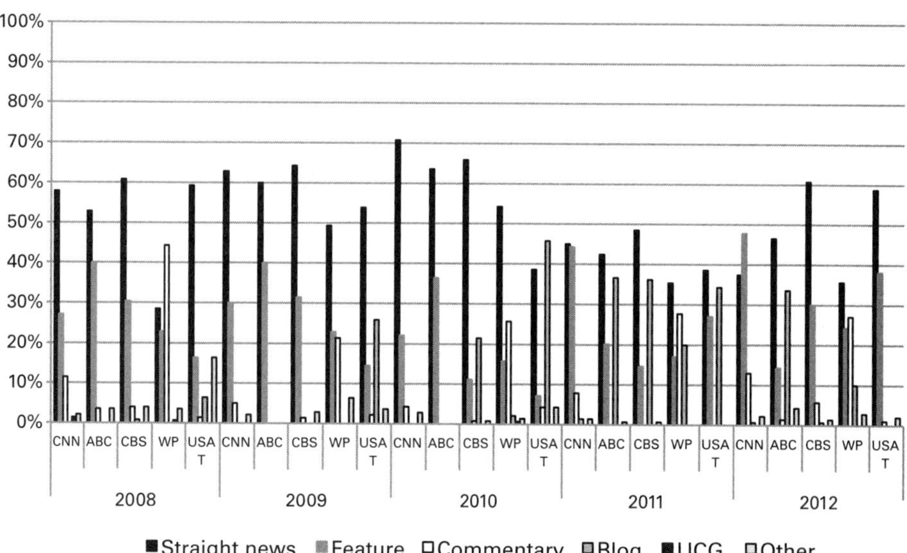


**Figure C.6**
Percentage of straight news, feature-style, commentary, blogs, and user-generated content in the stories most viewed by consumers on CNN, ABC, CBS, Washington Post, and USA Today, 2008, 2009, 2010, 2011, and 2012.

Feature style was the second-most-chosen storytelling format of the most newsworthy articles on most of the sites during most of the years, ranging from 6 percent on CBS in 2011 to 36 percent on CNN in 2012 and averaging 19 percent across the sites sampled. (See figure C.5.) It was also the second-most-popular format among consumers on most of the sites during most of the data-collection periods, with a low of 7 percent on USA Today in 2010 and Fox, a high of 48 percent on CNN in 2012, and an average of 26 percent. (See figure C.6.)

Commentary was the third-most-selected format by both journalists and consumers in 2008 and 2009, but fell to fourth place on most sites from 2010 on. On average, this format accounted for 5 percent of the most newsworthy stories, but there was wide variance in its prevalence. For instance, whereas on USA Today in 2008 and 2012 and on CBS in 2009 and 2011 there were no commentary stories among the top ten most newsworthy articles on any of the days on which we collected data, on Washington Post commentary accounted for at least 11 percent of the journalists' top choices in every year. (See figure C.5.) Commentary accounted for an average of 9 percent of the most clicked stories across sites. It also exhibited significant variance: absent from the top ten most clicked stories on ABC in 2009, 2010, and 2011, and from CBS and USA Today in 2011, it reached at least 21 percent on Washington Post during each of the five years of data collection. (See figure C.6.)

The various possible instantiations of user-generated content remained unpopular with both journalists and consumers on the five sites we studied. This format accounted for only 0.6 percent of the ten most newsworthy stories across sites during the five-year period. (See figure C.5.) It was not present at all among the ten most newsworthy stories on most of the sites during these years. Its highest occurrence was on Washington Post in 2009, when 5 percent of the top journalistic choices were user-generated stories. Articles employing this storytelling format were not among the most viewed stories on most of the sites during any of the five years. Its maximum popularity level, on CNN in 2008, was a meager 1 percent. On average, it accounted for 0.11 percent of the most clicked stories across sites and years. (See figure C.6.)

As we have already mentioned, the blogs on the five sites we studied experienced a noteworthy evolution from 2008 to 2012. This storytelling alternative increased in popularity in 2010 and 2011, overtaking commentary as the third most popular option in both the "most newsworthy" list and the "most viewed" list. However, its prevalence decreased considerably in 2012. Blogs reached an average of 14 percent among the ten most newsworthy stories across sites and years. (See figure C.5.) But the presence of this format exhibited significant inter-site and inter-annual variance, ranging from 32 percent on USA Today in 2011 to 0 percent on the same site the following year. Among the most viewed articles, blogs reached an average of 11 percent, and also showed wide variance. Blogs were absent from the "most viewed" lists on most sites in 2008 and 2009, but represented 46 percent of the most viewed articles on USA Today in 2011. (See figure C.6.)

The ups and downs in the popularity of blogs on the five sites, together with our impression during the content analysis that the presentation and the writing style of blogs changed during our five-year period of study, led us to conduct an additional analysis of this storytelling alternative. We wanted to ascertain whether the increase in the prevalence of blogs indicated greater interest in the new storytelling horizon represented by this format or whether it represented a displacement of straight-news content, and interest in it, into a new label. To that end, we examined the 841 blog posts that appeared on either the "most newsworthy" or "most viewed" lists in the 14 consecutive days we collected data in 2008, 2009, 2010, 2011, and 2012.[5] For each post, we assessed whether it had the distinct features of blogs—i.e., that it consisted of a dated entry arranged in reverse chronological order and written in an informal, conversational tone[6]—or whether it mimicked any of the traditional storytelling alternatives (straight news, feature-style, commentary).

Our analysis reveals that what was labeled as blog posts on the five news sites analyzed during the five-year period of our study changed. On the "most newsworthy" list, blogs employing the straight-news format increased from a low of 55 percent in 2008 to a high of 78 percent in 2011 (figure C.7a), whereas on the "most viewed" list that percentage went from a low of 60 in 2009 to high of 76 in 2011 (figure C.7b). This evolution of the blog format is consistent with research showing that mainstream news organizations have normalized or co-opted the blogging movement.[7] This suggests that in recent years blogs on mainstream news sites may have increasingly functioned as a secondary space either for quick dissemination of news that later receives fuller treatment in a traditional straight news story or for publication of brief stories that don't merit deeper treatment. Thus, what could have fostered a renewal in online storytelling seems to

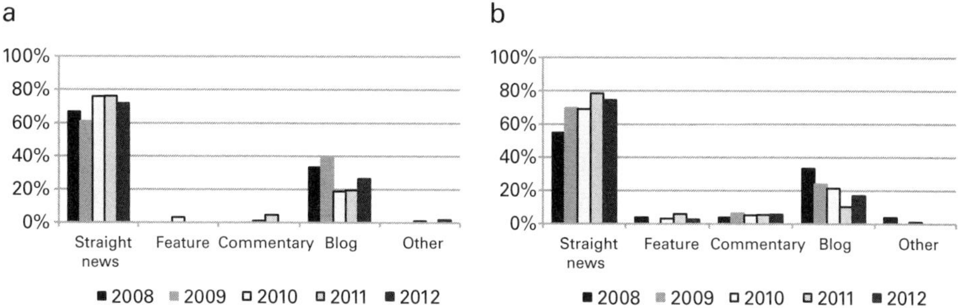


**Figure C.7**
Percentage of straight news, feature-style, commentary, blog, and alternative storytelling styles in the blog items deemed most newsworthy by journalists (a) and the stories most viewed by consumers (b) on the five sites combined, 2008, 2009, 2010, 2011, and 2012.

have recently become a reenactment of traditional journalistic storytelling, albeit with a different label.

This evolution of blogs is illustrated by changes that occurred in the Lifeline blog on USA Today. In 2008 that blog included mainly short, informal items about celebrities (such as Keith Olbermann's opinion of Ben Affleck's impersonation of him) presented in reverse chronological order. (See figure C.8.) The item on Olbermann opened with the well-known saying "Imitation is the sincerest form of flattery" and went on to state that "a 'flattered' Keith Olbermann is giving Ben Affleck high marks for his *Saturday Night Live* impersonation." By 2011, the Lifeline blog was covering entertainment in a more traditional way, featuring, for instance, a short post on the death of Gil Cates, producer of Academy Awards telecasts written in a straight-news format. The blog's author, Ann Oldenburg, was described as "having worn out many stilettos chasing celebs for USA Today." By 2012, the Lifeline blog had disappeared from USA Today, and Ann Oldenburg was now covering show business in a typical way. (One example is an article on morning news shows' "canceling their annual [Halloween] extravaganzas to focus on post-storm coverage" after Hurricane Sandy had hit the East Coast.)

If we add the data from this additional analysis of blogs to our larger examination of storytelling options during the 2008–2012 period, we find that straight news was most prevalent among the stories deemed most newsworthy by journalists, the percentage ranging from 58 in 2012 to 73 in 2011 and averaging 68 (figure C.9a). Feature style retained second position in each year; it increased substantially in 2012, but whether that represents the beginning of a trend remains to be seen. The dominance of straight news recurs among the most viewed items, ranging from 52 percent in 2008 to 69 percent in 2010 and averaging 60 percent (figure C.9b). Feature-style storytelling also came in second with consumers, but did not show the upsurge that was evident in journalists' choices in 2012.

An examination of the evolution of the format choices of journalists and consumers during the final months of the 2012 presidential campaign provides another perspective on whether their respective choices vary in relation to changes in the sociopolitical context. The storytelling preferences of both groups, thought not their thematic preferences, remained quite stable in the final months leading up to the election day and in the first few weeks that followed it. As the campaign progressed, there was no consistent increase or decrease in the odds of stories being presented as

LIFELINE LIVE Your ticket to all that's entertainment

USA TODAY

By Ann Oldenburg with staff contributions

E-mail me

Tuesday, November 4, 2008

Get Lifeline Live

Add Lifeline to your page

Subscribe with RSS

Get IM Alerts

Get Lifeline in your inbox

**Olbermann gives Affleck an 'A+'**

Imitation is the sincerest form of flattery, and a "flattered" Keith Olbermann is giving Ben Affleck high marks for his *Saturday Night Live* impersonation. "As a technical achievement, it was an A+," Olbermann told TV Newser's Gail Shister. "Ben got most of the facial expressions right, and the camera turns were hilarious."

He adds, "From the moment I heard about it as they rehearsed on Friday, I was flattered. I might nitpick the details, but there is a status implied by this. Especially running it before midnight. Especially having the host doing the impression. Also, you can kvetch now and again about criticism, and lord knows I do, but if you are insulted by something like this, it's time to become a Park Ranger."

LIFELINE LIVE

Your ticket to all that's entertainment

Home Archives Related Topics Forum About Search

« ABC announces Regis Philbin's first replacement

'Rock Center' opens to low ratings »

**Oscar producer Gil Cates, 77, found dead**

Comment 1

By Ann Oldenburg, USA TODAY

Updated

Longtime Oscar producer Gil Cates has died at age 77.

According to *The Hollywood Reporter*, Cates' body was found on Monday evening in a parking lot at UCLA, where he was once dean of the school of theater, film and television. Emergency medical personnel responded to a call on campus at about 5:50 p.m., but were unable to revive Cates. The Los Angeles County coroner is investigating the cause of death.

**About Ann Oldenburg**

Ann has worn out many stilettos chasing celebs for USA TODAY. She's covered the Oscars, the Emmys, the Golden Globes, and has interviewed stars ranging from Tom Cruise to Rosie O'Donnell. Ann knows entertainment news is best served as a hot dish to friends and she's hoping you'll dig right in. More about Ann

Advertisement

**Subscribe to Lifeline Live**

Subscribe to Lifeline Live via RSS

Subscribe

Sign up for Lifeline Live e-mail alerts

Subscribe

Delivered by FeedBurner

**Blogroll**

- Huffington Post
- Just Jared
- Marc Malkin
- People
- Pop Sugar
- Pop Watch

USA TODAY NEWS SPORTS LIFE MONEY TECH TRAVEL OPINION WEATHER

**'Today' and 'GMA' cancel Halloween shows**

Ann Oldenburg, USA TODAY 4:29p.m. EDT October 30, 2012

*Morning TV shows will focus on post-Sandy storm coverage.*

(Photo: Peter Kramer, AP)

STORY HIGHLIGHTS

Halloween is always big on the morning TV shows. But Sandy has ruined that fun.

Both *Today* and *Good Morning America* are canceling their annual extravaganzas to focus on post-storm coverage.

*Today*'s Halloween show on the plaza has been nixed "given the sensitivity of the storm," NBC tells us.

View Photos

**Figure C.8**

Lifeline Blog, USA Today, November 4, 2008 and November 1, 2011, and USA Today article on morning television shows canceling Halloween specials, October 30, 2012.

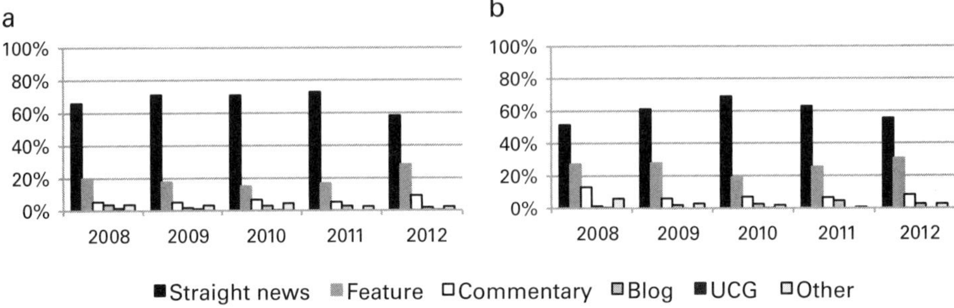


**Figure C.9**
Percentage of straight news, feature-style, commentary, blogs, and user-generated content in the stories deemed most newsworthy by journalists (a) and the stories most viewed by consumers (b) on the five sites combined, 2008, 2009, 2010, 2011, and 2012.

straight news, in feature style, or as commentary, either among journalists or among consumers.[8]

Thus, our account bolsters our arguments that there much less variability for storytelling than for content in the online news choices of journalists and consumers, and that straight news is the dominant option for both of them. It also shows a recent surge in the popularity of features for journalists that is not accompanied by a comparable variation in consumer choice and a certain denaturalization of blogs.

## Considering Content and Storytelling Online News Choices Jointly

When it comes to the content-and-storytelling combination of online news choices, the song remains the same across the five-year period we studied, at least on the five sites we examined: journalists oversupply public-affairs stories told as straight news, and undersupply non-public-affairs stories told in any fashion. That is, our analysis shows that the main gap between journalists and consumers consists of the journalists selecting as the most newsworthy stories of the day a substantially higher percentage of stories on public-affairs topics presented in a straight-news format than consumers select to view. This disparity is evident in all five of the years of our study, ranging from 7 percentage points in 2012 to 23 in 2011 and averaging 15 percentage points across all years, and is highest during non-election years.[9] (See figure C.10.) The gap is mostly offset by two other gaps

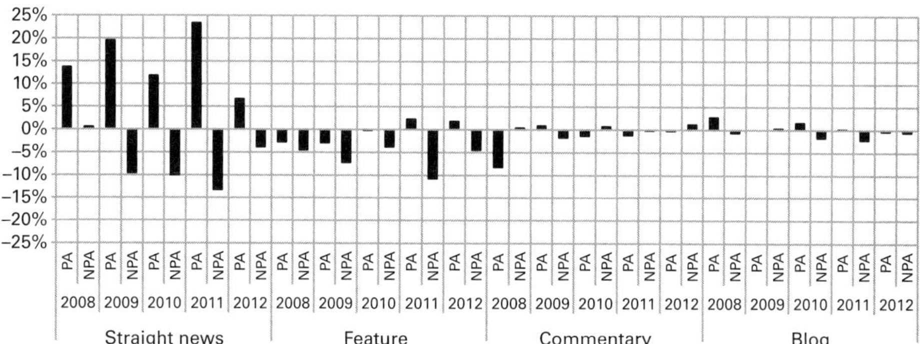


**Figure C.10**
Gaps in format and content choices between journalists and consumers on the five sites combined, 2008, 2009, 2010, 2011, and 2012.

of the reverse sign. First, consumers chose more non-public-affairs stories told in a straight-news format in every year except 2008. This gap ranged from 4 percentage points in 2012 to 13 in 2011, averaging 7 percentage points across the five years. A second gap in the same direction also applies to non-public-affairs stories told in feature style. This trend ranged from 4 percentage points in 2008, 2010, and 2012 to 11 in 2011, averaging 6 percentage points across sites. Taken together, these two gaps in the direction of consumers choosing more stories of a certain kind than journalists offset 13 of the 15 percentage points of the gap in which journalists select more public-affairs articles told in straight-news fashion than consumers select.

## Concluding Remarks

What does our analysis of journalistic and consumer online news choices during the most recent iteration of the typical five-year sequence in American politics mean for the media industry and for democracy? For the leading mainstream players in the industry, the sustained presence of the content gap and its cyclical nature call for rethinking the structure and the processes of news production. The current system neither meets the public where it is at nor takes it to a new destination. Therefore, it has the potential to reduce the business' vitality and its influence over the polity. Whether the current system would better be replaced with the flexible production system we proposed in chapter 6 or with another alternative remains to be seen, but something will probably have to be done if these sites are to remain viable over the long term. The alternatives that emerge, if any do emerge, will have to increase journalists' adaptability. Otherwise, the inertial pull of occupational cultures will continue to hinder the ability to innovate in a changing environment of high choice and high competition.

In contrast to what analysts and consultants have been saying for decades about the softening of the news and the possibility of smuggling public-affairs content through "soft" news formats, our study suggests that innovations in storytelling aren't likely to overcome the gap. Content is king online, and consumers remain steadily interested in non-public-affairs stories told in a straight-news style. The surge in the supply of feature-style news in 2012 wasn't accompanied by a comparable increase in interest in this storytelling option among consumers. Furthermore, the evolution of blogs on the five online news sites we studied from 2008 to 2012 is another worrisome sign of the industry's inability to innovate. The industry appears to have co-opted the new format, probably as a result of decreased resources for content production and increased pressure for immediacy and delivery of a high volume of stories. Finally, the remarkably low level of uptake of user-generated content among both journalists and consumers of these five sites suggests that there are no signs of a major trend toward peer production in the news—not, at least, within the leading mainstream media, which remain the largest providers of news content and the top destination of consumers of online news.

Regarding the role of the news media in the democratic process, our account suggests that the power of the media to set the agenda is cyclical and is tied to the ups and downs of the political environment. Therefore, the public is not highly likely to engage in informed deliberation and participation except during election campaigns and major national crises. Important as they are, elections and crises are relatively short and punctuated episodes. Many consequential events for the polity happen during normal times, however. Thus, the limited power of the media to set the agenda might mean a less-than-optimal level of information among consumers, and lower levels of public deliberation and participation than would be ideal for a vibrant democratic culture.

The continued dominance of straight news suggests that knowledge of public affairs is not likely to be increased by innovations in storytelling. More important, despite the optimistic picture often presented by pundits and advocates of peer production, the near absence of user-generated content from the most clicked stories on the five sites we studied suggests that bottom-up compensatory mechanisms might not be feasible alternatives either. In a context in which other kinds of user-generated content applications have become highly popular among a large segment of online users, the dismal performance of user-generated news content seems to suggest that the gap either alienates the public from media participation or provokes apathy rather than triggering a desire to produce a different kind of news.

With journalists and their organizations facing increased resource constraints and still exhibiting the rigidity that characterized their encounters with new media in the past four decades, and with the public considerably inattentive to public-affairs reportage and apparently unwilling to take the provision of online news into its own hands, a shadow of doubt emerges over the prospects of an informed citizenry for the digital age.

# Appendix

This technical appendix provides detailed information about the analyses presented in this book. The following abbreviations are used in the tables:

| | |
|---|---|
| PA | Public-affairs |
| NPA | Non-public-affairs |
| MCL | Most clicked |
| MEM | Most emailed |
| MCM | Most commented |
| MNW | Most newsworthy |
| UGC | User-generated content |

**Table A.1**

Percentage of public-affairs topics in stories deemed most newsworthy by journalists and the articles most viewed by consumers on Clarín, Nación Universal, Reforma, País, Mundo, Tagesspiegel, Welt, Guardian, Times, and Folha (all stories). (See figure 2.4.)

| Clarín | Journalists $N = 916$ | Consumers $N = 915$ | Nación | Journalists $N = 919$ | Consumers $N = 914$ |
|---|---|---|---|---|---|
| PA | 34.93% | 26.23% | PA | 67.90% | 51.2% |
| NPA | 65.07% | 73.77% | NPA | 32.10% | 48.8% |
| | $\chi^2 = 16.34$, d.f. = 1, $p < .000$ | | | $\chi^2 = 53.04$, d.f. = 1, $p < .000$ | |
| Universal | Journalists $N = 917$ | Consumers $N = 453$ | Reforma | Journalists $N = 916$ | Consumers $N = 368$ |
| PA | 73.17% | 54.97% | PA | 69.54% | 48.64% |
| NPA | 26.83% | 45.03% | NPA | 30.46% | 51.36% |
| | $\chi^2 = 45.57$, d.f. = 1, $p < .000$ | | | $\chi^2 = 49.51$, d.f. = 1, $p < .000$ | |

**Table A.1**
(Continued)

| País | Journalists $N = 908$ | Consumers $N = 908$ | Mundo | Journalists $N = 905$ | Consumers $N = 907$ |
|---|---|---|---|---|---|
| PA | 65.75% | 49.12% | PA | 52.60% | 29.66% |
| NPA | 34.25% | 50.88% | NPA | 47.40% | 70.34% |
| | $\chi^2 = 51.38$, d.f. = 1, $p < .000$ | | | $\chi^2 = 98.45$ d.f. = 1, $p < .000$ | |
| Tagesspiegel | Journalists $N = 906$ | Consumers $N = 908$ | Welt | Journalists $N = 904$ | Consumers $N = 906$ |
| PA | 53.53% | 39.32% | PA | 48.45% | 35.32% |
| NPA | 46.47% | 60.68% | NPA | 51.55% | 64.68% |
| | $\chi^2 = 36.84$, d.f. = 1, $p < .000$ | | | $\chi^2 = 32.06$, d.f. = 1, $p < .000$ | |
| Guardian | Journalists $N = 919$ | Consumers $N = 460$ | Times | Journalists $N = 920$ | Consumers $N = 367$ |
| PA | 66.16% | 34.78% | PA | 68.59% | 45.23% |
| NPA | 33.84% | 65.22% | NPA | 31.41% | 54.77% |
| | $\chi^2 = 133.30$, d.f. = 1, $p < .000$ | | | $\chi^2 = 60.69$, d.f. = 1, $p < .000$ | |
| Fohla | Journalists $N = 918$ | Consumers $N = 429$ | | | |
| PA | 44.12% | 19.17% | | | |
| NPA | 55.88% | 80.83% | | | |
| | $\chi^2 = 82.85$, d.f. = 1, $p < .000$ | | | | |

**Table A.2**
Percentage of public-affairs topics in stories deemed most newsworthy by journalists and the articles most viewed by consumers on CNN, Chicago, Seattle, and Yahoo (all stories). (See figure 2.5.)

| CNN | Journalists $N = 630$ | Consumers $N = 629$ | Chicago | Journalists $N = 630$ | Consumers $N = 630$ |
|---|---|---|---|---|---|
| PA | 45.87% | 32.43% | PA | 38.10% | 20.63% |
| NPA | 54.13% | 67.57% | NPA | 61.90% | 69.27% |
| | $\chi^2 = 23.87$, d.f. = 1, $p < .000$ | | | $\chi^2 = 46.30$, d.f. = 1, $p < .000$ | |
| Seattle | Journalists $N = 630$ | Consumers $N = 630$ | Yahoo | Journalists $N = 630$ | Consumers $N = 630$ |
| PA | 38.25% | 24.60% | PA | 57.14% | 44.13% |
| NPA | 61.75% | 75.40% | NPA | 42.86% | 55.87% |
| | $\chi^2 = 27.24$, d.f. = 1, $p < .000$ | | | $\chi^2 = 21.35$, d.f. = 1, $p < .000$ | |

**Table A.3**

Percentage of public-affairs topics in stories deemed most newsworthy by journalists and the articles most viewed by consumers on CNN, Chicago, Seattle, and Yahoo, excluding stories with overlap. (See figure 2.6.)

| CNN | Journalists $N = 165$ | Consumers $N = 165$ | Chicago | Journalists $N = 291$ | Consumers $N = 290$ |
|---|---|---|---|---|---|
| PA | 63.64% | 13.33% | PA | 56.36% | 18.28% |
| NPA | 36.36% | 86.67% | NPA | 43.64% | 81.72% |
| | $\chi^2 = 88.18$, d.f. = 1, $p < .000$ | | | $\chi^2 = 90.02$, d.f. = 1, $p < .000$ | |
| Seattle | Journalists $N = 381$ | Consumers $N = 381$ | Yahoo | Journalists $N = 424$ | Consumers $N = 424$ |
| PA | 40.68% | 17.85% | PA | 52.36% | 33.02% |
| NPA | 59.32% | 82.15% | NPA | 47.64% | 66.98% |
| | $\chi^2 = 47.98$, d.f. = 1, $p < .000$ | | | $\chi^2 = 32.41$, d.f. = 1, $p < .000$ | |

**Table A.4**

Percentage of public-affairs stories in the convergent news choices of journalists and consumers in United States, Germany, Mexico, Spain, United Kingdom, and Argentina.

| United States | Journalists $N = 539$ | Consumers $N = 485$ | Germany | Journalists $N = 261$ | Consumers $N = 102$ |
|---|---|---|---|---|---|
| PA | 55.84% | 35.46% | PA | 68.20% | 55.88% |
| NPA | 44.16% | 64.54% | NPA | 31.80% | 44.12% |
| | $\chi^2 = 42.66$, d.f. = 1, $p < .000$ | | | $\chi^2 = 4.87$, d.f. = 1, $p = .027$ | |
| Mexico | Journalists $N = 386$ | Consumers $N = 138$ | Spain | Journalists $N = 455$ | Consumers $N = 412$ |
| PA | 74.61% | 60.14% | PA | 70.55% | 44.66% |
| NPA | 25.39% | 39.86% | NPA | 29.45% | 55.34% |
| | $\chi^2 = 10.29$, d.f. = 1, $p = .001$ | | | $\chi^2 = 59.59$, d.f. = 1, $p < .000$ | |
| UK | Journalists $N = 475$ | Consumers $N = 110$ | Argentina | Journalists $N = 905$ | Consumers $N = 907$ |
| PA | 76.42% | 63.64% | PA | 58.91% | 51.20% |
| NPA | 23.58% | 36.36% | NPA | 41.09% | 48.80% |
| | $\chi^2 = 7.59$, d.f. = 1, $p = .006$ | | | $\chi^2 = 4.90$ d.f. = 1, $p = .027$ | |

**Table A.5**

Percentage of public-affairs topics in stories deemed most newsworthy by journalists and the articles most viewed by consumers in conservative and liberal/centrist online news sites. (See figure 2.7.)

| | | | |
|---|---|---|---|
| Conservative | | Journalists $N$ = 5481 | Consumers $N$ = 3921 |
| | PA | 58.58% | 38.00% |
| | NPA | 41.42% | 62.00% |
| | | $\chi^2 = 387.39$, d.f. = 1, $p < .000$ | |
| Liberal/Centrist | | Journalists $N$ = 4567 | Consumers $N$ = 3644 |
| | PA | 58.70% | 39.85% |
| | NPA | 41.30% | 60.15% |
| | | $\chi^2 = 288.31$, d.f. = 1, $p < .000$ | |

**Table A.6**

Percentage of public-affairs topics in stories deemed most newsworthy by journalists and the articles most viewed by consumers in Western Europe, Latin America, and United States. (See figure 2.8.)

| | | | |
|---|---|---|---|
| Western Europe | | Journalists $N$ = 5462 | Consumers $N$ = 4456 |
| | PA | 59.23% | 38.55% |
| | NPA | 40.77% | 61.45% |
| | | $\chi^2 = 419.49$, d.f. = 1, $p < .000$ | |
| Latin America | | Journalists $N$ = 4586 | Consumers $N$ = 3109 |
| | PA | 57.94% | 39.37% |
| | NPA | 42.06% | 60.63% |
| | | $\chi^2 = 255.54$, d.f. = 1, $p < .000$ | |
| United States | | Journalists $N$ = 2520 | Consumers $N$ = 2519 |
| | PA | 44.84% | 30.45% |
| | NPA | 55.16% | 59.55% |
| | | $\chi^2 = 111.17$, d.f. = 1, $p < .000$ | |

**Table A.7**

Percentage of public-affairs topics in stories deemed most newsworthy by journalists and the articles most viewed by consumers on CNN, CBS, Fox, Washington Post, ABC, and USA Today, 2008. (See figure 3.5.)

| | Journalists | Consumers | | Journalists | Consumers |
|---|---|---|---|---|---|
| CNN | $n$ = 140 | $n$ = 138 | CBS | $n$ = 139 | $n$ = 125 |
| PA | 76.09% | 59.29% | PA | 78.42 | 67.20 |
| NPA | 23.91% | 40.71% | NPA | 21.58 | 32.80 |
| | $\chi^2 = 8.97$, d.f. = 1, $p = .003$ | | | $\chi^2 = 4.21$, d.f. = 1, $p = .040$ | |
| Fox | $n$ = 140 | $n$ = 140 | Washington Post | $n$ = 140 | $n$ = 140 |
| PA | 75.00% | 25.00% | PA | 79.29 | 90.71 |
| NPA | 25.00% | 75.00% | NPA | 20.71 | 9.29 |
| | $\chi^2 = 70.00$, d.f. = 1, $p < .000$ | | | $\chi^2 = 7.17$, d.f. = 1, $p = .007$ | |
| ABC | $n$ = 140 | $n$ = 140 | USA Today | $n$ = 140 | $n$ = 140 |
| PA | 64.29% | 66.43% | PA | 75 | 62.86 |
| NPA | 35.71% | 33.57% | NPA | 25 | 37.14 |
| | $\chi^2 = 0.14$, d.f. = 1, $p = .706$ | | | $\chi^2 = 4.82$, d.f. = 1, $p = .028$ | |

**Table A.8**

Percentage of public-affairs topics in stories deemed most newsworthy by journalists and the articles most viewed by consumers on CNN, CBS, Fox, Washington Post, ABC, and USA Today, 2009. (See figure 3.10.)

| | Journalists | Consumers | | Journalists | Consumers |
|---|---|---|---|---|---|
| CNN | $n$ = 140 | $n$ = 140 | CBS | $n$ = 140 | $n$ = 140 |
| PA | 57.14 | 30 | PA | 68.57 | 45.71 |
| NPA | 42.86 | 70 | NPA | 31.43 | 54.29 |
| | $\chi^2 = 20.98$, d.f. = 1, $p < .000$ | | | $\chi^2 = 14.93$, d.f. = 1, $p < .000$ | |
| Fox | $n$ = 140 | $n$ = 140 | Washington Post | $n$ = 140 | $n$ = 140 |
| PA | 65 | 26.43 | PA | 82.14 | 68.57 |
| NPA | 35 | 73.57 | NPA | 17.86 | 31.43 |
| | $\chi^2 = 41.97$, d.f. = 1, $p < .000$ | | | $\chi^2 = 6.94$, d.f. = 1, $p = .008$ | |
| ABC | $n$ = 140 | $n$ = 140 | USA Today | $n$ = 140 | $n$ = 140 |
| PA | 47.86 | 30 | PA | 50 | 30.22 |
| NPA | 52.14 | 70 | NPA | 50 | 69.78 |
| | $\chi^2 = 9.39$, d.f. = 1, $p = .002$ | | | $\chi^2 = 11.36$, d.f. = 1, $p = .001$ | |

**Table A.9**

Fixed-effects logit regression of "content" on "week" and "site" in the journalists' lists across all sites, weeks 1–15 of 2008 study. (Election Day occurred during week 15). Base cases: CNN for "Site," week 1 for "Week." (See figure 3.11.)

| $N$ = 4070 | Coefficient | % change in odds of a story being about a PA topic | $Z$ | $p$ |
|---|---|---|---|---|
| Fox | –0.595 | –44.80 | 5.17 | 0.000 |
| ABC | –0.521 | –40.6 | –4.52 | 0.000 |
| CBS | 0.035 | 3.6 | 0.3 | 0.766 |
| Washington Post | 0.200 | 22.1 | 1.65 | 0.100 |
| USA Today | –0.235 | –20.9 | –2.01 | 0.044 |
| Week 2 | –0.143 | –13.40 | –0.63 | 0.526 |
| Week 3 | 0.120 | 12.7 | 0.53 | 0.597 |
| Week 4 | 0.171 | 18.7 | 0.76 | 0.450 |
| Week 5 | 0.576 | 78.0 | 2.67 | 0.008 |
| Week 6 | 0.716 | 104.6 | 3.2 | 0.001 |
| Week 7 | 0.328 | 38.9 | 1.44 | 0.149 |
| Week 8 | 0.472 | 60.3 | 2.06 | 0.039 |
| Week 9 | 0.453 | 57.4 | 1.98 | 0.047 |
| Week 10 | 0.620 | 86.0 | 2.69 | 0.007 |
| Week 11 | 0.959 | 160.9 | 4.06 | 0.000 |
| Week 12 | 0.540 | 71.5 | 2.35 | 0.019 |
| Week 13 | 0.529 | 69.7 | 2.39 | 0.017 |
| Week 14 | 0.840 | 131.7 | 3.92 | 0.000 |
| Week 15 | 1.251 | 249.3 | 5.68 | 0.000 |

**Table A.10**

Percentage of public-affairs stories in the journalists' lists across all sites, weeks 1–15 of 2008 study. (Election Day occurred during week 15.) (See figure 3.11.)

| Week | CNN | Fox | ABC | CBS | Washington Post | USA Today |
|---|---|---|---|---|---|---|
| 1 | 45% | 60% | 45% | 50% | 60% | 50% |
| 2 | 53% | 35% | 38% | 53% | 67% | 45% |
| 3 | 60% | 53% | 48% | 60% | 60% | 48% |
| 4 | 55% | 48% | 48% | 55% | 75% | 55% |
| 5 | 70% | 48% | 60% | 67% | 73% | 73% |
| 6 | 76% | 57% | 57% | 72% | 70% | 78% |
| 7 | 48% | 55% | 63% | 53% | 75% | 65% |
| 8 | 75% | 43% | 55% | 73% | 70% | 63% |
| 9 | 70% | 45% | 63% | 80% | 73% | 45% |
| 10 | 83% | 53% | 63% | 78% | 70% | 53% |

**Table A.10**
(Continued)

| Week | CNN | Fox | ABC | CBS | Washington Post | USA Today |
|---|---|---|---|---|---|---|
| 11 | 80% | 55% | 68% | 79% | 80% | 78% |
| 12 | 73% | 48% | 55% | 69% | 80% | 63% |
| 13 | 70% | 58% | 52% | 76% | 68% | 61% |
| 14 | 71% | 73% | 53% | 77% | 79% | 73% |
| 15 | 81% | 77% | 76% | 80% | 80% | 77% |
| 16 | 88% | 73% | 53% | 73% | 80% | 70% |
| 17 | 70% | 60% | 58% | 73% | 73% | 63% |
| 18 | 87% | 83% | 70% | 50% | 57% | 60% |

**Table A.11**
Fixed-effects logit regression of "content" on "week" and "site" in the consumers' lists across all sites, weeks 1–15 of 2008 study. (Election Day occurred during week 15.) Base cases: CNN for "Site," week 1 for "Week." (See figure 3.12.)

| $N$ = 3892 | Coefficient | % change in odds of a story being about a PA topic | $Z$ | $p$ |
|---|---|---|---|---|
| Fox | –1.255 | –71.50 | –10.1 | 0.000 |
| ABC | 0.264 | 30.2 | 2.37 | 0.018 |
| CBS | 0.767 | 115.3 | 6.19 | 0.000 |
| Washington Post | 1.737 | 468 | 13.34 | 0.000 |
| USA Today | 0.107 | 11.3 | 0.96 | 0.335 |
| Week 2 | 0.147 | 15.90 | 0.55 | 0.582 |
| Week 3 | 0.242 | 27.4 | 0.91 | 0.364 |
| Week 4 | 0.762 | 114.3 | 2.88 | 0.004 |
| Week 5 | 0.682 | 97.8 | 2.72 | 0.007 |
| Week 6 | 1.060 | 188.4 | 4.13 | 0.000 |
| Week 7 | 0.772 | 116.3 | 2.93 | 0.003 |
| Week 8 | 1.082 | 195.1 | 4.11 | 0.000 |
| Week 9 | 1.401 | 305.8 | 5.23 | 0.000 |
| Week 10 | 1.029 | 179.6 | 3.9 | 0.000 |
| Week 11 | 1.511 | 352.8 | 5.66 | 0.000 |
| Week 12 | 1.225 | 240.4 | 4.61 | 0.000 |
| Week 13 | 0.736 | 108.7 | 2.88 | 0.004 |
| Week 14 | 1.137 | 211.7 | 4.62 | 0.000 |
| Week 15 | 1.593 | 391.8 | 6.41 | 0.000 |

**Table A.12**

Percentage of public-affairs stories in the consumers' lists across all sites, weeks 1–15 of 2008 study. (Election Day occurred during week 15.) (See figure 3.12.)

| Week | CNN | Fox | ABC | CBS | Washington Post | USA Today |
|---|---|---|---|---|---|---|
| 1 | 30% | 10% | 32% | 40% | 75% | 15% |
| 2 | 30% | 13% | 32% | 50% | 68% | 30% |
| 3 | 35% | 20% | 33% | 52% | 65% | 28% |
| 4 | 43% | 23% | 43% | 67% | 80% | 45% |
| 5 | 40% | 17% | 48% | 66% | 75% | 43% |
| 6 | 44% | 20% | 58% | 86% | 84% | 48% |
| 7 | 45% | 18% | 60% | 52% | 80% | 43% |
| 8 | 58% | 20% | 70% | 56% | 80% | 53% |
| 9 | 60% | 23% | 58% | 91% | 95% | 58% |
| 10 | 43% | 25% | 48% | 75% | 85% | 58% |
| 11 | 56% | 45% | 65% | 82% | 85% | 58% |
| 12 | 48% | 33% | 63% | 69% | 90% | 55% |
| 13 | 44% | 2% | 42% | 60% | 86% | 60% |
| 14 | 47% | 27% | 56% | 64% | 93% | 57% |
| 15 | 71% | 23% | 77% | 70% | 89% | 69% |
| 16 | 58% | 15% | 55% | 61% | 93% | 43% |
| 17 | 70% | 18% | 55% | 58% | 78% | 43% |
| 18 | 70% | 30% | 57% | 36% | 70% | 27% |

**Table A.13**

Percentage of public-affairs stories in journalists' and consumers' choices on Clarín and Nación, by week. (See figure 3.13.)

| Week | Nación journalists | Nación consumers | Clarín journalists | Clarín consumers |
|---|---|---|---|---|
| 1 | 60% | 70% | 40% | 30% |
| 2 | 65% | 55% | 39% | 20% |
| 3 | 70% | 43% | 39% | 17% |
| 4 | 75% | 59% | 43% | 16% |
| 5 | 65% | 60% | 35% | 23% |
| 6 | 78% | 65% | 43% | 31% |
| 7 | 80% | 63% | 43% | 38% |
| 8 | 66% | 54% | 37% | 26% |
| 9 | 65% | 55% | 25% | 25% |
| 10 | 63% | 45% | 35% | 15% |
| 11 | 66% | 36% | 44% | 24% |
| 12 | 63% | 28% | 40% | 20% |

**Table A.13**
(Continued)

| Week | Nación journalists | Nación consumers | Clarín journalists | Clarín consumers |
|---|---|---|---|---|
| 13 | 65% | 38% | 35% | 35% |
| 14 | 65% | 25% | 30% | 25% |
| 15 | 72% | 29% | 26% | 24% |
| 16 | 74% | 63% | 30% | 41% |
| 17 | 63% | 43% | 20% | 13% |
| 18 | 72% | 52% | 30% | 28% |
| 19 | 72% | 78% | 44% | 49% |
| 20 | 68% | 58% | 25% | 30% |
| 21 | 62% | 56% | 34% | 26% |
| 22 | 58% | 50% | 28% | 20% |
| 23 | 75% | 60% | 40% | 45% |
| 24 | 55% | 63% | 20% | 10% |

**Table A.14**
News choices on journalists' and consumers' lists during periods of routine and heightened political activity on Clarín and Nación. (See figure 3.14.)

| | Routine political activity | Heightened political activity |
|---|---|---|
| Journalists | | |
| Clarín | $n = 666$ | $n = 250$ |
| PA | 35.59% | 33.20% |
| NPA | 64.41% | 66.80% |
| | $\chi^2 = 0.46$, d.f. = 1, $p = .500$ | |
| Nación | $n = 669$ | $n = 250$ |
| PA | 68.16% | 67.20% |
| NPA | 31.84% | 32.80% |
| | $\chi^2 = 0.08$, d.f. = 1, $p = .781$ | |
| Consumers | | |
| Clarín | $n = 666$ | $n = 249$ |
| PA | 24.02% | 32.13% |
| NPA | 75.98% | 67.87% |
| | $\chi^2 = 6.15$, d.f. = 1, $p = .013$ | |
| Nación | $n = 664$ | $n = 250$ |
| PA | 48.19% | 59.20% |
| NPA | 51.81% | 40.80% |
| | $\chi^2 = 8.81$, d.f. = 1, $p = .003$ | |

**Table A.15**

Average frequencies of different story-telling formats on all sites. (See table 4.1.)

| | Journalists | | Consumers | |
|---|---|---|---|---|
| | Average | S.D. | Average | S.D. |
| Straight news | 71.58% | 45.10% | 60.57% | 48.87% |
| | t-test = 19.9736, $p < .000$ | | | |
| Features | 14.45% | 35.17% | 23.93% | 42.67% |
| | *t*-test = –20.7747, $p < .000$ | | | |
| Commentary | 7.07% | 25.64% | 9.63% | 29.51% |
| | *t*-test = –7.9262, $p < .000$ | | | |
| Blogs | 3.61% | 18.66% | 2.50% | 15.59% |
| | *t*-test = 5.2560, $p < .000$ | | | |
| UGC | 1.42% | 11.81% | 0.26% | 5.34% |
| | *t*-test = 5.8882, $p < .000$ | | | |
| Other | 2.51% | 15.66% | 3.64% | 18.72% |
| | *t*-test = –3.1309, $p = .0017$ | | | |

Totals do not add up to 100% because the "blogs" category was coded only in the Western Europe, Latin America, and United States 2008 and 2009 samples, and the "UGC" category was coded only in the U.S. 2008 and 2009 samples.

**Table A.16**

Percentage of straight news, feature-style, commentary, and alternative formats in stories deemed most newsworthy by journalists on CNN, Seattle, Chicago, and Yahoo, 2007, and CNN, Fox, ABC, CBS, Washington Post, and USA Today, 2008 and 2009. (See figure 4.1.)

| | | Straight news | Feature | Commentary | Blog | UGC | Other |
|---|---|---|---|---|---|---|---|
| 2007 | CNN | 82.54% | 13.65% | 3.49% | | | 0.32% |
| | Chicago | 77.42% | 17.97% | 4.29% | | | 0.32% |
| | Seattle | 64.29% | 26.19% | 7.46% | | | 2.06% |
| | Yahoo | 74.76% | 22.70% | 1.43% | | | 1.11% |
| 2008 | CNN | 60.86% | 12.20% | 9.28% | 10.42% | 4.45% | 2.80% |
| | Fox | 93.54% | 4.69% | 0.25% | 0.51% | 0.25% | 0.76% |
| | ABC | 55.64% | 29.02% | 1.39% | 12.17% | 0.13% | 1.65% |
| | CBS | 79.80% | 12.33% | 2.03% | 3.30% | 0.00% | 2.54% |
| | Washington Post | 43.47% | 18.38% | 16.10% | 12.67% | 3.30% | 6.08% |
| | USA Today | 77.95% | 9.89% | 1.65% | 8.87% | 0.38% | 1.27% |

**Table A.16**
(Continued)

| | | Straight news | Feature | Commentary | Blog | UGC | Other |
|---|---|---|---|---|---|---|---|
| 2009 | CNN | 69.29% | 20.00% | 3.57% | 6.43% | 0% | 0.71% |
| | Fox | 90.00% | 7.14% | 0% | 2.14% | 0% | 0.71% |
| | ABC | 58.57% | 30.71% | 0.71% | 9.29% | 0.00% | 0.71% |
| | CBS | 87.86% | 10.71% | 0.00% | 0.71% | 0.00% | 0.71% |
| | Washington Post | 47.86% | 12.14% | 17.86% | 10.00% | 5.00% | 7.14% |
| | USA Today | 59.29% | 15.00% | 0.71% | 18.57% | 0.00% | 6.43% |

**Table A.17**
Percentage of straight news, feature-style, commentary, and alternative formats in stories deemed most newsworthy by journalists on Clarín, Nación, Folha, Welt, Tagesspiegel, Universal, Reforma, Mundo, País, Guardian, and Times. (See figure 4.2.)

| | Straight news | Feature | Commentary | Blog | Other |
|---|---|---|---|---|---|
| Tagesspiegel | 72.74% | 9.16% | 10.60% | 1.43% | 6.07% |
| Welt | 41.92% | 22.79% | 25.88% | 0.00% | 9.40% |
| Guardian | 80.09% | 9.36% | 1.20% | 3.70% | 5.66% |
| Times | 73.04% | 14.24% | 10.54% | 0.87% | 1.30% |
| País | 62.89% | 29.52% | 4.07% | 0.55% | 2.97% |
| Mundo | 57.79% | 27.85% | 1.88% | 2.87% | 9.61% |
| Folha | 77.78% | 17.65% | 3.70% | 0.00% | 0.87% |
| Clarín | 92.47% | 6.66% | 0.11% | 0.00% | 0.76% |
| Nación | 80.09% | 7.83% | 9.90% | 1.52% | 0.65% |
| Universal | 77.43% | 5.02% | 11.23% | 5.02% | 1.31% |
| Reforma | 82.31% | 4.04% | 11.24% | 1.09% | 1.31% |

**Table A.18**

Percentage of straight news, feature-style, commentary, and alternative formats in stories most viewed by consumers on CNN, Seattle, Chicago and Yahoo, 2007, and CNN, Fox, ABC, CBS, Washington Post, and USA Today, 2008 and 2009. (See figure 4.3.)

| | | Straight news | Feature | Commentary | Blog | UGC | Other |
|---|---|---|---|---|---|---|---|
| 2007 | CNN | 79.81% | 17.17% | 2.38% | | | 0.64% |
| | Chicago | 63.81% | 20.00% | 15.40% | | | 0.79% |
| | Seattle | 57.94% | 29.05% | 11.43% | | | 1.59% |
| | Yahoo | 77.94% | 18.41% | 1.90% | | | 1.75% |
| 2008 | CNN | 64.77% | 23.83% | 9.25% | 0% | 1.14% | 1.01% |
| | Fox | 89.97% | 7.97% | 1.03% | 0.39% | 0.00% | 0.64% |
| | ABC | 55.09% | 40.84% | 2.04% | 0.13% | 0.00% | 1.91% |
| | CBS | 63.25% | 26.66% | 5.63% | 0.99% | 0.00% | 3.48% |
| | Washington Post | 37.85% | 18.10% | 39.87% | 1.01% | 0.38% | 2.78% |
| | USA Today | 51.52% | 13.92% | 2.15% | 20.38% | 0.13% | 11.90% |
| 2009 | CNN | 62.86% | 30.00% | 5.00% | 0% | 0% | 2.14% |
| | Fox | 72.14% | 7.86% | 5.71% | 0% | 0% | 14.29% |
| | ABC | 60.00% | 40.00% | 0.00% | 0.00% | 0.00% | 0.00% |
| | CBS | 64.29% | 31.43% | 1.43% | 0.00% | 0.00% | 2.86% |
| | Washington Post | 49.29% | 22.86% | 21.43% | 0.00% | 0.00% | 6.43% |
| | USA Today | 53.96% | 14.39% | 2.16% | 25.90% | 0.00% | 3.60% |

**Table A.19**

Percentage of straight news, feature-style, commentary, and alternative formats in stories most viewed by consumers on Clarín, Nación, Folha, Welt, Tagesspiegel, Universal, Reforma, Mundo, País, Guardian, and Times. (See figure 4.4.)

| | Straight news | Feature | Commentary | Blog | Other |
|---|---|---|---|---|---|
| Tagesspiegel | 59.80% | 18.83% | 14.98% | 0.00% | 6.39% |
| Welt | 40.84% | 27.04% | 25.28% | 0.00% | 6.84% |
| Guardian | 50.43% | 27.61% | 10.22% | 6.74% | 5.00% |
| Times | 66.21% | 23.71% | 9.54% | 0.00% | 0.54% |
| País | 47.47% | 40.09% | 8.70% | 0.44% | 3.30% |
| Mundo | 50.94% | 37.38% | 4.63% | 5.07% | 1.98% |
| Folha | 63.92% | 17.86% | 18.30% | 0.00% | 0.22% |
| Clarín | 86.89% | 10.93% | 0.22% | 0.11% | 1.86% |
| Nación | 42.01% | 37.20% | 9.52% | 4.49% | 6.78% |
| Universal | 87.86% | 10.15% | 0.00% | 0.00% | 1.99% |
| Reforma | 91.30% | 8.15% | 0.00% | 0.00% | 0.54% |

**Table A.20**

Content and format of most newsworthy stories, Western Europe and Latin America. (See figure 4.5.)

| | Western Europe | | Latin America | |
|---|---|---|---|---|
| | PA<br>$N$ = 3235 | NPA<br>$N$ = 2227 | PA<br>$N$ = 2657 | NPA<br>$N$ = 1929 |
| Straight news | 74.40% | 50.88% | 83.48% | 79.99% |
| Features | 14.56% | 24.92% | 4.22% | 13.79% |
| Commentary | 7.20% | 11.63% | 10.58% | 2.64% |
| Blog | 1.05% | 2.33% | 1.58% | 1.45% |
| UGC | | | | |
| Other | 2.78% | 10.24% | 0.15% | 2.13% |
| | $\chi^2 = 356.52$, d.f. = 4, $p < .000$ | | $\chi^2 = 267.62$, d.f. = 4, $p < .000$ | |

**Table A.21**

Content and format of most newsworthy stories, United States, 2007, 2008, and 2009. (See figure 4.5.)

| | US 2007 | | US 2008 | | US 2009 | |
|---|---|---|---|---|---|---|
| | PA<br>$N$ = 1130 | NPA<br>$N$ = 1389 | PA<br>$N$ = 625 | NPA<br>$N$ = 612 | PA<br>$N$ = 520 | NPA<br>$N$ = 320 |
| Straight news | 79.91% | 70.55% | 63.84% | 71.23% | 68.65% | 69.06% |
| Features | 16.46% | 23.11% | 15.84% | 20.75% | 12.50% | 21.56% |
| Commentary | 3.01% | 5.11% | 4.96% | 1.42% | 5.19% | 1.56% |
| Blog | | | 10.72% | 4.72% | 10.77% | 3.13% |
| UGC | | | 1.60% | 0.47% | 0.58% | 1.25% |
| Other | 0.62% | 1.22% | 3.04% | 1.42% | 2.31% | 3.44% |
| | $\chi^2 = 29.90$, d.f. = 3, $p < .000$ | | $\chi^2 = 17.77$, d.f. = 5, $p = .003$ | | $\chi^2 = 33.79$, d.f. = 5, $p < .000$ | |

**Table A.22**

Content and format of most viewed stories, Western Europe and Latin America. (See figure 4.6.)

| | Western Europe | | Latin America | |
|---|---|---|---|---|
| | PA<br>$N$ = 2738 | NPA<br>$N$ = 1718 | PA<br>$N$ = 1224 | NPA<br>$N$ = 1885 |
| Straight news | 60.13% | 45.58% | 77.70% | 66.53% |
| Features | 25.20% | 32.87% | 14.62% | 22.23% |
| Commentary | 10.54% | 14.13% | 6.94% | 4.67% |
| Blog | 0.93% | 2.37% | 0.00% | 2.23% |
| UGC | | | | |
| Other | 3.20% | 5.04% | 0.74% | 4.35% |
| | $\chi^2 = 95.44$, d.f. = 4, $p < .000$ | | $\chi^2 = 102.68$, d.f. = 4, $p < .000$ | |

**Table A.23**

Content and format of most viewed stories, United States, 2007, 2008 and 2009. (See figure 4.6.)

| | US 2007 | | US 2008 | | US 2009 | |
|---|---|---|---|---|---|---|
| | PA<br>$N$ = 767 | NPA<br>$N$ = 1752 | PA<br>$N$ = 510 | NPA<br>$N$ = 315 | PA<br>$N$ = 323 | NPA<br>$N$ = 516 |
| Straight news | 78.88% | 65.92% | 50.98% | 63.49% | 60.06% | 60.66% |
| Features | 16.43% | 23.23% | 22.75% | 26.35% | 25.39% | 23.84% |
| Commentary | 3.78% | 9.53% | 17.45% | 0.63% | 8.98% | 4.07% |
| Blog | | | 2.55% | 5.40% | 3.10% | 5.04% |
| UGC | | | 0.39% | 0.32% | 0.00% | 0.00% |
| Other | 0.91% | 1.31% | 5.88% | 3.81% | 2.48% | 6.40% |
| | $\chi^2 = 47.87$, d.f. = 3, $p < .000$ | | $\chi^2 = 64.45$, d.f. = 5, $p < .000$ | | $\chi^2 = 16.23$, d.f. = 5, $p = .003$ | |

**Table A.24**

Gap in format choices between most newsworthy and most clicked articles, United States, 2007, 2008, and 2009.

| | US 2007 | | | US 2008 | | | US 2009 | | |
|---|---|---|---|---|---|---|---|---|---|
| | MNW | MCL | Gap | MNW | MCL | Gap | MNW | MCL | Gap |
| Straight news | 74.75% | 69.87% | 4.88% | 65.71% | 55.76% | 9.95% | 68.81% | 60.43% | 8.38% |
| | $\chi^2 = 95.44$, d.f. = 1, $p < .000$[a] | | | $\chi^2 = 17.27$, d.f. = 1, $p < .000$[a] | | | $\chi^2 = 12.89$, d.f. = 1, $p < .000$[a] | | |
| Features | 20.13% | 21.16% | –1.03% | 17.08% | 24.12% | –7.04% | 15.95% | 24.43% | –8.48% |
| | $\chi^2 = 0.81$, d.f. = 1, $p = .365$[b] | | | $\chi^2 = 12.59$, d.f. = 1, $p < .000$[b] | | | $\chi^2 = 18.74$, d.f. = 1, $p < .000$[b] | | |
| Commentary | 4.17% | 7.78% | –3.61% | 4.06% | 11.13% | –6.97% | 3.81% | 5.96% | –2.15% |
| | $\chi^2 = 29.26$, d.f. = 1, $p < .000$[c] | | | $\chi^2 = 29.00$, d.f. = 1, $p < .000$[c] | | | $\chi^2 = 4.18$, d.f. = 1, $p < .041$[c] | | |

a. To apply the $\chi^2$ test, categories were collapsed to straight news and all other formats.
b. To apply the $\chi^2$ test, categories were collapsed to feature-style news and all other formats.
c. To apply the $\chi^2$ test, categories were collapsed to commentary news and all other formats.

**Table A.25**
Gap in format choices between journalists and consumers, Western Europe and Latin America.

| | Western Europe | | | Latin America | | |
|---|---|---|---|---|---|---|
| | MNW | MCL | Gap | MNW | MCL | Gap |
| Straight news | 64.81% | 51.19% | 13.62% | 82.01% | 70.92% | 11.09% |
| | $\chi^2 = 187.82$, d.f. = 1, $p < .000$[a] | | | $\chi^2 = 130.75$, d.f. = 1, $p < .000$[a] | | |
| Features | 18.78% | 29.71% | −11.13% | 8.24% | 19.23% | −10.99% |
| | $\chi^2 = 167.71$, d.f. = 1, $p < .000$[b] | | | $\chi^2 = 202.14$, d.f. = 1, $p < .000$[b] | | |
| Commentary | 9.01% | 12.75% | −3.74% | 7.24% | 5.56% | 1.68% |
| | $\chi^2 = 35.94$, d.f. = 1, $p < .000$[c] | | | $\chi^2 = 8.48$, d.f. = 1, $p = .004$[c] | | |

a. To apply the $\chi^2$ test, categories were collapsed to straight news and all other formats.

b. To apply the $\chi^2$ test, categories were collapsed to feature-style news and all other formats.

c. To apply the $\chi^2$ test, categories were collapsed to commentary news and all other formats.

**Table A.26**
Gap in format and content choices between journalists and consumers, United States, 2007. (See figure 4.7.)

| | MNW | MCL | Gap |
|---|---|---|---|
| Straight news—PA | 35.83% | 24.01% | 11.83% |
| | $\chi^2 = 84.03$, d.f. = 1, $p < .000$[a] | | |
| Straight news—NPA | 38.93% | 45.83% | –6.90% |
| | $\chi^2 = 24.60$, d.f. = 1, $p < .000$[b] | | |
| Features—PA | 7.38% | 5.00% | 2.38% |
| | $\chi^2 = 12.27$, d.f. = 1, $p < .000$[c] | | |
| Features—NPA | 12.74% | 16.15% | –3.41% |
| | $\chi^2 = 11.87$, d.f. = 1, $p = .001$[d] | | |
| Commentary—PA | 1.35% | 1.15% | 0.20% |
| | $\chi^2 = 0.40$, d.f. = 1, $p = .526$[e] | | |
| Commentary—NPA | 2.82% | 6.63% | –3.81% |
| | $\chi^2 = 40.64$, d.f. = 1, $p < .000$[f] | | |

a. To apply the $\chi^2$ test, categories were collapsed to straight news/public affairs and all other format/content combinations.
b. To apply the $\chi^2$ test, categories were collapsed to straight news/non-public-affairs and all other format/content combinations.
c. To apply the $\chi^2$ test, categories were collapsed to features/public affairs and all other format/content combinations.
d. To apply the $\chi^2$ test, categories were collapsed to features/non-public-affairs and all other format/content combinations.
e. To apply the $\chi^2$ test, categories were collapsed to commentary/public affairs and all other format/content combinations.
f. To apply the $\chi^2$ test, categories were collapsed to commentary/non-public-affairs and all other format/content combinations.

**Table A.27**

Gap in format and content choices between journalists and consumers, United States, 2008. (See figure 4.7.)

| | MNW | MCL | Gap |
|---|---|---|---|
| Straight news—PA | 47.67% | 31.52% | 16.15% |
| | $\chi^2 = 45.32$, d.f. = 1, $p < .000$[a] | | |
| Straight news—NPA | 18.04% | 24.24% | –6.20% |
| | $\chi^2 = 9.59$, d.f. = 1, $p = .002$[b] | | |
| Features—PA | 11.83% | 14.06% | –2.23% |
| | $\chi^2 = 1.84$, d.f. = 1, $p = .175$[c] | | |
| Features—NPA | 5.26% | 10.06% | –4.80% |
| | $\chi^2 = 13.58$, d.f. = 1, $p < .000$[d] | | |
| Commentary—PA | 3.70% | 10.79% | –7.09% |
| | $\chi^2 = 31.13$, d.f. = 1, $p < .000$[e] | | |
| Commentary—NPA | 0.36% | 0.24% | 0.12% |
| | $\chi^2 = 0.19$, d.f. = 1, $p = .666$[f] | | |

a. To apply the $\chi^2$ test, categories were collapsed to straight news/public affairs and all other format/content combinations.
b. To apply the $\chi^2$ test, categories were collapsed to straight news/non-public-affairs and all other format/content combinations.
c. To apply the $\chi^2$ test, categories were collapsed to features/public affairs and all other format/content combinations.
d. To apply the $\chi^2$ test, categories were collapsed to features/non-public-affairs and all other format/content combinations.
e. To apply the $\chi^2$ test, categories were collapsed to commentary/public affairs and all other format/content combinations.
f. To apply the $\chi^2$ test, categories were collapsed to commentary/non-public-affairs and all other format/content combinations.

**Table A.28**

Gap in format and content choices between journalists and consumers, United States, 2009. (See figure 4.7.)

| | MNW | MCL | Gap |
|---|---|---|---|
| Straight news—PA | 42.50% | 23.12% | 19.38% |
| | $\chi^2 = 71.49$, d.f. = 1, $p < .000$[a] | | |
| Straight news—NPA | 26.31% | 37.31% | –11.00% |
| | $\chi^2 = 23.40$, d.f. = 1, $p < .000$[b] | | |
| Features—PA | 7.74% | 9.77% | –2.03% |
| | $\chi^2 = 2.18$, d.f. = 1, $p = .140$[c] | | |
| Features—NPA | 8.21% | 14.66% | –6.45% |
| | $\chi^2 = 17.22$, d.f. = 1, $p < .000$[d] | | |
| Commentary—PA | 3.21% | 3.46% | –0.25% |
| | $\chi^2 = 0.08$, d.f. = 1, $p = .782$[e] | | |
| Commentary- NPA | 0.60% | 2.50% | –1.90% |
| | $\chi^2 = 10.02$, d.f. = 1, $p = .002$[f] | | |

a. To apply the $\chi^2$ test, categories were collapsed to straight news/public affairs and all other format/content combinations.
b. To apply the $\chi^2$ test, categories were collapsed to straight news/non-public-affairs and all other format/content combinations.
c. To apply the $\chi^2$ test, categories were collapsed to features/public affairs and all other format/content combinations.
d. To apply the $\chi^2$ test, categories were collapsed to features/non-public-affairs and all other format/content combinations.
e. To apply the $\chi^2$ test, categories were collapsed to commentary/public affairs and all other format/content combinations.
f. To apply the $\chi^2$ test, categories were collapsed to commentary/non-public-affairs and all other format/content combinations.

**Table A.29**

Gap in format and content choices between journalists and consumers, Western Europe. (See figure 4.7.)

| | MNW | MCL | Gap |
|---|---|---|---|
| Straight news—PA | 44.07% | 23.18% | 20.89% |
| | $\chi^2 = 472.53$, d.f. = 1, $p < .000$[a] | | |
| Straight news—NPA | 20.74% | 28.01% | –7.27% |
| | $\chi^2 = 70.97$, d.f. = 1, $p < .000$[b] | | |
| Features—PA | 8.62% | 9.72% | –1.10% |
| | $\chi^2 = 3.55$, d.f. = 1, $p = .060$[c] | | |
| Features—NPA | 10.16% | 20.20% | –10.04% |
| | $\chi^2 = 197.46$, d.f. = 1, $p < .000$[d] | | |
| Commentary—PA | 4.27% | 4.06% | 0.21% |
| | $\chi^2 = 0.26$, d.f. = 1, $p = .614$[e] | | |
| Commentary—NPA | 4.74% | 8.68% | –3.94% |
| | $\chi^2 = 62.66$, d.f. = 1, $p < .000$[f] | | |

a. To apply the $\chi^2$ test, categories were collapsed to straight news/public affairs and all other format/content combinations.

b. To apply the $\chi^2$ test, categories were collapsed to straight news/non-public-affairs and all other format/content combinations.

c. To apply the $\chi^2$ test, categories were collapsed to features/public affairs and all other format/content combinations.

d. To apply the $\chi^2$ test, categories were collapsed to features/non-public-affairs and all other format/content combinations.

e. To apply the $\chi^2$ test, categories were collapsed to commentary/public affairs and all other format/content combinations.

f. To apply the $\chi^2$ test, categories were collapsed to commentary/non-public-affairs and all other format/content combinations.

**Table A.30**
Gap in format and content choices between journalists and consumers, Latin America. (See figure 4.7.)

| | MNW | MCL | Gap |
|---|---|---|---|
| Straight news—PA | 48.36% | 30.59% | 17.77% |
| | $\chi^2 = 241.71$, d.f. = 1, $p < .000$[a] | | |
| Straight news—NPA | 33.65% | 40.33% | –6.68% |
| | $\chi^2 = 25.83$, d.f. = 1, $p < .000$[b] | | |
| Features—PA | 2.44% | 5.76% | –3.32% |
| | $\chi^2 = 55.97$, d.f. = 1, $p < .000$[c] | | |
| Features—NPA | 5.80% | 13.48% | –7.68% |
| | $\chi^2 = 134.65$, d.f. = 1, $p < .000$[d] | | |
| Commentary—PA | 6.13% | 2.73% | 3.40% |
| | $\chi^2 = 47.10$, d.f. = 1, $p < .000$[e] | | |
| Commentary—NPA | 1.11% | 2.83% | –1.72% |
| | $\chi^2 = 30.85$, d.f. = 1, $p < .000$[f] | | |

a. To apply the $\chi^2$ test, categories were collapsed to straight news/public affairs and all other format/content combinations.
b. To apply the $\chi^2$ test, categories were collapsed to straight news/non-public-affairs and all other format/content combinations.
c. To apply the $\chi^2$ test, categories were collapsed to features/public affairs and all other format/content combinations.
d. To apply the $\chi^2$ test, categories were collapsed to features/non-public-affairs and all other format/content combinations.
e. To apply the $\chi^2$ test, categories were collapsed to commentary/public-affairs and all other format/content combinations.
f. To apply the $\chi^2$ test, categories were collapsed to commentary/non-public-affairs and all other format/content combinations.

**Table A.31**

Percentage of straight news, feature-style, commentary, blogs, user-generated content, and alternative formats in stories deemed most newsworthy by journalists and the articles most viewed by consumers in U.S. sample, 2008 and 2009. (See figure 4.8.)

| | MNW | | MCL | | | MNW | | MCL | |
|---|---|---|---|---|---|---|---|---|---|
| | 2008 | 2009 | 2008 | 2009 | | 2008 | 2009 | 2008 | 2009 |
| Straight news | 65.71% | 68.57% | 55.76% | 60.43% | Blog | 9.20% | 7.86% | 3.64% | 4.29% |
| | $\chi^2$ = 1.83, d.f. = 1, $p$ = .176[a] | | $\chi^2$ = 3.73, d.f. = 1, $p$ = .053[a] | | | $\chi^2$ = 0.97, d.f. = 1, $p$ = .325[d] | | $\chi^2$ = 0.47, d.f. = 1, $p$ = .494[d] | |
| Feature | 17.08% | 15.95% | 24.12% | 24.43% | UCG | 1.31% | 0.83% | 0.36% | 0.00% |
| | $\chi^2$ = 0.39, d.f. = 1, $p$ = .532[b] | | $\chi^2$ = 0.02, d.f. = 1, $p$ = .882[b] | | | $\chi^2$ = 0.91, d.f. = 1, $p$ = .339[e] | | $\chi^2$ = 3.06, d.f. = 1, $p$ = .080[e] | |
| Commentary | 4.06% | 3.81% | 11.03% | 5.96% | Other | 2.63% | 2.74% | 5.09% | 4.89% |
| | $\chi^2$ = 0.07, d.f. = 1, $p$ = .790[c] | | $\chi^2$ = 13.79, d.f. = 1, $p$ < .000[c] | | | $\chi^2$ = 0.02, d.f. = 1, $p$ = .889[f] | | $\chi^2$ = 0.04, d.f. = 1, $p$ = .848[f] | |

a. To apply the $\chi^2$ test, categories were collapsed to straight news and all other formats.

b. To apply the $\chi^2$ test, categories were collapsed to feature-style news and all other formats.

c. To apply the $\chi^2$ test, categories were collapsed to commentary news and all other formats.

d. To apply the $\chi^2$ test, categories were collapsed to blogs and all other formats.

e. To apply the $\chi^2$ test, categories were collapsed to UGC and all other formats.

f. To apply the $\chi^2$ test, categories were collapsed to other and all other formats.

**Table A.32**

Content and format of the stories deemed most newsworthy by journalists and the articles most viewed by consumers in U.S. sample, 2008 and 2009. (See figure 4.9.)

| | MNW | | | | MCL | | | |
|---|---|---|---|---|---|---|---|---|
| | PA | | NPA | | PA | | NPA | |
| | 2008 | 2009 | 2008 | 2009 | 2008 | 2009 | 2008 | 2009 |
| | *N* = 625 | *N* = 520 | *N* = 212 | *N* = 320 | *N* = 510 | *N* = 323 | *N* = 315 | *N* = 616 |
| Straight news | 63.84% | 68.65% | 71.23% | 69.06% | 50.98% | 60.06% | 63.49% | 60.66% |
| Features | 15.84% | 12.50% | 20.75% | 21.56% | 22.75% | 25.39% | 26.35% | 23.84% |
| Commentary | 4.96% | 5.19% | 1.42% | 1.56% | 17.45% | 8.98% | 0.63% | 4.07% |
| Blog | 10.72% | 10.77% | 4.72% | 3.13% | 2.55% | 3.10% | 5.40% | 5.04% |
| UGC | 1.60% | 0.58% | 0.47% | 1.25% | 0.39% | 0.00% | 0.32% | 0.00% |
| Other | 3.04% | 2.31% | 1.42% | 3.44% | 5.88% | 2.48% | 3.81% | 6.40% |
| | $\chi^2$ = 6.42, d.f. = 5 $p$ = .268 | | $\chi^2$ = 3.81, d.f. = 5 $p$ = .578 | | $\chi^2$ = 20.10, d.f. = 5 $p$ = .001 | | $\chi^2$ = 13.19, d.f. = 5 $p$ = .022 | |

**Table A.33**

Percentage of straight news, features, commentary articles, blog posts, user-generated content and "other" on journalists' list, August 1–December 1, 2008, United States, all sites, by week. (Election Day occurred during week 15.)

| Week | Straight news | Features | Commentary | Blogs | UGC | Other |
|---|---|---|---|---|---|---|
| 1 | 66.87% | 20.00% | 3.33% | 8.33% | 0.00% | 1.67% |
| 2 | 72.80% | 12.13% | 3.35% | 7.11% | 0.42% | 4.18% |
| 3 | 70.00% | 15.42% | 5.00% | 7.50% | 1.25% | 0.83% |
| 4 | 72.08% | 10.00% | 5.42% | 8.75% | 0.83% | 2.92% |
| 5 | 69.17% | 12.50% | 6.57% | 9.17% | 1.39% | 1.11% |
| 6 | 67.00% | 8.08% | 6.73% | 11.11% | 2.69% | 4.38% |
| 7 | 75.00% | 10.42% | 3.75% | 5.83% | 1.67% | 3.33% |
| 8 | 68.75% | 14.58% | 7.92% | 6.25% | 2.08% | 0.42% |
| 9 | 58.33% | 20.42% | 7.08% | 8.33% | 0.83% | 5.00% |
| 10 | 70.00% | 13.75% | 6.25% | 6.25% | 0.42% | 3.33% |
| 11 | 69.04% | 13.81% | 3.77% | 8.79% | 2.51% | 2.09% |
| 12 | 64.02% | 17.57% | 6.28% | 8.37% | 2.09% | 1.67% |
| 13 | 71.24% | 15.72% | 4.68% | 5.35% | 1.67% | 1.34% |
| 14 | 69.45% | 14.08% | 4.77% | 8.59% | 0.95% | 2.15% |
| 15 | 61.96% | 20.10% | 3.35% | 9.81% | 1.67% | 3.11% |
| 16 | 68.75% | 11.67% | 5.42% | 10.83% | 1.25% | 2.08% |
| 17 | 72.92% | 14.17% | 2.92% | 7.50% | 1.25% | 1.25% |
| 18 | 69.44% | 16.67% | 5.00% | 2.22% | 1.67% | 5.00% |

**Table A.34**

Fixed-effects logit regression of "straight news" on "week" and "site" on journalists' lists across all sites, weeks 1–15 of 2008 study. (Election Day occurred during week 15.) Base cases: CNN for "Site," week 1 for "Week."

| *N* = 4070 | Coefficient | % change in odds of a story being straight news | *Z* | *p* |
|---|---|---|---|---|
| Fox | 2.257 | 855.7 | 12.773 | 0.000 |
| ABC | −0.246 | −21.8 | −2.219 | 0.026 |
| CBS | 0.855 | 135.0 | 6.943 | 0.000 |
| Washington Post | −0.731 | −51.9 | −6.574 | 0.000 |
| USA Today | 0.790 | 120.3 | 6.491 | 0.000 |
| Week 2 | 0.328 | 38.8 | 1.264 | 0.206 |
| Week 3 | 0.177 | 19.4 | 0.690 | 0.490 |
| Week 4 | 0.293 | 34.0 | 1.132 | 0.258 |
| Week 5 | 0.132 | 14.1 | 0.547 | 0.584 |
| Week 6 | 0.019 | 1.9 | 0.075 | 0.940 |

**Table A.34**
(Continued)

| N = 4070 | Coefficient | % change in odds of a story being straight news | Z | p |
|---|---|---|---|---|
| Week 7 | 0.462 | 58.8 | 1.768 | 0.077 |
| Week 8 | 0.110 | 11.6 | 0.429 | 0.668 |
| Week 9 | –0.418 | –34.1 | –1.655 | 0.098 |
| Week 10 | 0.177 | 19.4 | 0.690 | 0.490 |
| Week 11 | 0.128 | 13.6 | 0.497 | 0.619 |
| Week 12 | –0.134 | –12.5 | –0.526 | 0.599 |
| Week 13 | 0.247 | 28.0 | 0.993 | 0.321 |
| Week 14 | 0.147 | 15.8 | 0.618 | 0.536 |
| Week 15 | –0.239 | –21.2 | –1.016 | 0.310 |

**Table A.35**
Fixed-effects logit regression of "feature" on "week" and "site" on journalists' lists across all sites, weeks 1–15 of 2008 study. (Election Day occurred during week 15.) Base cases: CNN for "Site," week 1 for "Week."

| N = 4070 | Coefficient | % change in odds of a story being told in feature style | Z | p |
|---|---|---|---|---|
| Fox | –0.928 | –60.5 | –4.290 | 0.000 |
| ABC | 1.181 | 225.9 | 7.951 | 0.000 |
| CBS | 0.155 | 16.7 | 0.925 | 0.355 |
| Washington Post | 0.610 | 84.0 | 3.897 | 0.000 |
| USA Today | –0.194 | –17.6 | –1.085 | 0.278 |
| Week 2 | –0.625 | –46.5 | –2.011 | 0.044 |
| Week 3 | –0.335 | –28.5 | –1.122 | 0.262 |
| Week 4 | –0.853 | –57.4 | –2.650 | 0.008 |
| Week 5 | –0.591 | –44.6 | –2.063 | 0.039 |
| Week 6 | –1.095 | –66.6 | –3.422 | 0.001 |
| Week 7 | –0.806 | –55.3 | –2.523 | 0.012 |
| Week 8 | –0.404 | –33.3 | –1.342 | 0.180 |
| Week 9 | 0.028 | 2.8 | 0.096 | 0.924 |
| Week 10 | –0.476 | –37.9 | –1.566 | 0.117 |
| Week 11 | –0.472 | –37.6 | –1.551 | 0.121 |
| Week 12 | –0.170 | –15.6 | –0.579 | 0.563 |
| Week 13 | –0.313 | –26.8 | –1.090 | 0.276 |
| Week 14 | –0.448 | –36.1 | –1.621 | 0.105 |
| Week 15 | 0.006 | 0.6 | 0.021 | 0.984 |

**Table A.36**

Fixed-effects logit regression of "commentary" on "week" and "site" on journalists' lists across all sites, weeks 1–15 of 2008 study. (Election Day occurred during week 15.) Base cases: CNN for "Site," week 1 for "Week."

| $N$ = 4070 | Coefficient | % change in odds of a story being told in commentary style | $Z$ | $p$ |
|---|---|---|---|---|
| Fox | –3.502 | –97.0 | –4.856 | 0.000 |
| ABC | –1.782 | –83.2 | –5.349 | 0.000 |
| CBS | –1.534 | –78.4 | –5.072 | 0.000 |
| Washington Post | 0.737 | 109.0 | 4.320 | 0.000 |
| USA Today | –1.694 | –81.6 | –5.268 | 0.000 |
| Week 2 | 0.015 | 1.5 | 0.023 | 0.981 |
| Week 3 | 0.448 | 56.5 | 0.741 | 0.459 |
| Week 4 | 0.539 | 71.4 | 0.899 | 0.369 |
| Week 5 | 0.779 | 117.8 | 1.377 | 0.169 |
| Week 6 | 0.787 | 119.6 | 1.370 | 0.171 |
| Week 7 | 0.128 | 13.7 | 0.205 | 0.838 |
| Week 8 | 0.983 | 167.3 | 1.700 | 0.089 |
| Week 9 | 0.850 | 134.0 | 1.456 | 0.145 |
| Week 10 | 0.703 | 102.0 | 1.191 | 0.234 |
| Week 11 | 0.130 | 13.9 | 0.207 | 0.836 |
| Week 12 | 0.705 | 102.4 | 1.194 | 0.232 |
| Week 13 | 0.372 | 45.0 | 0.627 | 0.531 |
| Week 14 | 0.397 | 48.8 | 0.695 | 0.487 |
| Week 15 | 0.005 | 0.5 | 0.009 | 0.993 |

**Table A.37**

Percentage of straight news, features, commentary articles, blog posts, user-generated content and "other" on consumers' list, August 1–December 1, 2008, United States, all sites, by week. (Election Day occurred during week 15.)

| Week | Straight news | Features | Commentary | Blogs | UGC | Other |
|---|---|---|---|---|---|---|
| 1 | 66.06% | 22.02% | 8.26% | 2.75% | 0.00% | 0.92% |
| 2 | 66.22% | 20.72% | 6.76% | 5.41% | 0.00% | 0.90% |
| 3 | 66.07% | 18% | 8.48% | 3.13% | 0.89% | 3.13% |
| 4 | 63.84% | 16.52% | 9.82% | 3.57% | 0.45% | 5.80% |
| 5 | 65.09% | 16.27% | 10.36% | 5.62% | 0.30% | 2.37% |
| 6 | 55.99% | 20.42% | 14.44% | 5.28% | 1.06% | 2.82% |
| 7 | 62.23% | 21.89% | 9.44% | 2% | 0.00% | 4.29% |
| 8 | 61.11% | 16.67% | 13.25% | 5.13% | 0.00% | 3.85% |

**Table A.37**
(Continued)

| Week | Straight news | Features | Commentary | Blogs | UGC | Other |
|---|---|---|---|---|---|---|
| 9 | 55.20% | 23.08% | 13.57% | 3.17% | 0.00% | 4.98% |
| 10 | 54.74% | 29.74% | 7.33% | 2.59% | 0.00% | 5.60% |
| 11 | 58% | 21.12% | 12.50% | 4.74% | 0.00% | 3.88% |
| 12 | 52.25% | 26.58% | 11.71% | 3.60% | 0.90% | 4.95% |
| 13 | 60.62% | 23.97% | 9.25% | 3.42% | 0.00% | 2.74% |
| 14 | 56.25% | 22.38% | 13.28% | 3.65% | 0.49% | 3.89% |
| 15 | 55.31% | 25.85% | 8.70% | 3.62% | 0.24% | 6.28% |
| 16 | 61.44% | 22.46% | 9.75% | 4.66% | 0.42% | 1.27% |
| 17 | 65.37% | 20.78% | 7.36% | 3.90% | 0.00% | 2.60% |
| 18 | 69.10% | 20.22% | 5.06% | 3.47% | 0.00% | 2.25% |

**Table A.38**
Fixed-effects logit regression of "straight news" on "week" and "site" on consumers' lists across all sites, weeks 1–15 of 2008 study. (Election Day occurred during week 15.) Base cases: CNN for "Site," week 1 for "Week."

| *N* = 3892 | Coefficient | % change in odds of a story being straight news | *Z* | *p* |
|---|---|---|---|---|
| Fox | 1.663 | 427.4 | 10.645 | 0.000 |
| ABC | –0.484 | –38.4 | –4.319 | 0.000 |
| CBS | –0.086 | –8.2 | –0.699 | 0.484 |
| Washington Post | –1.223 | –70.6 | –10.712 | 0.000 |
| USA Today | –0.624 | –46.4 | –5.580 | 0.000 |
| Week 2 | 0.004 | 0.4 | 0.016 | 0.987 |
| Week 3 | –0.003 | –0.3 | –0.011 | 0.991 |
| Week 4 | –0.112 | –10.6 | –0.428 | 0.669 |
| Week 5 | –0.051 | –5.0 | –0.208 | 0.836 |
| Week 6 | –0.484 | –38.4 | –1.933 | 0.053 |
| Week 7 | –0.197 | –17.9 | –0.763 | 0.445 |
| Week 8 | –0.252 | –22.3 | –0.976 | 0.329 |
| Week 9 | –0.515 | –40.2 | –1.984 | 0.047 |
| Week 10 | –0.550 | –42.3 | –2.136 | 0.033 |
| Week 11 | –0.409 | –33.5 | –1.585 | 0.113 |
| Week 12 | –0.594 | –44.8 | –2.299 | 0.022 |
| Week 13 | –0.275 | –24.1 | –1.100 | 0.271 |
| Week 14 | –0.484 | –38.3 | –2.016 | 0.044 |
| Week 15 | –0.526 | –40.9 | –2.195 | 0.028 |

**Table A.39**

Fixed-effects logit regression of "feature" on "week" and "site" on consumers' lists across all sites, weeks 1–15 of 2008 study. (Election Day occurred during week 15.) Base cases: CNN for "Site," week 1 for "Week."

| $N$ = 3892 | Coefficient | % change in odds of a story being told in feature style | $Z$ | $p$ |
|---|---|---|---|---|
| Fox | –1.362 | –74.4 | –7.750 | 0.000 |
| ABC | 0.877 | 140.3 | 7.270 | 0.000 |
| CBS | 0.207 | 23.1 | 1.530 | 0.126 |
| Washington Post | –0.272 | –23.8 | –2.020 | 0.043 |
| USA Today | –0.621 | –46.3 | –4.320 | 0.000 |
| Week 2 | –0.090 | –8.6 | –0.300 | 0.761 |
| Week 3 | –0.263 | –23.1 | –0.880 | 0.380 |
| Week 4 | –0.400 | –33.0 | –1.320 | 0.188 |
| Week 5 | –0.421 | –34.4 | –1.480 | 0.139 |
| Week 6 | –0.131 | –12.2 | –0.460 | 0.647 |
| Week 7 | –0.040 | –3.9 | –0.140 | 0.891 |
| Week 8 | –0.402 | –33.1 | –1.340 | 0.182 |
| Week 9 | 0.046 | 4.7 | 0.160 | 0.874 |
| Week 10 | 0.410 | 50.7 | 1.440 | 0.148 |
| Week 11 | –0.089 | –8.5 | –0.300 | 0.762 |
| Week 12 | 0.196 | 21.7 | 0.680 | 0.496 |
| Week 13 | 0.087 | 9.1 | 0.310 | 0.756 |
| Week 14 | –0.011 | –1.1 | –0.040 | 0.966 |
| Week 15 | 0.191 | 21.1 | 0.710 | 0.475 |

**Table A.40**

Fixed-effects logit regression of "commentary" on "week" and "site" on consumers' lists across all sites, weeks 1–15 of 2008 study. (Election Day occurred during week 15.) Base cases: CNN for "Site," week 1 for "Week."

| *N* = 3892 | Coefficient | % change in odds of a story being told in commentary style | *Z* | *p* |
|---|---|---|---|---|
| Fox | –2.292 | –89.9 | –5.695 | 0.000 |
| ABC | –1.467 | –76.9 | –5.136 | 0.000 |
| CBS | –0.450 | –36.3 | –1.993 | 0.046 |
| Washington Post | 1.926 | 586.3 | 12.490 | 0.000 |
| USA Today | –1.408 | –75.5 | –5.046 | 0.000 |
| Week 2 | –0.248 | –21.9 | –0.515 | 0.607 |
| Week 3 | 0.055 | 5.7 | 0.118 | 0.906 |
| Week 4 | 0.258 | 29.4 | 0.561 | 0.575 |
| Week 5 | 0.336 | 39.9 | 0.774 | 0.439 |
| Week 6 | 0.837 | 131.0 | 1.938 | 0.053 |
| Week 7 | 0.227 | 25.5 | 0.495 | 0.621 |
| Week 8 | 0.722 | 105.9 | 1.625 | 0.104 |
| Week 9 | 0.723 | 106.2 | 1.619 | 0.106 |
| Week 10 | –0.113 | –10.7 | –0.240 | 0.811 |
| Week 11 | 0.631 | 87.9 | 1.411 | 0.158 |
| Week 12 | 0.473 | 60.5 | 1.048 | 0.294 |
| Week 13 | 0.200 | 22.1 | 0.449 | 0.654 |
| Week 14 | 0.740 | 109.5 | 1.764 | 0.078 |
| Week 15 | 0.124 | 13.2 | 0.288 | 0.773 |

**Table A.41**
Percentage of public-affairs and non-public-affairs in the most clicked, most emailed, most commented on, and most newsworthy stories on CNN and Washington Post, 2008. (See figure 5.4.)

| | CNN | | | | Washington Post | | | |
|---|---|---|---|---|---|---|---|---|
| | MCL | MEM | MCM | MNW | MCL | MEM | MCM | MNW |
| PA | 49.94% | 40.03% | 84.16% | 70.52% | 82.41% | 81.01% | 98.61% | 72.62% |
| NPA | 50.06% | 59.97% | 15.84% | 29.48% | 17.59% | 18.99% | 1.39% | 27.38% |
| Sig. MCL-MEM | $\chi^2 = 15.59$, d.f. = 1, $p < .000$ | | | | $\chi^2 = 0.51$, d.f. = 1, $p = .474$ | | | |
| Sig. MCL-MCM | $\chi^2 = 205.87$, d.f. = 1, $p < .000$ | | | | $\chi^2 = 120.68$, d.f. = 1, $p < .000$ | | | |
| Sig. MCM-MEM | $\chi^2 = 320.44$, d.f. = 1, $p < .000$ | | | | $\chi^2 = 133.62$, d.f. = 1, $p < .000$ | | | |
| Sig. MNW-MCL | $\chi^2 = 69.69$, d.f. = 1, $p < .000$ | | | | $\chi^2 = 21.67$, d.f. = 1, $p < .000$ | | | |
| Sig. MNW-MEM | $\chi^2 = 147.58$, d.f. = 1, $p < .000$ | | | | $\chi^2 = 15.60$, d.f. = 1, $p < .000$ | | | |
| Sig. MNW-MCM | $\chi^2 = 41.19$, d.f. = 1, $p < .000$ | | | | $\chi^2 = 216.52$, d.f. = 1, $p < .000$ | | | |

**Table A.42**

Percentage of public-affairs and non-public-affairs in the most clicked, most emailed, most commented on, and most newsworthy stories on USA Today, 2008. (See figure 5.4.)

| | USA Today | | | |
|---|---|---|---|---|
| | MCL | MEM | MCM | MNW |
| PA | 48.38% | 44.83% | 74.27% | 63.88% |
| NPA | 51.62% | 55.17% | 25.73% | 36.12% |
| Sig. MCL-MEM | $\chi^2 = 2.09$, d.f. = 1, $p = .148$ | | | |
| Sig. MCL-MCM | $\chi^2 = 110.75$, d.f. = 1, $p < .000$ | | | |
| Sig. MCM-MEM | $\chi^2 = 140.74$, d.f. = 1, $p < .000$ | | | |
| Sig. MNW-MCL | $\chi^2 = 34.01$, d.f. = 1, $p < .000$ | | | |
| Sig. MNW-MEM | $\chi^2 = 57.15$, d.f. = 1, $p < .000$ | | | |
| Sig. MNW-MCM | $\chi^2 = 19.95$, d.f. = 1, $p < .000$ | | | |

**Table A.43**

Percentage of straight news, feature-style, commentary, and alternative formats in the most clicked, most emailed, most commented on, and most newsworthy stories on CNN. (See figure 5.5.)

| | MCL | MEM | MCM | MNW |
|---|---|---|---|---|
| Straight news | 64.77% | 45.91% | 26.23% | 60.86% |
| Feature | 23.83% | 42.58% | 15.45% | 12.20% |
| Commentary | 9.25% | 10.36% | 52.73% | 9.28% |
| Blog | 0% | 0.00% | 0.00% | 10.42% |
| UGC | 1.14% | 0.38% | 0.13% | 4.45% |
| Other | 1.01% | 0.77% | 5.45% | 2.80% |
| Sig. MCL-MEM | $\chi^2 = 70.58$, d.f. = 1, $p < .000$ | | | |
| Sig. MCL-MCM | $\chi^2 = 407.55$, d.f. = 1, $p < .000$ | | | |
| Sig. MCM-MEM | $\chi^2 = 399.45$, d.f. = 1, $p < .000$ | | | |
| Sig. MNW-MCL | $\chi^2 = 134.73$, d.f. = 1, $p < .000$ | | | |
| Sig. MNW-MEM | $\chi^2 = 266.61$, d.f. = 1, $p < .000$ | | | |
| Sig. MNW-MCM | $\chi^2 = 448.41$, d.f. = 1, $p < .000$ | | | |

**Table A.44**

Percentage of straight news, feature-style, commentary, and alternative formats in the most clicked, most emailed, most commented on, and most newsworthy stories on Washington Post. (See figure 5.5.)

| | MCL | MEM | MCM | MNW |
|---|---|---|---|---|
| Straight news | 37.85% | 30.51% | 41.77% | 43.47% |
| Feature | 18.10% | 23.42% | 10.76% | 18.38% |
| Commentary | 39.87% | 45.19% | 47.47% | 16.10% |
| Blog | 1.01% | 0.51% | 0.00% | 12.67% |
| UGC | 0.38% | 0.00% | 0.00% | 3.30% |
| Other | 2.78% | 0.38% | 0.00% | 6.08% |
| Sig. MCL-MEM | $\chi^2$ = 33.01, d.f. = 1, $p < .000$ | | | |
| Sig. MCL-MCM | $\chi^2$ = 54.50, d.f. = 1, $p < .000$ | | | |
| Sig. MCM-MEM | $\chi^2$ = 58.35, d.f. = 1, $p < .000$ | | | |
| Sig. MNW-MCL | $\chi^2$ = 189.26, d.f. = 1, $p < .000$ | | | |
| Sig. MNW-MEM | $\chi^2$ = 286.28, d.f. = 1, $p < .000$ | | | |
| Sig. MNW-MCM | $\chi^2$ = 312.42, d.f. = 1, $p < .000$ | | | |

**Table A.45**

Percentage of straight news, feature-style, commentary, and alternative formats in the most clicked, most emailed, most commented on, and most newsworthy stories on USA Today. (See figure 5.5.)

| | MCL | MEM | MCM | MNW |
|---|---|---|---|---|
| Straight news | 51.52% | 52.97% | 65.40% | 77.95% |
| Feature | 13.92% | 40.44% | 11.66% | 9.89% |
| Commentary | 2.15% | 2.07% | 1.52% | 1.65% |
| Blog | 20.38% | 0.13% | 20.15% | 8.87% |
| UGC | 0.13% | 0.00% | 0.25% | 0.38% |
| Other | 11.90% | 4.39% | 1.01% | 1.27% |
| Sig. MCL-MEM | $\chi^2$ = 284.48, d.f. = 1, $p < .000$ | | | |
| Sig. MCL-MCM | $\chi^2$ = 88.19, d.f. = 1, $p < .000$ | | | |
| Sig. MCM-MEM | $\chi^2$ = 307.31, d.f. = 1, $p < .000$ | | | |
| Sig. MNW-MCL | $\chi^2$ = 153.01, d.f. = 1, $p < .000$ | | | |
| Sig. MNW-MEM | $\chi^2$ = 265.58, d.f. = 1, $p < .000$ | | | |
| Sig. MNW-MCM | $\chi^2$ = 44.87, d.f. = 1, $p < .000$ | | | |

**Table A.46**

Content and format, most clicked, most emailed, most commented on, and most newsworthy stories, CNN, Washington Post, and USA Today, 2008. (See figure 5.6.)

| | MCL | | MEM | | MCM | | MNW | |
|---|---|---|---|---|---|---|---|---|
| | PA<br>$N$ = 1,428 | NPA<br>$N$ = 941 | PA<br>$N$ = 1,300 | NPA<br>$N$ = 1,046 | PA<br>$N$ = 2,013 | NPA<br>$N$ = 336 | PA<br>$N$ = 1,632 | NPA<br>$N$ = 733 |
| Straight news | 49.58% | 54.09% | 43.15% | 42.93% | 43.82% | 49.40% | 59.74% | 63.03% |
| Features | 15.69% | 23.06% | 22.92% | 50.96% | 10.53% | 25.00% | 10.48% | 20.19% |
| Commentary | 26.05% | 3.51% | 32.38% | 3.15% | 38.45% | 5.65% | 10.66% | 5.32% |
| Blog | 3.29% | 12.96% | 0.23% | 0.19% | 4.77% | 18.75% | 13.91% | 3.41% |
| UGC | 0.56% | 0.53% | 0.08% | 0.19% | 2.09% | 0.60% | 3.00% | 2.05% |
| Other | 4.83% | 5.84% | 1.23% | 2.58% | 0.35% | 0.60% | 2.21% | 6.00% |
| | $\chi^2 = 262.96$, d.f. = 5, $p < .000$ | | $\chi^2 = 390.90$, d.f. = 5, $p < .000$ | | $\chi^2 = 228.61$, d.f. = 5, $p < .000$ | | $\chi^2 = 127.89$, d.f. = 5, $p < .000$ | |

**Table A.47**

Gap in format and content choices between most newsworthy stories and most emailed articles.

| | MNW | MEM | Gap |
|---|---|---|---|
| Straight news—PA | 41.23% | 23.91% | 17.32% |
| | $\chi^2 = 160.65$, d.f. = 1, $p < .000$[a] | | |
| Straight news—NPA | 19.53% | 19.14% | 0.39% |
| | $\chi^2 = 0.12$, d.f. = 1, $p = .731$[b] | | |
| Features—PA | 7.23% | 12.70% | –5.47% |
| | $\chi^2 = 39.34$, d.f. = 1, $p < .000$[c] | | |
| Features—NPA | 6.26% | 22.72% | –16.47% |
| | $\chi^2 = 258.09$, d.f. = 1, $p < .000$[d] | | |
| Commentary—PA | 7.36% | 17.94% | –10.59% |
| | $\chi^2 = 119.65$, d.f. = 1, $p < .000$[e] | | |
| Commentary—NPA | 1.65% | 1.40% | 0.24% |
| | $\chi^2 = 0.46$, d.f. = 1, $p = .498$[f] | | |
| Blog—PA | 9.60% | 0.13% | 9.47% |
| | $\chi^2 = 227.46$, d.f. = 1, $p < .000$[g] | | |
| Blog—NPA | 1.06% | 0.08% | 0.97% |
| | $\chi^2 = 19.52$, d.f. = 1, $p < .000$[h] | | |
| UGC—PA | 2.07% | 0.04% | 2.03% |
| | $\chi^2 = 48.18$, d.f. = 1, $p < .000$[i] | | |
| UGC—NPA | 0.64% | 0.08% | 0.56% |
| | $\chi^2 = 9.87$, d.f. = 1, $p = .001$[j] | | |

a. To apply the $\chi^2$ test, categories were collapsed to straight news/public-affairs and all other format/content combinations.

b. To apply the $\chi^2$ test, categories were collapsed to straight news/non-public-affairs and all other format/content combinations.

c. To apply the $\chi^2$ test, categories were collapsed to features/public-affairs and all other format/content combinations.

d. To apply the $\chi^2$ test, categories were collapsed to features/non-public-affairs and all other format/content combinations.

e. To apply the $\chi^2$ test, categories were collapsed to commentary/public-affairs and all other format/content combinations.

f. To apply the $\chi^2$ test, categories were collapsed to commentary/non-public-affairs and all other format/content combinations.

g. To apply the $\chi^2$ test, categories were collapsed to blog/public-affairs and all other format/content combinations.

h. To apply the $\chi^2$ test, categories were collapsed to blog/non-public-affairs and all other format/content combinations.

i. To apply the $\chi^2$ test, categories were collapsed to UGC/public-affairs and all other format/content combinations.

j. To apply the $\chi^2$ test, categories were collapsed to UGC/non-public-affairs and all other format/content combinations.

**Table A.48**

Differences in format and content choices between most newsworthy stories and most commented on articles.

| | MNW | MCM | Gap |
|---|---|---|---|
| Straight news—PA | 41.23% | 37.55% | 3.67% |
| | $\chi^2 = 6.68$, d.f. = 1, $p = .010$[a] | | |
| Straight news—NPA | 19.53% | 7.06% | 12.47% |
| | $\chi^2 = 158.65$, d.f. = 1, $p < .000$[b] | | |
| Features—PA | 7.23% | 9.02% | –1.79% |
| | $\chi^2 = 5.09$, d.f. = 1, $p = .024$[c] | | |
| Features—NPA | 6.26% | 3.58% | 2.68% |
| | $\chi^2 = 18.12$, d.f. = 1, $p < .000$[d] | | |
| Commentary—PA | 7.36% | 32.95% | –25.60% |
| | $\chi^2 = 480.46$, d.f. = 1, $p < .000$[e] | | |
| Commentary—NPA | 1.65% | 0.81% | 0.84% |
| | $\chi^2 = 6.85$, d.f. = 1, $p = .009$[f] | | |
| Blog—PA | 9.60% | 4.09% | 5.51% |
| | $\chi^2 = 16.99$, d.f. = 1, $p < .000$[g] | | |
| Blog—NPA | 1.06% | 2.68% | –1.62% |
| | $\chi^2 = 19.52$, d.f. = 1, $p < .000$[h] | | |
| UGC—PA | 2.07% | 1.79% | 0.28% |
| | $\chi^2 = 0.50$, d.f. = 1, $p = .479$[i] | | |
| UGC—NPA | 0.64% | 0.09% | 0.55% |
| | $\chi^2 = 9.89$, d.f. = 1, $p = .002$[j] | | |

a. To apply the $\chi^2$ test, categories were collapsed to straight news/public-affairs and all other format/content combinations.
b. To apply the $\chi^2$ test, categories were collapsed to straight news/non-public-affairs and all other format/content combinations.
c. To apply the $\chi^2$ test, categories were collapsed to features/public-affairs and all other format/content combinations.
d. To apply the $\chi^2$ test, categories were collapsed to features/non-public-affairs and all other format/content combinations.
e. To apply the $\chi^2$ test, categories were collapsed to commentary/public-affairs and all other format/content combinations.
f. To apply the $\chi^2$ test, categories were collapsed to commentary/non-public-affairs and all other format/content combinations.
g. To apply the $\chi^2$ test, categories were collapsed to blog/public-affairs and all other format/content combinations.
h. To apply the $\chi^2$ test, categories were collapsed to blog/non-public-affairs and all other format/content combinations.
i. To apply the $\chi^2$ test, categories were collapsed to UGC/public-affairs and all other format/content combinations.
j. To apply the $\chi^2$ test, categories were collapsed to UGC/non-public-affairs and all other format/content combinations.

**Table A.49**

Percentage of public-affairs and non-public-affairs in the most clicked, most emailed, most commented on, and most newsworthy stories on CNN, USA Today, and Washington Post during fourteen days surrounding Election Day, 2008 and 2009. (See figure 5.7.)

| | MCL | | MEM | | MCM | | MNW | |
|---|---|---|---|---|---|---|---|---|
| | 2008 $N =$ 420 | 2009 $N =$ 419 | 2008 $N =$ 420 | 2009 $N =$ 419 | 2008 $N =$ 420 | 2009 $N =$ 419 | 2008 $N =$ 420 | 2009 $N =$ 419 |
| PA | 70.95% | 42.96% | 61.05% | 44.60% | 92.36% | 60.95% | 76.79% | 63.33% |
| NPA | 29.05% | 57.04% | 38.95% | 55.40% | 7.64% | 39.05% | 23.21% | 36.67% |
| | $\chi^2 = 67.05$, d.f. = 1, $p < .000$ | | $\chi^2 = 23.06$, d.f. = 1, $p < .000$ | | $\chi^2 = 114.26$, d.f. = 1, $p < .000$ | | $\chi^2 = 18.09$, d.f. = 1, $p < .000$ | |

**Table A.50**

Percentage of straight news, feature-style, commentary, and alternative formats in the most clicked, most emailed, most commented on, and most newsworthy stories on CNN, USA Today, and Washington Post during fourteen days surrounding Election Day, 2008 and 2009. (See figure 5.8.)

| | MCL | | MEM | | MCM | | MNW | |
|---|---|---|---|---|---|---|---|---|
| | 2008 | 2009 | 2008 | 2009 | 2008 | 2009 | 2008 | 2009 |
| Straight news | 44.52% | 55.37% | 44.18% | 36.39% | 34.48% | 47.62% | 57.66% | 58.81% |
| | $\chi^2 = 9.87$, d.f. = 1, $p = .002$[a] | | $\chi^2 = 5.08$, d.f. = 1, $p = .024$[a] | | $\chi^2 = 14.71$, d.f. = 1, $p < .000$[a] | | $\chi^2 = 0.11$, d.f. = 1, $p = .735$[a] | |
| Feature | 21.90% | 22.43% | 33.25% | 44.12% | 14.04% | 20.71% | 15.79% | 15.71% |
| | $\chi^2 = 0.03$, d.f. = 1, $p = .854$[b] | | $\chi^2 = 10.62$, d.f. = 1, $p = .001$[b] | | $\chi^2 = 6.39$, d.f. = 1, $p = .011$[b] | | $\chi^2 = 0.00$, d.f. = 1, $p = .976$[b] | |
| Commentary | 19.05% | 9.55% | 18.29% | 14.39% | 42.36% | 16.90% | 7.66% | 7.38% |
| | $\chi^2 = 15.45$, d.f. = 1, $p < .000$[c] | | $\chi^2 = 2.29$, d.f. = 1, $p = .131$[c] | | $\chi^2 = 64.45$, d.f. = 1, $p < .001$[c] | | $\chi^2 = 0.02$, d.f. = 1, $p = .880$[c] | |
| Blog | 6% | 9% | 0.24% | 3.84% | 7.14% | 9.05% | 12.44% | 11.67% |
| | $\chi^2 = 1.77$, d.f. = 1, $p = .184$[d] | | $\chi^2 = 13.69$, d.f. = 1, $p < .000$[d] | | $\chi^2 = 1.00$, d.f. = 1, $p = .316$[d] | | $\chi^2 = 0.12$, d.f. = 1, $p = .731$[d] | |
| UCG | 0.71% | 0.00% | 0.24% | 0.00% | 0.99% | 0.00% | 2.39% | 1.67% |
| | $\chi^2 = 3.00$, d.f. = 1, $p = .083$[e] | | $\chi^2 = 0.99$, d.f. = 1, $p = .320$[e] | | $\chi^2 = 4.15$ d.f. = 1, $p = .041$[e] | | $\chi^2 = 0.56$, d.f. = 1, $p = .456$[e] | |
| Other | 7.62% | 4.06% | 3.80% | 0.96% | 0.99% | 5.71% | 4.07% | 4.76% |
| | $\chi^2 = 4.84$, d.f. = 1, $p = .028$[f] | | $\chi^2 = 7.23$, d.f. = 1, $p = .007$[f] | | $\chi^2 = 14.10$, d.f. = 1, $p < .000$[f] | | $\chi^2 = 0.24$, d.f. = 1, $p = .624$[f] | |

a. To apply the $\chi^2$ test, categories were collapsed to straight news and all other formats.
b. To apply the $\chi^2$ test, categories were collapsed to feature-style news and all other formats.
c. To apply the $\chi^2$ test, categories were collapsed to commentary news and all other formats.
d. To apply the $\chi^2$ test, categories were collapsed to blogs and all other formats.
e. To apply the $\chi^2$ test, categories were collapsed to UGC and all other formats.
f. To apply the $\chi^2$ test, categories were collapsed to other and all other formats.

**Table A.51**

Content and format of most clicked stories on CNN, USA Today, and Washington Post during fourteen days surrounding Election Day, 2008 and 2009. (See figure 5.9.)

| | PA | | NPA | |
|---|---|---|---|---|
| | 2008<br>70.95% | 2009<br>42.96% | 2008<br>29.05% | 2009<br>57.04% |
| Straight news | 41.95% | 58.89% | 50.82% | 52.72% |
| Feature | 18.79% | 20.56% | 29.51% | 23.85% |
| Commentary | 26.85% | 13.33% | 0.00% | 6.69% |
| Blog | 3.02% | 5.56% | 13.93% | 10.88% |
| UGC | 0.67% | 0% | 0.82% | 0.00% |
| Other | 8.72% | 1.67% | 4.92% | 5.86% |
| | $\chi^2 = 28.50$, d.f. = 5, $p <$ .000 | | $\chi^2 = 11.95$, d.f. = 5, $p =$ .036 | |

**Table A.52**

Content and format of most emailed stories on CNN, USA Today, and Washington Post during fourteen days surrounding Election Day, 2008 and 2009. (See figure 5.9.)

| | PA | | NPA | |
|---|---|---|---|---|
| | 2008<br>61.05% | 2009<br>44.60% | 2008<br>38.95% | 2009<br>55.40% |
| Straight news | 39.69% | 46.24% | 51.22% | 29.00% |
| Feature | 27.63% | 27.42% | 42.07% | 57.58% |
| Commentary | 28.79% | 22.58% | 1.83% | 7.79% |
| Blog | 0.39% | 3.23% | 0.00% | 4.33% |
| UGC | 0.00% | 0.00% | 0.61% | 0.00% |
| Other | 3.50% | 0.54% | 4.27% | 1.30% |
| | $\chi^2 = 12.22$, d.f. = 4, $p <$ .016 | | $\chi^2 = 35.15$, d.f. = 5, $p <$ .000 | |

**Table A.53**

Content and format of most commented on stories on CNN, USA Today, and Washington Post during fourteen days surrounding Election Day, 2008 and 2009. (See figure 5.9.)

| | PA | | NPA | |
|---|---|---|---|---|
| | 2008 92.36% | 2009 60.95% | 2008 7.04% | 2009 39.05% |
| Straight news | 34.40% | 57.81% | 35.48% | 31.71% |
| Feature | 12.80% | 7.42% | 29.03% | 41.46% |
| Commentary | 45.60% | 25.78% | 3.23% | 3.05% |
| Blog | 5.07% | 7.42% | 32.26% | 11.59% |
| UGC | 1.07% | 0.00% | 0.00% | 0.00% |
| Other | 1.07% | 1.56% | 0.00% | 12.20% |
| | $\chi^2$ = 42.95, d.f. = 4, $p <$ .000 | | $\chi^2$ = 12.43, d.f. = 4, $p =$ .014 | |

**Table A.54**

Content and format of most newsworthy stories on CNN, USA Today, and Washington Post during fourteen days surrounding Election Day, 2008 and 2009. (See figure 5.9.)

| | PA | | NPA | |
|---|---|---|---|---|
| | 2008 76.79% | 2009 63.33% | 2008 23.21% | 2009 36.67% |
| Straight news | 54.52% | 58.27% | 68.04% | 59.74% |
| Feature | 14.96% | 12.03% | 18.56% | 22.08% |
| Commentary | 9.03% | 10% | 3.09% | 2.60% |
| Blog | 14% | 15.04% | 6.19% | 5.84% |
| UGC | 2.80% | 1.13% | 1.03% | 2.60% |
| Other | 4.36% | 3.38% | 3.09% | 7% |
| | $\chi^2$ = 3.87, d.f. = 4, $p =$ .568 | | $\chi^2$ = 3.56, d.f. = 4, $p <$ .615 | |

**Table A.55**

Gap in format and content choices between most newsworthy stories and most emailed articles on CNN, USA Today, and Washington Post, 2008 and 2009. (See figure 5.10a.)

| | 2008 | | | 2009 | | |
|---|---|---|---|---|---|---|
| | MNW | MEM | Gap | MNW | MEM | Gap |
| Straight news—PA | 41.87% | 24.23% | 17.64% | 36.90% | 20.62% | 16.28% |
| | $\chi^2 = 29.51$, d.f. = 1, $p < .000$[a] | | | $\chi^2 = 27.71$, d.f. = 1, $p < .000$[a] | | |
| Straight news—NPA | 15.79% | 19.95% | –4.16% | 21.90% | 16.07% | 5.84% |
| | $\chi^2 = 2.48$, d.f. = 1, $p = .116$[b] | | | $\chi^2 = 4.56$, d.f. = 1, $p = .033$[b] | | |
| Features—PA | 11.48% | 16.86% | –5.38% | 7.62% | 12.23% | –4.61% |
| | $\chi^2 = 4.99$, d.f. = 1, $p = .025$[c] | | | $\chi^2 = 5.03$, d.f. = 1, $p = .025$[c] | | |
| Features—NPA | 4.31% | 16.39% | –12.08% | 8.10% | 31.89% | –23.80% |
| | $\chi^2 = 32.95$, d.f. = 1, $p < .000$[d] | | | $\chi^2 = 74.53$, d.f. = 1, $p < .000$[d] | | |
| Commentary—PA | 6.94% | 17.58% | –10.64% | 6.43% | 10.07% | –3.64% |
| | $\chi^2 = 22.05$, d.f. = 1, $p < .000$[e] | | | $\chi^2 = 3.71$, d.f. = 1, $p = .054$[e] | | |
| Commentary—NPA | 0.72% | 0.71% | 0.01% | 0.95% | 4.32% | –3.36% |

| | | | | | | |
|---|---|---|---|---|---|---|
| | $\chi^2 = 0.001$, d.f. = 1, $p = .993$[f] | | | $\chi^2 = 9.29$, d.f. = 1, $p = .002$[f] | | |
| Blog—PA | 11.00% | 0.24% | 10.77% | 9.52% | 1.44% | 8.08% |
| | $\chi^2 = 45.98$, d.f. = 1, $p < .000$[g] | | | $\chi^2 = 26.25$, d.f. = 1, $p < .000$[g] | | |
| Blog—NPA | 1.44% | 0.00% | 1.44% | 2.14% | 2.40% | –0.26% |
| | $\chi^2 = 6.09$, d.f. = 1, $p = .014$[h] | | | $\chi^2 = 0.06$, d.f. = 1, $p = .800$[h] | | |
| UGC—PA | 2.15% | 0.00% | 2.15% | 0.71% | 0.00% | 0.71% |
| | $\chi^2 = 9.16$, d.f. = 1, $p = .002$[i] | | | $\chi^2 = 2.98$, d.f. = 1, $p = .004$[i] | | |
| UGC—NPA | 0.24% | 0.24% | 0.00% | 0.95% | 0.00% | 0.95% |
| | $\chi^2 = 0.00$, d.f. = 1, $p = .996$[j] | | | $\chi^2 = 3.98$, d.f. = 1, $p = .046$[j] | | |

a. To apply the $\chi^2$ test, categories were collapsed to straight news/public-affairs and all other format/content combinations.
b. To apply the $\chi^2$ test, categories were collapsed to straight news/non-public-affairs and all other format/content combinations.
c. To apply the $\chi^2$ test, categories were collapsed to features/public-affairs and all other format/content combinations.
d. To apply the $\chi^2$ test, categories were collapsed to features-non-public-affairs and all other format/content combinations.
e. To apply the $\chi^2$ test, categories were collapsed to commentary/public-affairs and all other format/content combinations.
f. To apply the $\chi^2$ test, categories were collapsed to commentary/non-public-affairs and all other format/content combinations.
g. To apply the $\chi^2$ test, categories were collapsed to blog/public-affairs and all other format/content combinations.
h. To apply the $\chi^2$ test, categories were collapsed to blog/non-public-affairs and all other format/content combinations.
i. To apply the $\chi^2$ test, categories were collapsed to UGC/public-affairs and all other format/content combinations.
j. To apply the $\chi^2$ test, categories were collapsed to UGC/non-public-affairs and all other format/content combinations.

**Table A.56**

Gap in format and content choices between most newsworthy stories and most commented on articles on CNN, USA Today, and Washington Post, 2008 and 2009. (See figure 5.10b.)

| | 2008 | | | 2009 | | |
|---|---|---|---|---|---|---|
| | MNW | MCM | Gap | MNW | MCM | Gap |
| Straight news—PA | 41.87% | 31.77% | 10.09% | 36.90% | 35.24% | 1.67% |
| | $\chi^2 = 9.01$, d.f. = 1, $p = .003$[a] | | | $\chi^2 = 0.33$, d.f. = 1, $p = .565$[a] | | |
| Straight news—NPA | 15.79% | 2.71% | 13.08% | 21.90% | 12.38% | 9.52% |
| | $\chi^2 = 41.60$, d.f. = 1, $p < .000$[b] | | | $\chi^2 = 12.68$, d.f. = 1, $p < .000$[b] | | |
| Features—PA | 11.48% | 11.82% | –0.34% | 7.62% | 4.52% | 3.10% |
| | $\chi^2 0.02$, d.f. = 1, $p = .879$[c] | | | $\chi^2 = 3.53$, d.f. = 1, $p = .060$[c] | | |
| Features—NPA | 4.31% | 2.22% | 2.09% | 8.10% | 16.19% | –8.10% |
| | $\chi^2 = 2.84$, d.f. = 1, $p = .092$[d] | | | $\chi^2 = 12.90$, d.f. = 1, $p < .000$[d] | | |
| Commentary—PA | 6.94% | 42.12% | –35.18% | 6.43% | 15.71% | –9.29% |
| | $\chi^2 = 138.68$, d.f. = 1, $p < .000$[e] | | | $\chi^2 = 18.39$, d.f. = 1, $p < .000$[e] | | |
| Commentary—NPA | 0.72% | 0.25% | 0.47% | 0.95% | 1.19% | –0.24% |

| | | | | | | |
|---|---|---|---|---|---|---|
| | $\chi^2 = 0.95$, d.f. = 1, $p = .330$[f] | | | $\chi^2 = 0.11$, d.f. = 1, $p = .738$[f] | | |
| Blog—PA | 11.00% | 4.68% | 6.32% | 9.52% | 4.52% | 5.00% |
| | $\chi^2 = 11.34$, d.f. = 1, $p = .001$[g] | | | $\chi^2 = 8.04$, d.f. = 1, $p = .005$[g] | | |
| Blog—NPA | 1.44% | 2.46% | –1.03% | 2.14% | 4.52% | –2.38% |
| | $\chi^2 = 1.14$, d.f. = 1, $p = .285$[h] | | | $\chi^2 = 3.69$, d.f. = 1, $p = .055$[h] | | |
| UGC—PA | 2.15% | 0.99% | 1.17% | 0.71% | 0.00% | 0.71% |
| | $\chi^2 = 1.81$, d.f. = 1, $p = .079$[i] | | | $\chi^2 = 3.01$, d.f. = 1, $p = .083$[i] | | |
| UGC—NPA | 0.24% | 0.00% | 0.24% | 0.95% | 0.00% | 0.95% |
| | $\chi^2 = 0.97$, d.f. = 1, $p = .324$[j] | | | $\chi^2 = 4.02$, d.f. = 1, $p < .045$[j] | | |

a. To apply the $\chi^2$ test, categories were collapsed to straight news/public-affairs and all other format/content combinations.
b. To apply the $\chi^2$ test, categories were collapsed to straight news/non-public-affairs and all other format/content combinations.
c. To apply the $\chi^2$ test, categories were collapsed to features/public-affairs and all other format/content combinations.
d. To apply the $\chi^2$ test, categories were collapsed to features-non-public-affairs and all other format/content combinations.
e. To apply the $\chi^2$ test, categories were collapsed to commentary/public-affairs and all other format/content combinations.
f. To apply the $\chi^2$ test, categories were collapsed to commentary/non-public-affairs and all other format/content combinations.
g. To apply the $\chi^2$ test, categories were collapsed to blog/public-affairs and all other format/content combinations.
h. To apply the $\chi^2$ test, categories were collapsed to blog/non-public-affairs and all other format/content combinations.
i. To apply the $\chi^2$ test, categories were collapsed to UGC/public-affairs and all other format/content combinations.
j. To apply the $\chi^2$ test, categories were collapsed to UGC/non-public-affairs and all other format/content combinations.

**Table A.57**

Percentage of public-affairs topics in "most clicked," "most emailed," "most commented," and "most newsworthy" lists on CNN, USA Today, and Washington Post, August 1–December 1, 2008, United States, by week. (Election Day occurred during week 15.) (See figure 5.11.)

| Week | MCL | MEM | MCM | MNW |
|---|---|---|---|---|
| 1 | 40.00% | 38.33% | 75.00% | 51.67% |
| 2 | 42.50% | 40.83% | 75.83% | 54.62% |
| 3 | 42.50% | 45.83% | 80.51% | 55.83% |
| 4 | 55.83% | 50.83% | 74.79% | 61.67% |
| 5 | 52.78% | 51.12% | 81.11% | 72.22% |
| 6 | 58.67% | 57.62% | 91.22% | 74.50% |
| 7 | 55.83% | 57.50% | 85.83% | 62.50% |
| 8 | 63.33% | 55.83% | 80.83% | 69.17% |
| 9 | 70.83% | 55.45% | 84.17% | 62.50% |
| 10 | 60.83% | 56.88% | 90.76% | 68.33% |
| 11 | 65.55% | 63.03% | 93.33% | 79.17% |
| 12 | 64.17% | 60.83% | 91.67% | 71.67% |
| 13 | 63.33% | 65.10% | 86.67% | 66.44% |
| 14 | 65.71% | 61.21% | 93.50% | 74.16% |
| 15 | 76.19% | 60.87% | 91.26% | 79.43% |
| 16 | 64.17% | 60.50% | 86.55% | 79.17% |
| 17 | 63.33% | 48.33% | 84.17% | 68.33% |
| 18 | 55.56% | 47.78% | 80.00% | 67.78% |

**Table A.58**

Fixed-effects logit regression of "content" on "week" and "site" in the "most clicked" list across all sites, weeks 1–15 of 2008 study. (Election Day occurred during week 15.) Base cases: CNN for "Site" and week 1 for "Week." (See figure 5.11.)

| $N = 2039$ | Coefficient | % change in odds of a story being about a PA topic | $Z$ | $p$ |
|---|---|---|---|---|
| Washington Post | 1.744 | 471.8 | 13.322 | 0.000 |
| USA Today | 0.115 | 12.1 | 1.028 | 0.304 |
| Week 2 | 0.121 | 12.8 | 0.347 | 0.729 |
| Week 3 | 0.121 | 12.8 | 0.347 | 0.729 |
| Week 4 | 0.742 | 110.0 | 2.141 | 0.032 |
| Week 5 | 0.601 | 82.4 | 1.836 | 0.066 |
| Week 6 | 0.874 | 139.6 | 2.603 | 0.009 |
| Week 7 | 0.742 | 110.0 | 2.141 | 0.032 |
| Week 8 | 1.095 | 199.0 | 3.138 | 0.002 |

**Table A.58**
(Continued)

| N = 2039 | Coefficient | % change in odds of a story being about a PA topic | Z | p |
|---|---|---|---|---|
| Week 9 | 1.472 | 335.9 | 4.148 | 0.000 |
| Week 10 | 0.976 | 165.3 | 2.805 | 0.005 |
| Week 11 | 1.198 | 231.3 | 3.414 | 0.001 |
| Week 12 | 1.135 | 211.3 | 3.249 | 0.001 |
| Week 13 | 1.095 | 199.0 | 3.247 | 0.001 |
| Week 14 | 1.211 | 235.7 | 3.734 | 0.000 |
| Week 15 | 1.771 | 487.8 | 5.337 | 0.000 |

**Table A.59**
Fixed-effects logit regression of "content" on "week" and "site" in the "most emailed" list across all sites, weeks 1–15 of 2008 study. (Election Day occurred during week 15.) Base cases: CNN for "Site" and week 1 for "Week." (See figure 5.11.)

| N = 2017 | Coefficient | % change in odds of a story being about a PA topic | Z | p |
|---|---|---|---|---|
| Washington Post | 1.969 | 616.0 | 15.235 | 0.000 |
| USA Today | 0.228 | 25.6 | 2.031 | 0.042 |
| Week 2 | 0.126 | 13.5 | 0.355 | 0.723 |
| Week 3 | 0.372 | 45.1 | 1.050 | 0.294 |
| Week 4 | 0.612 | 84.4 | 1.729 | 0.084 |
| Week 5 | 0.617 | 85.3 | 1.841 | 0.066 |
| Week 6 | 0.937 | 155.2 | 2.737 | 0.006 |
| Week 7 | 0.928 | 153.0 | 2.622 | 0.009 |
| Week 8 | 0.849 | 133.7 | 2.399 | 0.016 |
| Week 9 | 0.784 | 119.1 | 2.181 | 0.029 |
| Week 10 | 0.846 | 132.9 | 2.346 | 0.019 |
| Week 11 | 1.191 | 229.1 | 3.342 | 0.001 |
| Week 12 | 1.088 | 196.9 | 3.065 | 0.002 |
| Week 13 | 1.293 | 264.3 | 3.742 | 0.000 |
| Week 14 | 1.114 | 204.6 | 3.384 | 0.001 |
| Week 15 | 1.079 | 194.2 | 3.267 | 0.001 |

**Table A.60**

Fixed-effects logit regression of "content" on "week" and "site" in the "most commented" list across all sites, weeks 1–15 of 2008 study. (Election Day occurred during week 15.) Base cases: CNN for "Site" and week 1 for "Week." (See figure 5.11.)

| *N* = 2020 | Coefficient | % change in odds of a story being about a PA topic | *Z* | *p* |
|---|---|---|---|---|
| Washington Post | 2.551 | 1181.8 | 7.552 | 0.000 |
| USA Today | –0.636 | –47.1 | –4.450 | 0.000 |
| Week 2 | 0.053 | 5.4 | 0.133 | 0.895 |
| Week 3 | 0.365 | 44.0 | 0.897 | 0.370 |
| Week 4 | –0.015 | –1.5 | –0.038 | 0.970 |
| Week 5 | 0.411 | 50.9 | 1.080 | 0.280 |
| Week 6 | 1.367 | 292.2 | 3.109 | 0.002 |
| Week 7 | 0.792 | 120.7 | 1.871 | 0.061 |
| Week 8 | 0.391 | 47.8 | 0.963 | 0.336 |
| Week 9 | 0.648 | 91.2 | 1.558 | 0.119 |
| Week 10 | 1.300 | 266.9 | 2.836 | 0.005 |
| Week 11 | 1.680 | 436.4 | 3.403 | 0.001 |
| Week 12 | 1.428 | 317.0 | 3.052 | 0.002 |
| Week 13 | 0.868 | 138.2 | 2.125 | 0.034 |
| Week 14 | 1.705 | 450.3 | 3.911 | 0.000 |
| Week 15 | 1.372 | 294.4 | 3.342 | 0.001 |

**Table A.61**

Fixed-effects logit regression of "content" on "week" and "site" in the "most newsworthy" list across all sites, weeks 1–15 of 2008 study. (Election Day occurred during week 15.) Base cases: CNN for "Site," week 1 for "Week." (See figure 5.11.)

| *N* = 2035 | Coefficient | % change in odds of a story being about a PA topic | *Z* | *p* |
|---|---|---|---|---|
| Washington Post | 0.200 | 22.2 | 1.650 | 0.099 |
| USA Today | –0.236 | –21.0 | –2.016 | 0.044 |
| Week 2 | 0.121 | 12.9 | 0.381 | 0.703 |
| Week 3 | 0.169 | 18.4 | 0.531 | 0.595 |
| Week 4 | 0.412 | 51.0 | 1.285 | 0.199 |
| Week 5 | 0.895 | 144.8 | 2.903 | 0.004 |
| Week 6 | 1.013 | 175.3 | 3.158 | 0.002 |
| Week 7 | 0.448 | 56.5 | 1.394 | 0.163 |
| Week 8 | 0.747 | 111.0 | 2.287 | 0.022 |
| Week 9 | 0.448 | 56.5 | 1.394 | 0.163 |

**Table A.61**
(Continued)

| $N$ = 2035 | Coefficient | % change in odds of a story being about a PA topic | $Z$ | $p$ |
|---|---|---|---|---|
| Week 10 | 0.708 | 102.9 | 2.173 | 0.030 |
| Week 11 | 1.277 | 258.6 | 3.716 | 0.000 |
| Week 12 | 0.868 | 138.1 | 2.633 | 0.008 |
| Week 13 | 0.620 | 85.8 | 1.983 | 0.047 |
| Week 14 | 0.995 | 170.5 | 3.273 | 0.001 |
| Week 15 | 1.293 | 264.4 | 4.158 | 0.000 |

**Table A.62**
Percentage of "straight news" in "most clicked," "most emailed," "most commented," and "most newsworthy" lists on CNN, USA Today, and Washington Post, August 1–December 1, 2008, United States, by week. (Election Day occurred during week 15.)

| Week | MCL | MEM | MCM | MNW |
|---|---|---|---|---|
| 1 | 58.33% | 45.00% | 48.33% | 58.33% |
| 2 | 62.50% | 52.50% | 49.17% | 65.55% |
| 3 | 59.17% | 41.67% | 53.39% | 64.17% |
| 4 | 60.00% | 51.67% | 60.50% | 65.83% |
| 5 | 53.33% | 38.20% | 55.00% | 61.11% |
| 6 | 44.00% | 43.71% | 46.62% | 55.70% |
| 7 | 55.00% | 48.33% | 53.33% | 65.83% |
| 8 | 50.00% | 40.00% | 45.00% | 57.50% |
| 9 | 45.83% | 33.64% | 43.33% | 49.17% |
| 10 | 49.17% | 35.78% | 38.66% | 70.83% |
| 11 | 49% | 38% | 36.67% | 60.00% |
| 12 | 44.17% | 33.33% | 31.67% | 57.50% |
| 13 | 48.67% | 42.95% | 44.67% | 65.77% |
| 14 | 42.38% | 47.66% | 35.50% | 60.29% |
| 15 | 46.67% | 40.58% | 33.50% | 55.02% |
| 16 | 51.67% | 47.90% | 38.66% | 58.33% |
| 17 | 58.33% | 44.17% | 51.67% | 65.00% |
| 18 | 65.56% | 52.22% | 48.89% | 61.11% |

**Table A.63**

Fixed-effects logit regression of "straight news" on "week" and "site" in the "most clicked" list across all sites, weeks 1–15 of 2008 study. (Election Day occurred during week 15.) Base cases: CNN for "Site," week 1 for "Week."

| *N* = 2039 | Coefficient | % change in odds of a story being straight news | *Z* | *p* |
|---|---|---|---|---|
| Washington Post | –1.230 | –70.8 | –10.733 | 0.000 |
| USA Today | –0.627 | –46.6 | –5.594 | 0.000 |
| Week 2 | 0.185 | 20.3 | 0.556 | 0.578 |
| Week 3 | 0.036 | 3.7 | 0.110 | 0.912 |
| Week 4 | 0.073 | 7.6 | 0.221 | 0.825 |
| Week 5 | –0.216 | –19.4 | –0.694 | 0.488 |
| Week 6 | –0.614 | –45.9 | –1.926 | 0.054 |
| Week 7 | –0.144 | –13.4 | –0.438 | 0.662 |
| Week 8 | –0.357 | –30.1 | –1.087 | 0.277 |
| Week 9 | –0.535 | –41.4 | –1.625 | 0.104 |
| Week 10 | –0.393 | –32.5 | –1.194 | 0.232 |
| Week 11 | –0.406 | –33.3 | –1.231 | 0.218 |
| Week 12 | –0.607 | –45.5 | –1.840 | 0.066 |
| Week 13 | –0.414 | –33.9 | –1.302 | 0.193 |
| Week 14 | –0.684 | –49.5 | –2.236 | 0.025 |
| Week 15 | –0.499 | –39.3 | –1.636 | 0.102 |

**Table A.64**

Fixed-effects logit regression of "straight news" on "week" and "site" in the "most emailed" list across all sites, weeks 1–15 of 2008 study. (Election Day occurred during week 15.) Base cases: CNN for "Site," week 1 for "Week."

| *N* = 2017 | Coefficient | % change in odds of a story being straight news | *Z* | *p* |
|---|---|---|---|---|
| Washington Post | –0.799 | –55.0 | –6.897 | 0.000 |
| USA Today | 0.236 | 26.6 | 2.134 | 0.033 |
| Week 2 | 0.315 | 37.1 | 0.970 | 0.332 |
| Week 3 | –0.142 | –13.2 | –0.436 | 0.663 |
| Week 4 | 0.280 | 32.4 | 0.863 | 0.388 |
| Week 5 | –0.291 | –25.3 | –0.943 | 0.346 |
| Week 6 | –0.058 | –5.6 | –0.183 | 0.854 |
| Week 7 | 0.140 | 15.1 | 0.432 | 0.666 |
| Week 8 | –0.214 | –19.3 | –0.655 | 0.512 |

**Table A.64**
(Continued)

| *N* = 2017 | Coefficient | % change in odds of a story being straight news | *Z* | *p* |
|---|---|---|---|---|
| Week 9 | –0.461 | –36.9 | –1.371 | 0.170 |
| Week 10 | –0.360 | –30.3 | –1.076 | 0.282 |
| Week 11 | –0.307 | –26.4 | –0.934 | 0.350 |
| Week 12 | –0.514 | –40.2 | –1.553 | 0.120 |
| Week 13 | –0.086 | –8.2 | –0.272 | 0.785 |
| Week 14 | 0.103 | 10.9 | 0.343 | 0.732 |
| Week 15 | –0.186 | –17.0 | –0.617 | 0.538 |

**Table A.65**
Fixed-effects logit regression of "straight news" on "week" and "site" in the "most commented" list across all sites, weeks 1–15 of 2008 study. (Election Day occurred during week 15.) Base cases: CNN for "Site," week 1 for "Week."

| *N* = 2020 | Coefficient | % change in odds of a story being straight news | *Z* | *p* |
|---|---|---|---|---|
| Washington Post | 0.783 | 118.9 | 6.522 | 0.000 |
| USA Today | 1.703 | 449.3 | 13.909 | 0.000 |
| Week 2 | 0.037 | 3.8 | 0.112 | 0.911 |
| Week 3 | 0.212 | 23.6 | 0.631 | 0.528 |
| Week 4 | 0.544 | 72.3 | 1.611 | 0.107 |
| Week 5 | 0.300 | 34.9 | 0.947 | 0.343 |
| Week 6 | –0.089 | –8.5 | –0.273 | 0.785 |
| Week 7 | 0.224 | 25.2 | 0.669 | 0.503 |
| Week 8 | –0.150 | –13.9 | –0.448 | 0.654 |
| Week 9 | –0.226 | –20.2 | –0.672 | 0.501 |
| Week 10 | –0.434 | –35.2 | –1.284 | 0.199 |
| Week 11 | –0.537 | –41.5 | –1.584 | 0.113 |
| Week 12 | –0.784 | –54.3 | –2.286 | 0.022 |
| Week 13 | –0.165 | –15.2 | –0.510 | 0.610 |
| Week 14 | –0.634 | –47.0 | –2.014 | 0.044 |
| Week 15 | –0.707 | –50.7 | –2.248 | 0.025 |

**Table A.66**

Fixed-effects logit regression of "straight news" on "week" and "site" in the "most newsworthy" list across all sites, weeks 1–15 of 2008 study. (Election Day occurred during week 15.) Base cases: CNN for "Site," week 1 for "Week."

| $N$ = 2035 | Coefficient | % change in odds of a story being straight news | $Z$ | $p$ |
|---|---|---|---|---|
| Washington Post | –0.733 | –51.9 | –6.579 | 0.000 |
| USA Today | 0.792 | 120.7 | 6.499 | 0.000 |
| Week 2 | 0.327 | 38.7 | 0.964 | 0.335 |
| Week 3 | 0.268 | 30.8 | 0.794 | 0.427 |
| Week 4 | 0.348 | 41.6 | 1.025 | 0.305 |
| Week 5 | 0.126 | 13.4 | 0.398 | 0.691 |
| Week 6 | –0.117 | –11.1 | –0.363 | 0.717 |
| Week 7 | 0.348 | 41.6 | 1.025 | 0.305 |
| Week 8 | –0.037 | –3.7 | –0.112 | 0.911 |
| Week 9 | –0.405 | –33.3 | –1.213 | 0.225 |
| Week 10 | 0.598 | 81.9 | 1.738 | 0.082 |
| Week 11 | 0.075 | 7.8 | 0.224 | 0.822 |
| Week 12 | –0.037 | –3.7 | –0.112 | 0.911 |
| Week 13 | 0.350 | 41.9 | 1.069 | 0.285 |
| Week 14 | 0.089 | 9.3 | 0.285 | 0.776 |
| Week 15 | –0.148 | –13.7 | –0.476 | 0.634 |

**Table A.67**

Percentage of "feature-style articles" in "most clicked," "most emailed," "most commented," and "most newsworthy" lists on CNN, USA Today, and Washington Post, August 1–December 1, 2008, United States, by week. (Election Day occurred during week 15.)

| Week | MCL | MEM | MCM | MNW |
|---|---|---|---|---|
| 1 | 21.67% | 45.00% | 20.00% | 23.33% |
| 2 | 15.00% | 30.00% | 15.00% | 11.76% |
| 3 | 14% | 38% | 13% | 15.83% |
| 4 | 12.50% | 30.00% | 6.72% | 6.67% |
| 5 | 16.67% | 41.57% | 13.33% | 7.78% |
| 6 | 17.33% | 28.48% | 7.43% | 7.38% |
| 7 | 17.50% | 30.83% | 10.83% | 10.83% |
| 8 | 15.00% | 34.17% | 11.67% | 17.50% |
| 9 | 16.67% | 34.55% | 12.50% | 20.83% |

**Table A.67**
(Continued)

| Week | MCL | MEM | MCM | MNW |
|---|---|---|---|---|
| 10 | 25.83% | 37.61% | 15.13% | 10.00% |
| 11 | 15.13% | 35.29% | 8.33% | 14.17% |
| 12 | 20.00% | 41.67% | 20.00% | 13.33% |
| 13 | 24.00% | 36.24% | 14.67% | 14.09% |
| 14 | 21.43% | 30.84% | 13.50% | 12.92% |
| 15 | 22.38% | 35.75% | 14.56% | 18.66% |
| 16 | 19.17% | 36.97% | 12.61% | 12.50% |
| 17 | 19.17% | 44.17% | 10.83% | 15.83% |
| 18 | 17.78% | 33.33% | 7.78% | 15.56% |

**Table A.68**
Fixed-effects logit regression of "feature" on "week" and "site" in the "most clicked" list across all sites, weeks 1–15. of 2008 study. (Election Day occurred during week 15.) Base cases: CNN for "Site," week 1 for "Week."

| *N* = 2039 | Coefficient | % change in odds of a story being told in feature style | *Z* | *p* |
|---|---|---|---|---|
| Washington Post | –0.272 | –23.8 | –2.020 | 0.043 |
| USA Today | –0.622 | –46.3 | –4.320 | 0.000 |
| Week 2 | –0.454 | –36.5 | –1.116 | 0.264 |
| Week 3 | –0.521 | –40.6 | –1.270 | 0.204 |
| Week 4 | –0.666 | –48.6 | –1.589 | 0.112 |
| Week 5 | –0.327 | –27.9 | –0.876 | 0.381 |
| Week 6 | –0.280 | –24.4 | –0.732 | 0.464 |
| Week 7 | –0.268 | –23.5 | –0.675 | 0.499 |
| Week 8 | –0.454 | –36.5 | –1.116 | 0.264 |
| Week 9 | –0.327 | –27.9 | –0.819 | 0.413 |
| Week 10 | 0.233 | 26.3 | 0.616 | 0.538 |
| Week 11 | –0.441 | –35.7 | –1.085 | 0.278 |
| Week 12 | –0.102 | –9.7 | –0.262 | 0.793 |
| Week 13 | 0.134 | 14.3 | 0.363 | 0.717 |
| Week 14 | –0.014 | –1.4 | –0.040 | 0.968 |
| Week 15 | 0.042 | 4.3 | 0.118 | 0.906 |

**Table A.69**

Fixed-effects logit regression of "feature" on "week" and "site" in the "most emailed" list across all sites, weeks 1–15 of 2008 study. (Election Day occurred during week 15.) Base cases: CNN for "Site," week 1 for "Week."

| $N$ = 2017 | Coefficient | % change in odds of a story being told in feature style | $Z$ | $p$ |
|---|---|---|---|---|
| Washington Post | –0.840 | –56.8 | –6.982 | 0.000 |
| USA Today | –0.035 | –3.5 | –0.316 | 0.752 |
| Week 2 | –0.668 | –48.7 | –2.007 | 0.045 |
| Week 3 | –0.321 | –27.4 | –0.983 | 0.326 |
| Week 4 | –0.668 | –48.7 | –2.007 | 0.045 |
| Week 5 | –0.141 | –13.2 | –0.462 | 0.644 |
| Week 6 | –0.745 | –52.5 | –2.318 | 0.020 |
| Week 7 | –0.627 | –46.6 | –1.891 | 0.059 |
| Week 8 | –0.471 | –37.5 | –1.432 | 0.152 |
| Week 9 | –0.431 | –35.0 | –1.291 | 0.197 |
| Week 10 | –0.290 | –25.2 | –0.874 | 0.382 |
| Week 11 | –0.417 | –34.1 | –1.271 | 0.204 |
| Week 12 | –0.141 | –13.1 | –0.433 | 0.665 |
| Week 13 | –0.375 | –31.3 | –1.186 | 0.235 |
| Week 14 | –0.631 | –46.8 | –2.077 | 0.038 |
| Week 15 | –0.395 | –32.6 | –1.305 | 0.192 |

**Table A.70**

Fixed-effects logit regression of "feature" on "week" and "site" in the "most commented" list across all sites, weeks 1–15 of 2008 study. (Election Day occurred during week 15.). Base cases: CNN for "Site," week 1 for "Week."

| $N$ = 2020 | Coefficient | % change in odds of a story being told in feature style | $Z$ | $p$ |
|---|---|---|---|---|
| Washington Post | –0.281 | –24.5 | –1.731 | 0.083 |
| USA Today | –0.251 | –22.2 | –1.553 | 0.120 |
| Week 2 | –0.349 | –29.5 | –0.847 | 0.397 |
| Week 3 | –0.539 | –41.6 | –1.266 | 0.206 |
| Week 4 | –1.244 | –71.2 | –2.548 | 0.011 |
| Week 5 | –0.487 | –38.5 | –1.246 | 0.213 |
| Week 6 | –1.135 | –67.9 | –2.522 | 0.012 |
| Week 7 | –0.723 | –51.5 | –1.655 | 0.098 |

**Table A.70**
(Continued)

| *N* = 2020 | Coefficient | % change in odds of a story being told in feature style | *Z* | *p* |
|---|---|---|---|---|
| Week 8 | –0.639 | –47.2 | –1.485 | 0.138 |
| Week 9 | –0.561 | –42.9 | –1.319 | 0.187 |
| Week 10 | –0.340 | –28.8 | –0.824 | 0.410 |
| Week 11 | –1.014 | –63.7 | –2.193 | 0.028 |
| Week 12 | 0.000 | 0.0 | 0.000 | 1.000 |
| Week 13 | –0.376 | –31.3 | –0.945 | 0.344 |
| Week 14 | –0.463 | –37.1 | –1.206 | 0.228 |
| Week 15 | –0.380 | –31.6 | –1.004 | 0.315 |

**Table A.71**
Fixed-effects logit regression of "feature" on "week" and "site" on "most newsworthy" list across all sites, weeks 1–15 of 2008 study. (Election Day occurred during week 15.). Base cases: CNN for "Site," week 1 for "Week."

| *N* = 2035 | Coefficient | % change in odds of a story being told in feature style | *Z* | *p* |
|---|---|---|---|---|
| Washington Post | 0.615 | 84.9 | 3.912 | 0.000 |
| USA Today | –0.195 | –17.7 | –1.088 | 0.276 |
| Week 2 | –0.836 | –56.7 | –1.985 | 0.047 |
| Week 3 | –0.491 | –38.8 | –1.231 | 0.218 |
| Week 4 | –1.471 | –77.0 | –3.065 | 0.002 |
| Week 5 | –1.304 | –72.9 | –3.129 | 0.002 |
| Week 6 | –1.362 | –74.4 | –3.089 | 0.002 |
| Week 7 | –0.935 | –60.7 | –2.187 | 0.029 |
| Week 8 | –0.369 | –30.8 | –0.939 | 0.348 |
| Week 9 | –0.149 | –13.8 | –0.388 | 0.698 |
| Week 10 | –1.025 | –64.1 | –2.358 | 0.018 |
| Week 11 | –0.624 | –46.4 | –1.536 | 0.125 |
| Week 12 | –0.695 | –50.1 | –1.694 | 0.090 |
| Week 13 | –0.632 | –46.9 | –1.623 | 0.104 |
| Week 14 | –0.733 | –52.0 | –1.970 | 0.049 |
| Week 15 | –0.290 | –25.1 | –0.811 | 0.417 |

**Table A.72**

Percentage of "commentary articles" in "most clicked," "most emailed," "most commented," and "most newsworthy" lists on CNN, USA Today, and Washington Post, August 1–December 1, 2008, United States, by week. (Election Day occurred during week 15.)

| Week | MCL | MEM | MCM | MNW |
|---|---|---|---|---|
| 1 | 13.33% | 10.00% | 23.33% | 6.67% |
| 2 | 11.67% | 14.17% | 27.50% | 6.72% |
| 3 | 15.00% | 20.00% | 23.73% | 9.17% |
| 4 | 15.00% | 15.83% | 26.89% | 8.33% |
| 5 | 16.11% | 18.54% | 22.78% | 12.22% |
| 6 | 22.67% | 25.17% | 35.14% | 11.41% |
| 7 | 16.67% | 19.17% | 25.83% | 7.50% |
| 8 | 18.33% | 21.67% | 35.00% | 11.67% |
| 9 | 22.50% | 29.09% | 33% | 12.50% |
| 10 | 12.50% | 25.69% | 38.66% | 8.33% |
| 11 | 21.01% | 26.89% | 42.50% | 7.50% |
| 12 | 19.17% | 24.17% | 35.00% | 11.67% |
| 13 | 17.33% | 19.46% | 33.33% | 7.38% |
| 14 | 22.38% | 18.69% | 42.50% | 8.61% |
| 15 | 15.71% | 17.87% | 42.23% | 6.70% |
| 16 | 17.50% | 13.45% | 40.34% | 10.83% |
| 17 | 14.17% | 11.67% | 31.67% | 5.00% |
| 18 | 8.89% | 12.22% | 36.67% | 8.89% |

**Table A.73**

Fixed-effects logit regression of "commentary" on "week" and "site" in the "most clicked" list across all sites, weeks 1–15 of 2008 study. (Election Day occurred during week 15.) Base cases: CNN for "Site," week 1 for "Week."

| $N$ = 2039 | Coefficient | % change in odds of a story being told in commentary style | $Z$ | $p$ |
|---|---|---|---|---|
| Washington Post | 1.922 | 583.1 | 12.469 | 0.000 |
| USA Today | –1.407 | –75.5 | –5.044 | 0.000 |
| Week 2 | –0.178 | –16.3 | –0.347 | 0.729 |
| Week 3 | 0.164 | 17.8 | 0.328 | 0.743 |
| Week 4 | 0.164 | 17.8 | 0.328 | 0.743 |
| Week 5 | 0.266 | 30.5 | 0.567 | 0.571 |
| Week 6 | 0.802 | 123.0 | 1.707 | 0.088 |
| Week 7 | 0.316 | 37.2 | 0.640 | 0.522 |

**Table A.73**
(Continued)

| N = 2039 | Coefficient | % change in odds of a story being told in commentary style | Z | p |
|---|---|---|---|---|
| Week 8 | 0.459 | 58.3 | 0.937 | 0.349 |
| Week 9 | 0.789 | 120.2 | 1.634 | 0.102 |
| Week 10 | –0.087 | –8.3 | –0.171 | 0.864 |
| Week 11 | 0.669 | 95.3 | 1.378 | 0.168 |
| Week 12 | 0.528 | 69.6 | 1.082 | 0.279 |
| Week 13 | 0.374 | 45.4 | 0.784 | 0.433 |
| Week 14 | 0.780 | 118.2 | 1.717 | 0.086 |
| Week 15 | 0.230 | 25.9 | 0.497 | 0.619 |

**Table A.74**
Fixed-effects logit regression of "commentary" on "week" and "site" in the "most emailed" list across all sites, weeks 1–15 of 2008 study. (Election Day occurred during week 15.) Base cases: CNN for "Site," week 1 for "Week."

| N = 2017 | Coefficient | % change in odds of a story being told in commentary style | Z | p |
|---|---|---|---|---|
| Washington Post | 2.037 | 666.6 | 13.841 | 0.000 |
| USA Today | –1.673 | –81.2 | –5.781 | 0.000 |
| Week 2 | 0.466 | 59.4 | 0.858 | 0.391 |
| Week 3 | 0.991 | 169.5 | 1.870 | 0.061 |
| Week 4 | 0.627 | 87.3 | 1.165 | 0.244 |
| Week 5 | 0.860 | 136.3 | 1.685 | 0.092 |
| Week 6 | 1.406 | 307.8 | 2.744 | 0.006 |
| Week 7 | 0.922 | 151.4 | 1.735 | 0.083 |
| Week 8 | 1.126 | 208.3 | 2.133 | 0.033 |
| Week 9 | 1.527 | 360.6 | 2.913 | 0.004 |
| Week 10 | 1.283 | 260.7 | 2.434 | 0.015 |
| Week 11 | 1.507 | 351.5 | 2.880 | 0.004 |
| Week 12 | 1.320 | 274.2 | 2.512 | 0.012 |
| Week 13 | 0.942 | 156.4 | 1.818 | 0.069 |
| Week 14 | 0.912 | 148.9 | 1.815 | 0.070 |
| Week 15 | 0.800 | 122.6 | 1.586 | 0.113 |

**Table A.75**

Fixed-effects logit regression of "commentary" on "week" and "site" in the "most commented" list across all sites, weeks 1–15 of 2008 study. (Election Day occurred during week 15.) Base cases: CNN for "Site," week 1 for "Week."

| *N* = 2020 | Coefficient | % change in odds of a story being told in commentary style | *Z* | *p* |
|---|---|---|---|---|
| Washington Post | –0.319 | –27.3 | –2.848 | 0.004 |
| USA Today | –4.246 | –98.6 | –13.989 | 0.000 |
| Week 2 | 0.263 | 30.1 | 0.657 | 0.511 |
| Week 3 | 0.042 | 4.3 | 0.105 | 0.917 |
| Week 4 | 0.234 | 26.4 | 0.583 | 0.560 |
| Week 5 | –0.037 | –3.6 | –0.096 | 0.924 |
| Week 6 | 0.732 | 107.9 | 1.897 | 0.058 |
| Week 7 | 0.160 | 17.3 | 0.398 | 0.691 |
| Week 8 | 0.708 | 102.9 | 1.781 | 0.075 |
| Week 9 | 0.610 | 84.1 | 1.535 | 0.125 |
| Week 10 | 0.904 | 146.9 | 2.272 | 0.023 |
| Week 11 | 1.152 | 216.3 | 2.880 | 0.004 |
| Week 12 | 0.708 | 102.9 | 1.781 | 0.075 |
| Week 13 | 0.610 | 84.1 | 1.585 | 0.113 |
| Week 14 | 1.225 | 240.5 | 3.266 | 0.001 |
| Week 15 | 1.163 | 220.1 | 3.120 | 0.002 |

**Table A.76**

Fixed-effects logit regression of "commentary" on "week" and "site" on "most newsworthy" list across all sites, weeks 1–15 of 2008 study. (Election Day occurred during week 15.) Base cases: CNN for "Site," week 1 for "Week."

| *N* = 2035 | Coefficient | % change in odds of a story being told in commentary style | *Z* | *p* |
|---|---|---|---|---|
| Washington Post | 0.735 | 108.6 | 4.314 | 0.000 |
| USA Today | –1.693 | –81.6 | –5.265 | 0.000 |
| Week 2 | 0.017 | 1.7 | 0.027 | 0.979 |
| Week 3 | 0.360 | 43.3 | 0.582 | 0.561 |
| Week 4 | 0.251 | 28.5 | 0.401 | 0.689 |
| Week 5 | 0.700 | 101.3 | 1.214 | 0.225 |
| Week 6 | 0.617 | 85.3 | 1.046 | 0.296 |
| Week 7 | 0.131 | 14.0 | 0.207 | 0.836 |
| Week 8 | 0.643 | 90.3 | 1.068 | 0.285 |

**Table A.76**
(Continued)

| $N$ = 2035 | Coefficient | % change in odds of a story being told in commentary style | $Z$ | $p$ |
|---|---|---|---|---|
| Week 9 | 0.727 | 106.9 | 1.214 | 0.225 |
| Week 10 | 0.251 | 28.5 | 0.401 | 0.689 |
| Week 11 | 0.131 | 14.0 | 0.207 | 0.836 |
| Week 12 | 0.643 | 90.3 | 1.068 | 0.285 |
| Week 13 | 0.108 | 11.4 | 0.175 | 0.861 |
| Week 14 | 0.288 | 33.4 | 0.493 | 0.622 |
| Week 15 | 0.005 | 0.5 | 0.008 | 0.993 |

**Table A.77**
Percentage of Public-affairs topics in the stories deemed most newsworthy by journalists and the articles most viewed by consumers on CNN, CBS, Washington Post, ABC, and USA Today, 2008. (See figure C.1.)

| | Journalists | Consumers | | Journalists | Consumers |
|---|---|---|---|---|---|
| CNN | $n$ = 140 | $n$ = 138 | CBS | $n$ = 125 | $n$ = 139 |
| PA | 76.09% | 59.29% | PA | 78.42% | 67.20% |
| NPA | 23.91% | 40.71% | NPA | 21.58% | 32.80% |
| | $\chi^2$ = 8.97, d.f. = 1, $p$ = .003 | | | $\chi^2$ = 4.21, d.f. = 1, $p$ = .040 | |
| ABC | $n$ = 140 | $n$ = 140 | Washington Post | $n$ = 140 | $n$ = 140 |
| PA | 64.29% | 66.43% | PA | 79.29% | 90.71% |
| NPA | 35.71% | 33.57% | NPA | 20.71% | 9.29% |
| | $\chi^2$ = 0.14, d.f. = 1, $p$ = .706 | | | $\chi^2$ = 7.17, d.f. = 1, $p$ = .007 | |
| USA Today | $n$ = 140 | $n$ = 140 | | | |
| PA | 75% | 62.86% | | | |
| NPA | 25% | 37.14% | | | |
| | $\chi^2$ = 4.82, d.f. = 1, $p$ = .028 | | | | |

**Table A.78**

Percentage of public-affairs topics in the stories deemed most newsworthy by journalists and the articles most viewed by consumers on CNN, CBS, Washington Post, ABC, and USA Today, 2009. (See figure C.1.)

| | Journalists | Consumers | | Journalists | Consumers |
|---|---|---|---|---|---|
| CNN | $n$ = 140 | $n$ = 140 | CBS | $n$ = 140 | $n$ = 140 |
| PA | 57.14 | 30 | PA | 68.57 | 45.71 |
| NPA | 42.86 | 70 | NPA | 31.43 | 54.29 |
| | $\chi^2 = 20.98$, d.f. = 1, $p < .000$ | | | $\chi^2 = 14.93$, d.f. = 1, $p < .000$ | |
| ABC | $n$ = 140 | $n$ = 140 | Washington Post | $n$ = 140 | $n$ = 140 |
| PA | 47.86 | 30 | PA | 82.14 | 68.57 |
| NPA | 52.14 | 70 | NPA | 17.86 | 31.43 |
| | $\chi^2 = 9.39$, d.f. = 1, $p = .002$ | | | $\chi^2 = 6.94$, d.f. = 1, $p = .008$ | |
| USA Today | $n$ = 140 | $n$ = 140 | | | |
| PA | 50 | 30.22 | | | |
| NPA | 50 | 69.78 | | | |
| | $\chi^2 = 11.36$, d.f. = 1, $p = .001$ | | | | |

**Table A.79**

Percentage of public-affairs topics in the stories deemed most newsworthy by journalists and the articles most viewed by consumers on CNN, CBS, Washington Post, ABC, and USA Today, 2010. (See figure C.1.)

| | Journalists | Consumers | | Journalists | Consumers |
|---|---|---|---|---|---|
| CNN | $n$ = 140 | $n$ = 140 | CBS | $n$ = 140 | $n$ = 135 |
| PA | 72.14% | 48.57% | PA | 56.43% | 46.67% |
| NPA | 27.86% | 51.43% | NPA | 43.57% | 53.33% |
| | $\chi^2 = 16.25$, d.f. = 1, $p < .000$ | | | $\chi^2 = 2.62$, d.f. = 1, $p = .105$ | |
| ABC | $n$ = 140 | $n$ = 140 | Washington Post | $n$ = 138 | $n$ = 140 |
| PA | 39.29% | 32.14% | PA | 78.99% | 80% |
| NPA | 60.71% | 67.86% | NPA | 20.01% | 20% |
| | $\chi^2 = 1.56$, d.f. = 1, $p = .212$ | | | $\chi^2 = 0.04$, d.f. = 1, $p = .834$ | |
| USA Today | $n$ = 138 | $n$ = 140 | | | |
| PA | 62.32% | 39.29% | | | |
| NPA | 37.68% | 60.71% | | | |
| | $\chi^2 = 14.75$, d.f. = 1, $p < .000$ | | | | |

**Table A.80**

Percentage of public-affairs topics in the stories deemed most newsworthy by journalists and the articles most viewed by consumers on CNN, CBS, Washington Post, ABC, and USA Today, 2011. (See figure C.1.)

| | Journalists | Consumers | | Journalists | Consumers |
|---|---|---|---|---|---|
| CNN | $n$ = 140 | $n$ = 140 | CBS | $n$ = 140 | $n$ = 138 |
| PA | 60% | 33.57% | PA | 57.86% | 38.41% |
| NPA | 40% | 66.43% | NPA | 42.14% | 61.59% |
| | $\chi^2 = 19.64$, d.f. = 1, $p = .000$ | | | $\chi^2 = 10.53$, d.f. = 1, $p = 0.001$ | |
| ABC | $n$ = 140 | $n$ = 139 | Washington Post | $n$ = 140 | $n$ = 65 |
| PA | 47.14% | 19.42% | PA | 67.86% | 58.46% |
| NPA | 52.86% | 80.58% | NPA | 32.14% | 41.54% |
| | $\chi^2 = 24.12$, d.f. = 1, $p = .000$ | | | $\chi^2 = 1.71$, d.f. = 1, $p = 0.19$ | |
| USA Today | $n$ = 140 | $n$ = 70 | | | |
| PA | 52.86% | 18.57% | | | |
| NPA | 47.14% | 81.43% | | | |
| | $\chi^2 = 22.61$, d.f. = 1, $p = .000$ | | | | |

**Table A.81**

Percentage of public-affairs topics in the stories deemed most newsworthy by journalists and the articles most viewed by consumers on CNN, CBS, Washington Post, ABC, and USA Today, 2012. (See figure C.1.)

| | Journalists | Consumers | | Journalists | Consumers |
|---|---|---|---|---|---|
| CNN | $n$ = 140 | $n$ = 139 | CBS | $n$ = 140 | $n$ = 140 |
| PA | 75% | 57.55% | PA | 70% | 71.43% |
| NPA | 25% | 42.45% | NPA | 30% | 28.57% |
| | $\chi^2 = 9.50$, d.f. = 1, $p = .002$ | | | $\chi^2 = 0.069$, d.f. = 1, $p = 0.793$ | |
| ABC | $n$ = 140 | $n$ = 140 | Washington Post | $n$ = 140 | $n$ = 70 |
| PA | 63.57% | 57.86% | PA | 82.86% | 82.86% |
| NPA | 36.43% | 42.14% | NPA | 17.14% | 17.14% |
| | $\chi^2 = 0.96$, d.f. = 1, $p = .328$ | | | $\chi^2 = 0$, d.f. = 1, $p = 1$ | |
| USA Today | $n$ = 140 | $n$ = 97 | | | |
| PA | 62.14% | 48.45% | | | |
| NPA | 37.86% | 51.55% | | | |
| | $\chi^2 = 4.37$, d.f. = 1, $p = .037$ | | | | |

**Table A.82**

Percentage of public-affairs topics in the stories deemed most newsworthy by journalists and the articles most viewed by consumers on CNN, CBS, Washington Post, ABC, and USA Today, 2008, 2009, 2010, 2011 and 2012. (See figure C.2.)

| | Journalists | Consumers | | Journalists | Consumers |
|---|---|---|---|---|---|
| 2008 | $n = 697$ | $n = 685$ | 2009 | $n = 700$ | $n = 699$ |
| PA | 74.61% | 69.34% | PA | 61.14% | 40.92% |
| NPA | 25.39% | 30.66% | NPA | 38.86% | 59.08% |
| | $\chi^2 = 4.75$, d.f. = 1, $p = .029$ | | | $\chi^2 = 57.26$, d.f. = 1, $p < .000$ | |
| 2010 | $n = 696$ | $n = 695$ | 2011 | $n = 700$ | $n = 552$ |
| PA | 61.78% | 49.35% | PA | 57.14% | 32.25% |
| NPA | 38.22% | 50.65% | NPA | 43.86% | 67.75% |
| | $\chi^2 = 21.76$, d.f. = 1, $p < .000$ | | | $\chi^2 = 76.97$, d.f. = 1, $p < .000$ | |
| 2012 | $n = 700$ | $n = 586$ | | | |
| PA | 70.71% | 62.46% | | | |
| NPA | 29.29% | 37.54% | | | |
| | $\chi^2 = 9.83$, d.f. = 1, $p = .002$ | | | | |

**Table A.83**

Gap in format and content choices between most newsworthy stories and most viewed stories on CNN, ABC, CBS, USA Today, and Washington Post, 2008–2012. (See figure C.3.)

| | | Journalists | Consumers | Gap |
|---|---|---|---|---|
| 2008 | CNN | 76.09% | 59.29% | 16.80% |
| | ABC | 64.29% | 66.43% | –2.14% |
| | CBS | 78.42% | 67.20% | 11.22% |
| | Washington Post | 79.29% | 90.71% | –11.42% |
| | USA Today | 75% | 62.86% | 12.14% |
| | Average | 74.62% | 69.30% | 5.32% |
| 2009 | CNN | 57.14% | 30% | 27.14% |
| | ABC | 47.86% | 30% | 17.86% |
| | CBS | 68.57% | 45.71% | 22.86% |
| | WP | 82.14% | 68.57% | 13.57% |
| | USA T | 50% | 30.22% | 19.78% |
| | Average | 61.14% | 40.90% | 20.24% |
| 2010 | CNN | 72.14% | 48.57% | 23.57% |
| | ABC | 39.29% | 32.14% | 7.15% |
| | CBS | 56.43% | 46.67% | 9.76% |
| | WP | 78.99% | 80.00% | –1.01% |
| | USA T | 62.32% | 39.29% | 23.03% |
| | Average | 61.83% | 49.33% | 12.50% |

**Table A.83**
(Continued)

| | | Journalists | Consumers | Gap |
|---|---|---|---|---|
| 2011 | CNN | 60.00% | 33.57% | 26.43% |
| | ABC | 47.14% | 19.42% | 27.72% |
| | CBS | 57.86% | 38.41% | 19.45% |
| | Washington Post | 67.86% | 58.46% | 9.40% |
| | USA Today | 52.86% | 18.57% | 34.29% |
| | Average | 57.14% | 33.69% | 23.45% |
| 2012 | CNN | 75% | 57.55% | 17.45% |
| | ABC | 63.57% | 57.86% | 5.71% |
| | CBS | 70.00% | 71.43% | –1.43% |
| | WP | 82.86% | 82.86% | 0.00% |
| | USA T | 62.14% | 48.45% | 13.69% |
| | Average | 70.71% | 63.63% | 7.08% |

**Table A.84**
Percentage of public-affairs stories on the journalists' and consumers' lists across all sites, 2008 and 2012, weeks 1–18 (Election Day occurred during week 15), 2008 and 2012. (See figure C.4.)

| | 2008 | | 2012 | |
|---|---|---|---|---|
| Week | Journalists | Consumers | Journalists | Consumers |
| 1 | 50% | 38.20% | 48.50% | 33.75% |
| 2 | 50.75% | 41.21% | 47.50% | 36.88% |
| 3 | 55% | 41.85% | 57.50% | 43.40% |
| 4 | 57.50% | 54.35% | 59.67% | 48.54% |
| 5 | 68.67% | 53.60% | 67.33% | 52.30% |
| 6 | 70.56% | 62.55% | 64.80% | 54.77% |
| 7 | 60.50% | 55.96% | 72.80% | 56.50% |
| 8 | 67% | 63.40% | 58.79% | 51.27% |
| 9 | 66% | 70.33% | 51.33% | 35.83% |
| 10 | 69% | 60.94% | 60.50% | 49.10% |
| 11 | 76.88% | 68.75% | 53.60% | 43.69% |
| 12 | 67.84% | 64.58% | 61.20% | 47.39% |
| 13 | 65.46% | 58.26% | 55% | 48.79% |
| 14 | 70.49% | 63.34% | 64.29% | 54.76% |
| 15 | 78.74% | 75.29% | 77.14% | 70.21% |
| 16 | 72.50% | 61.73% | 66% | 47.56% |
| 17 | 67% | 60.73% | 53.77% | 29.70% |
| 18 | 64.67% | 52.03% | 52.84% | 29.22% |

**Table A.85**

Fixed-effects logit regression of "content" on "week" and "site" on the journalists' lists across all sites, weeks 1–15 (Election Day occurred during week 15) of 2008 study. Base cases: CNN for "Site" and week 1 for "Week."

| $N$ = 3391 | Coefficient | % change in odds of a story being about a PA topic | $Z$ | $p$ |
|---|---|---|---|---|
| ABC | –0.52 | –40.6 | –4.52 | 0.00 |
| CBS | 0.04 | 3.7 | 0.30 | 0.76 |
| Washington Post | 0.20 | 22.2 | 1.65 | 0.10 |
| USA Today | –0.24 | –21 | –2.01 | 0.04 |
| Week 2 | 0.03 | 3.3 | 0.13 | 0.90 |
| Week 3 | 0.20 | 22.6 | 0.82 | 0.41 |
| Week 4 | 0.31 | 35.9 | 1.24 | 0.22 |
| Week 5 | 0.80 | 121.8 | 3.36 | 0.00 |
| Week 6 | 0.89 | 142.6 | 3.61 | 0.00 |
| Week 7 | 0.43 | 54.2 | 1.74 | 0.08 |
| Week 8 | 0.72 | 105.3 | 2.85 | 0.00 |
| Week 9 | 0.67 | 96.1 | 2.68 | 0.01 |
| Week 10 | 0.81 | 125.3 | 3.20 | 0.00 |
| Week 11 | 1.22 | 238.7 | 4.64 | 0.00 |
| Week 12 | 0.76 | 113.5 | 3.00 | 0.00 |
| Week 13 | 0.65 | 91.3 | 2.68 | 0.01 |
| Week 14 | 0.88 | 142.1 | 3.78 | 0.00 |
| Week 15 | 1.33 | 277.5 | 5.52 | 0.00 |

**Table A.86**

Fixed-effects logit regression of "content" on "week" and "site" on the consumers' lists across all sites, weeks 1–15 (Election Day occurred during week 15) of 2008 study. Base cases: CNN for "Site" and week 1 for "Week."

| $N$ = 3224 | Coefficient | % change in odds of a story being about a PA topic | $Z$ | $p$ |
|---|---|---|---|---|
| ABC | 0.26 | 30.3 | 2.37 | 0.02 |
| CBS | 0.77 | 115.3 | 6.18 | 0.00 |
| Washington Post | 1.74 | 471.4 | 13.35 | 0.00 |
| USA Today | 0.11 | 11.4 | 0.97 | 0.33 |
| Week 2 | 0.14 | 14.5 | 0.48 | 0.63 |
| Week 3 | 0.17 | 18.0 | 0.59 | 0.55 |
| Week 4 | 0.73 | 106.5 | 2.61 | 0.01 |
| Week 5 | 0.69 | 99.4 | 2.62 | 0.01 |
| Week 6 | 1.09 | 196.7 | 4.03 | 0.00 |
| Week 7 | 0.78 | 119.0 | 2.84 | 0.01 |
| Week 8 | 1.12 | 205.9 | 4.02 | 0.00 |
| Week 9 | 1.47 | 336.0 | 5.16 | 0.00 |
| Week 10 | 1.01 | 174.0 | 3.63 | 0.00 |
| Week 11 | 1.37 | 294.6 | 4.87 | 0.00 |
| Week 12 | 1.18 | 224.2 | 4.21 | 0.00 |
| Week 13 | 0.89 | 142.4 | 3.30 | 0.00 |
| Week 14 | 1.11 | 204.7 | 4.30 | 0.00 |
| Week 15 | 1.72 | 455.8 | 6.48 | 0.00 |

**Table A.87**

Fixed-effects logit regression of "content" on "week" and "site" on journalists' lists across all sites, weeks 1–15 (Election Day occurred during week 15) of 2012 study. Base cases: CNN for "Site," week 1 for "Week."

| *N* = 3749 | Coefficient | % change in odds of a story being about a PA topic | *Z* | *p* |
|---|---|---|---|---|
| ABC | –0.46 | –36.6 | –4.28 | 0.00 |
| CBS | 0.17 | 18.1 | 1.53 | 0.13 |
| Washington Post | 0.69 | 99.9 | 6.00 | 0.00 |
| USA Today | –0.44 | –35.9 | –4.17 | 0.00 |
| Week 2 | –0.04 | –4.1 | –0.21 | 0.84 |
| Week 3 | 0.38 | 46 | 1.84 | 0.07 |
| Week 4 | 0.47 | 60.2 | 2.51 | 0.01 |
| Week 5 | 0.82 | 126.2 | 4.26 | 0.00 |
| Week 6 | 0.70 | 101.2 | 3.53 | 0.00 |
| Week 7 | 1.09 | 196.4 | 5.31 | 0.00 |
| Week 8 | 0.44 | 54.8 | 2.12 | 0.03 |
| Week 9 | 0.12 | 12.6 | 0.54 | 0.59 |
| Week 10 | 0.51 | 66.1 | 2.46 | 0.01 |
| Week 11 | 0.21 | 23.8 | 1.10 | 0.27 |
| Week 12 | 0.54 | 71.3 | 2.74 | 0.01 |
| Week 13 | 0.27 | 31.3 | 1.46 | 0.15 |
| Week 14 | 0.68 | 96.5 | 3.67 | 0.00 |
| Week 15 | 1.33 | 276.4 | 6.83 | 0.00 |

**Table A.88**

Fixed-effects logit regression of "content" on "week" and "site" on the consumers' lists across all sites, weeks 1–15 (Election Day occurred during week 15) of 2012 study. Base cases: CNN for "Site," week 1 for "Week."

| $N$ = 3052 | Coefficient | % change in odds of a story being about a PA topic | $Z$ | $p$ |
|---|---|---|---|---|
| ABC | –0.73 | –51.7 | –6.77 | 0.00 |
| CBS | –0.08 | –8.1 | –0.79 | 0.43 |
| Washington Post | 0.92 | 150.3 | 6.44 | 0.00 |
| USA Today | –0.84 | –56.6 | –6.59 | 0.00 |
| Week 2 | 0.15 | 15.8 | 0.61 | 0.55 |
| Week 3 | 0.44 | 54.9 | 1.83 | 0.07 |
| Week 4 | 0.66 | 93.4 | 3.02 | 0.00 |
| Week 5 | 0.82 | 127.1 | 3.75 | 0.00 |
| Week 6 | 0.93 | 152.5 | 4.08 | 0.00 |
| Week 7 | 1.00 | 171.9 | 4.40 | 0.00 |
| Week 8 | 0.78 | 118.9 | 3.28 | 0.00 |
| Week 9 | 0.10 | 10.3 | 0.38 | 0.71 |
| Week 10 | 0.71 | 103.5 | 3.01 | 0.00 |
| Week 11 | 0.47 | 60.5 | 2.09 | 0.04 |
| Week 12 | 0.64 | 90.4 | 2.87 | 0.00 |
| Week 13 | 0.69 | 100.2 | 3.19 | 0.00 |
| Week 14 | 0.96 | 161.1 | 4.54 | 0.00 |
| Week 15 | 1.66 | 424.9 | 7.62 | 0.00 |

**Table A.89**

Percentage of straight news, feature-style, commentary, blogs, and UGC in the stories deemed most newsworthy by journalists on CNN, ABC, CBS, Washington Post, and USA Today, 2008–2012. (See figure C.5.)

| | | Straight News | Feature | Commentary | Blog | UGC | other |
|---|---|---|---|---|---|---|---|
| 2008 | CNN | 57.97% | 10.87% | 9.42% | 13.77% | 4.35% | 3.62% |
| | ABC | 50.00% | 34.29% | 0.71% | 12.14% | 0.00% | 2.86% |
| | CBS | 77.70% | 16.55% | 0.72% | 4.32% | 0.00% | 0.72% |
| | Washington Post | 35.00% | 25.71% | 13.57% | 15.00% | 2.86% | 7.86% |
| | USA Today | 80.00% | 10.71% | 0.00% | 8.57% | 0.00% | 0.71% |
| 2009 | CNN | 69.29% | 20.00% | 3.57% | 6.43% | 0% | 0.71% |
| | ABC | 58.57% | 30.71% | 0.71% | 9.29% | 0.00% | 0.71% |
| | CBS | 87.86% | 10.71% | 0.00% | 0.71% | 0.00% | 0.71% |
| | Washington Post | 47.86% | 12.14% | 17.86% | 10.00% | 5.00% | 7.14% |
| | USA Today | 59.29% | 15.00% | 0.71% | 18.57% | 0.00% | 6.43% |
| 2010 | CNN | 67.86% | 13.57% | 4.29% | 8.57% | 0% | 5.71% |
| | ABC | 67.14% | 26.43% | 0.71% | 2.86% | 0% | 2.86% |
| | CBS | 82.14% | 8.57% | 0.71% | 7.86% | 0% | 0.71% |
| | Washington Post | 36.23% | 15.94% | 19.57% | 16.67% | 1.45% | 10.14% |
| | USA Today | 53.62% | 8.70% | 4.35% | 31.88% | 0% | 1.45% |
| 2011 | CNN | 48.57% | 23.57% | 5.71% | 18.57% | 0% | 3.57% |
| | ABC | 48.20% | 12.23% | 0% | 36.69% | 0% | 2.88% |
| | CBS | 64.29% | 7.14% | 0% | 25.71% | 0% | 2.86% |
| | Washington Post | 44.29% | 17.86% | 11.43% | 23.57% | 0% | 2.86% |
| | USA Today | 52.14% | 15.71% | 0.71% | 30.71% | 0% | 0.71% |
| 2012 | CNN | 25.00% | 35.71% | 16.43% | 20% | 0.71% | 2.14% |
| | ABC | 52.86% | 18.57% | 2.86% | 25.71% | 0 | 0% |
| | CBS | 64.29% | 27.14% | 5.71% | 0.71% | 0 | 2.14% |
| | Washington Post | 46.43% | 29.29% | 17.14% | 5% | 0.71% | 1.43% |
| | USA Today | 64.29% | 30% | 0% | 0 | 0 | 4.29% |

**Table A.90**

Percentage of straight news, feature-style, commentary, blogs, and UGC in the stories most viewed by consumers on CNN, ABC, CBS, Washington Post, and USA Today, 2008–2012. (See figure C.6.)

| | | Straight News | Feature | Commentary | Blog | UGC | other |
|---|---|---|---|---|---|---|---|
| 2008 | CNN | 57.86% | 27.14% | 11.43% | 0% | 1.43% | 2.14% |
| | ABC | 52.86% | 40.00% | 3.57% | 0.00% | 0.00% | 3.57% |
| | CBS | 60.80% | 30.40% | 4.00% | 0.80% | 0.00% | 4.00% |
| | Washington Post | 28.57% | 22.86% | 44.29% | 0.00% | 0.71% | 3.57% |
| | USA Today | 59.29% | 16.43% | 1.43% | 6.43% | 0.00% | 16.43% |
| 2009 | CNN | 62.86% | 30.00% | 5.00% | 0% | 0% | 2.14% |
| | ABC | 60.00% | 40.00% | 0.00% | 0.00% | 0.00% | 0.00% |
| | CBS | 64.29% | 31.43% | 1.43% | 0.00% | 0.00% | 2.86% |
| | Washington Post | 49.29% | 22.86% | 21.43% | 0.00% | 0.00% | 6.43% |
| | USA Today | 53.96% | 14.39% | 2.16% | 25.90% | 0.00% | 3.60% |
| 2010 | CNN | 70.71% | 22.14% | 4.29% | 0% | 0% | 2.86% |
| | ABC | 63.57% | 36.43% | 0% | 0% | 0% | 0% |
| | CBS | 65.93% | 11.11% | 0.74% | 21.48% | 0% | 0.74% |
| | Washington Post | 54.29% | 15.71% | 25.71% | 2.14% | 0.71% | 1.43% |
| | USA Today | 38.57% | 7.14% | 4.29% | 45.71% | 0% | 4.29% |
| 2011 | CNN | 45% | 44.29% | 7.86% | 1.43% | 0% | 1.43% |
| | ABC | 42.45% | 20.14% | 0% | 36.69% | 0% | 0.72% |
| | CBS | 48.55% | 14.49% | 0% | 36.23% | 0% | 0.72% |
| | Washington Post | 35.38% | 16.92% | 27.69% | 20% | 0% | 0% |
| | USA Today | 38.57% | 27.14% | 0% | 34.29% | 0% | 0% |
| 2012 | CNN | 37.41% | 47.76% | 12.95% | 0.72% | 0 | 2.16% |
| | ABC | 46.53% | 14.29% | 1.43% | 33.57% | 0 | 4.29% |
| | CBS | 60.71% | 30% | 5.71% | 0.71% | 0 | 1.43% |
| | Washington Post | 35.71% | 24.29% | 27.14% | 10% | 0 | 2.86% |
| | USA Today | 58.76% | 38.14% | 1.03% | 0 | 0 | 2.06% |

**Table A.91**

Percentage of straight news, feature-style, commentary, blog, and other story-telling styles in the blog items deemed most newsworthy by journalists on the five sites combined, 2008, 2009, 2010, 2011, and 2012. (See figure C.7.)

| | Straight News | Feature | Commentary | Blog | Other |
|---|---|---|---|---|---|
| 2008 (*N* = 75) | 54.67% | 4% | 4% | 33.33% | 4% |
| 2009 (*N* = 63) | 69.84% | 0% | 6.35% | 23.81% | 0% |
| 2010 (*N* = 94) | 69.15% | 3.19% | 5.32% | 21.28% | 1.06% |
| 2011 (*N* = 185) | 78.38% | 5.95% | 5.41% | 10.27% | 0% |
| 2012 (*N* = 71) | 74.65% | 2.82% | 5.63% | 16.90% | 0% |

**Table A.92**

Percentage of straight news, feature-style, commentary, blog, and other story-telling styles in the blog items most viewed by consumers on the five sites combined, 2008, 2009, 2010, 2011, and 2012. (See figure C.7.)

| | Straight News | Feature | Commentary | Blog | Other |
|---|---|---|---|---|---|
| 2008 (*N* = 30) | 66.67% | 0% | 0% | 33.33% | 0 |
| 2009 (*N* = 36) | 61.11% | 0% | 0% | 38.89% | 0 |
| 2010 (*N* = 96) | 76.04% | 3.13% | 1.04% | 18.75% | 1.04% |
| 2011 (*N* = 134) | 76.12% | 0% | 4.48% | 19.40% | 0 |
| 2012 (*N* = 57) | 71.93% | 0% | 0% | 26.32% | 1.75% |

**Table A.93**

Percentage of straight news, feature-style, commentary, blogs, UCG, and other storytelling styles in the stories deemed most newsworthy by journalists on the five sites combined, 2008, 2009, 2010, 2011, and 2012. (See figure C.9.)

| | Straight News | Feature | Commentary | Blog | UGC | Other |
|---|---|---|---|---|---|---|
| 2008 (*N* = 697) | 66% | 20.09% | 5.31% | 3.59% | 1.43% | 3.59% |
| 2009 (*N* = 700) | 71.14% | 17.71% | 5.14% | 1.86% | 1% | 3.14% |
| 2010 (*N* = 696) | 70.83% | 15.09% | 6.61% | 2.87% | 0.29% | 4.31% |
| 2011 (*N* = 700) | 72.71% | 16.86% | 5.14% | 2.71% | 0% | 2.57% |
| 2012 (*N* = 700) | 58.29% | 28.29% | 9.29% | 1.71% | 0.29% | 2.14% |

**Table A.94**

Percentage of straight news, feature-style, commentary, blogs, UCG and other storytelling styles in the stories most viewed by consumers on the five sites combined, 2008, 2009, 2010, 2011, and 2012. (See figure C.9.)

| | Straight News | Feature | Commentary | Blog | UGC | Other |
|---|---|---|---|---|---|---|
| 2008 (*N* = 685) | 51.68% | 27.30% | 13.14% | 1.46% | 0.44% | 5.99% |
| 2009 (*N* = 699) | 61.23% | 27.75% | 6.01% | 2% | 0 | 3% |
| 2010 (*N* = 695) | 69.06% | 18.99% | 7.19% | 2.59% | 0.14% | 2.01% |
| 2011 (*N* = 552) | 62.75% | 25.32% | 6.51% | 4.70% | 0 | 0.72% |
| 2012 (*N* = 586) | 55.46% | 30.89% | 8.36% | 2.56% | 0 | 2.73% |

**Table A.95**

Gaps in format and content choices between journalists and consumers, United States, 2008. (See figure C.10.)

| | Journalists | Consumers | Gap |
|---|---|---|---|
| Straight News—PA | 48.49% | 34.74% | 13.75% |
| | $\chi^2 = 26.87$, d.f. = 1, $p < .000$[a] | | |
| Straight News—NPA | 17.50% | 16.93% | 0.57% |
| | $\chi^2 = 0.08$, d.f. = 1, $p = .779$[b] | | |
| Features—PA | 13.92% | 16.64% | –2.72% |
| | $\chi^2 = 1.98$, d.f. = 1, $p = .16$[c] | | |
| Features—NPA | 6.17% | 10.66% | –4.49% |
| | $\chi^2 = 9.05$, d.f. = 1, $p = .003$[d] | | |
| Commentary—PA | 4.73% | 12.99% | –8.26% |
| | $\chi^2 = 29.27$, d.f. = 1, $p < .000$[e] | | |
| Commentary—NPA | 0.57% | 0.15% | 0.42% |
| | $\chi^2 = 1.75$, d.f. = 1, $p < .185$[f] | | |
| Blog—PA | 3.16% | 0.44% | 2.72% |
| | $\chi^2 = 14.37$, d.f. = 1, $p < .000$[g] | | |
| Blog—NPA | 0.43% | 1.02% | –0.59% |
| | $\chi^2 = 1.68$, d.f. = 1, $p = .195$[h] | | |

a. To apply the $\chi^2$ test, categories were collapsed to straight news/public affairs and all other format/content combinations.

b. To apply the $\chi^2$ test, categories were collapsed to straight news/non-public-affairs and all other format/content combinations.

c. To apply the $\chi^2$ test, categories were collapsed to features/public affairs and all other format/content combinations.

d. To apply the $\chi^2$ test, categories were collapsed to features/non-public-affairs and all other format/content combinations.

e. To apply the $\chi^2$ test, categories were collapsed to commentary/public affairs and all other format/content combinations.

f. To apply the $\chi^2$ test, categories were collapsed to commentary/non-public-affairs and all other format/content combinations.

g. To apply the $\chi^2$ test, categories were collapsed to blog/public affairs and all other format/content combinations.

h. To apply the $\chi^2$ test, categories were collapsed to blog/non-public-affairs and all other format/content combinations.

**Table A.96**

Gaps in format and content choices between journalists and consumers, United States, 2009. (See figure C.10.)

| | Journalists | Consumers | Gap |
|---|---|---|---|
| Straight News—PA | 44.86% | 25.32% | 19.54% |
| | $\chi^2 = 58.60$, d.f. = 1, $p < .000$[a] | | |
| Straight News—NPA | 26.39% | 35.91% | 9.52% |
| | $\chi^2 = 15.12$, d.f. = 1, $p < .000$[b] | | |
| Features—PA | 8.29% | 11.16% | –2.87% |
| | $\chi^2 = 3.29$, d.f. = 1, $p = .070$[c] | | |
| Features—NPA | 9.43% | 16.60% | –7.17% |
| | $\chi^2 = 15.87$, d.f. = 1, $p < .000$[d] | | |
| Commentary—PA | 4.29% | 3.43% | 0.86% |
| | $\chi^2 = .68$, d.f. = 1, $p = .408$[e] | | |
| Commentary—NPA | 0.86% | 2.58% | –1.72% |
| | $\chi^2 = 6.12$, d.f. = 1, $p = .013$[f] | | |
| Blog—PA | 1.29% | 1.29% | 0% |
| | $\chi^2 = 0$, d.f. = 1, $p = .998$[g] | | |
| Blog—NPA | 1.58% | 1.29% | 0.29% |
| | $\chi^2 = 0.200$, d.f. = 1, $p = .655$[h] | | |

a. To apply the $\chi^2$ test, categories were collapsed to straight news/public affairs and all other format/content combinations.

b. To apply the $\chi^2$ test, categories were collapsed to straight news/non-public-affairs and all other format/content combinations.

c. To apply the $\chi^2$ test, categories were collapsed to features/public affairs and all other format/content combinations.

d. To apply the $\chi^2$ test, categories were collapsed to features/non-public-affairs and all other format/content combinations.

e. To apply the $\chi^2$ test, categories were collapsed to commentary/public affairs and all other format/content combinations.

f. To apply the $\chi^2$ test, categories were collapsed to commentary/non-public-affairs and all other format/content combinations.

g. To apply the $\chi^2$ test, categories were collapsed to blog/public affairs and all other format/content combinations.

h. To apply the $\chi^2$ test, categories were collapsed to blog/non-public-affairs and all other format/content combinations.

**Table A.97**

Gaps in format and content choices between journalists and consumers, United States, 2010. (See figure C.10.)

| | Journalists | Consumers | Gap |
|---|---|---|---|
| Straight News—PA | 44.25% | 32.37% | 11.88% |
| | $\chi^2 = 20.76$, d.f. = 1, $p < .000$[a] | | |
| Straight News—NPA | 26.68% | 36.69% | −10.01% |
| | $\chi^2 = 16.44$, d.f. = 1, $p < .000$[b] | | |
| Features—PA | 8.76% | 8.92% | −0.16% |
| | $\chi^2 = 0.11$, d.f. = 1, $p = .918$[c] | | |
| Features—NPA | 6.32% | 10.07% | −3.75% |
| | $\chi^2 = 6.50$, d.f. = 1, $p = .011$[d] | | |
| Commentary—PA | 5.03% | 6.33% | −1.30% |
| | $\chi^2 = 1.10$, d.f. = 1, $p = .294$[e] | | |
| Commentary—NPA | 1.58% | 0.86% | 0.72% |
| | $\chi^2 = 1.48$, d.f. = 1, $p = .224$[f] | | |
| Blog—PA | 1.71% | 0.14% | 1.57% |
| | $\chi^2 = 9.38$, d.f. = 1, $p = .002$[g] | | |
| Blog—NPA | 0.14% | 1.86% | −1.72% |
| | $\chi^2 = 10.41$, d.f. = 1, $p = .001$[h] | | |

a. To apply the $\chi^2$ test, categories were collapsed to straight news/public affairs and all other format/content combinations.
b. To apply the $\chi^2$ test, categories were collapsed to straight news/non-public-affairs and all other format/content combinations.
c. To apply the $\chi^2$ test, categories were collapsed to features/public affairs and all other format/content combinations.
d. To apply the $\chi^2$ test, categories were collapsed to features/non-public-affairs and all other format/content combinations.
e. To apply the $\chi^2$ test, categories were collapsed to commentary/public affairs and all other format/content combinations.
f. To apply the $\chi^2$ test, categories were collapsed to commentary/non-public-affairs and all other format/content combinations.
g. To apply the $\chi^2$ test, categories were collapsed to blog/public affairs and all other format/content combinations.
h. To apply the $\chi^2$ test, categories were collapsed to blog/non-public-affairs and all other format/content combinations.

**Table A.98**

Gaps in format and content choices between journalists and consumers, United States, 2011. (See figure C.10.)

| | Journalists | Consumers | Gap |
|---|---|---|---|
| Straight News—PA | 43.43% | 20.07% | 23.36% |
| | $\chi^2 = 76.08$, d.f. = 1, $p < .000$[a] | | |
| Straight News—NPA | 29.29% | 42.50% | –13.21% |
| | $\chi^2 = 23.66$, d.f. = 1, $p < .000$[b] | | |
| Features—PA | 7.86% | 5.61% | 2.25% |
| | $\chi^2 = 2.45$, d.f. = 1, $p = .118$[c] | | |
| Features—NPA | 9% | 19.71% | –10.71% |
| | $\chi^2 = 29.93$, d.f. = 1, $p < .000$[d] | | |
| Commentary—PA | 3.86% | 5.06% | –1.20% |
| | $\chi^2 = 1.07$, d.f. = 1, $p = .301$[e] | | |
| Commentary—NPA | 1.29% | 1.45% | –0.16% |
| | $\chi^2 = 0.06$, d.f. = 1, $p = .807$[f] | | |
| Blog—PA | 1.43% | 1.27% | 0.16% |
| | $\chi^2 = 0.611$, d.f. = 1, $p = .805$[g] | | |
| Blog—NPA | 1.29% | 3.44% | –2.15% |
| | $\chi^2 = 6.54$, d.f. = 1, $p = .011$[h] | | |

a. To apply the $\chi^2$ test, categories were collapsed to straight news/public affairs and all other format/content combinations.

b. To apply the $\chi^2$ test, categories were collapsed to straight news/non-public-affairs and all other format/content combinations.

c. To apply the $\chi^2$ test, categories were collapsed to features/public affairs and all other format/content combinations.

d. To apply the $\chi^2$ test, categories were collapsed to features/non-public-affairs and all other format/content combinations.

e. To apply the $\chi^2$ test, categories were collapsed to commentary/public affairs and all other format/content combinations.

f. To apply the $\chi^2$ test, categories were collapsed to commentary/non-public-affairs and all other format/content combinations.

g. To apply the $\chi^2$ test, categories were collapsed to blog/public affairs and all other format/content combinations.

h. To apply the $\chi^2$ test, categories were collapsed to blog/non-public-affairs and all other format/content combinations.

**Table A.99**

Gaps in format and content choices between journalists and consumers, United States, 2012. (See figure C.10.)

| | Journalists | Consumers | Gap |
|---|---|---|---|
| Straight News—PA | 40.43% | 33.79% | 6.64% |
| | $\chi^2 = 6.01$, d.f. = 1, $p < .000$[a] | | |
| Straight News—NPA | 17.86% | 21.67% | -3.81% |
| | $\chi^2 = 2.95$, d.f. = 1, $p < .086$[b] | | |
| Features—PA | 19.57% | 17.75% | 1.82% |
| | $\chi^2 = 0.70$, d.f. = 1, $p = .404$[c] | | |
| Features—NPA | 8.71% | 13.14% | −4.43% |
| | $\chi^2 = 6.52$, d.f. = 1, $p = .011$[d] | | |
| Commentary—PA | 7.43% | 7.68% | −0.25% |
| | $\chi^2 = 0.03$, d.f. = 1, $p = .865$[e] | | |
| Commentary—NPA | 1.86% | 0.68% | 1.18% |
| | $\chi^2 = 3.37$, d.f. = 1, $p = .066$[f] | | |
| Blog—PA | 1.57% | 1.88% | −0.31% |
| | $\chi^2 = 0.18$, d.f. = 1, $p = .674$[g] | | |
| Blog—NPA | 0.14% | 0.68% | −0.54% |
| | $\chi^2 = 2.40$, d.f. = 1, $p = .121$[h] | | |

a. To apply the $\chi^2$ test, categories were collapsed to straight news/public affairs and all other format/content combinations.
b. To apply the $\chi^2$ test, categories were collapsed to straight news/non-public-affairs and all other format/content combinations.
c. To apply the $\chi^2$ test, categories were collapsed to features/public affairs and all other format/content combinations.
d. To apply the $\chi^2$ test, categories were collapsed to features/non-public-affairs and all other format/content combinations.
e. To apply the $\chi^2$ test, categories were collapsed to commentary/public affairs and all other format/content combinations.
f. To apply the $\chi^2$ test, categories were collapsed to commentary/non-public-affairs and all other format/content combinations.
g. To apply the $\chi^2$ test, categories were collapsed to blog/public affairs and all other format/content combinations.
h. To apply the $\chi^2$ test, categories were collapsed to blog/non-public-affairs and all other format/content combinations.

**Table A.100**

Fixed-effects logit regression of "straight news" on "week" and "site" on the journalists' lists across all sites, weeks 1–15 (Election Day occurred during week 15) of 2012 study. Base cases: CNN for "Site," week 1 for "Week."

| *N* = 3749 | Coefficient | % change in odds of a story being told as straight news | *Z* | *p* |
|---|---|---|---|---|
| ABC | 0.98 | 166.6 | 9.18 | 0.00 |
| CBS | 1.22 | 239.9 | 11.28 | 0.00 |
| Washington Post | 0.57 | 76.2 | 5.36 | 0.00 |
| USA Today | 0.67 | 95.1 | 6.32 | 0.00 |
| Week 2 | 0.09 | 8.9 | 0.41 | 0.68 |
| Week 3 | –0.17 | –15.5 | –0.82 | 0.41 |
| Week 4 | –0.28 | –24.4 | –1.49 | 0.14 |
| Week 5 | –0.24 | –21.2 | –1.27 | 0.20 |
| Week 6 | –0.26 | –22.9 | –1.34 | 0.18 |
| Week 7 | 0.13 | 13.8 | 0.66 | 0.51 |
| Week 8 | –0.34 | –28.5 | –1.64 | 0.10 |
| Week 9 | –0.10 | –9.4 | –0.44 | 0.66 |
| Week 10 | 0.02 | 2.2 | 0.10 | 0.92 |
| Week 11 | 0.08 | 8 | 0.39 | 0.70 |
| Week 12 | –0.06 | –5.8 | –0.30 | 0.76 |
| Week 13 | –0.36 | –30.5 | –1.94 | 0.05 |
| Week 14 | –0.32 | –27.2 | –1.74 | 0.08 |
| Week 15 | –0.22 | –19.9 | –1.22 | 0.22 |

**Table A.101**

Fixed-effects logit regression of "features" on "week" and "site" on the journalists' lists across all sites, weeks 1–15 (Election Day occurred during week 15) of 2012 study. Base cases: CNN for "Site," week 1 for "Week."

| *N* = 3749 | Coefficient | % change in odds of a story being told in feature style | *Z* | *p* |
|---|---|---|---|---|
| ABC | –0.84 | –57 | –6.47 | 0.00 |
| CBS | –0.48 | –38.3 | –3.96 | 0.00 |
| Washington Post | –0.21 | –19.1 | –1.81 | 0.07 |
| USA Today | –0.21 | –18.6 | –1.75 | 0.08 |
| Week 2 | –0.30 | –25.6 | –1.21 | 0.23 |
| Week 3 | –0.30 | –25.6 | –1.21 | 0.23 |
| Week 4 | –0.24 | –21.6 | –1.11 | 0.27 |
| Week 5 | –0.16 | –14.9 | –0.74 | 0.46 |
| Week 6 | –0.07 | –7 | –0.32 | 0.75 |

**Table A.101**
(Continued)

| *N* = 3749 | Coefficient | % change in odds of a story being told in feature style | *Z* | *p* |
|---|---|---|---|---|
| Week 7 | –0.80 | –55.2 | –3.18 | 0.00 |
| Week 8 | –0.23 | –20.8 | –0.96 | 0.34 |
| Week 9 | –0.64 | –47.4 | –2.26 | 0.02 |
| Week 10 | –0.06 | –5.4 | –0.24 | 0.81 |
| Week 11 | –0.10 | –9.1 | –0.43 | 0.67 |
| Week 12 | 0.12 | 13 | 0.56 | 0.58 |
| Week 13 | 0.27 | 30.5 | 1.27 | 0.20 |
| Week 14 | 0.23 | 25.4 | 1.11 | 0.27 |
| Week 15 | 0.15 | 16.7 | 0.76 | 0.45 |

**Table A.102**
Fixed-effects logit regression of "commentary" on "week" and "site" on the journalists' lists across all sites, weeks 1–15 (Election Day occurred during week 15) of 2012 study. Base cases: CNN for "Site," week 1 for "Week."

| *N* = 3749 | Coefficient | % change in odds of a story being told in commentary style | *Z* | *p* |
|---|---|---|---|---|
| ABC | –2.73 | –93.5 | –6.40 | 0.00 |
| CBS | –1.56 | –79 | –5.98 | 0.00 |
| Washington Post | 0.39 | 48.1 | 2.52 | 0.01 |
| USA Today | –1.95 | –85.7 | –6.41 | 0.00 |
| Week 2 | –0.27 | –23.9 | –0.64 | 0.52 |
| Week 3 | –0.62 | –46.3 | –1.34 | 0.18 |
| Week 4 | –0.06 | –5.4 | –0.15 | 0.88 |
| Week 5 | –0.38 | –31.5 | –0.96 | 0.34 |
| Week 6 | –0.52 | –40.5 | –1.22 | 0.22 |
| Week 7 | –0.42 | –34.5 | –1.02 | 0.31 |
| Week 8 | –0.27 | –23.9 | –0.64 | 0.52 |
| Week 9 | –0.62 | –46.3 | –1.22 | 0.22 |
| Week 10 | –0.27 | –23.9 | –0.64 | 0.52 |
| Week 11 | 0.03 | 3.3 | 0.09 | 0.93 |
| Week 12 | –0.03 | –3.3 | –0.09 | 0.93 |
| Week 13 | –0.06 | –5.4 | –0.15 | 0.88 |
| Week 14 | 0.39 | 47.2 | 1.13 | 0.26 |
| Week 15 | 0.11 | 11.9 | 0.32 | 0.75 |

**Table A.103**

Fixed-effects logit regression of "blog" on "week" and "site" on the journalists' lists across all sites, weeks 1–15 (Election Day occurred during week 15) of 2012 study. Base cases: CNN for "Site," week 1 for "Week."

| *N* = 3749 | Coefficient | % change in odds of a story being told in blog format | *Z* | *p* |
|---|---|---|---|---|
| ABC | 0.12 | 12.9 | 0.95 | 0.34 |
| CBS | –0.88 | –58.3 | –5.74 | 0.00 |
| Washington Post | –1.12 | –67.4 | –6.89 | 0.00 |
| USA Today | –0.16 | –14.5 | –1.19 | 0.24 |
| Week 2 | 0.47 | 60.4 | 1.52 | 0.13 |
| Week 3 | 1.04 | 184.3 | 3.57 | 0.00 |
| Week 4 | 0.94 | 154.9 | 3.38 | 0.00 |
| Week 5 | 0.94 | 154.9 | 3.38 | 0.00 |
| Week 6 | 0.91 | 147.7 | 3.18 | 0.00 |
| Week 7 | 0.98 | 166.5 | 3.46 | 0.00 |
| Week 8 | 1.04 | 184.3 | 3.57 | 0.00 |
| Week 9 | 1.15 | 215.2 | 3.76 | 0.00 |
| Week 10 | 0.26 | 29.2 | 0.80 | 0.43 |
| Week 11 | –0.09 | –9 | –0.29 | 0.77 |
| Week 12 | 0.00 | 0 | 0.00 | 1.00 |
| Week 13 | 0.30 | 35.3 | 1.03 | 0.31 |
| Week 14 | 0.06 | 6.5 | 0.21 | 0.83 |
| Week 15 | 0.00 | 0 | 0.00 | 1.00 |

**Table A.104**

Fixed-effects logit regression of "straight news" on "week" and "site" on the consumers' lists across all sites, weeks 1–15 (Election Day occurred during week 15) of 2012 study. Base cases: CNN for "Site," week 1 for "Week."

| *N* = 3052 | Coefficient | % change in odds of a story being told as straight news | *Z* | *p* |
|---|---|---|---|---|
| ABC | –0.18 | –16.7 | –1.76 | 0.08 |
| CBS | 0.06 | 6.3 | 0.59 | 0.55 |
| Washington Post | –0.65 | –47.6 | –4.97 | 0.00 |
| USA Today | –0.33 | –28.4 | –2.75 | 0.01 |
| Week 2 | 0.03 | 2.6 | 0.11 | 0.91 |
| Week 3 | –0.08 | –7.4 | –0.34 | 0.73 |
| Week 4 | 0.15 | 16.5 | 0.74 | 0.46 |
| Week 5 | 0.15 | 16.5 | 0.74 | 0.46 |
| Week 6 | –0.06 | –5.5 | –0.26 | 0.79 |

**Table A.104**
(Continued)

| *N* = 3052 | Coefficient | % change in odds of a story being told as straight news | *Z* | *p* |
|---|---|---|---|---|
| Week 7 | 0.32 | 37.7 | 1.49 | 0.14 |
| Week 8 | 0.14 | 15.1 | 0.62 | 0.53 |
| Week 9 | –0.16 | –15 | –0.66 | 0.51 |
| Week 10 | 0.39 | 48 | 1.75 | 0.08 |
| Week 11 | 0.24 | 27.6 | 1.15 | 0.25 |
| Week 12 | 0.33 | 39.3 | 1.57 | 0.12 |
| Week 13 | 0.07 | 7.3 | 0.35 | 0.73 |
| Week 14 | 0.10 | 11.1 | 0.53 | 0.60 |
| Week 15 | 0.14 | 15.4 | 0.72 | 0.47 |

**Table A.105**
Fixed-effects logit regression of "features" on "week" and "site" on the consumers' lists across all sites, weeks 1–15 (Election Day occurred during week 15) of 2012 study. Base cases: CNN for "Site," week 1 for "Week."

| *N* = 3052 | Coefficient | % change in odds of a story being told in feature style | *Z* | *p* |
|---|---|---|---|---|
| ABC | –0.66 | –48.3 | –5.61 | 0.00 |
| CBS | –0.49 | –38.7 | –4.26 | 0.00 |
| Washington Post | –0.39 | –32.2 | –2.77 | 0.01 |
| USA Today | –0.13 | –12.4 | –1.03 | 0.30 |
| Week 2 | –0.59 | –44.8 | –2.47 | 0.01 |
| Week 3 | –0.66 | –48.2 | –2.72 | 0.01 |
| Week 4 | –0.82 | –55.8 | –3.67 | 0.00 |
| Week 5 | –0.80 | –54.9 | –3.59 | 0.00 |
| Week 6 | –0.78 | –54 | –3.36 | 0.00 |
| Week 7 | –0.92 | –60.3 | –3.92 | 0.00 |
| Week 8 | –0.89 | –58.7 | –3.54 | 0.00 |
| Week 9 | –1.05 | –64.9 | –3.73 | 0.00 |
| Week 10 | –0.54 | –41.9 | –2.30 | 0.02 |
| Week 11 | –0.53 | –40.9 | –2.35 | 0.02 |
| Week 12 | –0.50 | –39.1 | –2.24 | 0.03 |
| Week 13 | –0.40 | –33.2 | –1.90 | 0.06 |
| Week 14 | –0.55 | –42.2 | –2.64 | 0.01 |
| Week 15 | –0.39 | –32.3 | –1.90 | 0.06 |

**Table A.106**

Fixed-effects logit regression of "commentary" on "week" and "site" on the consumers' lists across all sites, weeks 1–15 (Election Day occurred during week 15) of 2012 study. Base cases: CNN for "Site," week 1 for "Week."

| *N* = 3052 | Coefficient | % change in odds of a story being told in commentary style | *Z* | *p* |
|---|---|---|---|---|
| ABC | –2.17 | –88.6 | –6.38 | 0.00 |
| CBS | –1.63 | –80.4 | –5.95 | 0.00 |
| Washington Post | 0.99 | 168.6 | 5.71 | 0.00 |
| USA Today | –2.18 | –88.7 | –5.08 | 0.00 |
| Week 2 | 0.89 | 144.2 | 1.42 | 0.16 |
| Week 3 | 1.50 | 350.3 | 2.54 | 0.01 |
| Week 4 | 1.02 | 178.1 | 1.74 | 0.08 |
| Week 5 | 0.56 | 74.3 | 0.91 | 0.37 |
| Week 6 | 0.87 | 138.5 | 1.43 | 0.15 |
| Week 7 | 0.64 | 89.7 | 1.02 | 0.31 |
| Week 8 | 0.45 | 56.6 | 0.67 | 0.50 |
| Week 9 | 1.09 | 197.6 | 1.70 | 0.09 |
| Week 10 | 0.43 | 53.6 | 0.64 | 0.52 |
| Week 11 | 1.77 | 485.9 | 3.11 | 0.00 |
| Week 12 | 1.30 | 265.3 | 2.22 | 0.03 |
| Week 13 | 1.29 | 262.8 | 2.24 | 0.03 |
| Week 14 | 1.44 | 320.9 | 2.56 | 0.01 |
| Week 15 | 1.33 | 278.3 | 2.35 | 0.02 |

**Table A.107**

Fixed-effects logit regression of "blog" on "week" and "site" on the consumers' lists across all sites, weeks 1–15 (Election Day occurred during week 15) of 2012 study. Base cases: CNN for "Site," week 1 for "Week."

| $N$ = 3052 | Coefficient | % change in odds of a story being told in blog format | $Z$ | $p$ |
|---|---|---|---|---|
| ABC | 4.20 | 6535.9 | 8.24 | 0.00 |
| CBS | 3.76 | 4178 | 7.35 | 0.00 |
| Washington Post | 3.18 | 2314.9 | 6.02 | 0.00 |
| USA Today | 3.94 | 5032.6 | 7.62 | 0.00 |
| Week 2 | 0.74 | 108.8 | 2.14 | 0.03 |
| Week 3 | 0.78 | 118.5 | 2.28 | 0.02 |
| Week 4 | 0.75 | 112 | 2.34 | 0.02 |
| Week 5 | 0.93 | 154.4 | 2.94 | 0.00 |
| Week 6 | 1.11 | 203 | 3.43 | 0.00 |
| Week 7 | 0.83 | 130.4 | 2.54 | 0.01 |
| Week 8 | 1.08 | 193.4 | 3.21 | 0.00 |
| Week 9 | 1.34 | 282.1 | 3.85 | 0.00 |
| Week 10 | –0.22 | –19.8 | –0.56 | 0.57 |
| Week 11 | –0.46 | –36.7 | –1.17 | 0.24 |
| Week 12 | –0.41 | –33.6 | –1.07 | 0.28 |
| Week 13 | 0.04 | 4 | 0.12 | 0.91 |
| Week 14 | 0.14 | 15.5 | 0.44 | 0.66 |
| Week 15 | –0.24 | –21.6 | –0.70 | 0.48 |

# Notes

## Chapter 1

1. See Park 1981 [1940].

2. See Lippmann 1922 and 1925.

3. See Dewey 1927.

4. See ibid., p. 176.

5. The disregard for consumers' preferences was evident mostly in the behavior of journalists working in mainstream, quality organizations, as opposed to the popular press, such as the penny press in the nineteenth century or tabloid newspapers in the twentieth. See, e.g., Schudson 1978; Zelizer 2004.

6. See, e.g., Christians et al. 2009; Graber 2003; Schudson 2007.

7. According to agenda-setting theory (McCombs and Shaw 1972), the news media suggest which people, issues, or events are deserving of public attention.

8. According to the notion of monitorial citizenship (Schudson 1998), members of the public are neither widely knowledgeable about nor attuned to public affairs during periods of routine political activity, but turn their attention to this news when extraordinary dynamics affect the polity.

9. Some scholars have proposed that "soft" news and feature-style stories (i.e., stories that make use of narrative or other literary devices) have increased their presence in journalism and are important ways of conveying public-affairs information to the public. (See, e.g., Baum and Jamison 2006; Benson et al. 2012; Hollander 2005; Prior 2003; Taniguchi 2007.) Other scholars have proposed that blogs (frequently updated sections of news sites containing dated entries arranged in reverse chronological order and often employing an informal tone) and, especially, user-generated content (stories or material submitted by members of the public, which may include eyewitness footage or photos, accounts of experiences, and articles or commentary produced by members of the audience)

are transformative options to traditional journalistic narratives that can generate bottom-up alternative agendas and contributions to the public sphere. (See, e.g., Benkler 2006; Dutton 2009; Herring et al. 2005; Reese et al. 2007; Singer 2005; Thelwall et al. 2007.) In addition to these three storytelling formats, we also analyzed two other, popular formats: straight news (an authorial style that emphasizes important facts and is often told in a detached, non-personal way) and commentary (articles, with a pronounced point of view about a topic or a product, that feature opinions and value judgments rather than factual information and are differentiated from factual news articles by their presentation and placement).

10. See, e.g., Mindich 2005; Jensen 1990; Patterson 2000; Rosenstiel et al. 2007.

11. See, e.g., Butsch 2008; Habermas 1996; Page 1996.

12. See, e.g., Coronel 2010; Donohue et al. 1995; Iyengar and McGrady 2007; Skidmore 1993; Waisbord 2000.

13. See, e.g., Blumler and Gurevitch 1995; Curran 2000; Hunter and Van Wassenhove 2010.

14. See, e.g., Bogart 1989; Butsch 2008; Dayan and Katz 1992; Luhmann 1996; Morley 1980; Thompson 1995.

15. See, e.g., Barber 1984; Bennett and Entman 2001; Graber 1984; Habermas 1989; Page 1996.

16. See, e.g., Dean, Pertilla, and Belt 2007; Gans 2004; Mindich 2005; Singer 2011; Shoemaker and Cohen 2006; Zaller 1999.

17. See, e.g., Fishman 1980; Gans 2004; Jones 2009; Schudson 2003; Tuchman 1978.

18. See, e.g., Cook 1998; Davis 1995; Williams and Delli Carpini 2012.

19. See Gans 2004, p. 28.

20. See, e.g., Schudson 2003; Shoemaker and Cohen 2006.

21. See, e.g., Bennett, Lawrence, and Livingston 2007; Gitlin 1980.

22. See Zaller 1999, p. 22.

23. See Bennett 2002, p. 124.

24. See, e.g., Canel and Piqué 1998; Herscovitz and Cardoso 1998; Weischenberg et al. 1998.

25. See Darnton 1975, p. 122.

26. See, e.g., Frijters and Velamuri 2009; Gurevitch, Coleman, and Blumler 2009; Mindich 2005; Prior 2007; Schement and Curtis 1997; Stroud 2011; Williams and Delli Carpini 2011.

27. See, e.g., Dean, Pertilla, and Belt 2007; Patterson 1994; Schramm 1947; Shoemaker and Cohen 2006; Stone and Boudreau 1995.

28. See Jensen 1990, p. 73.

29. See Huang 2009, p. 122.

30. See, e.g., Bird 2003; Bogart 1989; Graber 1984; Hamilton 2004; Hollihan 2001; Prior 2007; Tewksbury 2003.

31. See Singer 2011, p. 634.

32. "Rational ignorance," a term coined by Anthony Downs (1957), refers to the situation in which an actor decides not to inform herself about a topic because doing so exceeds the perceived benefit of the learning outcome.

33. See, e.g., Baum 2002, 2003; Gans 2003; Heith 2010; Williams and Delli Carpini 2011.

34. See, e.g., Baum and Jamison 2006; Benson et al. 2012; Hollander 2005; Prior 2003; Taniguchi 2007.

35. See Baum 2003, p. 5.

36. See, e.g., Baum 2002; Brants and Neijens 1998; Heith 2010; Taniguchi 2007.

37. See, e.g., Boczkowski 2002; Pool 1983; Jenkins 2006; Lievrouw and Livingstone 2002; Sundar and Marathe 2010.

38. See, e.g., Ancu and Cozma 2009; Benkler 2006; Himelboim et al. 2009; Singer 2009; Song 2007; Tanner 2001.

39. See Ruiz et al. 2011, p. 575.

40. See, e.g., Gans 2007; Herring et al. 2005; Papacharissi 2007.

41. See Ornebring 2008, p. 780.

42. See Gans 2007, p. 163.

43. See, e.g., Bartels 1993; Price and Zaller 1993; Tewksbury 2003, 2006.

44. See, e.g., Epstein 1973; Fishman 1980; Sigal 1973; Tuchman 1978.

45. See, e.g., Lee et al. 2012; MacGregor 2007; Singer 2011; Thorson 2008.

46. There have been a few exceptions to this trend of studying separately the preferences of journalists and consumers. These exceptions have demonstrated the value of looking at the choices of both groups concurrently (Boczkowski 2010; Curtain et al. 2007; Shoemaker and Cohen 2006; Singer 2011).

47. See, e.g., Berkowitz 1992, 2000; Boyle et al. 2004; Tewksbury 2006.

48. See, e.g., Bartels 1993; Holbrook 1996; Smidt (manuscript).

49. See Williams and Delli Carpini 2011, p. 98.

50. See, e.g., Cho 2008; Holbrook 1996; Just et al. 1996; Tewksbury 2006.

51. See Schudson 1998.

52. Although closer attention to the bottom line transformed elite newspapers' management during the last three decades of the twentieth century (Bagdikian 1983; Blumler and Gurevitch 1995; Hamilton 2004; McManus 1995; Underwood 1995), until recently journalists at leading mainstream news organizations remained relatively sheltered from market pressures with respect to everyday editorial routines (Benson et al. 2012; Zaller 1999).

53. See, e.g., Baum and Kernell 1999; Clemons et al. 2002; Frijters and Velamuri 2009; Gurevitch et al. (2009; Kind et al. 2009; Thusssu 2007.

54. See Nielsen 2011, cited in Project for Excellence in Journalism 2011.

55. See, e.g., Bruns 2008; Gillmor 2004; Lowrey 2006; Robinson 2007; Singer 2006; Williams and Delli Carpini 2000.

56. See, e.g., Boczkowski 2010; MacGregor 2007; Thorsen 2008.

57. See, e.g., Schoenbach 2004; Schoenbach et al. 2005.

58. See, e.g., Prior 2007.

59. As of June 2012, ABC had 18.2 million monthly visitors (Project for Excellence in Journalism 2012), CBS 12.7 million (Project for Excellence in Journalism 2012), Chicago Tribune 7.3 million (Project for Excellence in Journalism 2012), Clarín 10.8 million ("Métricas: Usuarios de Internet," 2012, retrieved from http://www.iabargentina.com.ar), CNN 34.6 million (Project for Excellence in Journalism 2012), Folha had 19.4 million ("Folha.com bate recorde de visitantes em um mês," 2011, retrieved from http://www1.folha.uol.com.br), Fox 17.8 million (Project for Excellence in Journalism 2012), Guardian 63 million (Audit Bureau of Circulation Electronic Database, n.d., retrieved June 2012 from http://www.abc.org.uk), Mundo 13.1 million (Oficina de Justificacion de la Difusion, 2012), Nación 8.4 million (data provided by lanacion.com, available upon request), País 8 million ("*EL PAÍS, más líder de la información digital en España*," 2012, retrieved from http://sociedad.elpais.com), Seattle 4 million ("SeattlePI.com embraces three years of online-only news & teaming with Hearst Media Services," LocalEdge, April 13, 2012, retrieved from http://www.editorandpublisher.com), Reforma 2.6 million (Mediakit, 2012, retrieved from http://comercial.reforma.com), Taggespiegel.de 1.9 million (Arbeitsgemeinschaft Online Forschung Working Group for Online Media Research Aktuelle Rankings, 2012, retrieved from http://agof.de), Times 20.4 million (Audit Bureau of Circulation Electronic Database, n.d., retrieved June 2012 from http://www.abc.org.uk), Universal 15.5 million ("Debate en vivo," May 3, 2012, retrieved from http://mx.noticias.yahoo.com), USA Today 9.2 million (Project for Excellence in

Journalism 2012), Welt 8 million (Arbeitsgemeinschaft Online Forschung Working Group for Online Media Research Aktuelle Rankings, 2012, retrieved from http://agof.de), Yahoo 39 million (Project for Excellence in Journalism 2012), and Washington Post 11.2 million (Project for Excellence in Journalism 2012).

60. We focus on individual stories rather than on entire news outlets because most content selection takes place once consumers visit a website (Project for Excellence in Journalism 2012). Moreover, our empirical evidence has consistency in terms of brands (leading, elite news organizations in their respective countries) and variation across these brands (such as ideological orientation, type of legacy media, and country of origin).

61. We used these data because they were publicly available. Moreover, ethnographic evidence from other studies conducted by the authors indicates the use of other data sources within online newsrooms yield comparable findings regarding the presence and character of the gap (Boczkowski 2010; Raviola and Boczkowski 2012).

62. See Denzin 1978.

63. See, e.g., Benson et al. 2012; Kovach and Rosenstiel 2001; Picard 2004; Witschge and Nygren 2009; Zaller 1999.

64. Although we examine only the relative popularity of blogs and user-generated content within mainstream news sites, independent political websites and blogs don't appear to challenge news media's dominant position as providers of information. According to Hindman (2009, p. 66), "News and media sites still receive thirty times as many visits as political Web sites do."

65. See Lippmann 1922, p. 197.

## Chapter 2

1. "NATO bringt Mitrovica unter Kontrolle," Der Tagesspiegel, March 17, 2008, retrieved from http://www.tagesspiegel.de.

2. "Doppelmord an Ehepaar aufgeklärt," Der Tagesspiegel, March 17, 2008, retrieved from http://www.tagesspiegel.de.

3. "Crise vai durar 'bastante tempo' e terá 'graves conseqüências,'" diz FMI, Folha de S. Paulo, March 17, 2008, retrieved from http://www.folha.uol.com.br/.

4. "Ex-BBB Marcelo é antipático com Ana Maria Braga," Folha de S. Paulo, March 17, 2008, retrieved from http://www.folha.uol.com.br/.

5. Clarín had a monthly average of 7.37 million unique visitors during the data-collection period between November 2007 and April 2008 ("Métricas: Usuarios de Internetl," 2012, retrieved from http://www.iabargentina.com.ar). Its

print counterpart had an average daily circulation of more than 380,000 during the first semester of 2008 (Instituto Verificador de Circulaciones, cited at http://www.diariosobrediarios.com.ar. The news site has a centrist-populist ideology.

6. Nación had a monthly average of 4.06 million unique visitors during the data-collection period (Métricas: usuarios de Internet", retrieved from http://iabargentina.com.ar). Its print counterpart had an average daily circulation of more than 158,000 during the first semester of 2008 (Instituto Verificador de Circulaciones, cited at http://www.diariosobrediarios.com.ar. The news site has a conservative outlook.

7. Folha's print counterpart had a daily average circulation of 317,000 during the first semester of 2008 ("Congresso ANJ e crescimento dos jornais," 2008, retrieved from http://www.circulacao.org.br). The news site has a center-right stance.

8. Die Welt had a monthly average of 3.37 million unique visitors in the first quarter of 2008 (Arbeitsgemeinschaft Online Forschung Working Group for Online Media Research Aktuelle Rankings, 2008, retrieved from http://www.agof.de). Its print counterpart had an average daily circulation of more than 278,000 copies in the first quarter of 2008 (IVW, cited in "Zeitungen," 2009, retrieved from http://www.textintern.de). The news site has a conservative ideology.

9. Tagesspiegel had a monthly average of 880,000 unique visitors and was the sixth, top-ranked, quality online newspaper in the first quarter of 2008 (Arbeitsgemeinschaft Online Forschung Working Group for Online Media Research Aktuelle Rankings, 2008, retrieved from http://www.agof.de). Its print counterpart had an average daily circulation of more than 147,000 copies in the first quarter of 2008 (IVW, cited in retrieved from http://daten.ivw.eu). The news site has a liberal stance.

10. Universal is the top-ranked online newspaper and the second, top-ranked news site in Mexico according to Alexa rankings (Top sites by country, retrieved from http://www.alexa.com). Although there are no data available from third-party auditing of Mexican newspapers' circulation, its print counterpart is widely considered one of the most influential Mexican newspapers. The news site has a centrist outlook.

11. Reforma is a division of Grupo Reforma, the largest print media company in Mexico, which publishes nine newspapers in four cities. The print daily was founded in 1993 and is considered an independent, influential, and civic-oriented newspaper. The news site has a conservative ideology.

12. Mundo had more than 10 million unique visitors in July 2008 ("Buscador de publicaciones y medios electrónicos," n.d., retrieved from http://www.ojd.es). Its print counterpart had a daily circulation of more than 333,000 between July 2007 and June 2008 (ibid.). It has a conservative stance.

13. País is the second, top-ranked online newspaper in Spain, according to Alexa Rankings ("Top sites by country," retrieved from http://www.alexa.com), but its online readership wasn't audited by Spain's third-party news media auditor during the period of study. Its print counterpart has a daily circulation of more than 444,000 between July 2007 and June 2008 ("Buscador de publicaciones y medios electrónicos," n.d., retrieved June 2012 from http://www.ojd.es). The news site has a liberal outlook.

14. Guardian had a monthly average of more than 18 million unique visitors between November 2007 and May 2008 (Audit Bureau of Circulation Electronic Database, n.d., retrieved June 2012 from http://www.abc.org.uk). Its print counterpart had a daily circulation of more 355,000 in February 2008 (ibid.). The news site has a liberal ideology.

15. Times had a monthly average of more than 14 million unique visitors between November 2007 and May 2008 (Audit Bureau of Circulation Electronic Database, n.d., retrieved June 2012 from http://www.abc.org.uk). Its print coun terpart had a daily circulation of more 613,000 in February 2008 (cited in Audit Bureau of Circulations, National daily newspaper circulation, February 2009, at http://www.guardian.co.uk/media/table/2009/mar/06/abcs-national-newspapers). The news site has a conservative outlook.

16. Germany, Spain, and the United Kingdom are developed countries with stable democratic systems, and each represents one of Hallin and Mancini's (2004) three models of media systems: Germany represents the northern European or democratic-corporatist model, Spain the Mediterranean or polarized-pluralist model, and the United Kingdom the North Atlantic or liberal model. Argentina, Brazil, and Mexico are among the most populated and influential countries in Latin America. Each regained full democratic government between the 1980s and the early 1990s, a process that was tied to a modernization of the press (Alves 2005; Ferreira, 2006; Hughes 2003; Lawson 2002; Rockwell 2009; Waisbord 2000). The media systems in these three countries differ somewhat, but less than in the cases of Germany, Spain, and the United Kingdom. Moreover, unlike the three European countries, the Latin American countries lack a strong media tradition of public service and have relatively low newspaper circulation rates.

17. Data were collected on 92 randomly selected days over 25 weeks from November 10, 2007 to May 5, 2008, from Monday to Saturday, on four days per week on average. Sunday homepages weren't collected because some of the participating sites were affiliated with print newspapers that had no Sunday edition. A research assistant retrieved data at 10:00 a.m. U.S. Central Time, which was 10:00 a.m. in Mexico, 2:00 p.m. in Argentina and Brazil, 4:00 p.m. in the United Kingdom, and 5:00 p.m. in Germany and Spain. Data were collected once a day because in a previous study we found that collecting data at three different points in time

during each day (10 a.m., 4 p.m., and 10 p.m.) yielded no major, significant differences in the gaps of content and format across sites. Simultaneous data collection was chosen to compare cross-site coverage of similar events at a single point in time of their evolution. Although the data were gathered at different local times, in all cases they came from the peak time of activity of online news sites during the work week, i.e., during regular business hours (Boczkowski 2010). On each data-collection day, the top ten stories selected by journalists and the top ten, five, or four stories selected by consumers were identified and analyzed (Clarín, Nación, Tagesspiegel, Welt, Mundo, and País made ten stories from the consumers' list available; Folha, Universal, and Guardian made five; Reforma and Times made four). A total of 10,048 stories from the journalists' lists and 7,565 stories from the consumers' lists were analyzed from all the sites. The difference in the expected number of stories ($n$ = 10,120 for the journalists' lists and 7,636 for the consumers' lists) results from the retrieval of repeated stories that were later excluded from analysis (journalists' list). In addition, these sites posted fewer than ten, five, or four stories in their "most read" rankings (consumers' list) during a few days. The difference between the expected and actual number of stories is 1.45 percent for the journalists' list and 1.90 percent for the consumers' list.

18. Public-affairs stories included news about the activity of government, elected officials, political candidates; the economy and business developments; and events happening in other countries, about the state, or international organizations. Non-public-affairs stories referred to news about sports teams and events; criminal activity; arts and literature; medical, technological, and scientific matters; and weather information. If a story appeared to be a non-public-affairs subject, i.e., a scientific discovery, but its content dealt with public affairs, i.e., the political impact of this discovery, it was considered a public-affairs story for the purposes of this analysis.

19. Ten trained research assistants coded the stories. Intercoder agreement was assessed on a subset of 10 percent of the data. For story content, intercoder agreement levels averaged 90 percent, and Cohen's Kappa intercoder agreement levels averaged 0.79.

20. The sites examined didn't disclose the frequency with which they updated the "most read" list, nor the "look back" period of time used to calculate their most clicked rankings. However, the existence of a significant gap across all the sites suggests that the divergent pattern of journalistic and consumer choice is robust even despite potential cross-site variations in procedural matters.

21. We examined whether the difference between journalists' and consumers' lists could be due to the varying rate of updates on hard and factual news stories (which tend to be updated frequently and constitute the majority of journalists' choices in all the sites) and opinion articles and features pieces (which tend to be updated less

frequently and are the two other dominant format options). The analysis shows that the gap doesn't increase with the stories that are updated less frequently.

22. Anderson (2008) and Hindman (2009) have proposed that online readership follows Pareto or power-law distributions. Thus, the first stories in the consumers' list should receive a disproportionately larger number of clicks than the subsequent ones. Two analyses were performed to determine whether there was variation between the content of the stories placed in the first positions of the ranking and those placed further down. First was a crosstab of the content of the stories and their position in the ranking. According to the chi-square tests, there were no differences in the story depending on the position in the ranking in any of the sites. Second was a logistical regression of "content" on the ranking as dummy variables, with position 1 as the base case. The resulting coefficients weren't significant for any of the positions on Clarín, Reforma, Guardian, Nación, Pais, Reforma, Times, Universal, and Die Welt, and significant for only one position on Folha and Mundo. In conclusion, ranking position isn't a major factor affecting the supply-demand gap in information.

23. Chicago had nearly 3 million unique users in November 2006 ("NAA newspaper audience database report (Nadbase)," 2007, retrieved from http://www.marketingcharts.com). It is the online counterpart of the *Chicago Tribune*, which had an average daily circulation of about 567,000 for the period ending in September 2006 (Audit Bureau of Circulations, 2007 FAS-Fax report).

24. Seattle had 3.3 million unique users in November 2006 ("NAA newspaper audience database report (Nadbase)," 2007, retrieved from http://www.marketingcharts.com). It was the online counterpart of the *Seattle Post-Intelligencer*, which had an average daily circulation of about 128,000 for the period ending in September 2006 (Audit Bureau of Circulations, 2007 FAS-Fax report) and ceased print publication in the spring of 2009.

25. CNN had a monthly average of nearly 25 million monthly unique users in 2006, according to Nielsen measurements (Project for Excellence in Journalism 2007). It is the online counterpart of the Cable News Network, which had a median prime-time audience of 710,000 viewers during 2006 (Project for Excellence in Journalism 2007).

26. Yahoo had a monthly average of more than 28 million unique users in 2006, according to Nielsen measurements (Project for Excellence in Journalism 2007). It is affiliated with Yahoo, which runs the second-largest web search engine with more than 20 percent of the market share for July 2007 ("Nielsen//NetRatings announces July U.S. search share rankings," 2007, retrieved from http://www.marketwire.com).

27. "Bush veto forces Dems to weigh difficult concessions," CNN, May 2, 2007, retrieved from http://us.cnn.com.

28. "Britney Spears takes baby step back on stage," CNN, May 2, 2007, retrieved from http://us.cnn.com.

29. Data were gathered on 21 randomly selected days (three for each day of the week) during this period, for a total of three composite weeks. On each coding day, research assistants collected data at 10 a.m., 4 p.m., and 10 p.m. Central Time, yielding 63 distinct data-collection shifts (21 days × 3 times per day) for each site. At each shift for each site, they identified and collected the top ten stories selected by journalists and by consumers, respectively. Across the 63 data-collection shifts, each site yielded 1,260 stories—630 journalist-selected top stories and 630 consumer-selected top stories—or a total of 5,040 stories. All of the sites in this study made publicly available the list of the ten most viewed articles. Four trained research assistants coded the stories. Intercoder agreement was assessed a subset of 5 percent of the data. Intercoder agreement levels averaged 94 percent. Cohen's Kappa intercoder agreement levels averaged 0.88.

30. A similar analysis, including only the stories without overlap between journalists and consumers on each site, was also performed on the data from the study of Western European and Latin American media. It yielded a similar pattern of a widening of the gap across sites after the removal of the stories with overlap.

31. For details, see table A.4 in the appendix.

32. "Alonso será el nuevo portavoz parlamentario del PSOE en el Congreso 2008," El Mundo, March 24, retrieved from www.elmundo.es.

33. "Si se me rompe el bañador, a nadar sin él," El Mundo, March 23, 2008, retrieved from www.elmundo.es.

34. "Confirmado: El amor es ciego," El Pais, March 24, 2008, retrieved from www.elpais.com.

35. Byers 2008.

36. "Para la Justicia, los crímenes de la Triple A no prescriben," La Nación, March 17, 2008, retrieved from www.lanacion.com.

37. Alex Pell, "Hey, Facebook, just let go of me," Times (London), March 16, 2008 (retrieved from www.thetimes.co.uk).

38. Evangelina Himitian, "Los que logran sentirse jóvenes después de los 65," La Nación, March 17, 2008 (retrieved from www.lanacion.com).

39. See, e.g., Prior 2005; Prior 2007; Zaller 1999.

40. See, e.g., de Albuquerque 2005; Pfetsch and Esser 2004; Reese 2001; Swan son 2004.

41. See, e.g., Bielsa 2008; Hafez 2002; Hallin and Mancini 2004; Hantizch et al. 2011; Sanders and Canel 2006; Shoemaker and Cohen 2006.

42. See, e.g., Chan-Olmsted and Chang 2003; Murray 2005.

43. See, e.g., Arsenault and Castells 2008; Bennett 2004; Curran et al. 2009; Esser and D'Angelo 2006; Palmer 2008; Plasser 2005.

44. See, e.g., Gurevitch and Levy 1990; Merrill 2009; Wiley 2006.

45. See, e.g., Benson and Hallin 2007; Donsbach and Patterson 2004; Nelson and Paek 2007; Rössler 2004; Ruigrok and Van Atteveldt 2007.

46. The prevalence of public-affairs stories in the top choices of both journalists and consumers was different in news sites from countries in which the media systems share some structural characteristics, such as Argentina, Brazil, and Mexico. However, they didn't diverge as much in news sites from countries with different national media structures, such as Spain and Germany. (For a comparative analysis of media systems in Western Europe, see Hallin and Mancini 2004.) This suggests that the variations may be due to organizational and professional rather than structural factors. The importance of organizational and professional factors over national structural characteristics is reinforced by the stability in the site rank-order of prevalence of public-affairs stories in the top news choices of journalists and consumers.

47. See, e.g., Baum and Groeling 2008; Lee 2007.

48. See, e.g., Di Maggio et al. 2001; Iyengar and Hahn 2009; Stroud 2008, 2011.

49. See Prior 2007.

50. See, e.g., de Albuquerque 2005; Hafez 2002.

51. See Deuze, Neuberger, and Paulussen 2004.

52. See, e.g., Palmer 2008; Statham 2008.

53. Prior 2005, 2007.

54. See, e.g., Iyengar and Kinder 1987; McCombs and Shaw 1972; McCombs 2004.

55. See, e.g., Coleman and McCombs 2007; Roberts et al. 2002.

56. See, e.g., Althaus and Tewksbury 2002; Takeshita 2006.

57. See Boczkowski 2010.

58. See, e.g., Chaffee and Metzger 2001; Shaw and Hamm 1997; Takeshita 2006; Williams and Delli Carpini 2001.

## Chapter 3

1. See McDonald 2008.

2. See Matt Krantz, "Dow suffers its worst weekly drop ever," USA Today, October 14, 2008 (retrieved from www.usatoday.com).

3. See Bob Willis, "U.S. recession worst since Great Depression, revised data show," Bloomberg News, August 1, 2009 (retrieved from http://www.bloomberg.com).

4. See Collier 1993.

5. Shaver and Wilgoren 2008.

6. Dan Balz, "Polls show Obama with clear advantage," Washington Post, November 4, 2008 (retrieved from www.washingtonpost.com).

7. See Groshek 2008.

8. "Voters 'surprised,' 'excited' on historic election day," CNN, November 4, 2008 (retrieved from http://us.cnn.com).

9. Emanuella Grinberg, "Ballot hot buttons include abortion, same-sex marriage," CNN, November 4, 2008 (retrieved from http://us.cnn.com).

10. See, e.g., Farnsworth and Lichter 2005; C. R. Martin 2008.

11. See Groseclose and Milyo 2005.

12. See, e.g., Pew Research Center 2011; Stroud 2008.

13. ABC was the eighth-most-visited online news site in 2008, with a monthly average of 7.6 million unique uses that year (Project for Excellence in Journalism 2009). In 2008, the ABC network's nightly news program averaged more than 8 million viewers (ibid.). It is a generalist outlet with a heterogeneous audience that includes Democrats, Republicans, and Independents (Pew Research Center 2011).

14. CBS was the ninth-most-visited online news site in 2008, with a monthly average of 7.5 million unique users that year. In 2008, the CBS network's nightly newscast had more than 6 million viewers (Project for Excellence in Journalism 2009). It is a generalist outlet with a heterogeneous audience that includes Democrats, Republicans, and Independents (Pew Research Center 2011).

15. In 2008, CNN was the third-most-visited online news site in the United States, with a monthly average of more than 31 million unique users that year (Project for Excellence in Journalism 2009). It is the online counterpart of the Cable News Network, which had a median prime-time audience of 1.05 million viewers during 2008 (ibid.). It is a generalist outlet (Groshek 2008) whose audience includes mostly Democrats and Independents (Stroud 2008).

16. Fox was the seventh-most-visited online news site in 2008, with a monthly average of more than 8 million unique users that year (Project for Excellence in Journalism 2009). It is affiliated with Fox News, which was the top-rated cable news outlet of 2008, with a median prime-time audience of 1.79 million viewers (ibid.). Its consumers are mostly Republican (Bennett and Iyengar 2008; Iyengar and Hahn 2009; Pew Research Center 2011; Stroud 2008).

17. USA Today is a generalist outlet (Gladney 1993) with centrist leanings (Groseclose and Milyo 2005). It was the fourth-most-visited web site of a print newspaper in 2008, with more than 10.3 million unique users for November 2008 ("Nov. 2008: U.S. news sites see post-election growth," 2008, retrieved from http://blog

.nielsen.com). The print *USA Today* had an average daily circulation of 2,293,000 for the six-month period ending in September 2008 (Audit Bureau of Circulations, "Newspaper circulation falls 10.6% in H109," 2009, retrieved March 2012 from http://www.marketingcharts.com).

18. The *Washington Post* has liberal leanings (Groseclose and Milyo 2005) and a stronger focus on political coverage (Farnsworth and Lichter 2005; Martin 2008). Its website was the third-most-visited site of a print newspaper in 2008, with more than 11.1 million unique users for November of that year ("Nov. 2008: U.S. news sites see post-election growth," 2008, retrieved from http://blog.nielsen.com). The print *Washington Post* had an average daily circulation of approximately 623,000 for the six-month period ending in September 2008 (Audit Bureau of Circulations, "Newspaper circulation falls 10.6% in H109," retrieved March 2012 from http://www.marketingcharts.com).

19. On each data-collection day, a research assistant retrieved data from all six sites at 3:00 p.m. U.S. Central Time. Simultaneous data collection was chosen to compare cross-site coverage of similar events at a single point in time. Following the same procedure used for the studies conducted in the United States during 2007 and in Western Europe and Latin America in 2007 and 2008, we identified the top stories selected by journalists and consumers, respectively. The former consisted of each homepage's first ten stories (hereafter "journalists' list") counting from left to right and from the top down in a grid-like manner. The latter were the top five or ten stories in the "most read" list (hereafter "consumers' list") that each of these sites made publicly available. CNN, Fox, ABC, USA Today, and Washington Post made ten stories from the consumers' list available; and CBS made five to ten, depending on the day. (On average, CBS made eight stories available in the consumers' list during the data-collection period. The data on consumer choices were also analyzed, including only the top eight "most clicked" stories on all sites. There were no significant differences with the findings reported in this paper.) Data were collected on 79 days during 19 weeks—approximately four days for each of the weeks—from August 1 to December 1, 2008. Because this wave aimed to examine the difference between journalists' and consumers' online news choices during a period of heightened interest in politics, data were collected randomly during most of the weeks and purposively during periods of major, pre-scheduled political events. These latter periods include the Democratic Convention (August 25–28), the Republican Convention (September 1–4), the presidential debates (September 26, October 7, October 15). We analyzed 4,730 stories from the journalists' lists and 4,537 from the consumers' lists from all the sites. For each story, we examined whether the main topic was news about public-affairs or non-public-affairs matters. Three, trained, research assistants coded the stories. Intercoder agreement was assessed on a subset of 9 percent of the data. For story content, intercoder agreement levels averaged 87 percent, and Cohen's Kappa intercoder agreement was 0.75.

20. This second cycle of data collection included two gubernatorial elections; thus it had some electoral activity.

21. See, e.g., Bennett and Iyengar 2008; Iyengar and Hahn 2009; Stroud 2008, 2011.

22. Bacon and Franke-Ruta 2009.

23. Caitlin Gibson, "One daughter's secret revealed, ultimately too late," Washington Post, November 4, 2009 (retrieved from www.washingtonpost.com).

24. Alexander Mooney, "Fiorina jumps into high-profile California Senate race," CNN, November 4, 2009 (retrieved from http://us.cnn.com).

25. Jo Piazza, "Jessica Simpson finds a bosom buddy," CNN, November 4, 2009 (retrieved from http://us.cnn.com).

26. Dave Sheinin, "In fast company," Washington Post, August 1, 2008 (retrieved from www.washingtonpost.com).

27. Carrie Johnson, Del Quentin Wilber, and Carol Leonnig, "Md. anthrax scientist dies in suicide," Washington Post, August 1, 2008 (retrieved from www.washing tonpost.com).

28. Monica Hesse, "It's Hannah again. Should we take this?" Washington Post, August 1, 2008 (retrieved from www.washingtonpost.com).

29. Val Willingham, "Awake patient reads aloud during brain surgery," CNN, August 1, 2008 (retrieved from http://us.cnn.com).

30. "Decapitation suspect appears in court," CNN, August 1, 2008 (retrieved from http://us.cnn.com).

31. The analysis, a fixed-effects logistical regression of content of the stories on week, included all the stories in the journalists' lists across the six sites. The unit of analysis was the story, the dependent variable was the content of the story, and the independent variables were the site (base case: CNN) and the week on which the story was published (base case: week 1). For further details, see table A.9 in the appendix.

32. The analysis, a fixed-effects logistical regression of content of the stories on week, included all the stories on the consumers' lists across the six sites. The unit of analysis was the story, the dependent variable the content of the story, and the independent variables were the site (base case: CNN) and the week in which the story was published (base case: week 1). For further details, see table A.11 in the appendix.

33. "Murió Jorge Guinzburg," Clarín, March 1, 2008, retrieved from www.clarin.com.

34. "Cliente 9 y cuarto 871: un escándalo de sexo y política en Nueva York," Clarín, March 12, 2008 (retrieved from www.clarin.com).

35. CIA World Factbook 2012, retrieved from www.cia.gov.

36. *The Economist* Country Briefings, 2010, retrieved from www.economist.com.

37. "Tras el cacerolazo, el gobierno negó la posibilidad de cambios en la política de retenciones," *Clarín*, March 26, 2008, retrieved from www.clarin.com.

38. We collected data on 92 randomly selected days over 24 weeks—approximately four days for each of the weeks from 10 November 2007 to 5 May 2008, from Monday to Saturday, repeating the methodology described in the previous chapter. We analyzed 1,835 stories from the journalists' lists and 1,829 from the consumers' lists of both sites.

39. Interviews with journalists and consumers were loosely structured around a list of topics elaborated by the authors. The second author conducted interviews face-to-face in Buenos Aires between June and August of 2008. Twelve editors and editorial directors from six, top-ranked, Argentine online newspapers were recruited for the interviews with journalists. The news sites (Clarín.com, Lanacion.com.ar, Infobae.com, Criticadigital.com, Perfil.com, and Pagina12.com.ar) were selected according to their online readership as measured by Alexa Rankings and Google Web Trends. They also provide a wide spectrum of ideological orientation and type of audience. Five interviewees were editorially in charge of their respective sites, and seven were editors directly involved with management of the homepage. For the interviews with consumers, snowballing sampling yielded a convenience sample of 25 respondents. Recruitment of news consumers was undertaken through a referral network of contacts, in part following a process developed by the first author for a previous book (Boczkowski 2010). Initially, twelve distant acquaintances who didn't know any of the authors personally were invited to be interviewed. At the end of the interview, each interviewee was asked to name three acquaintances who met three criteria: regular Internet use; diversity in terms of gender, age group, and occupation; and membership in relatively different social networks. Approximately half of the interviewees named acquaintances to be contacted for additional interviews, and thirteen contacts were recruited. This procedure yielded a convenience sample of 25 respondents in terms of gender and age group who loosely mirrored the adult population who accessed the Internet in Argentina at the time of the study. There were eleven women and fourteen men. There were thirteen people between the ages of 18 and 29, eight between 30 and 49, and four who were at least 50 years old. The interviewees in the final sample represented a broad spectrum of occupations, and each had at least finished high school. The interviews lasted an average of 40 minutes and were recorded and transcribed in their entirety for analysis.

40. Personal communication July 25, 2008.

41. Personal communication, July 18, 2008.

42. Personal communication, August 8, 2008.

43. Personal communication, August 4, 2008.

44. Personal communication, July 29, 2008.

45. Personal communication, July 30, 2008.

46. Personal communication, July 22, 2008.

47. Personal communication, August 15, 2008.

48. Personal communication, July 3, 2008.

49. Personal communication, July 24, 2008.

50. Personal communication, August 15, 2008.

51. Personal communication, July 24, 2008.

52. Personal communication, July 18, 2008.

53. Personal communication, August 8, 2008.

54. Personal communication, August 4, 2008.

55. Personal communication, July 29, 2008.

56. Personal communication, July 29, 2008.

57. Personal communication, July 24, 2008.

58. Personal communication, August 4, 2008.

59. Personal communication, July 3, 2008.

60. Personal communication, July 29, 2008.

61. Personal communication, July 22, 2008.

62. Personal communication, July 22, 2008.

63. Here D'Atri refers to "the Homer," a car designed by Homer Simpson in "Oh Brother, Where Art Thou?" (the fifteenth episode in the second season).

64. Personal communication, July 22, 2008.

65. Personal communication, August 15, 2008.

66. Personal communication, July 30, 2008.

67. Personal communication, July 24, 2008.

68. For accounts of the tension between the logics of the occupation and the market in the history of journalism, see Cohen 2002; MacGregor 2007; McManus 1994; Sumpter 2000; Underwood 1993.

69. Personal communication, July 8, 2008.

70. Personal communication, July 10, 2008.

71. Personal communication, July 23, 2008.

72. Personal communication, July 4, 2008.

73. Personal communication, July 14, 2008.

74. Personal communication, July 30, 2008.

75. Personal communication, June 27, 2008.

76. Personal communication, August 5, 2008.

77. Personal communication, July 4, 2008.

78. Personal communication, June 25, 2008.

79. Personal communication, July 4, 2008.

80. Personal communication, July 2, 2008.

81. Personal communication, July 11, 2008.

82. Personal communication, July 23, 2008.

83. Personal communication, August 8, 2008.

84. Personal communication, July 2, 2008.

85. Personal communication, July 8, 2008.

86. Personal communication, July 10, 2008.

87. Personal communication, July 4, 2008.

88. Personal communication, July 22, 2008.

89. Personal communication, July 8, 2008.

90. Personal communication, August 13, 2008.

91. Personal communication, July 22, 2008.

92. Personal communication, July 23, 2008.

93. Personal communication, August 5, 2008.

94. Personal communication, July 31, 2008.

95. See, e.g., Bennett 2003; Fishman 1980; Gans 2004; Schudson 2003; Tuchman 1978; Zaller 1999.

96. See Downs 1957.

97. See, e.g., Bird 2003; Hamilton 2004; Hollihan 2001; Tewksbury 2003.

98. See, e.g., Cho 2008; Graber 2004; Holbrook 1996; Tewksbury 2006.

99. See Chaffee and Metzger 2001.

100. See Zaller 2003.

101. See, e.g., Bennett 2003; Patterson 2000.

102. See, e.g., Barabas and Jerit 2005; Graber 2004; Parker-Stephen 2009.

103. See, e.g., Blekesaune et al. 2012; Butsch 2008; V. B. Martin 2008; Poindexter et al. 2001; Wilson et al. 2003.

104. See, e.g., Albrecht 2006; Best and Krueger 2005; Chadwick 2006; Papacharissi 2002.

105. See Prior 2007.

106. See, e.g., Baum 2002, 2003; Baum and Jamison 2006; Gans 2003.

## Chapter 4

1. See, e.g., Bennett 2002; Boczkowski 2009; Patterson 2000; Quandt 2008; Schudson 2003; Williams and Delli Carpini 2011.

2. See, e.g., Baum 2002; Heith 2010; Hollander 2005; Prior 2003; Taniguchi 2011.

3. We use the notion of "soft news" to refer to characteristics of the stories, such as the use of narrative or other literary devices, as opposed to the sparse, fact-loaded, traditional journalistic style. We seek to engage in conversation with the literature on the softening of news, which has tended to focus on product features rather than production issues. For this reason, we depart from the definition employed in Boczkowski 2010, a work that addressed the temporal dimension of production dynamics.

4. See, e.g., Benkler 2006; Dutton 2009; Herring et al. 2005; Reese et al. 2007; Singer 2005; Thelwall et al. 2007.

5. See, e.g., Barnhurst and Mutz 1997; Benson et al. 2012; Singer 2008; Tuchman 1972.

6. Allegra Stratton, "Tibet protesters disrupt Olympic flame ceremony," The Guardian, March 24, 2008 (retrieved from www.guardian.co.uk).

7. See, e.g., Garrison 2009; Shapiro 2005; Steensen 2009; Williamson 1975.

8. See, e.g., Hamilton 2004; Schramm 1947; Shapiro 2006.

9. Susan Donaldson James, "Virginity pledges can work for some," ABC News, September 29, 2008 (retrieved from www.abcnews.go.com).

10. See, e.g., Damas and Barber 2010; Kovach and Rosenstiel 2001.

11. Gerard Baker, "Obama: Is America ready for this dangerous left-winger?" Times (London), February 22, 2008 (retrieved from www.thetimes.co.uk).

12. In the first U.S. study, which gathered data in 2007, no distinction was made among blogs, user-generated content, and other formats such as photo

galleries. In the Western Europe and Latin America study, "blogs" was coded as a separate category. In the U.S. studies that collected data from 2008 and 2007, "blogs" and "user-generated content" were coded as two separate categories.

13. See, e.g., Herring et al. 2005; Lowrey 2006; Trammell and Keshelashvili 2005; Tremayne 2007.

14. "Nicole Kidman: 'I've explored strange sexual fetish stuff,'" USA Today, November 4, 2009 (retrieved from http://www.usatoday.com/).

15. See, e.g., Hermida and Thurman 2008; Ornebring 2008; Vujnovic et al. 2010; Williams et al. 2010.

16. Katie Hawkins, "Turning 50 isn't what it used to be," CNN, August 16, 2008 (retrieved from http://us.cnn.com).

17. "John Edwards admits having an affair," CBS News, August 8, 2008 (retrieved from www.cbsnews.com).

18. Simon Crerar, "Harry Potter split more painful than divorce, says JK Rowling," Times (London), January 29, 2008 (retrieved from www.thetimes.co.uk).

19. For further details, see tables A.24 and A.25.

20. Rick Jervis, "Gulf Coast residents flee Gustav," USA Today, August 31, 2008 (retrieved from www.usatoday.com).

21. We ran three analyses for the journalists' list and three for the consumer0s' list. Each analysis consisted of a fixed-effects logistical regression of format of the articles one week, with one of the format categories (straight news, feature, commentary) as a binary dependent variable. The unit of analysis was the story, the dependent variable was the content of the story, and the independent variables were the site (base case: CNN) and the week in which the story was published (base case: week 1). For further details, see tables A.33–A.40 in the appendix.

22. See, e.g., Bucy 2004; Deuze 2006; Matheson 2004; Robinson 2006; Singer 2006.

23. See, e.g., Bennett 2002; Gans 2004; Scott and Gobetz 1992; Times Mirror Center 1990.

24. See Baum and Jamison 2003.

25. See, e.g., Bird 2003; Bogart 1989; Hagen 1994; Hamilton 2004; Prior 2007.

26. See, e.g., Dean et al. 2007; Jensen 1990; atterson 2000; Stone and Boudreau 1995.

27. See, e.g., Herring et al. 2005; Reese et al. 2007; Singer 2005; Thelwall et al. 2007.

28. See, e.g., Benkler 2006; Dutton 2009; McCoy 2001; Tremayne 2007.

29. See, e.g., Boczkowski 2004; Thurman 2008; Williams et al. 2010; Ye and Li 2006.

30. See, e.g., Boczkowski 2010; Chung and Nah 2009; Goode 2009; Hujanen and Pietikainen 2004.

31. See, e.g., Johnston and Forde 2011; Lewis et al. 2008; Paterson 2005.

32. See, e.g., Christians et al. 2009; Gans 2004; Tuchman 1978.

33. See, e.g., Baum 2003; Baum 2007; Baum and Jamison 2006; Hollander 2005; Moy et al. 2006.

34. See, e.g., Gladney 1993; Liebes 1995; Prichard 1987.

35. See, e.g., Benkler 2006; Chadwick 2011; Hermida 2010; Jenkins 2006; Perry 1993; Rosen 1999.

## Chapter 5

1. It should be noted that the same population of online news users doesn't select the three sets of stories analyzed—most clicked, most emailed, and most commented on. Previous research suggests that a relatively small percentage of news consumers email and comment on stories from the much larger universe of consumers who click on the stories available on online news sites (Boczkowski 2010; Davis 2009; Goss 2007; Schultz 2000.

2. See Boczkowski 2002; Pool 1983; Jenkins 2006; Lievrouw and Livingstone 2002. Interactivity is a contested concept (Heeter 1989; Jensen 1998; Kiousis 2002; McMillan 2002; Rafaeli 1988). The definition we use focuses on media attributes (Ahren et al. 2000; Massey and Levy 1999; Schultz 2000; Sundar 2004) rather than on users' perceptions (Downes and McMillan 2000; Morrison 1998; Newhagen et al. 1995).

3. See, e.g., Bucy 2004; Chung and Yoo 2008; Massey and Levy 1999a; Stromer-Galley 2000.

4. See, e.g., Chung 200; Jensen 1998; Massey and Levy 1999b; McMillan 2002.

5. The "most emailed" and "most commented" lists weren't collected in the 2007 U.S. study or in the Latin America and Western Europe studies. The three sites we look at in this chapter allowed commenting on all their articles. The remaining three sites in the 2008 and 2009 U.S. studies (ABC, CBS, and Fox) didn't make their "most clicked," "most emailed," and "most commented" lists publicly available. For each data-collection day, three types of stories were gathered and identified. They included (1) the top ten most clicked stories made publicly available by each of these sites, usually under rubrics such as the most popular and most viewed stories; (2) the top ten most emailed stories, also publicly available on each site; and (3) the top ten most commented on stories displayed on each of these sites. The analysis included 2,789 most clicked stories (2,370 from 2008 and 419 from 2009), 2,763 most emailed articles (2,347 from 2008 and 416 from 2009), and 2,770 most commented on stories (2,350 from 2008 and 420 from 2009) from the three sites.

6. "Decapitation suspect appears in court," CNN, August 1, 2008 (retrieved from http://us.cnn.com).

7. "Foreclosed home caused 44-pound cat's abandonment," USA Today, August 1, 2008 (retrieved from www.usatoday.com).

8. Dana Milbank, "President Obama continues hectic victory tour," Washington Post, July 3, 2008 (retrieved from www.washingtonpost.com).

9. For further details, see tables A.47 and A.48.

10. Gabe Oppenheim, "The beer that takes you back . . . millions of years," Washington Post, September 1, 2008 (retrieved from www.washingtonpost.com).

11. Brown 2008.

12. Anne Godlasky, "New ways to mitigate migraines," USA Today, November 4, 2008 (retrieved from www.usatoday.com).

13. Jessica Leving, "Beer with extra buzz on tap up to 16%," USA Today, November 4, 2009 (retrieved from www.usatoday.com).

14. David Broder, Dan Balz, and Chris Cillizza, "The state of the races," Washington Post, November 4, 2008 (retrieved from www.washingtonpost.com).

15. Dan Balz, "Contests serve as warning to Democrats: It's not 2008 anymore," Washington Post, November 4, 2009 (retrieved from www.washingtonpost.com).

16. The analysis, a fixed-effects logistical regression of content of the stories on week, included all the stories in the "most clicked" lists across the three sites. The unit of analysis was the story, the dependent variable the content of the story, and the independent variables were the site (base case: CNN) and the week in which the story was published (base case: week 1). For further details, see table A.58.

17. The analysis, a fixed-effects logistical regression of content of the stories on week, included all the stories in the "most emailed" lists across the three sites. The unit of analysis was the story, the dependent variable the content of the story, and the independent variables were the site (base case: CNN) and the week in which the story was published (base case: week 1). For further details, see table A.59.

18. The analysis, a fixed-effects logistical regression of content of the stories on week, included all the stories in the "most commented" lists across the three sites. The unit of analysis was the story, the dependent variable the content of the story, and the independent variables were the site (base case: CNN) and the week in which the story was published (base case: week 1). For further details, see table A.60.

19. The analysis, a fixed-effects logistical regression of content of the stories on week, included all the stories in the "most newsworthy" lists across the three sites. The unit of analysis was the story, the dependent variable the content of the story, and the independent variables were the site (base case: CNN) and the week in which the story was published (base case: week 1). For further details, see table A.61.

20. Three analyses were run for the "most newsworthy" list, three for the "most clicked" list, three for the "most emailed" list, and three for the "most commented" list. Each analysis consisted of a fixed-effects logistical regression of format of the articles each week, with one of the format categories (straight-news, feature-style, commentary) as a binary dependent variable. The unit of analysis was the story, the dependent variable the format of the story, and the independent variables were the site (base case: CNN) and the week in which the story was published (base case: week 1). For further details, see tables A.62–A.76.

21. See, e.g., Althaus and Tewksbury 2002; Berger and Milkman 2010; Domingo 2008; Goss 2007; Schultz 2000.

22. See, e.g., Chung 2007; Jensen 1998; Massey and Levy 1999a; McMillan 2002.

23. See, e.g., Boczkowski 2010; Jensen 1990; Ling and Thrane 2002; Palmgreen et al. 2002.

24. See, e.g., Bohman 2004; Min 2007; Price 2006; Stromer-Galley 2001.

25. Although we didn't examine content of readers' comments, there are conflicting accounts of the quality of news audiences' comments. One camp maintains that they lack rationality and civility (Al-Saggaf 2006; Constantinescu and Tedesco 2007; Mitchelstein 2011; Schultz 2000; Singer and Ashman 2009). The opposite camp finds that political debate on the Internet allows the expression of different positions and rational argumentation (Papacharissi 2004; Price and Cappella 2002; Ruiz et al.,2011; Stromer-Galley 2001; Wright and Street 2007).

26. See, e.g., Barabas and Jerit 2005; Graber 2004; Parker-Stephen 2009; Schudson 1998; Zaller 2003.

27. See, e.g., Lazarsfeld et al. 1948; Katz and Lazarsfeld 1955.

28. See, e.g., Arnold 2006; Prior 2007.

29. See Chaffee and Metzger 2001.

## Chapter 6

1. See, e.g., Barnhurst and Nerone 2001; Carey 2002; Graber 1984; Williams and Nicholas 2001.

2. See, e.g., Boczkowski 2010; Jensen 1990; Ling and Thrane 2002; V. B. Martin 2008; Palgreem et al. 1980.

3. See, e.g., Bohman 2004; Min 2007; Price 2006; Stromer-Galley 2001.

4. See, e.g., Carlson 2007; Hong 2012; Qayyum et al. 2010; Weeks and Southwell 2010.

5. See Katz and Lazersfeld 1955.

6. See Prior 2007.

7. See Zaller 2003.

8. See, e.g., Bennett 2003; Patterson 2000.

9. See, e.g., Bausinger 1984; Berger and Milkman 2010; Boczkowski 2010.

10. See Boczkowski 2010.

11. See Hindman 2009.

12. See, e.g., Habermas 1989; Papacharissi 2002; Statham 2008; Witschge 2004.

13. See, e.g., Barber 1984; Dewey 1946; Fishkin 1991.

14. See, e.g., Butsch 2008; Habermas 1996; Page 1996.

15. See, e.g., Bucy and Gregson 2001; Min 2007; Nah et al. 2006; Nisbet and Scheufele 2004.

16. See Habermas 2006, p. 423.

17. See, e.g., Coronel 2010; Donohue et al. 1995; Iyengar and McGrady 2007; Skidmore 1993; Waisbord 2000.

18. See, e.g., Jensen 2010; Mill 1991; Thompson 1995.

19. See, e.g., Norris 2004; Waisbord 2000.

20. See, e.g., Blumler and Gurevitch 1995; Curran 2000; Hunter and Van Wassenhove 2010.

21. See Waisbord 2010, p. 321.

22. See Park 1981 [1940].

23. See Saussure 1956.

24. See Marx and Engels 1906.

## Coda

1. This total includes 835 most newsworthy articles in 2010, 840 in 2011, and 6,123 in 2012 and 835 most viewed articles in 2010, 692 in 2011, and 3,627 in 2012. The decrease in the number of most viewed articles is due to Washington Post's reducing its "most viewed" list from 10 to 5 items in 2011 and 2012 and USA Today's reducing its "most viewed" list to 5 items in 2011 and approximately 6 items (it varied according to the day) in 2012. The very small difference with the expected number of most newsworthy stories ($n$ = 6,130, from [(6 × 10 × 14) + (6 × 10 × 14) + (5 × 10 × 89)] and most viewed articles ($n$ = 5189, from {(6 × 10 × 14 in 2010) + [(4 × 10 × 14) + (2 × 5 × 14) in 2011] + [(3 × 10 × 89) + (1 × 5 × 89) + (1 × 6 × 89) in 2012]},

considering that USA Today made, on average, six stories available to the public in the most viewed stories in 2012) results from the retrieval of repeated stories that were later excluded from analysis (most newsworthy articles) and that these sites posted fewer than five, fewer than six, or fewer than ten stories in their "most viewed" rankings during a few days. Intercoder agreement was assessed on a subset of 8 percent of the data. For story content, intercoder agreement levels averaged 93 percent, and Cohen's Kappa intercoder agreement was 0.84. For storytelling format, intercoder agreement levels averaged 84 percent, and Cohen's Kappa intercoder agreement was 0.76.

2. See Liptak 2012.

3. The analysis, a fixed-effects logistical regression of content of the stories one week, included all the stories in the journalists' lists across the six sites. The unit of analysis was the story, the dependent variable was the content of the story, and the independent variables were the site (base case: CNN) and the week on which the story was published (base case: week 1). See tables A.86 and A.87 for further details.

4. The analysis, a fixed-effects logistical regression of content of the stories one week, included all the stories in the journalists' lists across the six sites. The unit of analysis was the story, the dependent variable was the content of the story, and the independent variables were the site (base case: CNN) and the week on which the story was published (base case: week 1). See tables A.88 and A.89 for further details.

5. 488 on the "most newsworthy" list (75 in 2008, 63 in 2009, 94 in 2010, 185 in 2011, and 71 in 2012), and 353 on the "most viewed" list (30 in 2008, 36 in 2009, 96 in 2010, 134 in 2011, and 57 in 2012).

6. See, e.g., Herring et al. 2005; Lowrey 2006; Trammell and Keshelashvili 2005; Tremayne 2007.

7. See, e.g., Allan 2006; Hermida and Thurman 2008; Lowrey and Anderson 2005; Reese et al. 2007; Singer 2005.

8. We ran three analyses for the journalists' list and three for the consumers' list. Each analysis consisted of a fixed-effects logistical regression of format of the articles one week, with one of the format categories (straight news, features-style, commentary) as a binary dependent variable. The unit of analysis was the story, the dependent variable was the content of the story, and the independent variables were the site (base case: CNN) and the week in which the story was published (base case: week 1). See tables A.103–A.110 for further details.

9. These calculations draw upon the recoded blog data. The figures change slightly with the blog data before it was recoded, but the main patterns remain.

# References


Ahren, R., Stromer-Galley, J., and Neuman, W. 2000. Interactivity and Structured Issue Comparisons on the Political Web: An Experimental Study of the 2000 New Hampshire Presidential Primary. Paper presented at meeting of International Communication Association, Acapulco.

Albrecht, S. 2006. Whose voice is heard in online deliberation? A study of participation and representation in political debates on the internet. *Information Communication and Society* 9 (1): 62–82.

Alonso será el nuevo portavoz parlamentario del PSOE en el Congreso 2008. El Mundo (www.elmundo.es), March 24.

Al-Saggaf, Y. 2006. The online public sphere in the Arab world: The war in Iraq on the Al Arabiya website. *Journal of Computer-Mediated Communication* 12 (1), article 16.

Althaus, S. L., and D. Tewksbury. 2002. Agenda setting and the "new" news—Patterns of issue importance among readers of the paper and online versions of the New York Times. *Communication Research* 29(2): 180–207.

Alves, R. C. 2005. From lapdog to watchdog: The role of the press in Latin America's democratization. In *Making Journalists*, ed. H. De Burgh. Routledge.

Ancu, M., and R. Cozma. 2009. MySpace politics: Uses and gratifications of befriending candidates. *Journal of Broadcasting & Electronic Media* 53 (4): 567–583.

Anderson, C. 2008. *The Long Tail: Why the Future of Business Is Selling Less of More.* Revised and updated edition. Hyperion.

Arnold, R. D. 2006. *Congress, The Press, and Political Accountability.* Russell Sage Foundation.

Arsenault, A., and M. Castells. 2008. Switching power: Rupert Murdoch and the global business of media politics: A sociological analysis. *International Sociology* 23 (4): 488–513.

Bacon, P., and G. Franke-Ruta. Steele assumes "the Heisman position." Washington Post (www.washingtonpost.com), November 4, 2009.

Bagdikian, B. H. 1983. *The Media Monopoly*. Beacon.

Baker, G. Obama: Is America ready for this dangerous left-winger? Times (www.thetimes.co.uk), February 22, 2008.

Balz, D. Polls show Obama with clear advantage. Washington Post (www.washingtonpost.com ), November 4, 2008.

Balz, D. Contests serve as warning to Democrats: It's not 2008 anymore. Washington Post (www.washingtonpost.com), November 4, 2009.

Barabas, J., and J. Jerit. 2005. Surveillance Knowledge and the Mass Media. Paper presented at meeting of American Political Science Association, Washington.

Barber, B. 1984. *Strong Democracy*. University of California Press.

Barnhurst, K. G., and D. Mutz. 1997. American journalism and the decline in event-centered reporting. *Journal of Communication* 47 (4): 27–53.

Barnhurst, K. G., and J. C. Nerone. 2001. *The Form of News: A History*. Guilford.

Bartels, L. M. 1993. Messages received: The political impact of media exposure. *American Political Science Review* 87 (2): 267–285.

Baum, M. A. 2002. Sex, lies, and war: How soft news brings foreign policy to the inattentive public. *American Political Science Review* 96 (1): 91–110.

Baum, M. A. 2003. *Soft News Goes to War: Public Opinion and American Foreign Policy in the New Media Age*. Princeton University Press.

Baum, M. A. 2007. Soft news and foreign policy: How expanding the audience changes the policies. *Japanese Journal of Political Science* 8: 115–145.

Baum, M., and T. Groeling. 2008. New media and the polarization of American political discourse. *Political Communication* 25 (4): 345–365.

Baum, M. A., and A. S. Jamison. 2006. The Oprah effect: How soft news helps inattentive citizens vote consistently. *Journal of Politics* 68 (4): 946–959.

Baum, M. A., and S. Kernell. 1999. Has cable ended the golden age of presidential television? *American Political Science Review* 93 (1): 99–114.

Bausinger, H. 1984. Media, technology and daily life. *Media Culture & Society* 6: 343–351.

Benkler, Y. 2006. *The Wealth of Networks: How Social Production Transforms Markets and Freedom*. Yale University Press.

Bennett, W. L. 2002. *News: The Politics of Illusion*. Fifth edition. Longman.

Bennett, W. L. 2003. The burglar alarm that just keeps ringing: A response to Zaller. *Political Communication* 20 (2): 131–138.

Bennett, W. L. 2004. Global media and politics: Transnational communication regimes and civic cultures. *Annual Review of Political Science* 7 (1): 125–148.

Bennett, W. L., and R. Entman. 2001. Mediated politics: An introduction. In *Mediated Politics: Communication in the Future of Democracy*, ed. L. Bennett and R. Entman. Cambridge University Press.

Bennett, W. L., and S. Iyengar. 2008. A new era of minimal effects? The changing foundations of political communication. *Journal of Communication* 58 (4): 707–731.

Bennett, W. L., R. G. Lawrence, and S. Livingston. 2007. *When the Press Fails: Political Power and the News Media from Iraq to Katrina*. University of Chicago Press.

Benson, R., M. Blach-Ørsten, M. Powers, I. Willig, and S. V. Zambrano. 2012. Media systems online and off: Comparing the form of news in the United States, Denmark, and France. *Journal of Communication* 62 (1): 21–38.

Benson, R., and D. C. Hallin. 2007. How states, markets and globalization shape the news: The French and US national press, 1965–97. *European Journal of Communication* 22 (1): 27–48.

Berger, J., and K. Milkman. 2010. Social Transmission, Emotion, and the Virality of Online Content. Research paper, Wharton School, University of Pennsylvania.

Berkowitz, D. 1992. Routine newswork and the what-a-story: A case study of organizational adaptation. *Journal of Broadcasting & Electronic Media* 36 (1): 45.

Berkowitz, D. 2000. Doing double duty: Paradigm repair and the Princess Diana what-a-story. *Journalism* 1 (2): 125–143.

Best, S. J., and B. S. Krueger. 2005. Analyzing the representativeness of Internet political participation. *Political Behavior* 27 (2): 183–216.

Bielsa, E. 2008. The pivotal role of news agencies in the context of globalization: A historical approach. *Global Networks* 8 (3): 347–366.

Bird, S. E. 2003. *The Audience in Everyday Life: Living in a Media World*. Routledge.

Blekesaune, A., E. Elvestad, and T. Aalberg. 2012. Tuning out the world of news and current affairs: An empirical study of Europe's disconnected citizens. *European Sociological Review* 28 (1): 110–126.

Blumler, J. G., and M. Gurevitch. 1995. *The Crisis of Public Communication*. Routledge.

Boczkowski, P. J. 2002. The development and use of online newspapers: What research tells us and what we might want to know. In *Handbook of New Media: Social Shaping and Consequences of ICTs*, ed. L. A. Lievrouw and S. Livingstone. Sage.

Boczkowski, P. J. 2004. *Digitizing the News: Innovation in Online Newspapers*. MIT Press.

Boczkowski, P. J. 2009. Rethinking hard and soft news production: From common ground to divergent paths. *Journal of Communication* 59 (1): 98–116.

Boczkowski, P. J. 2010. *News at Work: Imitation in an Age of Information Abundance*. University of Chicago Press.

Boczkowski, P. J., and E. Mitchelstein. 2010. Is there a gap between the news choices of journalists and consumers? A relational and dynamic approach. *International Journal of Press/Politics* 15 (4): 420–440.

Boczkowski, P. J., and E. Raviola. Newssroom meets community in journalism: An account of institutional innovation in a French news site. Manuscript.

Bogart, L. 1989. *Press and Public: Who Reads What, When, Where, and Why in American newspapers*. Erlbaum.

Bohman, J. 2004. Expanding dialogue: The Internet, the public sphere and prospects for global democracy. *Sociological Review* 52 (1): 131–155.

Boyle, M. P., M. Schmierbach, C. L. Armstrong, D. M. McLeod, D. V. Shah, and Z. D. Pan. 2004. Information seeking and emotional reactions to the September 11 terrorist attacks. *Journalism & Mass Communication Quarterly* 81 (1): 155–167.

Brants, K., and P. Neijens. 1998. The infotainment of politics. *Political Communication* 15 (2): 149–164.

Britney Spears takes baby steps back on stage. CNN (http://us.cnn.com), May 2, 2007.

Broder, D., D. Balz and C. Cillizza. The state of the races. Washington Post (www.washingtonpost.com), November 4, 2008.

Brown, C. 2008. Sexist treatment of Palin must end. CNN (http://us.cnn.com), September 24.

Bruns, A. 2008. The active audience: transforming journalism from gatekeeping to gatewatching. In *Making Online News: The Ethnography of New Media Production*, ed. C. A. Paterson and D. Domingo. Peter Lang.

Bucy, E. 2004. Second generation net news: Interactivity and information accessibility in the online environment. *International Journal on Media Management* 6 (1): 102–113.

Bucy, E. P., and K. S. Gregson. 2001. Media participation: A legitimizing mechanism of mass democracy. *New Media & Society* 3 (3): 357–380.

Bush veto forces Dems to weigh difficult concessions. CNN (http://us.cnn.com), May 2, 2007.

Butsch, R. 2008. *The Citizen Audience: Crowds, Publics and Individuals*. Routledge.

Byers, D. Kosovo rioting forces UN peacekeepers out of Serb-dominated Mitrovica. Times (www.thetimes.co.uk), March 17, 2008.

Canel, M., and A. Piqué. 1998. Journalists in emerging democracies: The case of Spain. In *The Global Journalist: News People Around the World*, ed. D. Weaver. Hampton.

Carey, J. 2002. A cultural approach to communication. In *McQuail's Reader in Mass Communication Theory*, ed. D. McQuail. Sage.

Carlson, D. 2003. The history of online journalism. In *Digital Journalism: Emerging Media and the Changing Horizons OF Journalism*, ed. K. Kawamoto. Rowman & Littlefield.

Chadwick, A. 2006. *Internet politics: states, citizens, and new communication technologies*. Oxford University Press.

Chadwick, A. 2011. The political information cycle in a hybrid news system: The British prime minister and the "Bullygate" affair. *International Journal of Press/Politics* 16 (1): 3–29.

Chaffee, S. H., and M. J. Metzger. 2001. The end of mass communication? *Mass Communication & Society* 4 (4): 365–379.

Chan-Olmsted, S. M., and B.-H. Chang. 2003. Diversification strategy of global media conglomerates: Examining its patterns and determinants. *Journal of Media Economics* 16 (4): 213–233.

Cho, J. H. 2008. Political ads and citizen communication. *Communication Research* 35 (4): 423–451.

Christians, C., T. Glasser, D. McQuail, K. Nordenstreng, and R. White. 2009. *Normative Theories of the Media: Journalism in Democratic Societies*. University of Illinois Press.

Chung, D. S. 2007. Profits and perils: Online news producers' perceptions of interactivity and uses of interactive features. *Convergence* 13 (1): 43–61.

Chung, D. S., and S. Nah. 2009. The effects of interactive news presentation on perceived user satisfaction of online community newspapers. *Journal of Computer-Mediated Communication* 14 (4): 855–874.

Chung, D. S., and C. Y. Yoo. 2008. Audience motivations for using interactive features: Distinguishing use of different types of interactivity on an online newspaper. *Mass Communication & Society* 11 (4): 375–397.

Clemons, E. K., B. Gu, and K. R. Lang. 2002. Newly vulnerable markets in an age of pure information products: An analysis of online music and online news. *Journal of Management Information Systems* 19 (3): 17–41.

Cliente 9 y cuarto 871: Un escándalo de sexo y política en Nueva York. Clarín (www.clarin.com), March 12, 2008.

Coleman, R., and M. McCombs. 2007. The young and agenda-less? Exploring age-related differences in agenda setting on the youngest generation, baby boomers and the civic generation. *Journalism & Mass Communication Quarterly* 84 (3): 495–508.

Collier, D. 1993. The comparative method. In *Political Science: The State of the Discipline II*, ed. A. Finifter. American Political Science Association.

Confirmado: 'El amor es ciego.' El País (www.elpais.com), March 24, 2008.

Constantinescu, A. R., and J. C. Tedesco. 2007. Framing a kidnapping. *Journalism Studies* 8 (3): 444–464.

Cook, T. 1998. *Governing with the News: The News Media as a Political Institution.* University of Chicago Press.

Coronel, S. 2010. Corruption and the watchdog role of the news media. In *Public Sentinel: News Media and Governance Reform*, ed. P. Norris. World Bank.

Crerar, S. 2008. Harry Potter split more painful than divorce, says JK Rowling. Times (www.thetimes.co.uk), January 29.

Crise vai durar 'bastante tempo' e terá "graves conseqüências," diz FMI. Folha de S. Paulo (http://www.folha.uol.com.br/), March 17, 2008.

Cronkite, W. 1998. Reporting presidential campaigns: A journalist's view. In *The Politics of News: The News of Politics*, ed. D. Graber, D. McQuail, and P. Norris. CQ Press.

Curran, J. 2000. Rethinking media and democracy. In *Mass Media and Society*, ed. J. Curran and M. Gurevitch. Arnold.

Curran, J., S. Iyengar, A. Brink Lund, and I. Salovaara-Moring. 2009. Media system, public knowledge and democracy: A comparative study. *European Journal of Communication* 24 (1): 5–26.

Curtain, P., E. Dougall, and R. Mersey. 2007. Study compares Yahoo! news story preferences. *Newspaper Research Journal* 28 (4): 22.

Damas, S. H., and C. M. Barber. 2010. Journalists and citizens faced with the mixture of information and opinion in the journalistic messages. Field research in the community of Madrid (2007–2009). *Estudios sobre el mensaje periodístico* 16: 185–208.

Darnton, R. 1975. Writing news and telling stories. *Daedalus* 104 (2): 175–194.

Davis, R. 1995. *The Press and American Politics: The New Mediator.* Longman.

Davis, R. 2009. *Typing Politics: The Role of Blogs in American Politics.* Oxford University Press.

Dayan, D., and E. Katz. 1992. *Media Events: The Live Broadcasting of History.* Harvard University Press.

De Albuquerque, A. 2005. Another "fourth branch": Press and political culture in Brazil. *Journalism* 6 (4): 486–504.

Dean, W., A. Pertilla, and T. Belt. 2007. The myths that dominate local TV news: The X-structure, and the fallacy of the hook-and-hold method of TV news. In *We Interrupt This Newscast: How to Improve Local News and Win Ratings, Too*, ed. T. Rosenstiel, M. Just, T. Belt, A. Pertilla, W. Dean, and D. Chinni. Cambridge University Press.

Decapitation suspect appears in court. CNN (http://us.cnn.com), August 1, 2008.

Denzin, N. K. 1978. *The Research Act: A Theoretical Introduction to Sociological Methods*. McGraw-Hill.

Deuze, M. 2006. Participation, remediation, bricolage: Considering principal components of a digital culture. *Information Society* 22 (2): 63–75.

Deuze, M., Bruns, A., and C. Neuberger. 2007. Preparing for an age of participatory news *Journalism Practice* 1 (3): 322–338.

Deuze, M., C. Neuberger, and S. Paulussen. 2004. Journalism education and online journalists in Belgium, Germany, and the Netherlands. *Journalism Studies* 5 (1): 19–29.

Dewey, J. 1927. *The Public and Its Problems*. Gateway Books.

DiMaggio, P., E. Hargittai, W. R. Neuman, and J. P. Robinson. 2001. Social implications of the Internet. *Annual Review of Sociology* 27 (1): 307–336.

Domingo, D. 2008. Interactivity in the daily routines of online newsrooms: Dealing with an uncomfortable myth. *Journal of Computer-Mediated Communication* 13 (3): 680–704.

Donaldson James, S. 2008. Virginity pledges can work for some. ABC News (www.abcnews.go.com), September 2.

Donohue, G. A., P. J. Tichenor, and C. N. Olien. 1995. A guard dog perspective on the role of media. *Journal of Communication* 45 (2): 115–132.

Donsbach, W., and T. Patterson. 2004. Political news journalists: Partisanship, professionalism, and political roles in five countries. In *Comparing Political Communication: Theories, Cases, and Challenges*, ed. F. Esser and B. Pfetsch. Cambridge University Press.

Doppelmord an Ehepaar aufgeklärt. Der Tagesspiegel (www.tgaesspiegel.de), March 17, 2008.

Downes, E., and S. McMillan. 2000. Defining interactivity. *New Media & Society* 2 (2): 157.

Downs, A. 1957. *An Economic Theory of Democracy*. Harper & Row.

Dutton, W. H. 2009. The fifth estate emerging through the network of networks. *Prometheus* 27 (1): 1–15.

Epstein, E. J. 1973. *News from Nowhere: Television and the News*. Random House.

Esser, F., and P. D'Angelo. 2006. Framing the press and publicity process in U.S., British, and German general election campaigns: A comparative study of metacoverage. *Harvard International Journal of Press/Politics* 11 (3): 44–66.

ExBBB Marcelo é antipático com Ana Maria Braga. Folha de S. Paulo (http://www.folha.uol.com.br), March 17, 2008.

Farnsworth, S. J., and S. R. Lichter. 2005. The mediated congress: Coverage of Capitol Hill in the New York Times and the Washington Post. *Harvard International Journal of Press/Politics* 10 (2): 94–107.

Farnsworth, S. J., and S. R. Lichter. 2007. *The Nightly News Nightmare: Television's Coverage of US Presidential Elections, 1988–2004*. Rowman & Littlefield.

Ferreira, L. 2006. *Centuries of Silence: The Story of Latin American Journalism*. Praeger.

Fishkin, J. S. 1991. *Democracy and Deliberation: New Directions For Democratic Reform*. Yale University Press.

Fishman, M. 1980. *Manufacturing the News*. University of Texas Press.

Foreclosed home caused 44-pound cat's abandonment. USA Today (www.usatoday.com), August 1, 2008.

Frijters, P., and M. Velamuri. 2009. Is the Internet bad news? The online news era and the market for high-quality news. *Review of Network Economics* 9 (2): 32.

Gans, H. J. 2003. *Democracy and the News*. Oxford University Press.

Gans, H. J. 2004. Deciding What's News: A Study of *CBS Evening News, NBC Nightly News, Newsweek,* and *Time*. 25th anniversary edition. Northwestern University Press.

Gans, H. J. 2007. Everyday news, newsworkers, and professional journalism. *Political Communication* 24 (2): 161–166.

Garrison, B. 2009. *Professional Feature Writing*. Taylor & Francis.

Gibson, C. 2009. One daughter's secret revealed, ultimately too late. Washington Post (www.washingtonpost.com), November 4.

Gillmor, D. 2004. *We the Media: Grassroots Journalism by the People, for the People*. O'Reilly Media.

Gitlin, T. 1980. *The Whole World Is Watching*. University of California Press.

Gladney, G. A. 1993. USA Today, its imitators, and its critics: Do newsroom staffs face an ethical dilemma? *Journal of Mass Media Ethics* 8 (1): 17.

Godlasky, A. 2008. New ways to mitigate migraines. USA Today (www.usatoday.com), November 4.

Goode, L. 2009. Social news, citizen journalism and democracy. *New Media & Society* 11 (8): 1287–1305.

Goss, B. M. 2007. Online "Looney Tunes." *Journalism Studies* 8: 365–381.

Graber, D. 1984. *Processing the News: How People Tame the Information Tide*. Longman.

Graber, D. 2003. The media and democracy: Beyond myths and stereotypes. *Annual Review of Political Science* 6 (1): 139–160.

Graber, D. 2004. Mediated politics and citizenship in the twenty-first century. *Annual Review of Psychology* 55: 545–571.

Grinberg, E. 2008. Ballot hot buttons include abortion, same-sex marriage. CNN (http://us.cnn.com), November 4.

Groseclose, T., and J. Milyo. 2005. A measure of media bias. *Quarterly Journal of Economics* 120 (4): 1191–1237.

Groshek, J. 2008. Homogenous agendas, disparate frames: CNN and CNN international coverage online. *Journal of Broadcasting & Electronic Media* 52 (1): 52–68.

Gurevitch, M., S. Coleman, and J. Blumler. 2009. Political communication: Old and new media relationships. *Annals of the American Academy of Political and Social Science* 625 (1): 164–181.

Gurevitch, M., and M. Levy. 1990. The global newsroom. *British Journalism Review* 2 (1): 27–37.

Habermas, J. 1989. *The Structural Transformation of the Public Sphere: An Inquiry into a Category of Bourgeois Society*. MIT Press.

Habermas, J. 1996. *Between Facts and Norms: Contributions to a Discourse Theory of Law and Democracy*. MIT Press.

Habermas, J. 2006. Political communication in media society: Does democracy still enjoy an epistemic dimension? The impact of normative theory on empirical research. *Communication Theory* 16 (4): 411–426.

Hafez, K. 2002. Journalism ethics revisited: A comparison of ethics codes in Europe, North Africa, the Middle East, and Muslim Asia. *Political Communication* 19: 225–250.

Hagen, I. 1994. The ambivalences of TV news viewing: Between ideals and everyday practices. *European Journal of Communication* 9 (2): 193–220.

Hallin, D., and P. Mancini. 2004. *Comparings Media Systems: Three Models of Media and Politics*. Cambridge University Press.

Hamilton, J. 2004. *All the News That's Fit to Sell: How the Market Transforms Information into News*. Princeton University Press.

Hanitzsch, T., et al. 2011. Mapping journalism cultures across nations. *Journalism Studies* 12 (3): 273–293.

Hawkins, K. 2008. Turning 50 isn't what it used to be. CNN (http://us.cnn.com), August 16.

Heeter, C. 1989. Implications of new interactive technologies for conceptualizing communication. In *Media Use in the Information Age: Emerging Patterns of Adoption and Consumer Use*, ed. J. L. Salvaggio and J. Bryant. Erlbaum.

Heith, D. J. 2010. Reaching women: Soft media in the 2004 presidential election. *Journal of Women, Politics & Policy* 31 (1): 22–43.

Hermida, A. 2010. Twittering the news: The emergence of ambient journalism. *Journalism* 4 (3): 297–308.

Hermida, A., and N. Thurman. 2008. A clash of cultures. *Journalism Practice* 2 (3): 343–356.

Herring, S. C., L. A. Scheidt, E. Wright, and S. Bonus. 2005. Weblogs as a bridging genre. *Information Technology & People* 18 (2): 142–171.

Herscovitz, H., and A. Cardoso. 1998. The Brazilian journalist. In *The Global Journalist: News People Around the World*, ed. D. Weaver. Hampton.

Hesse, M. 2008. It's Hannah again. Should we take this? Washington Post (www.washingtonpost.com), August 1.

Himelboim, I., E. Gleave, and M. Smith. 2009. Discussion catalysts in online political discussions: Content importers and conversation starters. *Journal of Computer-Mediated Communication* 14 (4): 771–789.

Himitian, E. 2008. Los que logran sentirse jóvenes después de los 65. La Nación (www.lanacion.com), March 17.

Hindman, M. 2009. *The Myth OF Digital Democracy*. Princeton University Press.

Holbrook, T. M. 1996. *Do Campaigns Matter?* Sage.

Hollander, B. A. 2005. Late-night learning: Do entertainment programs increase political campaign knowledge for young viewers? *Journal of Broadcasting & Electronic Media* 49 (4): 402–415.

Hollihan, T. 2001. *Uncivil Wars: Political Campaigns in a Media Age*. Bedford/St. Martin's.

Hong, S. M. 2012. Online news on Twitter: Newspapers' social media adoption and their online readership. *Information Economics and Policy* 24 (1): 69–74.

Huang, E. 2009. The causes of youths' low news consumption and strategies for making youths happy news consumers. *Convergence* 15 (1): 105–122.

Hughes, S. 2003. From the inside out: How institutional entrepreneurs transformed Mexican journalism. *Harvard International Journal of Press/Politics* 8 (3): 87–117.

Hujanen, J., and S. Pietikainen. 2004. Interactive uses of journalism: Crossing between technological potential and young people's news-using practices. *New Media & Society* 6 (3): 383–401.

Hunter, M., and L. Van Wassenhove. 2010. Disruptive News Technologies: Stakeholder Media and the Future of Watchdog Journalism Business Models. Working paper, INSEAD.

Iyengar, S., and K. S. Hahn. 2009. Red media, blue media: Evidence of ideological selectivity in media use. *Journal of Communication* 59 (1): 19–39.

Iyengar, S., and D. R. Kinder. 1987. *News That Matters*. University of Chicago Press.

Iyengar, S., and J. McGrady. 2007. *Media Politics: A Citizen's Guide*. Norton.

Jarvis, R. 2008. Gulf Coast residents flee Gustav. USA Today (www.usatoday.com), August 31.

Jenkins, H. 2006. *Convergence Culture: Where Old and New Media Collide*. NYU Press.

Jensen, E. 2010. Between credulity and scepticism: Envisaging the fourth estate in 21st-century science journalism. *Media Culture & Society* 32 (4): 615–630.

Jensen, J. 1998. Interactivity. *Nordicom Review* 19 (2): 185–204.

Jensen, K. 1990. The politics of polysemy: Television news, everyday consciousness and political action. *Media Culture & Society* 12 (1): 57–77.

John Edwards admits having an affair. CBS News (www.cbsnews.com), August 8, 2008.

Johnson, C., Q. Wilber, and C. Leonning. 2008. MD anthrax scientist dies in suicide. Washington Post (www.washingtonpost.com), August 1.

Johnston, J., and S. Forde. 2011. The silent partner: News agencies and 21st century news. *International Journal of Communication* 5: 195–214.

Jones, A. S. 2009. *Losing the News: The Future of the news That Feeds Democracy*. Oxford University Press.

Just, M., A. Crigler, D. Alger, T. Cook, M. Kern, and D. West. 1996. *Crosstalk: Citizens, Candidates, and the Media in a Presidential Election*. University of Chicago Press.

Katz, E., and P. F. Lazarsfeld. 1955. *Personal Influence: The Part Played by People in the Flow of Mass Communications*. Free Press.

Kind, H. J., T. Nilssen, and L. Sorgard. 2009. Business Models for Media Firms: Does Competition Matter for How They Raise Revenue? Working Paper 2713, CESifo.

Kiousis, S. 2002. Interactivity: A concept explication. *New Media & Society* 4 (3): 355–383.

Knobloch-Westerwick, S., N. Sharma, D. L. Hansen, and S. Alter. 2005. Impact of popularity indications on readers' selective exposure to online news. *Journal of Broadcasting & Electronic Media* 49 (3): 296–313.

Kovach, B., and T. Rosenstiel. 2001. *The Elements of Journalism: What Newspeople Should Know and the Public Should Expect*. Three Rivers.

Krantz, M. 2008. Dow suffers its worst weekly drop ever. USA Today (www.usatoday.com), October 14.

Lawson, C. 2002. *Building the Fourth Estate: Democratization and the Rise of a Free Press in Mexico*. University of California Press.

Lee, J. K. 2007. The effect of the Internet on homogeneity of the media agenda: A test of the fragmentation thesis. *Journalism & Mass Communication Quarterly* 84 (4): 745–760.

Leaving, J. 2008. Beer with extra buzz on tap up to 16%. USA Today (www.usatoday.com), November 4.

Lewis, J., A. Williams, and B. Franklin. 2008. A compromised fourth estate? *Journalism Studies* 9 (1): 1–20.

Liebes, T. 1994. Narrativization of the news: An introduction. *Journal of Narrative and Life History* 4 (1): 1–8.

Lievrouw, L., and S. Livingstone. 2002. Introduction: The social shaping and consequences of ICTs. In *The Handbook of New Media*, ed. L. Lievrouw and S. Livingstone. Sage.

Ling, R., and K. Thrane. 2002. "I don't watch TV to like learn anything": The leisure use of TV and the Internet. *First Monday* 7 (1) (http://firstmonday.org).

Lippman, W. 1922. *Public Opinion*. Macmillan.

Lippmann, W. 1925. *The Phantom Public*. Harcourt, Brace.

Liptak, K. 2012. Reports show turnout lower than 2008 and 2004. CNN (http//us.cnn.com), November 8.

Lowrey, W. 2006. Mapping the journalism-blogging relationship. *Journalism* 7 (4): 477–500.

Lowrey, W., and W. Anderson. 2005. The journalists behind the curtain. *Journal of Computer-Mediated Communication* 10 (3), article 13.

Luhmann, N. 1996. *The Reality of the Mass Media*. Stanford University Press.

MacGregor, P. 2007. Tracking the online audience. *Journalism Studies* 8 (2): 280–298.

Martin, C. R. 2008. "Upscale" news audiences and the transformation of labor news. *Journalism Studies* 9 (2): 178–194.

Martin, V. B. 2008. Attending the news: A grounded theory about a daily regimen. *Journalism* 9 (1): 76–94.

Marx, K., and F. Engels. 1906. *Manifesto of the Communist Party*. Kerr.

Massey, B., and M. Levy. 1999a. Interactivity, online journalism, and English-language web newspapers in Asia. *Journalism & Mass Communication Quarterly* 76 (1): 138–151.

Massey, B., and M. Levy. 1999b. Interactive online journalism at English-language web newspapers in Asia: A dependency theory analysis. *International Communication Gazette* 61 (6): 523–538.

Matheson, D. 2004. Weblogs and the epistemology of the news: Some trends in online journalism. *New Media & Society* 6 (4): 443–468.

McCartney, J. 1997. News lite. *American Journalism Review* 19 (5): 18–25.

McCombs, M. 2004. *Setting the Agenda: The Mass Media and Public Opinion*. Polity.

McCombs, M., and D. Shaw. 1972. The agenda setting function of mass media. *Public Opinion Quarterly* 36 (2): 176.

McCoy, M. E. 2001. Dark alliance: News repair and institutional authority in the age of the Internet. *Journal of Communication* 51 (1): 164–193.

McDonald, M. P. 2008. The return of the voter: Voter turnout in the 2008 presidential election. *The Forum* 6 (4) (http://www.clas.ufl.edu).

McManus, J. 1995. A market-based model of news production. *Communication Theory* 5 (4): 301–338.

McMillan, S. 2002. Exploring models of interactivity from multiple research traditions: Users, documents, and systems. In *Handbook of New Media*, volume 2. ed. L. Lievrouw and S. Livingston. Sage.

Merrill, J. C. 2009. In *Global Journalism: Topical Issues and Media Systems*, ed. A. S. de Beer. Pearson.

Milbank, D. President Obama continues hectic victory tour. Washington Post (www.washingtonpost.com), July 3, 2008.

Mill, J. S. [1869] 1991. On liberty. In On Liberty *in Focus*, ed. J. Gray and G. Smith. Routledge.

Min, S. J. 2007. Online vs. face-to-face deliberation: Effects on civic engagement. *Journal of Computer-Mediated Communication* 12 (4): 11.

Mindich, D. T. Z. 2005. *Tuned Out: Why Americans under 40 Don't Follow the News.* Oxford University Press.

Mitchelstein, E. 2011. Catharsis and community: Divergent motivations for audience participation in online newspapers and blogs. *International Journal of Communication* 5: 2014–2034.

Mooney, A. 2009. Fiorina jumps into high-profile California Senate race. CNN (http://us.cnn.com), November 4.

Morley, D. 1992. *Television, Audiences, and Cultural Studies.* Routledge.

Morrison, M. 1998. A look at interactivity from a consumer perspective. *Developments in Marketing Science* 21: 149–154.

Moy, P., M. A. Xenos, and V. K. Hess. 2006. Priming effects of late-night comedy. *International Journal of Public Opinion Research* 18 (2): 198–210.

Murió Jorge Guinzburg. Clarín (www.clarin.com), March 1, 2008.

Murray, S. 2005. Brand loyalties: Rethinking content within global corporate media. *Media Culture & Society* 27 (3): 415–435.

Nah, S., A. S. Veenstra, and D. V. Shah. 2006. The Internet and anti-war activism: A case study of information, expression, and action. *Journal of Computer-Mediated Communication* 12 (1).

NATO bringt Mitrovica unter knotrolle. Der Tagesspiegel (http://www.tagesspiegel.de), March 17, 2008.

Nelson, M., and H. Paek. 2007. A content analysis of advertising in a global magazine across seven countries. *International Marketing Review* 24 (1): 64–86.

Newhagen, J., J. Cordes, and M. Levy. 1995. Nightly@nbc.com: Audience scope and the perception of interactivity in viewer mail on the Internet. *Journal of Communication* 45 (3): 164–175.

Nisbet, M. C., and D. A. Scheufele. 2004. Political talk as a catalyst for online citizenship. *Journalism & Mass Communication Quarterly* 81 (4): 877–896.

Norris, P. 2004. Global political communication: Good governance, human development, and mass communication. In *Comparing Political Communication: Theories, Cases, and Challenges*, ed. F. Esser and B. Pfetsch. Cambridge University Press.

Oppenheim, G. The beer that takes you back . . . millions of years. Washington Post (www.washingtonpost.com), September 1, 2008.

Ornebring, H. 2008. The consumer as a producer—of what? User-generated tabloid content in The Sun (UK) and Aftonbladet (Sweden). *Journalism Studies* 9: 771–785.

Page, B. I. 1996. *Who Deliberates? Mass Media IN Modern Democracy*. University of Chicago Press.

Palmer, M. 2008. International news from Paris- and London-based newsrooms. *Journalism Studies* 9 (5): 813–821.

Palmgreen, P., L. A. Wenner, and J. D. Rayburn. 1980. Relations between gratifications sought and obtained: A study of television news. *Communication Research* 7 (2): 161–192.

Papacharissi, Z. 2002. The virtual sphere: The internet as a public sphere. *New Media & Society* 4 (1): 9–27.

Papacharissi, Z. 2004. Democracy online: Civility, politeness, and the democratic potential of online political discussion groups. *New Media & Society* 6 (2): 259–283.

Papacharissi, Z. 2007. The blogger revolution? Audiences as media producers: Content analysis of 260 blogs. In *Blogging, Citizenship and the Future of Media*, ed. M. Tremayne. Routledge.

Para la Justicia, los crímenes de la Triple A no prescriben. La Nación (www.lanacion.com), March 17, 2008.

Park, R. 1981 [1940]. Introduction. In *News and the Human Interest Story*, ed. H. Hughes. Transaction.

Parker-Stephen, E. 2009). Contextual Effects on Mass Perception: Sometimes You Think Like You Feel, Sometimes You Don't. Paper presented at meeting of Midwest Political Association, Chicago.

Paterson, C. 2005. News agency dominance in international news on the Internet. In *Converging Media, Diverging Politics: A Political Economy of News Media in the United States and Canada*, ed. D. Skinner, J. Compton, and M. J. Gasher. Lexington Books.

Patterson, T. 1994. *Out of Order*. Vintage.

Patterson, T. 2000. Doing Well and Doing Good: How Soft News and Critical Journalism Are Shrinking the News Audience and Weakening Democracy—And What News Outlets Can Do About It. Faculty Research Working Paper, John F. Kennedy School of Government, Harvard University.

Pell, A. Hey Facebook, just let go of me. Times (www.thetimes.com.uk), March 16, 2008.

Pew Research Center for the People and the Press. 2011. *The Internet and Campaign 2010*.

Pfetsch, B., and F. Esser. 2004. Comparing political communication: Reorientations in a changing world. In *Comparing Political Communication*, ed. F. Esser and B. Pfetsch. Cambridge University Press.

Piazza, J. 2009. Jessica Simpson finds a bosom buddy. CNN (http://us.cnn.com), November 4.

Picard, R. G. 2004. *Strategic Responses to Media Market Changes*, volume 2004-2. Jönköping International Business School.

Plasser, F. 2005. From hard to soft news standards? How political journalists in different Media systems evaluate the shifting quality of news. *Harvard International Journal of Press/Politics* 10 (2): 47.

Poindexter, P. M., and M. E. McCombs. 2001. Revisiting the civic duty to keep informed in the new media environment. *Journalism & Mass ommunication Quarterly* 78 (1): 113–126.

Pool, I. de Sola. 1983. *Technologies of Freedom*. Belknap.

Price, V. 2006. Citizens deliberating online: Theory and some evidence. In *Online Deliberation: Design, Research, and Practice*, ed. T. Davies and B. Noveck. University of Chicago Press.

Price, V., and J. N. Cappella. 2002. Online deliberation and its influence: The Electronic Dialogue Project in campaign 2000. *IT and Society* 1 (1): 303–329.

Price, V., and J. Zaller. 1993. Who gets the news: Alternative measures of news reception and their implications for research. *Public Opinion Quarterly* 57: 133–164.

Prichard, P. 1987. *The Making of McPaper: The Inside Story of* USA Today. Andrews, McMeel & Parker.

Prior, M. 2003. Any good news in soft news? The impact of soft news preference on political knowledge. *Political Communication* 20 (2): 149–171.

Prior, M. 2005. News vs. entertainment: How increasing media choice widens gaps in political knowledge and turnout. *American Journal of Political Science* 49 (3): 577–592.

Prior, M. 2007. *Post-Broadcast Democracy: How Media Choice Increases Inequality in Political Involvement and Polarizes Elections*. Cambridge University Press.

Project for Excellence in Journalism. 2007. The State of the News Media 2007: An Annual Report on American Journalism. http://stateofthemedia.org.

Project for Excellence in Journalism. 2009. The State of the News Media 2009: An Annual Report on American Journalism. http://stateofthemedia.org.

Project for Excellence in Journalism. 2011. The State of the News Media 2011: An Annual Report on American Journalism. http://stateofthemedia.org.

Project for Excellence in Journalism. 2012. The State of the News Media 2012: An Annual Report on American Journalism. http://stateofthemedia.org.

Qayyum, M. A., K. Williamson, Y. H. Liu, and P. Hider. 2010. Investigating the news seeking behavior of young adults. *Australian Academic & Research Libraries* 41 (3): 178–191.

Quandt, T. 2008. (No) news on the World Wide Web? *Journalism Studies* 9: 717–738.

Rafaeli, S. 1988. Interactivity: From new media to communication. *Sage Annual Review of Communication Research: Advancing Communication Science* 16: 110–134.

Reese, S. D. 2001. Understanding the global journalist: A hierarchy-of-influences approach. *Journalism Studies* 2: 173–187.

Reese, S. D., L. Rutigliano, K. Hyun, and J. Jeong. 2007. Mapping the blogosphere: Professional and citizen-based media in the global news arena. *Journalism* 8 (3): 235–261.

Roberts, M., W. Wanta, and T.-H. Dzwo. 2002. Agenda setting and issue salience online. *Communication Research* 29 (4): 452–465.

Robinson, M. J. 1976. Public affairs television and the growth of political malaise: The case of "The selling of the Pentagon." *American Political Science Review* 70 (2): 409–432.

Robinson, S. 2006. The mission of the j-blog: Recapturing journalistic authority online. *Journalism* 7 (1): 65–83.

Robinson, S. 2007. Someone's gotta be in control here. *Journalism Practice* 1 (3): 305–321.

Rockwell, R. 2009. Latin America. In *Global Journalism: Topical Issues and Media Systems*, ed. A. S. De Beer. Pearson.

Rosen, J. 1999. The action of the idea: Public journalism in built form. In *The Idea of Public Journalism*, ed. T. Glasser. Guilford.

Rosenstiel, T., M. Just, W. Dean, T. Belt, and A. Pertilla. 2007. *We Interrupt This Newscast: How to Improve Local News and Win Ratings, Too*. Cambridge University Press.

Rössler, P. 2004. Political communication messages: Pictures of our world on international television news. In *Comparing Political Communication: Theories, Cases, and Challenges*, ed. F. Esser and B. Pfetsch. Cambridge University Press.

Ruigrok, N., and W. Van Atteveldt. 2007. Global angling with a local angle: How U.S., British, and Dutch newspapers frame global and local terrorist attacks. *Harvard International Journal of Press/Politics* 12 (1): 68–90.

Ruiz, C., D. Domingo, J. L. Mico, J. Diaz-Noci, K. Meso, and P. Masip. 2011. Public sphere 2.0? The democratic qualities of citizen debates in online newspapers. *International Journal of Press/Politics* 16 (4): 463–487.

Sanders, K., and M. J. Canel. 2006. A scribbling tribe: Reporting political scandal in Britain and Spain. *Journalism* 7 (4): 453–476.

Saussure, F. de. 1956. *Course in General Linguistics*. Columbia University Press.

Schement, J., and T. Curtis. 1997. *Tendencies and Tensions of the Information Age: The Production and Distribution of Information in the United States*. Transaction.

Schoenbach, K. 2004. A balance between imitation and contrast: What makes newspapers successful? A summary of internationally comparative research. *Journal of Media Economics* 17 (3): 219–227.

Schoenbach, K., E. de Waal, and E. Lauf. 2005. Research note: Online and print newspapers. *European Journal of Communication* 20 (2): 245–258.

Schramm, W. 1947. Measuring another dimension of newspaper readership. *Journalism Quarterly* 24: 293–306.

Schudson, M. 1978. *Discovering the News: A Social History of American Newspapers*. Basic Books.

Schudson, M. 1998. *The Good Citizen: A History of American Civic Life*. Martin Kessler Books.

Schudson, M. 2003. *The Sociology of News*. Norton.

Schudson, M. 2007. Citizens, consumers, and the good society. *Annals of the American Academy of Political and Social Science* 611 (1): 236–249.

Schultz, T. 2000. Mass media and the concept of interactivity: An exploratory study of online forums and reader email. *Media Culture & Society* 22 (2): 205–221.

Scott, D. K., and R. H. Gobetz. 1992. Hard news/soft news content of the national broadcast networks, 1972–1987. *Journalism & Mass Communication Quarterly* 69 (2): 406–412.

Shapiro, S. 2005. *Reinventing the Feature Story: Mythic Cycles in American Literary Journalism*. Apprentice House.

Shapiro, S. 2006. Return of the sob sisters. *American Journalism Review* 28 (3): 50.

Shaver, D., and D. Wilgoren. Voters encounter long lines, minor problems. Washington Post (www.washingtonpost.com), November 4, 2008.

Shaw, D. L., and B. J. Hamm. 1997. How individuals are using media to reshape American society. In *Communication and Democracy: Exploring the Intellectual Frontiers in Agenda-Setting Theory*, ed. M. McCombs, D. L. Shaw, and A. J. Weaver. Erlbaum.

Sheinin, D. In fast company. Washington Post (www.washingtonpost.com), August 1, 2008.

Shoemaker, P. J., and A. A. Cohen. 2006. *News Around the World: Content, Practitioners, and the Public*. Routledge.

Si se me rompe el bañador, a nadar sin él. El Mundo (www.elmundo.es), March 23, 2008.

Sigal, L. V. 1973. *Reporters and Officials: The Organization and Politics of Newsmaking*. Heath.

Singer, J. B. 2005. The political j-blogger: "Normalizing" a new media form to fit old norms and practices. *Journalism* 6 (2): 173–198.

Singer, J. B. 2006. Stepping back from the gate: Online newspaper editors and the co-production of content in campaign 2004. *Journalism & Mass Communication Quarterly* 83 (2): 265–280.

Singer, J. B. 2008. Five ws and an h: Digital challenges in newspaper newsrooms and boardrooms. *International Journal on Media Management* 10 (3): 122–129.

Singer, J. B. 2009. Separate spaces: Discourse about the 2007 Scottish elections on a national newspaper web site. *International Journal of Press/Politics* 14 (4): 477–496.

Singer, J. B. 2011. Community service: Editor pride and user preference on local newspaper websites. *Journalism Practice* 5 (6): 623–642.

Singer, J. B., and I. Ashman. 2009. "Comment is free, but facts are sacred": User-generated content and ethical constructs at the Guardian. *Journal of Mass Media Ethics: Exploring Questions of Media Morality* 24 (1): 3–21.

Skidmore, T. E. 1993. Politics and the media in a democratizing Latin America. In *Television, Politics, and the Transition to Democracy in Latin America*, ed. T. E. Skidmore. Johns Hopkins University Press.

Smidt, C. D. Manuscript. Can the Free Media be Bought? Senate Candidate Influence on News Media Campaign Coverage.

Song, Y. 2007. Internet news media and issue development: A case study on the roles of independent online news services as agenda-builders for anti-US protests in South Korea. *New Media & Society* 9 (1): 71–92.

Statham, P. 2008. Making Europe news: How journalists view their role and media performance. *Journalism* 9 (4): 398–422.

Steensen, S. 2009. Online feature journalism: A clash of discourses. *Journalism Practice* 3 (1): 13–29.

Stone, G., and T. Boudreau. 1995. Camparison of reader content preferences. *Newspaper Research Journal* 16: 13–28.

Straton, A. 2008. Tibet protester disrupt Olympic flame ceremony. The Guardian (www.guardian.co.uk), March 24.

Stromer-Galley, J. 2000. On-line interaction and why candidates avoid it. *Journal of Communication* 50 (4): 111–132.

Stromer-Galley, J. 2001. New Voices in the Public Sphere: A Comparative Analysis of Interpersonal and Online Political Talk. Paper presented at European Institute of Communication and Culture Colloquium (Euricom), Piran, Slovenia.

Stroud, N. J. 2008. Media use and political predispositions: Revisiting the concept of selective exposure. *Political Behavior* 30 (3): 341–366.

Stroud, N. J. 2011. *Niche News: The Politics of News Choice*. Oxford University Press.

Sundar, S. S. 2004. Theorizing interactivity's effects. *Information Society* 20 (5): 385–389.

Sundar, S. S., and S. S. Marathe. 2010. Personalization versus customization: The importance of agency, privacy, and power usage. *Human Communication Research* 36 (3): 30.

Sundar, S. S., and C. Nass. 2001. Conceptualizing sources in online news. *Journal of Communication* 51 (1): 52–72.

Swanson, D. 2004. Transnational trends in political communication. In *Comparing Political Communication. Theories, Cases, and Challenges*, ed. F. Esser and B. Pfetsch. Cambridge University Press.

Takeshita, T. 2006. Current critical problems in agenda-setting research. *International Journal of Public Opinion Research* 18 (3): 275–296.

Taniguchi, M. 2007. Changing media, changing politics in Japan. *Japanese Journal of Political Science* 8 (1): 147–166.

Tanner, E. 2001. Chilean conversations: Internet forum participants debate Augusto Pinochet's detention. *Journal of Communication* 51 (2): 383–403.

Tewksbury, D. 2003. What do Americans really want to know? Tracking the behavior of news readers on the Internet. *Journal of Communication* 53 (4): 694–710.

Tewksbury, D. 2006. Exposure to the newer media in a presidential primary campaign. *Political Communication* 23 (3): 313–332.

Thelwall, M., A. Byrne, M. Goody. 2007. Which types of news story attract bloggers? *Information Research 12*(4).

Thompson, J. B. 1995. *The Media and Modernity: A Social Theory of the Media*. Polity.

Thorsen, E. 2008. Journalistic objectivity redefined? Wikinews and the neutral point of view. *New Media & Society* 10 (6): 935–954.

Thurman, N. 2008. Forums for citizen journalists? Adoption of user generated content initiatives by online news media. *New Media & Society* 10 (1): 139–157.

Thussu, D. K. 2007. The "Murdochization" of news? The case of Star TV in India. *Media Culture & Society* 29 (4): 593–611.

Times Mirror Center for The People and The Press. 1990. *The Age Of Indifference: A Study of Young Americans and How They View the News.*

Trammell, K. D., and A. Keshelashvili. 2005. Examining the new influencers: A self-presentation study of A-list blogs. *Journalism & Mass Communication Quarterly* 82 (4): 968–982.

Tras el cacerolazo, el gobierno negó la posibilidad de cambios en la política de retenciones. Clarín (www.clarin.com), March 26, 2008.

Tremayne, M. 2007. Harnessing the active audience: Synthesing blog research and lessons for the future of media. In *Blogging, Citizenship and the Future of Media*, ed. M. Tremayne. Routledge.

Tuchman, G. 1972. Objectivity as strategic ritual: An examination of newsmen's notions of objectivity. *American Journal of Sociology* 77 (4): 660–679.

Tuchman, G. 1978. *Making News*. Free Press.

Underwood, D. 1995. *When MBAs Rule the Newsroom: How the Marketers and Managers Are Reshaping Today's Media*. Columbia University Press.

Voters 'surprised,' 'excited' on historic election day. CNN (http://us.cnn.com), November 4, 2008.

Vujnovic, M., J. Singer, S. Paulussen, A. Heinonen, Z. Reich, T. Quandt, A. Hermida, and D. Domingo. 2010. Exploring the political-economic factors of participatory journalism. *Journalism Practice* 4 (3): 1–12.

Waisbord, S. 2000. *Watchdog Journalism in South America: News, Accountability, and Democracy*. Columbia University Press.

Waisbord, S. 2010. Latin America. In *Public Sentinel: News Media and Governance Reform*, ed. P. Norris. World Bank.

Weeks, B., and B. Southwell. 2010. The symbiosis of news coverage and aggregate online search behavior: Obama, rumors, and presidential politics. *Mass Communication & Society* 13 (4): 341–360.

Weischenberg, S., M. Löffelholz, and A. Scholl. 1998. Journalism in Germany. In *The Global Journalist: News People Around the World*, ed. D. Weaver. Hampton.

Weldon, M. 2008. *Everyman News: The Changing American Front Page*. University of Missouri Press.

Wiley, S. B. C. 2006. Transnation: Globalization and the reorganization of Chilean television in the early 1990s. *Journal of Broadcasting & Electronic Media* 50 (3): 400–420.

Williams, A., Wardle, C., and K. Wahl-Jorgensen. 2010. "Have they got news for us?" Audience revolution or business as usual at the BBC? *Journalism Practice* 5 (1): 85–99.

Williams, B. A., and M. X. Deli Carpini. 2000. Unchained reaction: The collapse of media gatekeeping and the Clinton-Lewinsky scandal. Journalism 1 (1): 61–85.

Williams, B. A., and M. X. Delli Carpini. 2011. *After Broadcast News: Media Regimes, Democracy, and the New Information Environment.* Cambridge University Press.

Williams, P., and D. Nicholas. 2001. Navigating the news net: How news consumers read the electronic version of a daily newspaper. *Libri* 51 (1): 8–16.

Williamson, D. R. 1975. *Feature Writing for Newspapers*. Hastings House.

Willingham, V. Awake patient reads aloud during brain surgery. CNN (http://us.cnn.com), August 1, 2008.

Wilson, T., A. Hamzah, and U. Khattab. 2003. The "cultural technology of clicking" in the hypertext era: Electronic journalism reception in Malaysia. *New Media & Society* 5 (4): 523–545.

Witschge, T. 2004. Online deliberation: Possibilities of the Internet for deliberative democracy. In *Democracy Online: The Prospects for Political Renewal through the Internet*, ed. P. M. Shane. Routledge.

Witschge, T., and G. Nygren. 2009. Journalism: A profession under pressure? *Journal of Media Business Studies* 6 (1): 37–59.

Wright, S., and J. Street. 2007. Democracy, deliberation and design: The case of online discussion forums. *New Media & Society* 9 (5): 849–869.

Ye, X., and X. Li. 2006. Internet newspapers' public forum and user involvement. In *Internet Newspapers: The Making of a Mainstream Medium*, ed. X. Li. Erlbaum.

Zaller, J. 1999. A Theory of Media Politics. http://www.sscnet.ucla.edu.

Zaller, J. 2003. A new standard of news quality: Burglar alarms for the monitorial citizen. *Political Communication* 20 (2): 109.

Zelizer, B. 2004. *Taking Journalism Seriously: News and the Academy*. Sage.

# Index